GROWING UP
IN AMERICA

ISSN 1534-1631

GROWING UP IN AMERICA

Melissa J. Doak

INFORMATION PLUS® REFERENCE SERIES
Formerly published by Information Plus, Wylie, Texas

THOMSON

GALE

Detroit • New York • San Francisco • San Diego • New Haven, Conn. • Waterville, Maine • London • Munich

Growing Up in America

Melissa J. Doak

Paula Kepos, Series Editor

Project Editor
John McCoy

Permissions
Margaret Abendroth, Edna Hedblad, Emma Hull

Composition and Electronic Prepress
Evi Seoud

Manufacturing
Drew Kalasky

Cover photograph reproduced by permission of PhotoDisc.

While every effort has been made to ensure the reliability of the information presented in this publication, Thomson Gale does not guarantee the accuracy of the data contained herein. Thomson Gale accepts no payment for listing; and inclusion in the publication of any organization, agency, institution, publication, service, or individual does not imply endorsement of the editors or publisher. Errors brought to the attention of the publisher and verified to the satisfaction of the publisher will be corrected in future editions.

LIBRARY OF CONGRESS CATALOGING-IN-PUBLICATION DATA

ISBN 0-7876-5103-6 (set)
ISBN 0-7876-9074-0
ISSN 1534-1631

Printed in the United States of America
10 9 8 7 6 5 4 3 2 1

TABLE OF CONTENTS

PREFACE

Growing Up in America is one of the latest volumes in the *Information Plus Reference Series*. The purpose of each volume of the series is to present the latest facts on a topic of pressing concern in modern American life. These topics include today's most controversial and most studied social issues: abortion, capital punishment, care for the elderly, crime, health care, the environment, immigration, minorities, social welfare, women, youth, and many more. Although written especially for the high school and undergraduate student, this series is an excellent resource for anyone in need of factual information on current affairs.

By presenting the facts, it is Thomson Gale's intention to provide its readers with everything they need to reach an informed opinion on current issues. To that end, there is a particular emphasis in this series on the presentation of scientific studies, surveys, and statistics. These data are generally presented in the form of tables, charts, and other graphics placed within the text of each book. Every graphic is directly referred to and carefully explained in the text. The source of each graphic is presented within the graphic itself. The data used in these graphics are drawn from the most reputable and reliable sources, in particular from the various branches of the U.S. government and from major independent polling organizations. Every effort has been made to secure the most recent information available. The reader should bear in mind that many major studies take years to conduct, and that additional years often pass before the data from these studies is made available to the public. Therefore, in many cases the most recent information available in 2005 dated from 2002 or 2003. Older statistics are sometimes presented as well, if they are of particular interest and no more-recent information exists.

Although statistics are a major focus of the *Information Plus Reference Series*, they are by no means its only content. Each book also presents the widely held positions and important ideas that shape how the book's subject is discussed in the United States. These positions are explained in detail and, where possible, in the words of their proponents. Some of the other material to be found in these books includes: historical background; descriptions of major events related to the subject; relevant laws and court cases; and examples of how these issues play out in American life. Some books also feature primary documents, or have pro and con debate sections giving the words and opinions of prominent Americans on both sides of a controversial topic. All material is presented in an even-handed and unbiased manner; the reader will never be encouraged to accept one view of an issue over another.

HOW TO USE THIS BOOK

Childhood and adolescence are perhaps the most critical period in any person's life. The education one receives during this time, the environment one is raised in, and the way one is treated by family, friends, and society, go a long way towards determining how the rest of an individual's life will turn out. Most Americans, and indeed the American society as a whole, place tremendous importance on protecting children from harm and giving them an upbringing that will enable them to become happy and productive adults. It comes as no surprise that many private organizations and governmental bodies make a close study of American youth. This book presents the latest information available on America's children and adolescents. Its particular focus is on problematic and controversial issues such as juvenile delinquency, teenage sexuality, and the quality of the U.S. public school system. The leisure activities, spending habits, and opinions of American youth are also discussed.

Growing Up in America consists of eleven chapters and three appendices. Each chapter covers a major issue related to youths in America; for a summary of the information covered in each chapter, please see the synopses provided in the Table of Contents at the front of the book. Chapters generally begin with an overview of the basic facts and background information on the chapter's topic, then proceed to examine sub-topics of particular interest. For example, Chapter 4: Children, Teens, and Money begins by describing the median income of different types of families. It then moves on to examine the issue of child poverty, with sections on the overall child poverty rate and the poverty rate for children of different races and ethnicities. Government programs aimed at helping poor children are described and their effectiveness examined. Next, the chapter examines single-parent homes and child support payments. The chapter concludes with an examination of the working and spending habits of American teenagers. Readers can find their way through a chapter by looking for the section and sub-section headings, which are clearly set off from the text. Or, they can refer to the book's extensive index if they already know what they are looking for.

Statistical Information

The tables and figures featured throughout *Growing Up in America* will be of particular use to the reader in learning about this topic. These tables and figures represent an extensive collection of the most recent and important statistics on children and adolescents; for example: the average cost of raising a child in the United States, the amount and types of interaction that American children typically have with their parents, and the percentage of high school students who admit to using illegal drugs. Thomson Gale believes that making this information available to the reader is the most important way in which we fulfill the goal of this book: to help readers understand the topic of youth in America and reach their own conclusions about controversial issues related to growing up in the United States.

Each table or figure has a unique identifier appearing above it, for ease of identification and reference. Titles for the tables and figures explain their purpose. At the end of each table or figure, the original source of the data is provided.

In order to help readers understand these often complicated statistics, all tables and figures are explained in the text. References in the text direct the reader to the relevant statistics. Furthermore, the contents of all tables and figures are fully indexed. Please see the opening section of the index at the back of this volume for a description of how to find tables and figures within it.

Appendices

In addition to the main body text and images, *Growing Up in America* has three appendices. The first is the Important Names and Addresses directory. Here the reader will find contact information for a number of organizations that study children, adolescents, and families. The second appendix is the Resources section, which can also assist the reader in conducting his or her own research. In this section, the author and editors of *Growing Up in America* describe some of the sources that were most useful during the compilation of this book. The final appendix is this book's index.

ADVISORY BOARD CONTRIBUTIONS

The staff of Information Plus would like to extend their heartfelt appreciation to the Information Plus Advisory Board. This dedicated group of media professionals provides feedback on the series on an ongoing basis. Their comments allow the editorial staff who work on the project to continually make the series better and more user-friendly. Our top priorities are to produce the highest-quality and most useful books possible, and the Advisory Board's contributions to this process are invaluable.

The members of the Information Plus Advisory Board are:

- Kathleen R. Bonn, Librarian, Newbury Park High School, Newbury Park, California

- Madelyn Garner, Librarian, San Jacinto College—North Campus, Houston, Texas

- Anne Oxenrider, Media Specialist, Dundee High School, Dundee, Michigan

- Charles R. Rodgers, Director of Libraries, Pasco-Hernando Community College, Dade City, Florida

- James N. Zitzelsberger, Library Media Department Chairman, Oshkosh West High School, Oshkosh, Wisconsin

COMMENTS AND SUGGESTIONS

The editors of the *Information Plus Reference Series* welcome your feedback on *Growing Up in America*. Please direct all correspondence to:

Editors
Information Plus Reference Series
27500 Drake Rd.
Farmington Hills, MI 48331-3535

CHAPTER 1
HOW MANY CHILDREN?

DEFINING CHILDHOOD AND ADULTHOOD

Exactly when childhood ends and adulthood begins differs among cultures and over periods of time within cultures. People in some societies believe that adulthood begins with the onset of puberty, arguing that people who are old enough to have children also are old enough to assume adult responsibilities. This stage of life is often solemnized with special celebrations. In Jewish tradition, for example, the bar mitzvah ceremony for thirteen-year-old boys and the bat mitzvah ceremony for twelve-year-old girls commemorates the attainment of adult responsibility for observing Jewish law.

Modern American society identifies an interim period of life between childhood and adulthood known as adolescence, during which teens reach a series of milestones when they accept increasing amounts of adult responsibility. At age sixteen most Americans can be licensed to drive. At eighteen most young people leave the public education system and are eligible to vote. At that time they can be tried as adults in the court system and join the military without parental permission. There are contradictions in the rights and privileges conferred, however. In many states teens under the age of eighteen can marry but cannot see X-rated movies.

In general, American society recognizes twenty-one as the age of full adulthood. At twenty-one young men and women are considered legally independent of their parents and are completely responsible for their own decisions. They are allowed to buy alcoholic beverages and become eligible to apply for some jobs in the federal government.

BIRTH INDICATORS

Historical events greatly influence the number of children born in a society, and two events during recent American history—the Great Depression and World War II—have shaped present-day demographics in the United States. During the early years of the Great Depression (1929–39),

fewer babies were born because most people could not support large families. The small number of births during this time resulted in a relatively small population who were in their late forties and early fifties during the 1980s.

In contrast, the birth rate boomed during the years following World War II (1939–45). After ten years of economic hardship and four years of war, many Americans who had delayed starting a family wanted to have children during the post-war economic boom. During the period from 1946 to 1964 the United States recorded its highest-ever number of births. Figure 1.1, Figure 1.2, and Figure 1.3 are population pyramids, graphical representations of the age and gender distribution of a population. In the pyramids the letters BB represent the age groups that are part of the baby boom generation. The bulge representing baby boomers moves higher on the pyramid as decades pass and baby boomers age. Boomers were in their mid-twenties to mid-forties during the 1990s, their mid-thirties to mid-fifties in 2000, and will be in their sixties and seventies by the year 2025.

According to the Federal Interagency Forum on Child and Family Statistics (*America's Children in Brief: Key National Indicators of Well-Being, 2004,* Washington, DC, 2004, http://childstats.gov/ac2004/tables [accessed August 24, 2004]), in 2002 72.9 million children younger than the age of eighteen lived in the United States. This number is expected to increase to 80.3 million in 2020. However, because the country's entire population will increase, the percentage of children in the population will actually remain fairly steady, decreasing slightly from 25% in 2002 to 24% by 2020.

Family and Household Size

The composition of households in American society changed markedly in the twentieth century. According to the 2002 Census Bureau Report on demographic trends in the twentieth century, in 1950 families accounted for 89.4% of all households. By 2000 that number had decreased to

FIGURE 1.1

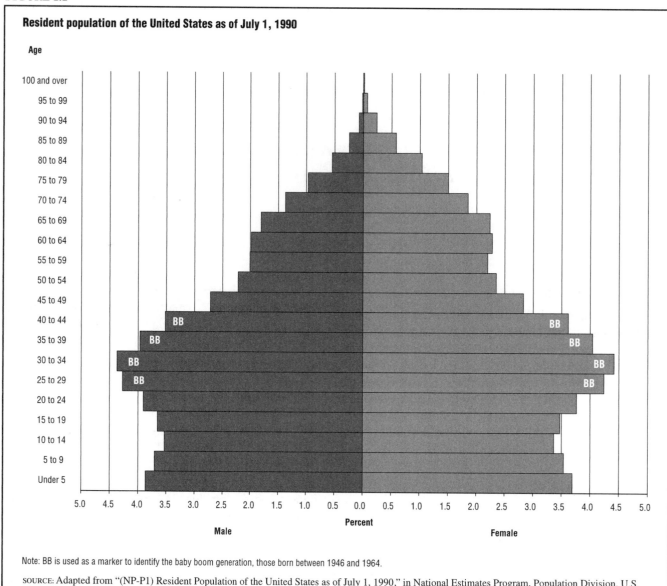

Resident population of the United States as of July 1, 1990

Note: BB is used as a marker to identify the baby boom generation, those born between 1946 and 1964.

SOURCE: Adapted from "(NP-P1) Resident Population of the United States as of July 1, 1990," in National Estimates Program, Population Division, U.S. Census Bureau, 2000, http://www.census.gov/population/www/projections/np_p1.pdf (accessed August 24, 2004)

68.1%. The proportion of married-couple households that included at least one child under the age of eighteen has also decreased. In 1960 59.3% of married-couple households included at least one child under the age of eighteen, but by 2000 only 45.3% of these households had a child under eighteen living at home. (See Figure 1.4.)

The American family shrank in size during the twentieth century. In 1900 most households consisted of five or more people. By 1950 two-person families became the most common family type and remained so to the end of the century. The proportion of one- and two-person households increased from 1950 to 2000, while the proportion of households with three or more people steadily decreased. (See Figure 1.5.) Average household size declined from 4.6 people per household at the beginning of the century to 2.6 people in 2000. This was true partly because the population was getting older.

AN AGING POPULATION

The median age (half are older and half are younger) of the American population has risen quickly. According to the U.S. Census Bureau in *Census 2000 PHC-T-9. Population by Age, Sex, Race, and Hispanic or Latino Origin for the United States: 2000*, median age increased from thirty years in 1980 to 35.3 years in 2000. Within a ten-year span, from 1990 to 2000, the median age jumped from 32.9 years to 35.3 years. This rapid increase in the median age is the result of three separate trends:

• Americans are having fewer children than their parents did.

• Baby boomers are reaching middle age and leaving their childbearing years.

• Americans are living longer because of health consciousness and medical advances.

FIGURE 1.2

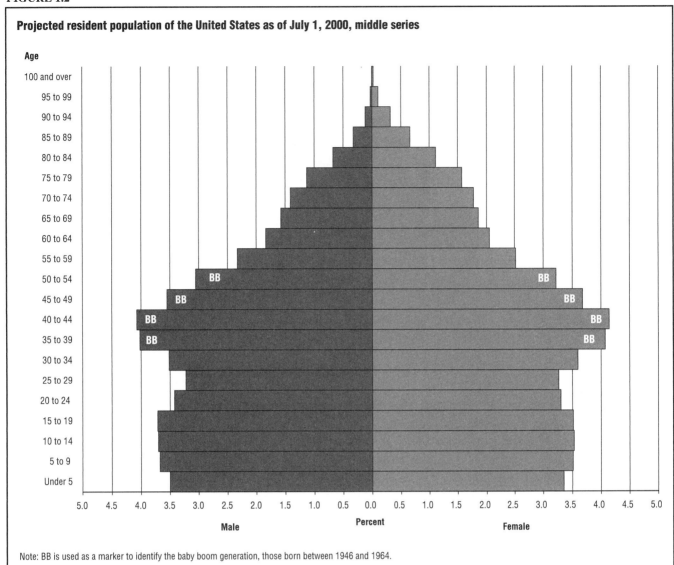

Projected resident population of the United States as of July 1, 2000, middle series

Note: BB is used as a marker to identify the baby boom generation, those born between 1946 and 1964.

SOURCE: Adapted from "(NP-P2) Projected Resident Population of the United States as of July 1, 2000," in National Estimates Program, Population Division, U.S. Census Bureau, 2000, http://www.census.gov/population/www/projections/np_p2.pdf (accessed August 24, 2004)

RACIAL AND ETHNIC DIFFERENCES

Birth and Fertility Rates

Fertility is measured in a number of ways. One such measure, called the crude birth rate, is the number of live births per one thousand women in the population, regardless of their age. In 2001 the national birth rate was 14.1 live births per one thousand women. The birth rate for Hispanic women (of any race) was considerably higher (23) than for non-Hispanic African-American women (16.6), Asian/Pacific Islander women (16.4), Native American/ Alaska Native women (13.7), and non-Hispanic white women (11.8). (See Table 1.1.)

Another way to measure the number of births is the fertility rate, the number of live births per one thousand women in the population between the ages of fifteen and forty-four years. These are the years generally considered to be a woman's reproductive age range. During the first ten years of the baby boom, fertility rates were well over one hundred births per one thousand women. In contrast, the fertility rate for American women in 2001 was 65.3 births per one thousand women, just over half the 1960 fertility rate of 118 births per one thousand women. In 2001 the fertility rate for Hispanic women was 96 births per one thousand women; non-Hispanic white women, 57.7; non-Hispanic African-American women, 69.1; and Asian/Pacific Islander women, 64.2. (See Table 1.1.)

A third way to measure fertility is the total fertility rate (TFR), or the total number of children one thousand women will have during their childbearing years if current fertility rates continue (in other words, the number of children one thousand women will have from the year they are fifteen through the year they are forty-four). A population will replace itself if this rate is 2,100 children per one thousand women or 2.1 children per woman, on average. This is

FIGURE 1.3

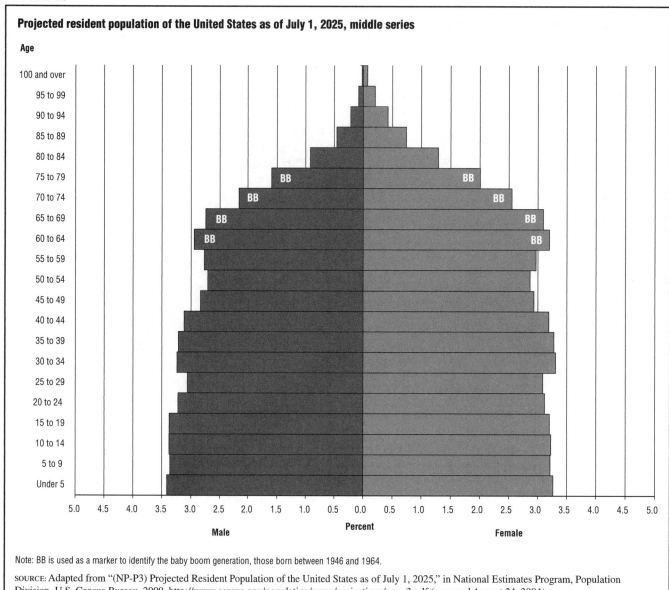

Projected resident population of the United States as of July 1, 2025, middle series

Note: BB is used as a marker to identify the baby boom generation, those born between 1946 and 1964.

SOURCE: Adapted from "(NP-P3) Projected Resident Population of the United States as of July 1, 2025," in National Estimates Program, Population Division, U.S. Census Bureau, 2000, http://www.census.gov/population/www/projections/np_p3.pdf (accessed August 24, 2004)

known as the population replacement rate. The TFR has not reached 2,100 since the 1980s. (See Table 1.2.)

Birth Trends

According to the U.S. Census Bureau, fertility rates among racial and ethnic groups are expected to differ markedly in the twenty-first century ("Projected Total Fertility Rates by Race and Hispanic Origin, 1999 to 2100," January 13, 2000). The white fertility rate is expected to rise slightly through the century but not to reach the population replacement rate. The fertility rate for African-American, non-Hispanic women will remain steady at about the population replacement rate. Native American and Asian fertility rates are expected to decrease slightly but remain well above the population replacement rate through the twenty-first century. The Hispanic fertility rate is also expected to decrease from a high of 2,920.5 births

per one thousand women in 1999 to 2,333.8 births per one thousand women in 2100—a rate still well above the population replacement rate and well above the rates of other ethnic and racial groups.

After 2020, Hispanic births are expected to add more people each year to the United States population than all other nonwhite racial/ethnic groups combined. By 2010 the Hispanic-origin population likely will become the nation's second-largest group. The white, non-Hispanic population will drop from 69.4 percent of the total population in 2000 to 50.1 percent in 2050, while the Hispanic population will rise from 12.6 percent of the total population in 2000 to 24.4 percent in 2050. (See Table 1.3.)

Increasing Diversity among Youth

The youth segment of the American population is becoming more racially diverse. Between 1980 and 2002

FIGURE 1.4

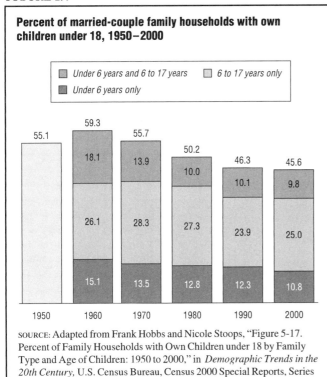

Percent of married-couple family households with own children under 18, 1950–2000

FIGURE 1.5

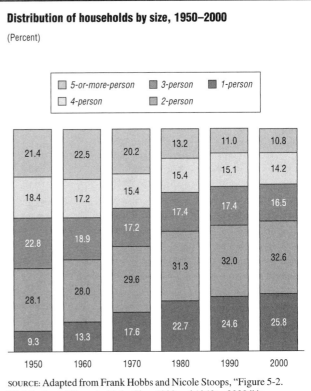

Distribution of households by size, 1950–2000

(Percent)

the non-Hispanic white share of the under-eighteen population dropped from 74% to 60%. (See Figure 1.6.) During the same period the non-Hispanic African-American share of this population remained stable at about 15%. The Native American/Alaska Native share stayed at 1%. In contrast, the Asian/Pacific Islander share of the under-eighteen population increased from 2% in 1980 to 4% in 2000. The Hispanic share of the under-eighteen population showed the highest increase, from 9% in 1980 to 18% in 2002. According to the U.S. Census Bureau, as of the 2000 Census, one of every six children in the United States (17%) was of Hispanic origin.

Median Age

The median ages of minority populations are significantly younger than the median age of the non-Hispanic white population, a natural consequence of more babies per woman born in these populations. In 2000 the median age of Hispanics was 25.8 years, Native Americans/Alaska Natives 28 years, Asians 32.7 years, non-Hispanic African-Americans 30.2 years, and non-Hispanic whites 37.7 years. Among people from one racial/ethnic background, people of Hispanic origin had the youngest population, with 35% under age eighteen, compared with 31% of the African-American population and 23.5% of the white population.

Evidence also suggests that racial and ethnic lines became less rigid in the United States in the last two decades of the twentieth century, as people from different ethnic and racial backgrounds parented children together. People who reported in the 2000 Census that they came from more than one ethnic or racial background had a significantly younger median age than all single-race groups, at 22.7 years. Almost one in two people (41.9%) with a mixed ethnic or racial background were under the age of eighteen. (See Figure 1.7.) This finding may indicate that distinctions between racial and ethnic groups in America will continue to blur in the twenty-first century.

TABLE 1.1

Crude birth rates, fertility rates, and birth rates by age of mother, according to race and Hispanic origin, selected years, 1950–2001

(Data are based on birth certificates)

Race, Hispanic origin, and year	Crude birth rate[1]	Fertility rate[2]	10–14 years	15–19 years Total	15–17 years	18–19 years	20–24 years	25–29 years	30–34 years	35–39 years	40–44 years	45–54 years[3]
All races					Live birth per 1,000 women							
1950	24.1	106.2	1.0	81.6	40.7	132.7	196.6	166.1	103.7	52.9	15.1	1.2
1960	23.7	118.0	0.8	89.1	43.9	166.7	258.1	197.4	112.7	56.2	15.5	0.9
1970	18.4	87.9	1.2	68.3	38.8	114.7	167.8	145.1	73.3	31.7	8.1	0.5
1980	15.9	68.4	1.1	53.0	32.5	82.1	115.1	112.9	61.9	19.8	3.9	0.2
1985	15.8	66.3	1.2	51.0	31.0	79.6	108.3	111.0	69.1	24.0	4.0	0.2
1990	16.7	70.9	1.4	59.9	37.5	88.6	116.5	120.2	80.8	31.7	5.5	0.2
1995	14.6	64.6	1.3	56.0	35.5	87.7	107.5	108.8	81.1	34.0	6.6	0.3
1996	14.4	64.1	1.2	53.5	33.3	84.7	107.8	108.6	82.1	34.9	6.8	0.3
1997	14.2	63.6	1.1	51.3	31.4	82.1	107.3	108.3	83.0	35.7	7.1	0.4
1998	14.3	64.3	1.0	50.3	29.9	80.9	108.4	110.2	85.2	36.9	7.4	0.4
1999	14.2	64.4	0.9	48.8	28.2	79.1	107.9	111.2	87.1	37.8	7.4	0.4
2000	14.4	65.9	0.9	47.7	26.9	78.1	109.7	113.5	91.2	39.7	8.0	0.5
2001	14.1	65.3	0.8	45.3	24.7	76.1	106.2	113.4	91.9	40.6	8.1	0.5
Race of child:[4] white												
1950	23.0	102.3	0.4	70.0	31.3	120.5	190.4	165.1	102.6	51.4	14.5	1.0
1960	22.7	113.2	0.4	79.4	35.5	154.6	252.8	194.9	109.6	54.0	14.7	0.8
1970	17.4	84.1	0.5	57.4	29.2	101.5	163.4	145.9	71.9	30.0	7.5	0.4
1980	14.9	64.7	0.6	44.7	25.2	72.1	109.5	112.4	60.4	18.5	3.4	0.2
Race of mother:[5] white												
1980	15.1	65.6	0.6	45.4	25.5	73.2	111.1	113.8	61.2	18.8	3.5	0.2
1985	15.0	64.1	0.6	43.3	24.4	70.4	104.1	112.3	69.9	23.3	3.7	0.2
1990	15.8	68.3	0.7	50.8	29.5	78.0	109.8	120.7	81.7	31.5	5.2	0.2
1995	14.1	63.6	0.8	49.5	29.7	80.0	104.7	117.7	83.3	34.2	6.4	0.3
1996	13.9	63.3	0.7	47.5	28.0	77.4	105.3	117.7	84.6	35.3	6.7	0.3
1997	13.7	62.8	0.7	45.5	26.6	74.8	104.5	111.3	85.7	36.1	6.9	0.3
1998	13.8	63.6	0.6	44.9	25.6	73.9	105.4	113.6	88.5	37.5	7.3	0.4
1999	13.7	64.0	0.6	44.0	24.5	72.8	105.0	114.9	90.7	38.5	7.4	0.4
2000	13.9	65.3	0.6	43.2	23.3	72.3	106.6	116.7	94.6	40.2	7.9	0.4
2001	13.7	65.0	0.5	41.2	21.4	70.8	103.7	117.0	95.8	41.3	8.0	0.5
Race of child:[4] black or African American												
1960	31.9	153.5	4.3	156.1	—	—	295.4	218.6	137.1	73.9	21.9	1.1
1970	25.3	115.4	5.2	140.7	101.4	204.9	202.7	136.3	79.6	41.9	12.5	1.0
1980	22.1	88.1	4.3	100.0	73.6	138.8	146.3	109.1	62.9	24.5	5.8	0.3
Race of mother:[5] black or African American												
1980	21.3	84.9	4.3	97.8	72.5	135.1	140.0	103.9	59.9	23.5	5.6	0.3
1985	20.4	78.8	4.5	95.4	69.3	132.4	135.0	100.2	57.9	23.9	4.6	0.3
1990	22.4	86.8	4.9	112.8	82.3	152.9	160.2	115.5	68.7	28.1	5.5	0.3
1995	17.8	71.0	4.1	94.4	68.6	134.6	133.7	95.6	63.0	28.4	6.0	0.3
1996	17.3	69.2	3.5	89.6	63.4	130.1	133.2	94.3	62.0	28.7	6.1	0.3
1997	17.1	69.0	3.1	86.3	59.4	127.4	135.2	95.0	62.6	29.3	6.5	0.3
1998	17.1	69.4	2.8	83.5	55.5	124.3	138.4	97.5	63.2	30.0	6.6	0.3
1999	16.8	68.5	2.5	79.1	50.7	120.1	137.9	97.3	62.7	30.2	6.5	0.3
2000	17.0	70.0	2.3	77.4	49.0	118.8	141.3	100.3	65.4	31.5	7.2	0.4
2001	16.3	67.6	2.0	71.8	43.9	114.0	133.2	99.2	64.8	31.6	7.2	0.4
American Indian or Alaska Native mothers[5]												
1980	20.7	82.7	1.9	82.2	51.5	129.5	143.7	106.6	61.8	28.1	8.2	*
1985	19.8	78.6	1.7	79.2	47.7	124.1	139.1	109.6	62.6	27.4	6.0	*
1990	18.9	76.2	1.6	81.1	48.5	129.3	148.7	110.3	61.5	27.5	5.9	*
1995	15.3	63.0	1.6	72.9	44.7	121.8	123.1	91.6	56.5	24.3	5.5	*
1996	14.9	61.8	1.6	68.2	42.7	112.9	123.5	91.1	56.5	24.4	5.5	*
1997	14.7	60.8	1.5	65.2	41.1	106.8	122.5	91.6	56.0	24.4	5.4	0.3
1998	14.8	61.3	1.5	64.7	39.8	106.5	125.1	92.0	56.8	24.6	5.3	*
1999	14.2	59.0	1.4	59.9	36.5	97.9	120.7	90.6	53.8	24.3	5.7	0.3
2000	14.0	58.7	1.1	58.3	34.1	97.1	117.2	91.8	55.5	24.6	5.7	0.3
2001	13.7	58.1	1.0	56.3	31.4	94.8	115.0	90.4	55.9	24.7	5.7	0.3

TABLE 1.1

Crude birth rates, fertility rates, and birth rates by age of mother, according to race and Hispanic origin, selected years, 1950–2001 [CONTINUED]

(Data are based on birth certificates)

Race, Hispanic origin, and year	Crude birth rate[1]	Fertility rate[2]	10–14 years	15–19 years			20–24 years	25–29 years	30–34 years	35–39 years	40–44 years	45–54 years[3]
				Total	15–17 years	18–19 years						
Asian or Pacific Islander mothers[5]												
1980	19.9	73.2	0.3	26.2	12.0	46.2	93.3	127.4	96.0	38.3	8.5	0.7
1985	18.7	68.4	0.4	23.8	12.5	40.8	83.6	123.0	93.6	42.7	8.7	1.2
1990	19.0	69.6	0.7	26.4	16.0	40.2	79.2	126.3	106.5	49.6	10.7	1.1
1995	16.7	62.6	0.7	25.5	15.1	42.2	64.2	103.7	102.3	50.1	11.8	0.8
1996	16.5	62.3	0.6	23.5	14.3	38.6	63.5	102.8	104.1	50.2	11.9	0.8
1997	16.2	61.3	0.5	22.3	13.5	37.0	61.2	101.6	102.5	51.0	11.5	0.9
1998	15.9	60.1	0.5	22.2	13.2	36.9	59.2	98.7	101.6	51.4	11.8	0.9
1999	15.9	60.9	0.4	21.4	11.8	36.5	58.9	100.8	104.3	52.9	11.3	0.9
2000	17.1	65.8	0.3	20.5	11.6	32.6	60.3	108.4	116.5	59.0	12.6	0.8
2001	16.4	64.2	0.2	19.8	10.3	32.8	59.1	106.4	112.6	56.7	12.3	0.9
Hispanic of Latino mothers[5,6,7]												
1980	23.5	95.4	1.7	82.2	52.1	126.9	156.4	132.1	83.2	39.9	10.6	0.7
1990	26.7	107.7	2.4	100.3	65.9	147.7	181.0	153.0	98.3	45.3	10.9	0.7
1995	24.1	98.8	2.6	99.3	67.9	146.7	171.9	140.4	90.5	43.7	10.7	0.6
1996	23.8	97.5	2.4	94.6	64.1	140.5	170.2	140.7	91.3	43.9	10.7	0.6
1997	23.0	94.2	2.1	89.6	61.0	132.9	162.6	137.5	89.6	43.4	10.7	0.6
1998	22.7	93.2	1.9	87.9	58.4	131.7	159.3	136.1	90.5	43.4	10.8	0.6
1999	22.5	93.0	1.9	86.8	56.9	129.8	157.3	135.8	92.3	44.5	10.6	0.6
2000	23.1	95.9	1.7	87.3	55.5	132.6	161.3	139.9	97.1	46.6	11.5	0.6
2001	23.0	96.0	1.6	86.4	52.8	135.5	163.5	140.4	97.6	47.9	11.6	0.7
White, not Hispanic or Latino mothers[5,6,7]												
1980	14.2	62.4	0.4	41.2	22.4	67.7	105.5	110.6	59.9	17.7	3.0	0.1
1990	14.4	62.8	0.5	42.5	23.2	66.6	97.5	115.3	79.4	30.0	4.7	0.2
1995	12.5	57.5	0.4	39.3	22.0	65.9	90.2	105.1	81.5	32.8	5.9	0.3
1996	12.3	57.1	0.4	37.6	20.6	63.8	90.1	104.9	82.8	33.9	6.2	0.3
1997	12.2	56.8	0.4	36.0	19.4	61.9	90.0	104.8	84.3	34.8	6.5	0.3
1998	12.2	57.6	0.3	35.3	18.4	60.8	91.2	107.4	87.2	36.4	6.8	0.4
1999	12.1	57.7	0.3	34.1	17.1	59.3	90.6	108.6	89.5	37.3	6.9	0.4
2000	12.2	58.5	0.3	32.6	15.8	57.5	91.2	109.4	93.2	38.8	7.3	0.4
2001	11.8	57.7	0.3	30.3	14.0	54.8	87.1	108.9	94.3	39.8	7.5	0.4
Black or African American, not Hispanic or Latino mothers[5,6,7]												
1980	22.9	90.7	4.6	105.1	77.2	146.5	152.2	117.7	65.2	25.8	5.8	0.3
1990	23.0	89.0	5.0	116.2	84.9	157.5	165.1	118.4	70.2	28.7	5.6	0.3
1995	18.2	72.8	4.2	97.2	70.6	138.5	137.8	98.5	64.4	28.8	6.1	0.3
1996	17.6	70.7	3.6	91.9	65.0	133.4	137.0	96.7	63.2	29.1	6.2	0.3
1997	17.4	70.3	3.2	88.3	60.9	130.4	138.8	97.2	63.6	29.6	6.5	0.3
1998	17.5	70.9	2.9	85.7	57.0	127.4	142.5	99.9	64.4	30.4	6.7	0.3
1999	17.1	69.9	2.6	81.0	52.0	123.1	142.1	99.8	63.9	30.6	6.5	0.3
2000	17.3	71.4	2.4	79.2	50.1	121.9	145.4	102.8	66.5	31.8	7.2	0.4
2001	16.6	69.1	2.1	73.5	44.9	116.7	137.2	102.1	66.2	32.1	7.3	0.4

— Data not available.

*Rates based on fewer than 20 births are considered unreliable and are not shown.

[1]Live births per 1,000 population.

[2]Total number of live births regardless of age of mother per 1,000 women 15–44 years of age.

[3]Prior to 1997 data are for live births to mothers 45–49 years of age per 1,000 women 45–49 years of age. Starting in 1997 data are for live births to mothers 45–54 years of age per 1,000 women 45–49 years of age.

[4]Live births are tabulated by race of child.

[5]Live births are tabulated by race and/or Hispanic origin of mother.

[6]Prior to 1993, data from states lacking an Hispanic-origin item on the birth certificate were excluded. Interpretation of trend data should take into consideration expansion of reporting areas and immigration.

[7]Rates in 1985 were not calculated because estimates for the Hispanic and non-Hispanic populations were not available.

Notes: Data are based on births adjusted for underregistration for 1950 and on registered births for all other years. Beginning in 1970, births to persons who were not residents of the 50 states and the District of Columbia are excluded. The population estimates used to compute rates for 1991 through 2000 differ from those used previously. Starting with *Health, United States, 2003,* rates for 1991–99 were revised using intercensal population estimates based on Census 2000. Rates for 2000 were computed using Census 2000 counts and rates for 2001 were computed using 2000-based postcensal estimates. Estimates of intercensal populations used to compute birth rates for teenagers 15–17 and 18–19 years are based on adjustments of the revised populations for the 5-year age group, 15–19 years. The race groups, white, black, American Indian or Alaska Native, and Asian or Pacific Islander, include persons of Hispanic and non-Hispanic origin. Persons of Hispanic origin may be of any race.

SOURCE: "Crude Birth Rates, Fertility Rates, and Birth Rates by Age of Mother, According to Race and Hispanic Origin: United States, Selected Years 1950–2001," in *Health, United States, 2003,* Centers for Disease Control and Prevention, National Center for Health Statistics, 2003, http://www.cdc.gov/nchs/data/hus/tables/2003/03hus003.pdf (accessed August 24, 2004)

TABLE 1.2

Children ever born per 1,000 women 40–44 years old, selected years, 1976–2002

(Numbers in thousands)

Year	Number of women	Children ever born per 1,000 women	Percent distribution of women by number of children ever born						
			Total	None	1 child	2 children	3 children	4 children	5 or more children
1976	5,684	3,091	100.0	10.2	9.6	21.7	22.7	15.8	20.1
1980	5,983	2,988	100.0	10.1	9.6	24.6	22.6	15.5	17.6
1985	7,226	2,447	100.0	11.4	12.6	32.9	23.1	10.9	9.1
1990	8,905	2,045	100.0	16.0	16.9	35.0	19.4	8.0	4.8
1995	10,244	1,961	100.0	17.5	17.6	35.2	18.5	7.4	3.9
1998	11,113	1,877	100.0	19.0	17.3	35.8	18.2	6.1	3.5
2000	11,447	1,913	100.0	19.0	16.4	35.0	19.1	7.2	3.3
2002	11,561	1,930	100.0	17.9	17.4	35.4	18.9	6.8	3.6

SOURCE: Barbara Downs, "Table 2. Children Ever Born per 1,000 Women 40 to 44 Years Old: Selected Years, 1976 to 2002," in *Fertility of American Women: June 2002,* Current Population Reports, P20-548, U.S. Census Bureau, 2003, http://www.census.gov/prod/2003pubs/p20-548.pdf (accessed August 24, 2004)

TABLE 1.3

Projected population of the United States, by race and Hispanic origin, 2000–50

(In thousands except as indicated. As of July 1. Resident population.)

Population or percent and race or Hispanic origin	2000	2010	2020	2030	2040	2050
Population total	**282,125**	**308936**	**335,806**	**363,584**	**391,946**	**419,854**
White alone	228,548	244,995	260,629	275,731	289,690	302,626
Black alone	35,818	40,454	45,365	50,442	55,876	61,361
Asian alone*	10,684	14,241	17,988	22,580	27,992	33,430
All other races	7,075	9,246	11,822	14,831	18,388	22,437
Hispanic (of any race)	35,622	47,756	59,756	73,055	87,585	102,560
White alone, not Hispanic	195,729	201,112	205,936	209,176	210,331	210,283
	100.0	**100.0**	**100.0**	**100.0**	**100.0**	**100.0**
White alone	81.0	79.3	77.6	75.8	73.9	72.1
Black alone	12.7	13.1	13.5	13.9	14.3	14.6
Asian alone	3.8	4.6	5.4	6.2	7.1	8.0
All other races*	2.5	3.0	3.5	4.1	4.7	5.3
Hispanic (of any race)	12.6	15.5	17.8	20.1	22.3	24.4
White alone, not Hispanic	69.4	65.1	61.3	57.5	53.7	50.1

*Includes American Indian and Alaska Native alone, Native Hawaiian and Other Pacific Islander alone, and two or more races.

SOURCE: "Table 1a. Projected Population of the United States, by Race and Hispanic Origin: 2000 to 2050," from *U.S. Interim Projections by Age, Sex, Race, and Hispanic Origin,* U.S. Census Bureau, March 18, 2004, http://www.census.gov/ipc/www/usinterimproj/natprojtab01a.pdf (accessed August 24, 2004)

FIGURE 1.6

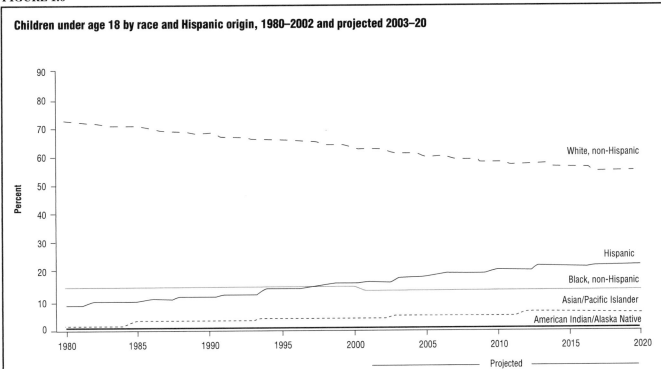

Children under age 18 by race and Hispanic origin, 1980–2002 and projected 2003–20

Note: All population figures for the year 2000 shown here are estimates based on the 1990 U.S. Census; they do not reflect Census 2000 counts. Population figures for 2001–20 are projections.

SOURCE: "Table POP 3. Percentage of U.S. Children under Age 18 by Race and Hispanic Origin, Selected Years 1980–2002 and Projected 2003–2020," in *America's Children: Key National Indicators of Well-Being, 2004,* Federal Interagency Forum on Child and Family Statistics, 2004, http://childstats.gov/ac2004/pop3.asp (accessed August 24, 2004)

FIGURE 1.7

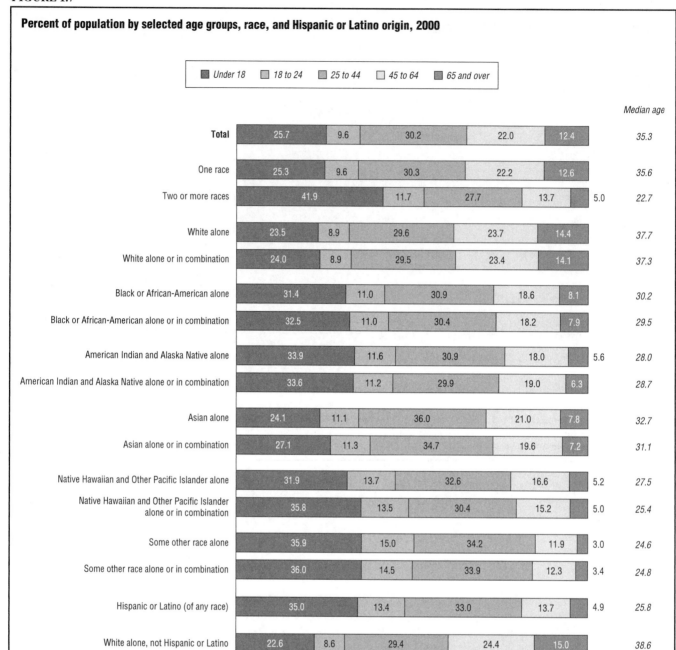

Percent of population by selected age groups, race, and Hispanic or Latino origin, 2000

Legend: ■ Under 18 ■ 18 to 24 ■ 25 to 44 □ 45 to 64 ■ 65 and over

Group	Under 18	18 to 24	25 to 44	45 to 64	65 and over	Median age
Total	25.7	9.6	30.2	22.0	12.4	35.3
One race	25.3	9.6	30.3	22.2	12.6	35.6
Two or more races	41.9	11.7	27.7	13.7	5.0	22.7
White alone	23.5	8.9	29.6	23.7	14.4	37.7
White alone or in combination	24.0	8.9	29.5	23.4	14.1	37.3
Black or African-American alone	31.4	11.0	30.9	18.6	8.1	30.2
Black or African-American alone or in combination	32.5	11.0	30.4	18.2	7.9	29.5
American Indian and Alaska Native alone	33.9	11.6	30.9	18.0	5.6	28.0
American Indian and Alaska Native alone or in combination	33.6	11.2	29.9	19.0	6.3	28.7
Asian alone	24.1	11.1	36.0	21.0	7.8	32.7
Asian alone or in combination	27.1	11.3	34.7	19.6	7.2	31.1
Native Hawaiian and Other Pacific Islander alone	31.9	13.7	32.6	16.6	5.2	27.5
Native Hawaiian and Other Pacific Islander alone or in combination	35.8	13.5	30.4	15.2	5.0	25.4
Some other race alone	35.9	15.0	34.2	11.9	3.0	24.6
Some other race alone or in combination	36.0	14.5	33.9	12.3	3.4	24.8
Hispanic or Latino (of any race)	35.0	13.4	33.0	13.7	4.9	25.8
White alone, not Hispanic or Latino	22.6	8.6	29.4	24.4	15.0	38.6

SOURCE: Julie Meyer, "Figure 4. Percent of Population by Selected Age Groups, Race, and Hispanic or Latino Origin: 2000," in *Age: 2000,* Census 2000 Briefs, C2KBR/01-12, U.S. Census Bureau, 2001, http://www.census.gov/prod/2001pubs/c2kbr01-12.pdf (accessed August 24, 2004)

CHAPTER 2

FAMILY AND LIVING ARRANGEMENTS

FEWER "TRADITIONAL" FAMILIES

One of the more significant social changes to occur in the last decades of the twentieth century was a shift away from the "traditional" family structure—a married couple with their own child or children living in the home. The U.S. Census Bureau divides households into two major categories: family households (defined as groups of two or more people living together related by birth, marriage, or adoption) and nonfamily households (consisting of a person living alone or an individual living with others to whom he or she is not related). As a percentage of all households, family households declined over the period 1950 to 2000. According to the U.S. Census Bureau, in 1950 family households accounted for 89.4% of all households. By 2000 that figure had dropped to 68.1%. The rise in nonfamily households is the result of many factors, some of the most prominent being:

- People are postponing marriage until later in life and are thus living alone or with nonrelatives for a longer period of time.

- A rising divorce rate translates into more people living alone or with nonrelatives.

- A rise in the number of people who cohabit before or instead of marriage results in higher numbers of non-family households.

- The oldest members of our population are living longer and often live in nonfamily households as widows/widowers or in institutional settings.

Although family households were a smaller proportion of all households in 2000 than in 1950, they were still the majority of households. The Census Bureau breaks family households into three categories: (1) married couples with their own children, (2) married couples without children, and (3) other family households. The last category includes single-parent households and households made up of relatives (such as siblings) who live together or grandparents who live with grandchildren without members of the middle generation being present.

Of the three categories, the "other family household" grew the most between 1970 and 2000, growing from 10.6% of all households in 1970 to 16% in 2000. The "traditional" family household experienced the greatest decline during the period. Married couples with their own children made up 40.3% of households in 1970 but only 24.1% in 2000. (See Figure 2.1.)

One- and Two-Parent Families

Among all families with children, two-parent families accounted for 87.2% of families in 1970 and 68.3% in 2002. (See Table 2.1.) Overall, most households with children are still headed by married couples. But the decline in the percentage of children being raised in two-parent households has been the subject of much study and attention.

In 2002 31.7% of families with children were maintained by just one parent, compared to 12.8% in 1970. (See Table 2.1.) In 2002 mothers were single parents 4.5 times as often as fathers. In 1970 that figure was 8.7 times as often; in 1970 there were very few single-father families. During that thirty-two-year period, the number of single-father families increased more than fivefold while single-mother households increased 2.9 times.

The proportion of families headed by a single parent increased from 1980 to 2003 in all racial and ethnic groups. African-American children were the least likely of all racial and ethnic groups to live in two-parent households (36% in 2003). (See Table 2.2.)

The rise in single-parent families is the result of several factors, all pointing to a change in American lifestyles and values. Among these changes are an escalating divorce rate and an increase in the number of children born to unmarried women.

TABLE 2.1

Family households, 1970 and 2002

(Numbers in thousands)

Year	Total with own children under 18	All family groups				Two-parent families as percent of total
		Two-parent	One parent			
			Total	Maintained by		
				Mother	Father	
All races						
2002	38,472	26,271	12,201	9,969	2,232	68.3
1970	29,626	25,823	3,803	3,410	393	87.2
White						
2002	30,550	22,381	8,169	6,423	1,746	73.3
1970	26,115	23,477	2,638	2,330	307	89.9
Black						
2002	5,635	2,179	3,456	3,067	389	38.7
1970	3,219	2,071	1,148	1,063	85	64.3
Hispanic origin*						
2002	6,050	3,936	2,114	1,704	410	65.1
1980	2,194	1,626	568	526	42	74.1
1970	(NA)	(NA)	(NA)	(NA)	(NA)	(NA)

*Persons of Hispanic origin may be of any race.
(NA) Data not available.
Notes: Data for 2002 use population controls based on Census 2000 and an expanded sample of households designed to improve state estimates of children with health insurance. Family groups with children include all parent-child situations (two-parent and one-parent): those that maintain their own household (family households with own children); those that live in the home of a relative (related subfamilies); and those that live in the home of a nonrelative (unrelated subfamilies). Data based on the Current Population Survey (CPS).

SOURCE: Adapted from "FM-2. All Parent/Child Situations, by Type, Race, and Hispanic Origin of Householder or Reference Person: 1970 to Present," in Families and Living Arrangements: March 2002," *Current Population Survey Reports,* U.S. Census Bureau, June 12, 2003, http://www.census.gov/population/socdemo/hh-fam/tabFM-2.pdf (accessed August 24, 2004)

FIGURE 2.1

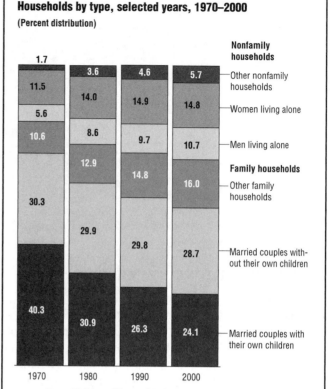

Households by type, selected years, 1970–2000

(Percent distribution)

SOURCE: Jason Fields and Lynne M. Casper, "Figure 1: Households by Type: Selected Years, 1970 to 2000," in *America's Families and Living Arrangements 2000,* U.S. Census Bureau, June 2001, http://www.census.gov/prod/2001pubs/p20-537.pdf (accessed August 24, 2004)

According to the 2002 American Community Survey, in that year the number of divorced individuals reached 22.1 million, more than five times the 4.3 million divorces in 1970. According to the National Center for Health Statistics (NCHS), every year since 1972 more than one million children have experienced their parents' divorce. The NCHS also reports that the rate of children whose parents divorce has risen. During the 1950s only six out of every thousand children experienced parental divorce during a given year, compared with nineteen per thousand in the 1990s.

The rise in the number of single-parent family households can also be attributed to the dramatic rise in the number of births to unmarried women. In its publication *Births: Final Data for 2002,* the Centers for Disease Control and Prevention reported that 34% of births in 2002 were to unmarried women. Nonmarital birth rates differed significantly by race and ethnicity. Unmarried Hispanic women had the highest birthrate in 2002, at 87.9 births per one thousand women of childbearing age. (See Table 2.3.) The birthrate for unmarried African-American women that year was 66.2 births per one thousand women, which had fallen steeply from a birthrate of 90.5 births per one thousand women in 1990. The rate for unmarried, non-Hispanic white women was 27.8 births per one thou-

sand women. The rate of births to unmarried women was highest among women in their twenties; the birth rate for unmarried women ages twenty to twenty-four years was 70.5 births per one thousand women, and the rate for women ages twenty-five to twenty-nine was 61.5 births per one thousand women. Unmarried teen birth rates had fallen steadily since the 1990s.

LIVING ARRANGEMENTS OF CHILDREN

Single-Parent Families

Many children who live in single-parent households face significant challenges that can be exacerbated by racial and ethnic inequalities. According to the Census Bureau, in 2002 the poverty rate for African-American households was 24.1% and for Hispanic households 21.8%, but for non-Hispanic white households it was only 8%. Children who lived in minority families with a single parent were likely to have greatly reduced economic, educational, and social opportunities. Single parents were more likely to have a low income and less education and were more likely to be unemployed and to be renting a home or apartment or living in public housing.

Non-Traditional Families

Many single-parent families, however, are not single adult families; some single parents maintain a household

TABLE 2.2

Percentage of children under age 18 by presence of married parents in household, race, and Hispanic origin, selected years, 1980–2003

Race, Hispanic origin, and family type	1980	1981	1982	1983	1984	1985	1986	1987	1988	1989	1990	1991	1992	1993	1994	1995	1996	1997	1998	1999	2000	2001	2002	2003
Total																								
Two married parents[a]	77	76	75	75	75	74	74	73	73	73	73	72	71	71	69	69	68	68	68	68	69	69	69	68
Mother only[b]	18	18	20	20	20	21	21	21	21	22	22	22	23	23	23	23	24	24	23	23	22	22	23	23
Father only[b]	2	2	2	2	2	2	2	3	3	3	3	2	3	3	3	4	4	4	4	4	4	4	5	5
No parent	4	4	3	3	3	3	3	3	3	3	3	3	3	3	4	4	4	4	4	4	4	4	4	4
White, non-Hispanic[c]																								
Two married parents[a]	—	—	—	—	—	—	—	—	—	—	81	80	79	79	79	78	77	77	76	77	77	78	77	77
Mother only[b]	—	—	—	—	—	—	—	—	—	—	15	15	16	16	16	16	16	17	16	16	16	16	16	16
Father only[b]	—	—	—	—	—	—	—	—	—	—	3	3	4	3	3	4	4	4	5	4	4	4	4	4
No parent	—	—	—	—	—	—	—	—	—	—	2	2	1	1	3	3	3	3	3	3	3	2	3	3
Black[c]																								
Two married parents[a]	42	43	42	41	41	39	41	40	39	38	38	36	36	36	33	33	33	35	36	35	38	38	38	36
Mother only[b]	44	43	47	51	50	51	51	50	51	51	51	54	54	54	53	52	53	52	51	52	49	48	48	51
Father only[b]	2	3	2	2	3	3	2	3	3	3	4	4	3	3	4	4	4	5	4	4	4	5	5	5
No parent	12	11	8	6	6	7	6	7	7	7	8	7	7	7	10	11	9	8	9	10	9	10	8	9
Hispanic[d]																								
Two married parents[a]	75	70	69	68	70	68	66	66	66	67	67	66	65	65	63	63	62	64	64	63	65	65	65	65
Mother only[b]	20	23	25	27	25	27	28	28	27	28	27	27	28	28	28	28	29	27	27	27	25	25	25	25
Father only[b]	2	2	2	2	2	2	3	3	3	3	3	3	4	4	4	4	4	4	4	5	4	5	5	6
No parent	3	4	4	3	3	3	3	4	4	2	3	4	3	4	5	4	5	5	5	5	5	6	5	5

— Not available.

[a]Excludes families where parents are not living as a married couple.

[b]Because of data limitations, includes some families where both parents are present in the household but living as unmarried partners.

[c]Beginning in 2003, the Current Population Survey asked respondents to choose one or more races. All race groups discussed in this table from 2003 onward refer to people who indicated only one racial identity within the racial category presented. The use of the single-race population in this table does not imply that it is the preferred method of presenting or analyzing data.

[d]Persons of Hispanic origin may be of any race.

Note: Data for 1999, 2000, and 2001 use Census 2000 population controls. Data for 2000 onward are from the expanded Current Population Survey sample. Family structure refers to the presence of biological, adoptive, and stepparents in the child's household. Thus, a child with a biological mother and stepfather living in the household is said to have two married parents.

Two married parents family:

In the Current Population Survey, children live in a two-parent family if they are living with a parent who is married with his or her spouse present. This is not an indicator of the biological relationship between the child and the parents. The parent who is identified could be a biological, step, or adoptive parent. If a second parent is present and not married to the first parent, then the child is identified as living with a single parent.

Single parent family:

A "single" parent is defined as a parent who is not currently living with a spouse. Single parents may be married and not living with their spouse, they may be divorced, widowed, or never married. As with the identification of two parents described above, if a second parent is present and not married to the first, then the child is identified as living with a single parent.

SOURCE: "Table POP6. Family Structure and Children's Living Arrangements: Percentage of Children under Age 18 by Presence of Married Parents in Household, Race, and Hispanic Origin, Selected Years 1980–2003," in *America's Children in Brief: Key National Indicators of Well-Being, 2004*, Federal Interagency Forum on Child and Family Statistics, 2004, http://childstats.gov/ac2004/tables/pop6.asp (accessed August 24, 2004)

TABLE 2.3

Number, birth rate, and percentage of births to unmarried women, by age, race, and Hispanic origin of mother, 2002

Measure and age of mother	All races[1]	White Total[2]	White Non-Hispanic	Black Total[2]	Black Non-Hispanic	American Indian[2,3]	Asian or Pacific Islander[2]	Hispanic[4]
				Number				
All ages	1,365,966	904,461	528,535	404,864	395,538	25,297	31,344	381,466
Under 15 years	7,093	3,683	1,446	3,174	3,119	129	107	2,266
15–19 years	340,186	228,407	135,313	99,375	97,282	6,678	5,726	94,483
15 years	17,629	10,672	4,811	6,293	6,150	399	265	5,970
16 years	38,888	25,531	12,816	12,015	11,728	774	568	12,954
17 years	66,274	44,829	25,344	19,053	18,637	1,329	1,063	19,774
18 years	95,259	64,580	39,359	27,131	26,589	1,880	1,668	25,547
19 years	122,136	82,795	52,983	34,883	34,178	2,296	2,162	30,238
20–24 years	527,657	349,161	214,529	158,274	155,080	9,548	10,672	136,369
25–29 years	268,312	176,055	94,304	79,946	77,952	4,993	7,318	83,035
30–34 years	139,208	91,688	50,150	40,375	39,193	2,475	4,670	42,254
35–39 years	66,036	43,684	25,472	18,958	18,299	1,176	2,218	18,566
40 years and over	17,474	11,783	7,321	4,760	4,613	298	633	4,493
			Rate per 1,000 unmarried women in specified group					
15–44 years[5]	43.7	38.9	27.8	66.2	—	—	21.3	87.9
15–19 years	35.4	30.4	22.1	64.8	—	—	13.4	66.1
15–17 years	20.8	17.5	11.5	39.9	—	—	7.5	43.0
18–19 years	58.6	51.0	38.8	104.1	—	—	22.2	105.3
20–24 years	70.5	61.6	46.1	119.2	—	—	26.5	131.4
25–29 years	61.5	56.8	38.5	85.9	—	—	27.5	123.1
30–34 years	40.8	38.3	26.0	49.9	—	—	28.6	88.1
35–39 years	20.8	19.4	13.5	24.9	—	—	18.7	51.3
40–44 years[6]	5.4	5.0	3.7	6.3	—	—	6.8	12.6
			Percent of births to unmarried women					
All ages	34.0	28.5	23.0	68.2	68.4	59.7	14.9	43.5
Under 15 years	97.0	94.8	96.9	99.6	99.6	97.0	97.3	93.6
15–19 years	80.0	74.6	75.4	95.7	95.9	86.6	71.5	73.9
15 years	94.3	91.5	93.8	99.3	99.3	98.3	89.5	89.8
16 years	90.1	86.5	88.9	99.0	99.0	96.1	81.3	84.6
17 years	86.2	82.0	83.9	98.2	98.2	91.5	80.5	79.8
18 years	80.3	75.1	76.9	96.0	96.1	86.9	73.6	72.7
19 years	72.7	66.7	67.4	92.7	92.8	79.7	63.2	65.7
20–24 years	51.6	44.6	41.3	81.3	81.5	66.6	35.5	51.4
25–29 years	25.3	20.7	15.3	58.5	58.7	49.2	11.7	35.2
30–34 years	14.6	11.8	8.1	42.5	42.5	39.1	6.6	26.8
35–39 years	14.5	11.8	8.6	39.2	39.1	39.5	6.8	26.0
40 years and over	17.3	14.5	11.2	39.6	39.6	40.7	8.9	28.8

— Data not available.

[1] Includes races other than white and black and origin not stated.

[2] Race and Hispanic origin are reported separately on the birth certificate. Race categories are consistent with the 1977 Office of Management and Budget guidelines. Data for persons of Hispanic origin are included in the data for each race group according to the mother's reported race.

[3] Includes births to Aleuts and Eskimos.

[4] Includes all persons of Hispanic origin of any race.

[5] Birth rates computed by relating total births to unmarried mothers, regardless of age of mother, to unmarried women aged 15–44 years.

[6] Birth rates computed by relating births to unmarried mothers aged 40 years and over to unmarried women aged 40–44 years.

Notes: For 48 states and the District of Columbia, marital status is reported on the birth certificate; for Michigan and New York, mother's marital status is inferred. Rates cannot be computed for unmarried non-Hispanic black women or for American Indian women because the necessary populations are not available.

SOURCE: Joyce A. Martin, Brady E. Hamilton, Paul D. Sutton, Stephanie J. Venture, Fay Menacher, and Martha L. Munson, "Table 17. Number, Birth Rate, and Percent of Births to Unmarried Women by Age, Race, and Hispanic Origin of Mother: United States, 2002," in "Births: Final Data for 2002," *National Vital Statistics Reports,* vol. 52, no. 10, National Center for Health Statistics, 2002, http://www.cdc.gov/nchs/data/nvsr/nvsr52/nvsr52_10.pdf (accessed August 24, 2004)

with an unmarried partner. In 1990 the Census Bureau sought to reflect changing lifestyles in America by asking for the first time whether unmarried couples maintained households together. Although in 2000 a slight majority of U.S. households (52%) were headed by married couples, a significant number of unmarried couples also maintained households together. According to the 2000 Census, 5.5 million unmarried couples cohabited in the United States. Most of these couples were opposite-sex couples, but one in nine of them were same-sex couples.

A significant portion of all coupled households in 2000 contained children under the age of eighteen. Nearly half (45.6%) of all married-couple households had children living within them, and almost as many opposite-sex partnered households, 43.1%, contained children. Same-sex partnered households also often contained children; nearly a quarter (22.3%) of households headed by male partners had children living in them, and a third (34.3%) of households headed by female partners had children living with them.

This Census data shows that many children are living in nontraditional family situations; in 2002 more than two million children lived in unmarried-couple households. This number represented a significant increase over previ-

FIGURE 2.2

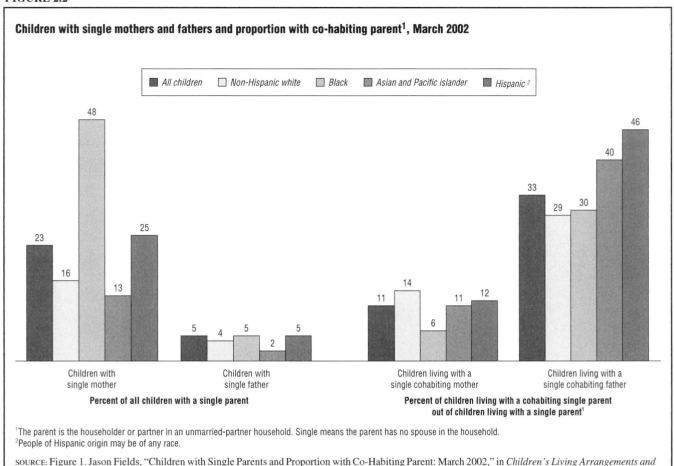

Children with single mothers and fathers and proportion with co-habiting parent[1], March 2002

Legend: ■ All children □ Non-Hispanic white ▨ Black ▨ Asian and Pacific islander ▨ Hispanic [2]

Children with single mother: 23, 16, 48, 13, 25
Children with single father: 5, 4, 5, 2, 5

Percent of all children with a single parent

Children living with a single cohabiting mother: 11, 14, 6, 11, 12
Children living with a single cohabiting father: 33, 29, 30, 40, 46

Percent of children living with a cohabiting single parent out of children living with a single parent[1]

[1]The parent is the householder or partner in an unmarried-partner household. Single means the parent has no spouse in the household.
[2]People of Hispanic origin may be of any race.

SOURCE: Figure 1. Jason Fields, "Children with Single Parents and Proportion with Co-Habiting Parent: March 2002," in *Children's Living Arrangements and Characteristics: March 2002,* U.S. Census Bureau, June 2003, http://www.census.gov/prod/2003pubs/p20-547.pdf (accessed August 24, 2004)

ous decades. According to the 1960 Census, only 197,000 children under the age of fifteen lived in opposite-sex, unmarried partner households; by 2002 this number had reached 1,654,000—more than eight times as many.

Figure 2.2 shows the dramatic differences in the proportion of children living with single parents and cohabiting single parents by race and ethnic group. Children from all backgrounds were much more likely to be living with a single mother (23%) than a single father (5%). But 33% of children living with single fathers also lived with cohabiting partners, compared to only 11% of children living with single mothers.

Grandparents

Grandparents sometimes provide housing for, and sometimes reside in, the homes of their children and grandchildren. According to the U.S. Census Bureau ("Grandchildren Living in the Home of their Grandparents: 1970 to Present," June 12, 2003), in 2002 3,681,000 grandchildren under the age of eighteen lived with grandparents. Of these, 1,658,000 lived with their mothers and grandparents; 275,000 lived with their fathers and grandparents; and nearly 1.3 million, or 1.8% of all children, lived with grandparents only with no parents present. This

percentage remained fairly steady from 1970 to 2002, varying from a low of 1.3% in 1992 to a high of 2.1% in 1995. These caretaking grandparents were responsible for most of the basic needs (food, shelter, clothing) of one or more of the grandchildren living with them.

Living and caretaking arrangements of grandparents and grandchildren varied by race and ethnicity in 2002. African-American, Native American, and Hispanic grandparents were four times more likely to live with their grandchildren than white grandparents. However, Hispanic grandparents (34.7%) were less likely than African-American (51.7%) or Native American (56.1%) grandparents to be the primary caregivers for those grandchildren. Asian grandparents (20%) were least likely of all groups to be the primary caretakers for the grandchildren with whom they resided. (See Table 2.4.)

Grandparents also play a significant role in the lives of children living with a single parent. One out of ten children who lived with single mothers in 2002 were the grandchildren of the householder; 8% of children who lived with single fathers were living in a grandparent's household. When neither parent was present, 44% of the time children lived with and were cared for by their grandparents.

TABLE 2.4

Grandparents living with grandchildren, responsible for coresident grandchildren, and duration of responsibility, by race and Hispanic origin, 2000

Characteristic	Total	Race							Hispanic origin		
		White alone	Black or African American alone	American Indian and Alaska Native alone	Asian alone	Native Hawaiian and Other Pacific Islander alone	Some other race alone	Two or more races	Hispanic or Latino (of any race)	Not Hispanic or Latino	
										Total	White alone, not Hispanic or Latino
Population 30 years old and over	158,881,037	126,715,472	16,484,644	1,127,455	5,631,301	169,331	5,890,748	2,862,086	14,618,891	144,262,146	119,063,492
Grandparents living with grandchildren	5,771,671	3,219,409	1,358,699	90,524	359,709	17,014	567,486	158,830	1,221,661	4,550,010	2,654,788
Percent of population 30 and over	3.6	25	8.2	8.0	6.4	10.0	9.6	5.5	8.4	3.2	2.2
Responsible for grandchildren	2,426,730	1,340,809	702,595	50,765	71,791	6,587	191,107	63,076	424,304	2,002,426	1,142,006
Percent of coresident grandparents	42.0	41.6	51.7	56.1	20.0	38.7	33.7	39.7	34.7	44.0	43.0
By duration of care (percent)*											
Total	**100.0**	**100.0**	**100.0**	**100.0**	**100.0**	**100.0**	**100.0**	**100.0**	**100.0**	**100.0**	**100.0**
Less than 6 months	12.1	12.6	9.8	13.0	13.6	12.7	15.6	13.5	14.6	11.5	12.4
6 to 11 months	10.8	11.6	9.3	10.5	11.0	8.4	11.4	11.2	11.2	10.7	11.6
1 to 2 years	23.2	23.8	21.2	22.5	25.2	23.8	26.1	23.4	25.1	22.8	23.6
3 to 4 years	15.4	15.8	14.6	13.9	17.6	11.7	15.7	16.0	15.8	15.3	15.7
5 years to more	38.5	36.3	45.2	40.0	32.7	43.3	31.1	35.9	33.3	39.6	36.6

*Percent duration based on grandparents responsible for grandchildren. Percent distribution may not sum to 100 percent because of rounding.

SOURCE: Tavia Simmons and Jane Lawler Dye, "Table 1. Grandparents Living with Grandchildren, Responsible for Coresident Grandchildren, and Duration of Responsibility by Race and Hispanic Origin, 2000," in *Grandparents Living with Grandchildren: 2000*, U.S. Census Bureau, http://www.census.gov/prod/2003pubs/c2kbr-31.pdf (accessed August 24, 2004)

The homes maintained by grandparents without parents present were more likely to experience economic hardship than families with a parent present. According to the U.S. Census (*Children's Living Arrangements and Characteristics: March 2002)*, of all grandchildren, 18% lived below the poverty line in 2002), 23% were not covered by health insurance, and 9% received public assistance. Among children who lived with their grandparents with their parents absent, the numbers were much higher: 30% were below the poverty line, 36% were not covered by health insurance, and 17% received public assistance. These numbers suggest that children who live with their grandparents without a parent present are at an economic disadvantage; grandchildren's presence in their grandparents' homes without an economic contribution from the middle generation appears to severely tax the economic resources of grandparents.

Foster Care and Adoption

There is currently no comprehensive federal registry system for adoptions, which can be arranged by government agencies, private agencies, and through private arrangements between birth mothers and adoptive parents with the assistance of lawyers. The federally funded National Center for Social Statistics collected information on all finalized adoptions from 1957 to 1975, but with the dissolution of the Center, very limited statistical information is now available. With the passage of the Adoption and Safe Families Act of 1997, there was a renewed effort to improve the data available about adoption. The U.S. Department of Health and Human Services, through the Adoption and Foster Care Analysis and Reporting System (AFCARS), now tracks adoptions arranged through the foster care system.

AFCARS reported that on September 30, 2001, 542,000 children were living in foster homes with foster parents. Foster parents are trained people supervised by local social service agencies who provide space in their homes and care for children who have been neglected, abused, or abandoned, or whose parents are unable to care for them. According to the American Public Welfare Association, foster care is the most common type of substitute care, but children needing substitute care might also live in group homes, emergency shelters, child-care facilities, hospitals, correctional institutions, or on their own. It is becoming more difficult to place children in foster care. The number of potential foster care families is down, due in part to the fact that women, the primary givers of foster care, are entering the paid labor force in greater numbers.

AFCARS estimated that in fiscal year 2001, 290,000 children eighteen years old and younger entered foster care, with an average age of 8.6 years. A disproportionate share of children entering foster care were African-American—28% of children entering foster care were African-American, but only 17% of all Americans under age eighteen were African-American. White children were underrepresented among those entering foster care—46% were white, compared to the 64% of all children under the age of eighteen who were white. Hispanic and Native American/Alaska Native children were proportionally represented—16% entering foster care were Hispanic, and 3% were Native American/Alaska Native.

A child's stay in foster care can vary from just a few days to many years. Almost one in five of the children who left foster care in fiscal year 2001 had been in care less than a month (19%). Almost a third had been in care from one to eleven months (31%), another one-fifth in care from one to two years (19%), and almost a third had lived in foster care for more than two years (31%). (See Table 2.5.)

According to the AFCARS report, more than half of the children who left foster care in fiscal year 2001 were reunited with their parents (57%). (See Table 2.5.) Some of these children moved to a relative's or guardian's home (13%). Seven percent "aged out" of the system when they turned eighteen years old. Almost one out of five of the children who left foster care were adopted (18%). (See Table 2.6.) Of those adopted children, 25,117 were male and 24,883 were female. Foster parents adopted 59% of these children, relatives other than parents adopted 23%, and nonrelatives adopted 17%. While "traditional families"—married couples—made up two-thirds of those who adopted children from foster care (67%), a significant share were nontraditional families—30% of adopters were single women, 2% were single men, and 1% were unmarried couples.

In 1996 the federal government began to provide incentives to both potential adoptive parents and to states to move children into adoptive homes more quickly by instituting a $5,000 tax credit for adoptive parents to cover adoption expenses; the credit was $6,000 if the adopted child had special needs. Children with special needs were defined as those with physical, mental, or emotional problems; children needing to be adopted with siblings; or children who were difficult to place because of age, race, or ethnicity. In 2002 the tax credit was increased to $10,000 to cover adoption expenses for children without special needs; adoptive parents of special-needs children, including many children from foster care, received the full amount of the tax credit regardless of incurred expenses.

In addition, Congress passed the Adoption and Safe Families Act (PL 105–200) in 1997, providing fiscal incentives to states to move children from foster care into adoptive families more quickly. States that increase the number of adoptions of foster children (in a given year over a base year) receive a standard payment of $4,000 per adopted child and $6,000 for the adoption of a special-needs child.

TABLE 2.5

Children who exited foster care, 2001

WHAT WERE THE AGES OF THE CHILDREN WHO EXITED CARE DURING FISCAL YEAR 2001?

Mean years	10.1	
Median years	10.2	
Less than 1 year	4%	10,923
1–5 years	27%	70,395
6–10 years	23%	59,544
11–15 years	24%	63,881
16–18 years	20%	53,253
19 or more years	2%	5,005

WHAT WERE THE LENGTHS OF STAY OF THE CHILDREN WHO EXITED FOSTER CARE DURING FISCAL YEAR 2001?

Mean months	22.1	
Median months	11.8	
Less than 1 month	19%	50,300
1–5 months	17%	44,969
6–11 months	14%	37,707
12–17 months	11%	29,270
18–23 months	8%	20,833
24–29 months	6%	15,234
30–35 months	5%	12,146
3–4 years	11%	28,604
5 or more years	9%	23,936

WHAT WAS THE RACE/ETHNICITY OF THE CHILDREN WHO EXITED CARE DURING FISCAL YEAR 2001?

American Native non-Hispanic	2%	6,544
Asian non-Hispanic	1%	2,689
Black non-Hispanic	30%	79,308
Hawaiian/Pacific Islander non-Hispanic	0%	1,046
Hispanic	15%	40,346
White non-Hispanic	45%	117,377
Unknown/unable to determine	4%	9,602
Two or more races non-Hispanic	2%	6,087

WHAT WERE THE OUTCOMES FOR THE CHILDREN EXITING FOSTER CARE DURING FISCAL YEAR 2001?

Reunification with parent(s) or primary caretaker(s)	57%	148,606
Living with other relative(s)	10%	26,084
Adoption	18%	46,668
Emancipation	7%	19,008
Guardianship	3%	8,969
Transfer to another agency	3%	7,918
Runaway	2%	5,219
Death of child	0%	528

Notes: Deaths are attributable to a variety of causes including medical conditions, accidents and homicide. Using U.S. Bureau of the Census standards, children of Hispanic origin may be of any race. Beginning in fiscal year 2000, children could be identified with more than one race designation.

SOURCE: Adapted from "How Many Children Exited Foster Care during FY 2001?" in *Adoption and Foster Care Analysis and Reporting System (AFCARS), no. 8,* U.S. Department of Health and Human Services, Administration for Children and Families, March 2003, http://www.acf.hhs.gov/programs/cb/publications/afcars/report8.pdf (accessed August 24, 2004)

Despite these incentives, many children who enter foster care will never have a permanent family, but instead will age out of the system. On September 30, 2001, there were 126,000 children living in foster homes whose parents' rights had been terminated. These "waiting children" were disproportionately African-American. While 17% of all children under eighteen were African-American and 28% of children entering foster care were African-American, almost half (45%) of waiting children were African-American. The majority of these children lived in foster

TABLE 2.6

Children adopted from the public foster care system, 2001

HOW MANY CHILDREN WERE ADOPTED FROM THE PUBLIC FOSTER CARE SYSTEM IN FY 2001?

		50,000

WHAT IS THE GENDER DISTRIBUTION OF THE CHILDREN ADOPTED FROM THE PUBLIC FOSTER CARE SYSTEM?

Male	50%	25,117
Female	50%	24,883

HOW OLD WERE THE CHILDREN WHEN THEY WERE ADOPTED FROM THE PUBLIC FOSTER CARE SYSTEM?

Mean years	6.9	
Median years	6.3	
Less than 1 year	2%	993
1–5 years	46%	22,942
6–10 years	34%	16,759
11–15 years	16%	8,075
16–18 years	2%	1,181
19 or more years	0%	51

WHAT PROPORTION OF THE CHILDREN ADOPTED ARE RECEIVING AN ADOPTION SUBSIDY?

Yes	88%	44,013
No	12%	5,987

WHAT IS THE FAMILY STRUCTURE OF THE CHILD'S ADOPTIVE FAMILY?

Married couple	67%	33,251
Unmarried couple	1%	664
Single female	30%	14,975
Single male	2%	1,110

WHAT IS THE RACIAL/ETHNIC* DISTRIBUTION OF THE CHILDREN ADOPTED FROM THE PUBLIC FOSTER CARE SYSTEM?

American Indian/Alaska Native non-Hispanic	1%	715
Asian non-Hispanic	1%	260
Black non-Hispanic	35%	17,606
Hawaiian/Pacific Islander non-Hispanic	0%	164
Hispanic	16%	8,033
White non-Hispanic	38%	19,139
Unknown/unable to determine	5%	2,583
Two or more races non-Hispanic	3%	1,502

TABLE 2.6

Children adopted from the public foster care system, 2001 [CONTINUED]

HOW MANY MONTHS DID IT TAKE AFTER TERMINATION OF PARENTAL RIGHTS FOR THE CHILDREN TO BE ADOPTED?

Mean months	16	
Median months	12	
Less than 1 month	3%	1,749
1–5 months	17%	8,683
6–11 months	28%	13,845
12–17 months	20%	9,954
18–23 months	12%	6,153
24–29 months	7%	3,722
30–35 months	4%	2,027
3–4 yrs	6%	2,922
5 or more yrs	2%	945

WHAT WAS THE RELATIONSHIP OF THE ADOPTIVE PARENTS TO THE CHILD PRIOR TO THE ADOPTION?

Non-relative	17%	8,699
Foster parent	59%	29,501
Step-parent	0%	131
Other relative	23%	11,670

*Using U.S. Bureau of the Census standards, children of Hispanic origin may be of any race. Beginning in FY 2000, children could be identified with more than one race designation.

Notes: The number of adoptions reported here do not equal the number of adoption discharges reported under foster care exits because the adoptions reported here include adoptions of some children who were not in foster care but received other support from the public agency. In addition, states have historically underreported adoption discharges. In contrast, states tend to more accurately report the adoptions to the AFCARS adoption database because those are the adoptions used to calculate adoption incentive awards. Some percentages do not total 100% and/or the estimated numbers do not add up to the total number in the category due to rounding.

SOURCE: Adapted from *Adoption and Foster Care Analysis and Reporting System (AFCARS), Report Number 8*, U.S. Department of Health and Human Services, Administration for Children and Families, March 2003, http://www.acf.hhs.gov/programs/cb/publications/afcars/report8.pdf (accessed August 24, 2004)

homes with nonrelatives while waiting to be adopted (59%). (See Table 2.7.)

LIVING ARRANGEMENTS OF YOUNG ADULTS

A young person's transition into adult independence does not necessarily occur at age eighteen. The marriage age has risen since the 1950s, and, as obtaining a college education has become the norm, young people have delayed finding employment that allows them to support themselves independently of their parents. A growing portion of young adults older than eighteen continue to live in, or return to, their parents' homes. Some young people live with their parents until their mid-twenties, and others are likely to return home after moving out, especially after college or service in the military. Many young adults also share households with others.

Socioeconomic experts attribute this phenomenon to the rising cost of living in the United States. Wages have not increased at the same rate as the cost of living; therefore, the same amount of money buys less than in previous years. Real estate prices, particularly in the most populous states (New York, California, Florida, and Texas), have skyrocketed. This is good news for homeowners but bad news for renters and first-time homebuyers, a large percentage of whom are young adults.

Living with Parents

In 2002 13.7 million young adults between the ages of eighteen and twenty-four lived in their parents' homes. (See Table 2.8. This figure includes those who were living in college dormitories who were still counted as residing at their parental residences.) Males in the age group were more likely (55.3%) than females (46%) to live with their parents. This was primarily because men tend to marry at a later age than women do. Almost all men and women in this age group who lived with their parents had never been married. Table 2.9 shows that the percentage of both men and women ages fifteen to twenty-four and twenty-five to thirty-four that had never married rose steadily from 1950 to 2000, but the percentage of men who had never married was consistently higher.

Young adults who live by themselves for any length of time are unlikely to return home after experiencing independence. Those who move in with roommates, on the other hand, or who cohabit without marrying, are more likely to return to the parental home if the relation-

TABLE 2.7

Children waiting to be adopted on September 30, 2001

WHAT IS THE GENDER DISTRIBUTION OF THE WAITING CHILDREN?

Male	53%	66,175
Female	47%	59,825

HOW OLD WERE THE WAITING CHILDREN WHEN THEY WERE REMOVED FROM THEIR PARENTS OR CARETAKERS?

Mean years	4.7	
Median years	4.0	
Less than 1 year	26%	33,052
1–5 years	38%	48,026
6–10 years	27%	34,144
11–15 years	8%	10,515
16–18 years	0%	263

HOW MANY MONTHS HAVE THE WAITING CHILDREN BEEN IN CONTINUOUS FOSTER CARE?

Mean months	44	
Median months	35	
Less than 1 month	1%	725
1–5 months	4%	4,946
6–11 months	8%	9,567
12–17 months	10%	12,889
18–23 months	11%	13,420
24–29 months	10%	13,194
30–35 months	8%	10,692
36–59 months	24%	30,503
60 or more months	24%	30,064

WHAT IS THE RACIAL/ETHNIC DISTRIBUTION OF THE WAITING CHILDREN?

American Native non-Hispanic	2%	2,146
Asian non-Hispanic	0%	484
Black non-Hispanic	45%	56,306
Hawaiian/Pacific Islander non-Hispanic	0%	400
Hispanic	12%	15,253
White non-Hispanic	34%	42,913
Unknown/unable to determine	4%	5,602
Two or more races non-hispanic	2%	2,895

HOW OLD WERE THE CHILDREN ON SEPTEMBER 30, 2001?

Mean years	8.3	
Median years	8.3	
Less than 1 year	3%	4,206
1–5 years	32%	40,848
6–10 years	32%	40,648
11–15 years	28%	34,724
16–18 years	4%	5,573

WHERE WERE THE WAITING CHILDREN LIVING ON SEPTEMBER 30, 2001?

Pre-adoptive home	12%	15,141
Foster family home (relative)	19%	24,247
Foster family home (non-relative)	59%	73,992
Group home	3%	4,087
Institution	6%	7,638
Supervised independent living	0%	94
Runaway	0%	437
Trial home visit	0%	364

Notes: Waiting children are identified as children who have a goal of adoption and/or whose parental rights have been terminated. Children 16 years old and older whose parental rights have been terminated and who have a goal of emancipation have been excluded from the estimate. Using U.S. Bureau of the Census standards, children of Hispanic origin may be of any race. Beginning in fiscal year 2000, children could be identified with more than one race designation.

SOURCE: Adapted from "How Many Children Were Waiting to Be Adopted on September 30, 2001?" in *Adoption and Foster Care Analysis and Reporting System (AFCARS), no. 8*, U.S. Department of Health and Human Services, Administration for Children and Families, March 2003, http://www.acf.hhs.gov/programs/cb/publications/afcars/report8.pdf (accessed August 24, 2004)

TABLE 2.8

Young adults living at home, 1960–2002

(Numbers in thousands.)

	Male			Female		
Age	Total	Child of householder	Percent	Total	Child of householder	Percent
18 to 24 years						
2002	13,696	7,575	55.3	13,602	6,252	46.0
2001*	13,412	7,385	55.1	13,361	6,068	45.4
2000	13,291	7,593	57.1	13,242	6,232	47.1
1999	12,936	7,440	57.5	13,031	6,389	49.0
1998	12,633	7,399	58.6	12,568	5,974	47.5
1997	12,534	7,501	59.8	12,452	6,006	48.2
1996	12,402	7,327	59.0	12,441	5,955	48.0
1995	12,545	7,328	58.4	12,613	5,896	46.7
1994	12,683	7,547	59.5	12,792	5,924	46.3
1993	12,049	7,145	59.3	12,260	5,746	46.9
1992	12,083	7,296	60.4	12,351	5,929	48.0
1991	12,275	7,385	60.2	12,627	6,163	48.8
1990	12,450	7,232	58.1	12,860	6,135	47.7
1989	12,574	7,308	58.1	13,055	6,141	47.0
1988	12,835	7,792	60.7	13,226	6,398	48.4
1987	13,029	7,981	61.3	13,433	6,375	47.5
1986	13,324	7,831	58.8	13,787	6,433	46.7
1985	13,695	8,172	59.7	14,149	6,758	47.8
1984	14,196	8,764	61.7	14,482	6,779	46.8
1983	14,344	8,803	61.4	14,702	7,001	47.6
1982	14,368	(NA)	(NA)	14,815	(NA)	(NA)
1981	14,367	(NA)	(NA)	14,848	(NA)	(NA)
1980 Census	14,278	7,755	54.3	14,844	6,336	42.7
1970 Census	10,398	5,641	54.3	11,959	4,941	41.3
1960 Census	6,842	3,583	52.4	7,876	2,750	34.9
25 to 34 years						
2002	19,220	2,610	13.6	19,428	1,618	8.3
2001*	19,308	2,520	13.1	19,527	1,583	8.1
2000	18,563	2,387	12.9	19,222	1,602	8.3
1999	18,924	2,636	13.9	19,551	1,690	8.6
1998	19,526	2,845	14.6	19,828	1,680	8.5
1997	20,039	2,909	14.5	20,217	1,745	8.6
1996	20,390	3,213	16.0	20,528	1,810	9.0
1995	20,589	3,166	15.4	20,800	1,759	8.5
1994	20,873	3,261	15.6	21,073	1,859	8.8
1993	20,856	3,300	15.8	21,007	1,844	8.8
1992	21,125	3,225	15.3	21,368	1,874	8.8
1991	21,319	3,172	14.9	21,586	1,887	8.7
1990	21,462	3,213	15.0	21,779	1,774	8.1
1989	21,461	3,130	14.6	21,777	1,728	7.9
1988	21,320	3,207	15.0	21,649	1,791	8.3
1987	21,142	3,071	14.5	21,494	1,655	7.7
1986	20,956	2,981	14.2	21,097	1,686	8.0
1985	20,184	2,685	13.3	20,673	1,661	8.0
1984	19,876	2,626	13.2	20,297	1,548	7.6
1983	19,438	2,664	13.7	19,903	1,520	7.6
1982	19,090	(NA)	(NA)	19,614	(NA)	(NA)
1981	18,625	(NA)	(NA)	19,203	(NA)	(NA)
1980 Census	18,107	1,894	10.5	18,689	1,300	7.0
1970 Census	11,929	1,129	9.5	12,637	829	6.6
1960 Census	10,896	1,185	10.9	11,587	853	7.4

*Data for March 2001 and later use population controls based on Census 2000 and an expanded sample of households designed to improve state estimates of children with health insurance.
Notes: Unmarried college students living in dormitories are counted as living in their parent(s) home. NA=Not available.

SOURCE: Adapted from "Table AD-1. Young Adults Living at Home: 1960 to Present," U.S. Census Bureau, June 12, 2003, http://www.census.gov/population/socdemo/hh-fam/tabAD-1.pdf (accessed August 24, 2004)

ship fails. Some young people struggle on their own only to return home for respite from financial pressures, loneliness, or because they need emotional support or security.

Even if they do not settle into careers immediately, most young adults living at home work for wages. Those young people who lived away from home and then moved back were more likely to pay rent or make some financial contribution to the household

TABLE 2.9

Percentage of the population aged 15 and over, by sex, age, and marital status, 1950–2000

(Data based on sample)

Sex and year	15 to 24 years, never married	25 to 34 years			35 to 59 years		60 years and over		
		Never married	Divorced	Separated	Divorced	Separated	Married	Divorced or separated	Widowed
Men									
1950	77.4	18.7	1.9	1.6	2.7	2.0	68.6	3.8	19.1
1960	77.2	16.2	2.0	1.6	2.9	1.8	73.1	4.1	15.1
1970	77.9	15.5	3.1	1.9	3.7	1.9	74.8	4.8	13.2
1980	82.8	23.9	7.6	2.7	7.4	2.4	79.1	5.5	11.4
1990	88.0	36.1	7.3	2.5	11.8	2.7	76.3	7.1	11.4
2000	87.5	39.1	6.4	2.1	13.2	2.5	74.9	9.3	11.2
Women									
1950	56.4	11.3	2.8	2.5	3.4	2.5	42.2	2.7	46.5
1960	58.6	8.6	2.9	2.8	4.0	2.5	43.3	3.6	44.8
1970	63.8	10.0	4.6	3.4	5.4	2.9	42.7	4.9	44.5
1980	70.9	16.3	10.1	3.9	10.0	3.3	44.9	6.0	44.1
1990	78.9	25.0	9.8	3.8	15.0	3.5	44.5	7.7	42.5
2000	81.8	29.7	8.5	3.3	16.3	3.4	46.4	10.3	38.9

SOURCE: Rose M. Kreider and Tavia Simmons, "Table 4. Percent of the Population Aged 15 and Over by Sex and Age in Specified Marital Status: 1950 to 2000," in *Marital Status: 2000,* U.S. Census Bureau, October 2003, http://www.census.gov/prod/2003pubs/c2kbr-30.pdf (accessed August 24, 2004)

than those who never lived on their own, even if they were employed.

HOW LONG DO THEY STAY? Young men are more likely than young women to stay with their parents indefinitely. This may be because young men typically lose less of their autonomy when they return home than young women do. Young women report that they have more responsibility to help around the house and more rules to obey than do their young male counterparts.

HOMELESS CHILDREN AND YOUTH

Families with Children

Homelessness is on the rise in the United States. In 2002 the U.S. Conference of Mayors surveyed twenty-five cities and reported that requests for emergency shelter by homeless people had increased 19% over the previous year (*A Status Report on Hunger and Homelessness in America's Cities 2002: A 25-City Survey,* Washington, DC, December 2002). The most frequent reasons given by participating cities for homelessness were a lack of affordable housing; mental illness and substance abuse (and the lack of available services for both); low-paying jobs or unemployment; domestic violence; and cuts in public assistance programs.

The survey concluded that families with children accounted for 41% of the homeless population, 9% higher than a decade earlier, when families with children accounted for 32% of the homeless population. Three-quarters (73%) of these homeless families were headed by single parents.

Shelters

The 2002 Conference of Mayors survey found that emergency shelters in 60% of cities surveyed had to turn away homeless families due to a lack of resources. Nearly a third (30%) of shelter requests by homeless people could not be met, and an even higher percentage of shelter requests by families were not met (38%). In 40% of the surveyed cities, some homeless families had to break up in order to be accommodated in emergency shelters, because some shelters for women and children will not allow men (including husbands of women residents) to stay with their families.

Unaccompanied Youth

In 2002 the U.S. Conference of Mayors reported that 5% of the homeless in the surveyed cities were unaccompanied youths. Burlington, Vermont, reported the highest rate of homeless unaccompanied youth (9%), followed by Chicago, Illinois; Louisville, Kentucky; Nashville, Tennessee; New Orleans, Louisiana; Phoenix, Arizona; and San Antonio, Texas, at 5% each. Young people are among the least studied of the homeless population. Comparing studies is difficult because inconsistent terms are used to define homeless youth, including runaways, pushouts, throwaways, and unaccompanied youth. The U.S. Department of Health and Human Services (HHS) notes that much more research is needed to get a complete picture of homeless youth, evaluate programs designed for them, and design interventions to prevent homelessness among at-risk youth.

CHAPTER 3
CARING FOR CHILDREN

SOCIETAL CHANGES AND WORKING MOTHERS

In the second half of the twentieth century the "stay-at-home mom" became less common. In the early twenty-first century women with young children were much more likely to work outside the home than they had been three decades previously. In 1976 31% of women ages fifteen to forty-four with a child under twelve months old worked; by 2003 that percentage had increased to 53.7%, down from a high of 58.7% in 1998 (*Fertility of American Women: June 2002*, U.S. Census Bureau, 2003, and "Labor Force Participation of Mothers with Infants in 2003," *Monthly Labor Review*, April 22, 2004). In 2003 62.8% of mothers with children under age six and 77.8% of mothers with school-age children worked outside the home. (See Table 3.1.)

Legislation passed in the late 1970s made it more possible for women to return to work after the birth of a child. In 1976 tax code changes allowed families a tax credit on child care costs, making it more financially feasible for women to return to work. In 1978 the Pregnancy Discrimination Act was passed, making it illegal for employers to discriminate in hiring, firing, promotions, or pay levels based on pregnancy or childbirth. And in 1993 the Family and Medical Leave Act (FMLA) was passed, requiring employers to give eligible employees up to twelve weeks of unpaid leave for childbearing or family care each year.

Societal changes also contributed to the greater number of women with young children participating in the labor force. In *Maternity Leave and Employment Patterns, 1961–1995* (U.S. Census Bureau, Current Population Reports, P70-79, November 2001), Kirsten Smith and her colleagues reviewed the changing demographic profile of first-time mothers between the 1960s and 1990s to explain in part the increase. The report emphasized that during that period the incidence of first-time motherhood at age thirty or older tripled, and that first-time mothers in the 1990s

tended to be better educated than their 1960 counterparts. These older, well-educated mothers often viewed their jobs as long-term careers and believed time lost could adversely affect their ability to hold a position and earn promotions and could decrease contributions to retirement funds.

Furthermore, the increasing number of single mothers meant that more women must work to support their families. In 1970 3,410,000 women maintained single-parent households; by 2002 that number had almost tripled, to 9,969,000. Changes in government programs providing assistance to poor families also resulted in increasing numbers of single mothers entering the workforce. In 1996 the federal government abolished Aid to Families with Dependent Children (AFDC) and replaced it with a new program, Temporary Assistance to Needy Families (TANF). TANF placed a two-year time limit on benefits, requiring poor parents to work even if they had to place young children in day care. In 2003 two-thirds (65.4%) of single mothers with children under three years old were in the labor force, with a 16.7% unemployment rate. (See Table 3.2.)

Married women have also entered the workforce in larger numbers. A decline in men's real wages plus a rising cost of living has led some two-parent families to decide to maintain two incomes in order to meet financial obligations and pay for their children's future college expenses. According to the U.S. Census Bureau's Current Population Survey, 2003 Annual Social and Economic Supplement, the median income in 2002 for married couples with the wife in the paid labor force was $87,496, significantly higher than the $58,379 median income for married-couple families in which the wife was not in the paid labor force. Table 3.1 shows that 68.6% of married women with children under eighteen were in the labor force in 2003, and Table 3.2 shows that 56.8% of married women with children under age three were in the labor force in that year. Many families have come to depend upon women's economic contributions to the household.

TABLE 3.1

Employment status of population, by sex, marital status, and presence and age of own children under 18, 2003

(Numbers in thousands)

Characteristic	2003 Total	Men	Women
With own children under 18 years			
Civilian noninstitutional population	64,932	28,402	36,530
Civilian labor force	52,727	26,739	25,988
Participation rate	81.2	94.1	71.1
Employed	50,103	25,638	24,466
Employment-population ratio	77.2	90.3	67.0
Full-time workers[1]	42,880	24,762	18,118
Part-time workers[2]	7,223	876	6,347
Unemployed	2,624	1,101	1,523
Unemployment rate	5.0	4.1	5.9
Married, spouse present			
Civilian noninstitutional population	52,476	26,049	26,427
Civilian labor force	42,776	24,638	18,138
Participation rate	81.5	94.6	68.6
Employed	41,128	23,712	17,416
Employment-population ratio	78.4	91.0	65.9
Full-time workers[1]	35,315	22,954	12,360
Part-time workers[2]	5,813	757	5,056
Unemployed	1,648	926	722
Unemployment rate	3.9	3.8	4.0
Other marital status[3]			
Civilian noninstitutional population	12,455	2,354	10,102
Civilian labor force	9,950	2,100	7,850
Participation rate	79.9	89.2	77.7
Employed	8,975	1,926	7,050
Employment-population ratio	72.1	81.8	69.8
Full-time workers[1]	7,566	1,807	5,759
Part-time workers[2]	1,411	118	1,291
Unemployed	976	175	800
Unemployment rate	9.8	8.3	10.2
With own children 6 to 17 years, none younger			
Civilian noninstitutional population	35,943	15,653	20,290
Civilian labor force	30,362	14,572	15,790
Participation rate	84.5	93.1	77.8
Employed	29,040	14,008	15,032
Employment-population ratio	80.8	89.5	74.1
Full-time workers[1]	25,116	13,558	11,557
Part-time workers[2]	3,925	450	3,475
Unemployed	1,322	564	758
Unemployment rate	4.4	3.9	4.8
With own children under 6 years			
Civilian noninstitutional population	28,988	12,749	16,240
Civilian labor force	22,365	12,167	10,198
Participation rate	77.2	95.4	62.8
Employed	21,063	11,630	9,433
Employment-population ratio	72.7	91.2	58.1
Full-time workers[1]	17,764	11,203	6,561
Part-time workers[2]	3,299	426	2,872
Unemployed	1,302	538	765

WHO CARES FOR AMERICA'S CHILDREN?

School-Age Children

The Forum on Child and Family Statistics reported in *America's Children: Key National Indicators of Well-Being, 2003* that about half of children in kindergarten through eighth grade were cared for by someone other than their parents in 2001. Younger children were more likely to receive home-based care or center-based care for before or after-school hours; children in grades four and up were less likely to receive these types of care and more likely to care for themselves. (See Figure 3.1.) Only 2.8% of children in kindergarten through third grade cared for

TABLE 3.1

Employment status of population, by sex, marital status, and presence and age of own children under 18, 2003 [CONTINUED]

(Numbers in thousands)

Characteristic	2003 Total	Men	Women
With no own children under 18 years			
Civilian noninstitutional population	154,714	76,510	78,204
Civilian labor force	92,319	50,036	42,284
Participation rate	59.7	65.4	54.1
Employed	86,233	46,294	39,939
Employment-population ratio	55.7	60.5	51.1
Full-time workers[1]	69,073	39,245	29,827
Part-time workers[2]	17,160	7,049	10,111
Unemployed	6,087	3,741	2,345
Unemployment rate	6.6	7.5	5.5

[1]Usually work 35 hours or more a week at all jobs.
[2]Usually work less than 35 hours a week at all jobs.
[3]Includes never-married, divorced, separated, and widowed persons.

SOURCE: Adapted from "Table 5. Employment Status of the Population by Sex, Marital Status, and Presence and Age of Own Children under 18, 2002–03 Annual Averages," in *Employment Characteristics of Families in 2003,* United States Department of Labor, Bureau of Labor Statistics, April 20, 2004, http://www.bls.gov/news.release/pdf/famee.pdf (accessed August 24, 2004)

themselves regularly, while 25% of older children did. (See Table 3.3.)

SELF-CARE—"LATCHKEY KIDS." The phrase "latchkey kids" is used to describe children left alone or unsupervised either during the day or before or after school. These are children five to fourteen years of age whose parents report "child cares for self" as either the primary or secondary child care arrangement. In 1999 6.4 million grade-school-age children cared for themselves on a regular basis without adult supervision. (See Table 3.4.) Most of these children are twelve or older, but 443,000 children eight years of age and younger regularly took care of themselves. And the number of children in self-care may be rising; in 2002 the Annie E. Casey Foundation estimated in *Kids Count Data Book: State Profiles of Child Wellbeing* that eight million children between ages five and fourteen spend some time alone at home each week.

TWENTY-FIRST-CENTURY COMMUNITY LEARNING CENTERS. More than half of all families use after-school programs, and in many families parents rely on after-school care to provide a safe and nurturing place for their children while they are working. In response to concerns about the availability of quality after-school programs, the U.S. Department of Education initiated Twenty-First-Century Community Learning Centers (CCLC), authorized under Title X, Part I, of the Elementary and Secondary Education Act and reauthorized under Title IV, Part B, of the No Child Left Behind Act. This initiative gives grants to low-performance middle and elementary schools in rural and urban areas to provide after-school opportunities for their students, both educational and

TABLE 3.2

Employment status of mothers with own children under three years old, by single year of age of youngest child and marital status, 2003

(Numbers in thousands)

		Civilian labor force							
				Employed				Unemployed	
Characteristic	Civilian noninstitutional population	Total	Percent of population	Total	Percent of population	Full-time workers[1]	Part-time workers[2]	Number	Percent of labor force
2002									
Total mothers									
With own children under 3 years old	9,350	5,632	60.2	5,181	55.4	3,513	1,667	451	8.0
2 years	2,949	1,895	64.3	1,758	59.6	1,234	524	137	7.2
1 year	3,310	2,003	60.5	1,852	56.0	1,241	610	151	7.5
Under 1 year	3,091	1,734	56.1	1,571	50.8	1,038	533	163	9.4
Married, spouse present									
With own children under 3 years old	7,073	4,071	57.6	3,869	54.7	2,572	1,297	203	5.0
2 years	2,201	1,333	60.6	1,274	57.9	870	404	59	4.4
1 year	2,509	1,446	57.6	1,379	55.0	902	477	67	4.6
Under 1 year	2,363	1,292	54.7	1,216	51.5	800	416	77	6.0
Other marital status[3]									
With own children under 3 years old	2,278	1,562	68.6	1,313	57.6	941	372	248	15.9
2 years	748	562	75.1	484	64.7	364	120	77	13.7
1 year	802	557	69.5	473	59.0	340	134	84	15.1
Under 1 year	728	443	60.9	356	48.9	237	118	87	19.6
2003									
Total mothers									
With own children under 3 years old	9,450	5,563	58.9	5,115	54.1	3,430	1,685	446	8.0
2 years	2,987	1,896	63.5	1,752	58.7	1,205	547	143	7.5
1 year	3,353	1,997	59.6	1,842	54.9	1,223	619	154	7.7
Under 1 year	3,110	1,670	53.7	1,521	48.9	1,002	519	149	8.9
Married, spouse present									
With own children under 3 years old	7,165	4,068	56.8	3,872	54.0	2,529	1,342	197	4.8
2 years	2,243	1,350	60.2	1,281	57.1	853	428	69	5.1
1 year	2,541	1,458	57.4	1,395	54.9	906	488	64	4.4
Under 1 year	2,381	1,260	52.9	1,196	50.2	770	426	64	5.1
Other marital status[3]									
With own children under 3 years old	2,287	1,495	65.4	1,244	54.4	902	341	250	16.7
2 years	744	546	73.4	471	63.3	352	118	75	13.7
1 year	813	539	66.3	448	55.1	317	131	91	16.9
Under 1 year	730	410	56.2	325	44.5	233	92	84	20.5

[1]Usually work 35 hours or more a week at all jobs.
[2]Usually work less than 35 hours a week at all jobs.
[3]Includes never-married, divorced, separated, and widowed persons.
Notes: Own children include sons, daughters, step-children, and adopted children. Not included are nieces, nephews, grandchildren, and other related and unrelated children. Detail may not sum to totals due to rounding.

SOURCE: "Table 6. Employment Status of Mothers with Own Children under Three Years Old by Single Year of Age of Youngest Child and Marital Status, 2002–03 Annual Averages," in *Employment Characteristics of Families in 2003,* United States Department of Labor, Bureau of Labor Statistics, April 20, 2004, http://www.bls.gov/news.release/pdf/famee.pdf (accessed August 24, 2004)

recreational. The budget for the CCLC program was raised from $1 million in 1997 to $40 million in 1998, $453 million in 2000, and $846 million in 2001. In fiscal year 2004 Congress appropriated $999 million in funding for CCLC. According to the U.S. Department of Education's Web site, by 2003 CCLC supported after-school programs in about 6,800 rural and inner-city public schools in 1,420 communities.

However, Duncan Chaplin and Michael J. Puma, in "What 'Extras' Do We Get with Extracurriculars? Technical Research Consideration" (Urban Institute, September 30, 2003), offered a cautionary note about claims that these programs may give disadvantaged students an academic boost. The researchers found that extracurricular activities included in after-school programs that do not specifically target academic outcomes (for example, arts, music, drama, and language classes) had no affect on academic achievement. The authors suggested more rigorous evaluation of after-school programs that target disadvantaged youth be conducted before further money is spent on these programs, as that money might be spent on potentially more effective educational programs for disadvantaged youth.

Children Younger Than Five (Preschoolers)

In 2002 mothers with children under twelve months old were much less likely to be employed full-time than were mothers with children older than twelve months. Roughly a third of mothers with an infant (34%) were employed full-time, compared to more than half of mothers with older children (51%). (See Figure 3.2.) Almost

FIGURE 3.1

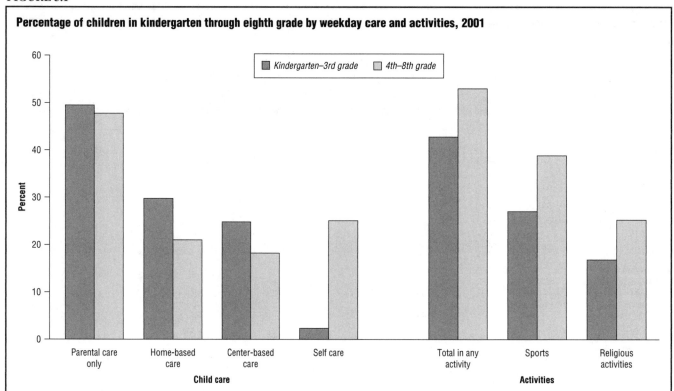

Percentage of children in kindergarten through eighth grade by weekday care and activities, 2001

SOURCE: "Figure POP8C. Percentage of Children in Kindergarten through Eighth Grade by Weekday Care and Activities, 2001," in *America's Children in Brief: Key National Indicators of Well-Being, 2004,* Federal Interagency Forum on Child and Family Statistics, 2004, http://childstats.gov/ac2004/pop8.asp (accessed August 24, 2004)

half the mothers with an infant were not in the labor force at all (45%), while only a little more than a quarter of mothers with older children (28%) were not in the labor force. Unemployment and part-time employment were relatively equal in the two groups of mothers.

In 2001 52% of children under age two and 74% of children ages three to six were in nonparental care at least some of the time. (See Table 3.5.) These preschoolers were more likely to be cared for in a center-based program (33%) than any other child-care arrangement. Relatives provided care for 23% of preschoolers and nonrelatives for 16% of preschoolers in 2001.

But care arrangements for preschoolers varied greatly according to the age of the child. As their children grow from infancy to school age, working mothers often change child-care arrangements to meet the needs of their children, their families, and their employers. Making child-care arrangements for infants and toddlers is often more difficult than for older children, because fewer organized child-care facilities admit infants and very young children, primarily due to the cost involved in hiring a sufficient number of workers and adapting facilities to care adequately for babies. In addition, many parents prefer, if possible, to keep their infants in a home environment as long as possible. In 2001 only 17% of children under age two were in center-based programs, compared with 56% of older preschoolers. (See Table 3.5.)

FACTORS THAT AFFECT CHILD CARE

Preschool Child Care

RACIAL AND ETHNIC DIFFERENCES. In 2001 African-American and Hispanic mothers of preschoolers relied more heavily on relatives to provide child care than did white mothers. Of those children in nonparental care, 34% of African-American preschoolers and 23% of Hispanic preschoolers were cared for by relatives, compared with 20% of white preschoolers. (See Table 3.5.) Both white (54%) and African-American preschoolers (55%) were more likely to be cared for by nonrelatives or in center-based programs than were Hispanic preschoolers (32%).

POVERTY MAKES A DIFFERENCE. In 2002 72.8% of preschoolers with employed mothers were regularly in nonparental care, but the type of care varied according to the income levels of those families. Jeffrey Capizzano and Gina Adams found in "Snapshots of America's Families III: Children in Low-Income Families Are Less Likely to Be in Center-Based Child Care" (Urban Institute, No. 16, November 2003) that preschoolers from lower-income families (families with an income less than 200% of the poverty line) were less likely to be in center-based care (24.9%) than children from higher-income families (31.2%). (See Table 3.6.) The authors suggest the lower percentage of lower-income children in center care reflects the lower cost of home-based care. At the same

TABLE 3.3

Percentage of children in kindergarten through eighth grade by weekday care and before- and after-school activities, by grade level, poverty, race, and Hispanic origin, 2001

Care arrangement or grade level and activity	Total	Poverty status		Race and Hispanic origin[1]			
		Below poverty	At or above poverty	White, non-Hispanic	Black, non-Hispanic	Hispanic	Other, non-Hispanic
Kindergarten through 3rd grade							
Care arrangements							
Parental care only	50.6	54.1	49.7	53.9	35.1	52.8	49.3
Nonparental care[2]	49.4	45.9	50.3	46.1	64.9	47.2	50.7
Home-based care[3]	29.6	26.6	30.4	27.9	39.0	29.9	22.8
Center-based care	23.3	23.4	23.3	21.1	32.2	21.0	30.6
Self care	2.8	3.0	2.8	1.8	6.7	3.0	3.7
Activities							
Any activity[2]	43.2	20.1	49.2	53.8	26.7	22.6	35.8
Arts[d]	14.7	6.1	17.0	17.4	12.3	6.6	17.4
Sports	27.7	7.2	33.0	36.6	10.8	13.5	21.3
Clubs	2.6	1.6	2.9	3.1	1.5	2.4	0.9
Academic activities[5]	4.0	1.4	4.6	4.4	3.9	2.7	3.7
Community services	3.7	0.9	4.5	5.0	2.2	1.6	1.0
Religious activities	17.9	8.5	20.4	21.4	13.8	10.5	13.7
Scouts	13.1	4.6	15.3	18.0	5.9	4.3	6.2
4th through 8th grade							
Care arrangements							
Parental care only	47.7	43.1	48.8	52.0	33.4	46.3	48.3
Nonparental care[2]	52.3	56.9	51.2	48.0	66.6	53.7	51.7
Home-based care[3]	20.8	24.7	20.0	18.9	28.0	22.6	16.2
Center-based care	17.8	22.7	16.7	13.6	28.5	22.3	20.3
Self care	25.0	24.5	25.2	23.8	31.9	22.1	25.5
Activities							
Any activity[2]	52.6	28.5	58.1	62.3	34.7	33.1	50.4
Arts[4]	22.2	8.9	25.3	26.6	15.4	10.7	24.4
Sports	38.5	15.7	43.7	46.8	23.6	22.0	35.0
Clubs	7.4	3.1	8.3	9.1	3.5	4.5	7.1
Academic activities[5]	9.1	7.0	9.5	8.9	11.1	6.2	12.2
Community services	11.2	4.6	12.7	13.3	6.6	6.5	13.9
Religious activities	26.4	13.5	29.3	31.8	17.0	15.9	22.1
Scouts	9.4	3.0	10.8	12.7	3.5	3.2	6.4

[1]Persons of Hispanic origin may be of any race.

[2]Children may have multiple nonparental child care arrangements, as well as be involved in more than one activity; thus the total of the three kinds of nonparental arrangements may not sum to the category, "Nonparental care category"; likewise, the seven activities listed may not sum to the category "Any activity category." Activities include organized programs a child participates in outside of school hours that are not part of a before- or after-school program.

[3]Home-based care includes care that takes place in a relative or nonrelative's private home.

[4]Arts includes activities such as music, dance, and painting.

[5]Academic activities includes activities such as tutoring or math lab.

SOURCE: "Table POP8C. Percentage of Children in Kindergarten through 8th Grade by Weekday Care and Before- and After-School Activities by Grade Level, Poverty, Race and Hispanic Origin, 2001," in *America's Children in Brief: Key National Indicators of Well-Being, 2004,* Federal Interagency Forum on Child and Family Statistics, 2004, http://childstats.gov/ac2004/tables/pop8c.asp (accessed August 24, 2004)

time, they argue that there is evidence that quality, center-based care plays a big role in helping preschoolers make a successful transition to school, and that low-income children are in large part missing this opportunity. The Children's Defense Fund also stressed the importance of providing low-income families with child care assistance to help their children succeed ("Good Child Care Assistance Policies Help Low-Income Working Families Afford Quality Care and Help Children Succeed," in *Key Facts: Essential Information about Child Care, Early Education and School-Age Care,* Children's Defense Fund, 2003).

REGIONAL DIFFERENCES. Using data from the 1997 National Survey of America's Families (NSAF), the Urban Institute calculated the number of hours that preschool children spend in institutional care by state

(*The Hours That Children under Five Spend in Child Care: Variation across States,* Jeffery Capizzano and Gina Adams, http://newfederalism.urban.org/html/series_b/b8/b8.html [accessed July 9, 2004]). Nationwide, 41% of preschool children with employed mothers were in institutional care for thirty-five or more hours per week and another 25% were in care fifteen to thirty-four hours per week. The percentages vary widely by state. Alabama and Mississippi had the highest percentages of children in full-time care (59% and 56%, respectively). Texas also ranked high, at 46%. On the other hand, California, Massachusetts, and Washington had the lowest percentages of children in full-time care, with fewer than one in three children in care for thirty-five hours or more per week (29%, 29%, and 33%, respectively). California and Washington had the highest proportions of children who spent no time in child care (30% and 26%, respectively).

TABLE 3.4

Prevalence of self-care among grade-school-age children, by child and family characteristics, 1999

(Numbers in thousands)

	Total number of children by age in years					
	Employment status					
	Not employed			Employed		
	Age of child			Age of child		
	5 to 8	9 to 11	12 to 14	5 to 8	9 to 11	12 to 14
Characteristic	Total number	Total number	Total number	Total number	Total number	Total number
Total children 5 to 14 years, in thousands	6,423	4,284	3,617	9,755	8,031	7,987
Number in self care, in thousands	134	389	872	309	1,294	3,400

	Percent of children in self care by age in years					
	Not employed			Employed		
	Age of child			Age of child		
	5–8 years Self care percent	9–11 years Self care percent	12–14 years Self care percent	5–8 years Self care percent	9–11 years Self care percent	12–14 years Self care percent
	2.1	9.1	24.1	3.2	16.1	42.6
Marital status						
Married	2.1	8.1	24.8	2.8	15.4	41.6
Widowed, separated, divorced	0.5	11.2	23.7	2.7	19.9	46.8
Never married	3.7	13.0	18.2	5.9	12.9	37.7
Race						
White	1.9	9.3	25.5	2.9	17.7	44.9
Black	1.9	9.6	19.1	3.9	9.7	32.5
Native American	13.9	6.7	26.6	9.1	34.3	41.8
Asian and Pacific Islander	3.4	3.8	12.5	3.8	6.2	32.9
White, non-Hispanic						
Other	1.8	6.1	16.1	3.3	9.6	32.7
White, non-Hispanic	2.3	11.2	29.3	3.1	19.6	47.4
Hispanic origin						
Non-Hispanic	2.5	10.7	27.2	3.4	17.5	44.4
Hispanic	0.6	4.1	12.9	1.9	8.0	30.5
Age of parent						
15–24 years	2.4	6.5	15.6	2.9	14.4	35.4
25–34 years	1.9	11.0	24.5	3.9	15.7	41.6
35+ years	1.5	9.9	27.0	2.9	18.0	45.6
Education level of parent						
Less than high school	1.1	6.9	16.5	2.1	7.5	31.3
High school diploma	2.2	7.4	20.3	3.7	14.1	40.5
College 1–3 years	2.3	11.7	28.3	3.2	17.4	44.2
College 4+ years	2.8	12.2	39.3	3.0	22.0	49.4
Family poverty level						
Below poverty line	1.7	7.3	18.6	3.9	12.3	32.1
On or above poverty line	2.1	10.2	27.2	3.1	16.8	43.8
Less than 100% poverty	1.7	7.3	18.6	3.9	12.3	32.1
100 to 200% poverty	2.4	7.8	20.9	3.1	12.4	31.9
200% and above poverty	1.8	11.5	31.3	3.1	18.4	47.6
Missing	5.3	3.3	14.8	2.1	—	37.9

Note: Because of multiple arrangements, numbers and percentages may exceed the total number of children.
— Represents or rounds to zero.

SOURCE: Adapted from "PPL Table 4. Family and Child Characteristics of Children in Self Care by Age of Child and Employment Status of Designated Parent," in *Who's Minding the Kids? Child Care Arrangements: Spring 1999,* U.S. Census Bureau, January 24, 2003, http://www.census.gov/population/socdemo/child/ppl-168/tab04.pdf (accessed August 24, 2004)

FORMAL CHILD CARE FACILITIES

While no comprehensive data exist on the types or quality of child-care facilities in the United States, the Children's Foundation, a Washington, D.C.-based private national educational nonprofit organization, estimated that in 2004 there were 117,284 regulated child-care centers in the fifty states, District of Columbia, Puerto Rico, and Virgin Islands, a 26% percent increase since 1991.

These facilities, which most often provide a school-like environment, serve five to six million children. Many more unlicensed child care facilities exist, but because they are not regulated, no reliable statistics are collected.

In 2001 almost two out of three preschool children spent time in nonparental care each week. (See Table 3.5.) Their care providers are major influences in their lives. Many

FIGURE 3.2

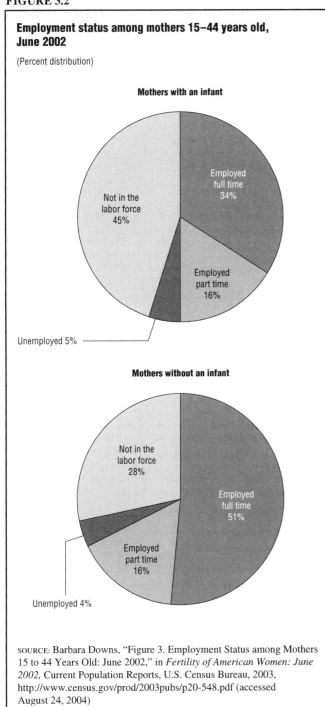

Employment status among mothers 15–44 years old, June 2002

(Percent distribution)

Mothers with an infant

Employed full time 34%
Not in the labor force 45%
Employed part time 16%
Unemployed 5%

Mothers without an infant

Not in the labor force 28%
Employed full time 51%
Employed part time 16%
Unemployed 4%

SOURCE: Barbara Downs, "Figure 3. Employment Status among Mothers 15 to 44 Years Old: June 2002," in *Fertility of American Women: June 2002,* Current Population Reports, U.S. Census Bureau, 2003, http://www.census.gov/prod/2003pubs/p20-548.pdf (accessed August 24, 2004)

working parents discover that quality and affordable care is very difficult to find. In some communities child care is hard to find at any cost. Shortages of child care for infants, sick children, children with special needs, and for school children before and after school pose problems for many parents.

Child Care during Nonstandard Hours

Many parents choose to have one parent work nonstandard hours to allow both parents to provide child care at different times of the day. According to the Bureau of Labor Statistics ("Workers on Flexible and Shift Sched-

ules in 2001," Press Release, April 18, 2002, http://www.bls.gov/news.release/flex.nr0.htm [accessed July 10, 2004]), in 2001 twenty-nine million workers, or 28.8%, worked flexible hours and were able to vary their work hours to fit their schedules. That number was nearly twice as many workers as ten years earlier. Flexible schedules were most common among professionals, and were more common among white workers (30.0%) than African-American (21.2%) or Hispanic workers (19.8%).

On the other hand, the percentage of those who worked an evening or overnight shift had fallen from 18% in 1991 to 14.5% in 2001. When asked why they worked a non-daytime schedule, 8.9% of shift or flexible schedule workers answered they did so for better family or child-care arrangements. (See Table 3.7.)

Regulations and Quality of Care

In 1988 Congress passed the Family Support Act (FSA) (PL 100-485), which included several provisions affecting Aid to Families with Dependent Children (AFDC) and the regulation of child-care services. The legislation specified that by 1990 all states had to establish child-care programs for AFDC recipients, including the guarantee of child care for families participating in the Job Opportunities and Basic Skills Training programs (JOBS). The FSA also made grants available to states to improve their child-care licensing and registration requirements.

Federal assistance to low-income families to pay for child care eroded in the late twentieth century, however, at the same time that the government imposed requirements that more low-income parents work. The 1996 welfare reform law, the Personal Responsibility and Work Opportunity Reconciliation Act (PL 104-193), eliminated the guarantee that families on welfare would receive subsidized child care and replaced it with the Child Care and Development Block Grant (CCDBG) to states. While the legislation gave states wide discretion in the use of these funds, it also imposed penalties if states failed to meet criteria for getting low-income parents into the workforce.

This legislation pushed the issue of regulation of child-care facilities to the forefront. In 1989 the National Institute of Child Health and Human Development (NICHD) initiated the Study of Early Child Care (SECC). This comprehensive ongoing longitudinal study was designed to answer many questions about the relationship between child-care experiences and children's developmental outcomes. The 1999 phase of the study examined whether the amount of time children spent in child care affected their interactions with their mothers. Results showed that the number of hours infants and toddlers spent in child care was modestly linked to the sensitivity of the mother to her child, as well as to the engagement of the child with the mother in play activities. Children in consistent quality day care showed less problem behavior, while those who switched day-care

TABLE 3.5

Percentage of preschool children by type of care arrangement and child and family characteristics, 2001

Characteristic	Parental care only	Type of nonparental care arrangement			
		Total in nonparental care[2]	Care in a home[1]		Center-based program[3]
			By a relative	By a nonrelative	
Total	39	61	23	16	33
Age/grade in school					
Ages 0–2	48	52	23	18	17
Ages 3–6, not yet in kindergarten	26	74	23	14	56
Race and Hispanic origin					
White, non-Hispanic	38	62	20	19	35
Black, non-Hispanic	26	74	35	13	40
Hispanic[4]	52	48	23	12	21
Other, non-Hispanic	35	65	23	15	37
Poverty status					
Below poverty	45	55	27	10	27
At or above poverty	37	63	22	18	35
Mother's highest level of education[5]					
Less than high school	55	45	22	8	21
High school graduate/GED	42	58	26	13	28
Vocational/technical or some college	37	63	25	15	35
College graduate	31	69	17	24	42
Mother's employment status[5]					
35 hours or more per week	15	85	34	26	42
Less than 35 hours per week	29	71	32	20	36
Looking for work	57	43	17	10	25
Not in the labor force	68	32	7	5	24

[1]Relative and nonrelative care can take place in either the child's own home or another home.
[2]Some children participate in more than one type of nonparental care arrangement. Thus, details do not sum to the total percentage of children in nonparental care.
[3]Center-based programs include day care centers, pre-kindergartens, nursery schools, Head Start programs, and other early childhood education programs.
[4]Persons of Hispanic origin may be of any race.
[5]Children without a mother in the home are excluded from estimates of mother's highest level of education and mother's employment status.
Note: Some children participate in more than one type of arrangement, so the sum of all arrangement types exceeds the total percentage in nonparental care. Center-based programs include day care centers, pre-kindergartens, nursery schools, Head Start programs, and other early childhood education programs. Relative and nonrelative care can take place in either the child's own home or another home.

SOURCE: Adapted from "Table POP8A. Child Care: Percentage of Children from Birth through Age 6, Not Yet in Kindergarten, by Type of Care Arrangement and Child and Family Characteristics, 1995 and 2001," in *America's Children in Brief: Key National Indicators of Well-Being, 2004,* Federal Interagency Forum on Child and Family Statistics, 2004, http://childstats.gov/ac2004/tables/pop8a.asp (accessed August 24, 2004)

arrangements showed more problem behaviors. Children in quality care centers had higher cognitive and language development than those in lower-quality centers.

As more children receive nonparental care at younger ages, research into the importance of quality care has shown that poor care at young ages can lead to poor adjustment and performance in school (Sheri Azer et al., National Center for Early Development and Learning, "Regulation of Child Care," *Briefs*, vol. 2, no. 1, Winter 2002). But regulation of child-care facilities varies considerably from state to state. (See Table 3.8.) No system for monitoring unlicensed care exists, and in thirty-four states child-care homes with fewer than three children are not regulated at all. In 2001 only 14% of child-care centers and 13% of family child-care homes nationwide were rated as good quality, and a large proportion were rated as being of poor quality and probably harmful to children. While there had been some improvements in the quality of child care available since 1986, especially in child/staff ratios and training requirements, the authors made several recommendations, including:

- All child-care facilities should be licensed by states, and states should employ enough staff to adequately enforce licensing standards in child-care facilities.

- Staff of child-care facilities should have training specific to the age group they supervise.

- Directors of child-care facilities should have management and child development training.

- All child-care workers should be required to complete annual training.

THE COST OF CHILD CARE

In 2000 the Children's Defense Fund (CDF) published *The High Cost of Child Care Puts Quality Care out of Reach for Many Families* (Washington, DC), which surveyed child-care costs across the country. The survey showed that child care could easily cost a family $4,000 to $6,000 per year, and in some areas more than $10,000 per year. Child-care costs for a four-year-old ranged from $3,380 annually in Mississippi to a high of $8,121 in Mass-

TABLE 3.6

Primary child care arrangements for children under age 5 with employed mothers, by age and family income

	All children under 5		Children under 3		3- and 4-year-olds	
	Low-income[a]	Higher-income[a]	Low-income	Higher-income	Low-income	Higher-income
Nonparental	68.7	74.6	62.3	67.6	77.0	84.1
Center-based	24.9	31.2	16.2	20.6	36.4	45.5
Family child care	10.7	14.2	11.0	14.7	10.3	13.6
Nanny/baby-sitter	3.5	5.3	3.3	6.5	3.8	3.7
Relative	29.5	23.9	31.7	25.8	26.5	21.3
Parent/other[b]	31.3	25.4	37.7	32.4	23.0	15.9

Note: Percentages for nonparental care may differ from sum of subcategory percentages due to rounding.
[a]Low-income is defined as below 200 percent of the federal poverty thresholds and higher-income as 200 percent of the federal poverty thresholds and above.
[b]Parent/other category contains children whose mothers did not report the use of any regular child care arrangement while they worked.

SOURCE: Jeffrey Capizzano and Gina Adams, "Table 1. Primary Child Care Arrangements for Children under Age 5 with Employed Mothers, by Age and Family Income (Percent)," in *Snapshots3 of America's Families: Children in Low-Income Families Are Less Likely to Be in Center-Based Child Care*, no. 16, The Urban Institute, November 2003, http://www.urban.org/UploadedPDF/310923_snapshots3_no16.pdf (accessed August 24, 2004)

TABLE 3.7

Full-time shift workers by reason for working a non-daytime schedule, May 2001

(Percent distribution)

Reason for working a non-daytime schedule	Total workers[1]	Shift					
		Evening	Night	Rotating	Split	Arranged	Other
Number[2] (thousands)	14,461	4,816	3,318	2,315	446	2,804	706
Percent[2]	100.0	100.0	100.0	100.0	100.0	100.0	100.0
Better arrangements for family or childcare	8.9	12.1	14.9	3.0	7.1	2.5	5.8
Better pay	6.9	7.8	11.2	5.7	4.5	2.6	4.1
Allows time for school	3.3	6.1	2.5	2.1	2.1	1.2	.8
Could not get any other job	6.6	9.1	8.9	3.4	4.6	3.2	3.6
Nature of the job	53.3	38.9	32.0	76.8	65.1	79.5	67.2
Personal preference	13.3	17.3	21.5	3.3	10.2	6.4	10.0
Some other reason	6.2	7.2	7.2	4.8	5.9	4.2	8.5

[1]Includes persons who worked a non-daytime schedule, but did not report the shift worked.
[2]Includes persons who worked a non-daytime schedule, but did not report a reason.
Note: Data relate to the sole or principal job of full-time wage and salary workers and exclude all self-employed persons, regardless of whether or not their businesses were incorporated.

SOURCE: "Table 6. Full-Time Wage and Salary Shift Workers by Reason for Working a Non-Daytime Schedule, May 2001," in *Workers on Flexible and Shift Schedules in 2001*, Bureau of Labor Statistics, April 18, 2002, http://www.bls.gov/news.release/flex.t06.htm (accessed August 24, 2004)

---

achusetts. For a twelve-month-old child, annual costs jumped to $3,692 in Mississippi and $12,978 in Massachusetts. And child care in urban care centers was so expensive that it could cost more than public college tuition.

Low-Income Families

At the beginning of the twenty-first century, a low-income family with two parents working full time, fifty-two weeks a year, at the federal minimum wage earned $21,424 per year before taxes. The Children's Defense Fund estimated that such families could afford to pay no more than 10% of their income ($2,142 annually) on child care. The Census Bureau estimated that in 1999 the average family with a preschool child spent 8.6% of its income on child-care (*Who's Minding the Kids? Child Care Arrangements: Spring 1999*, January 23, 2003). Even if able to save 10% of their income for child care, many low-income families were forced to enroll their children in low-cost, and often poor-quality, child-care

centers. As a result, these children spent much of their day in unstimulating and possibly unsafe environments.

GOVERNMENT INVOLVEMENT

Recognizing that child-care assistance helps contribute to a productive workforce, federal and state governments subsidize some child care for those on welfare and for low-income working families. However, the Children's Defense Fund noted in *State Developments in Child Care, Early Education, and School-Age Care, 2001* that only one in seven children eligible for child-care assistance received it.

Block Grants

In 1990 the 101st Congress passed what many consider the nation's first comprehensive child-care legislation—The Child Care and Development Block Grant, or CCDBG (PL 101-508). Federal funding for the CCDBG for fiscal year 2004 was almost $2.1 billion. Money is allocated to

TABLE 3.8

State child care licensing regulations, 2001

State	Infants (9 months)		Four-year-olds		Center teacher ECE training requirements (lowest alternative)		Center director ECE & administrative training requirements (lowest alternative)	
	Child:staff ratio	Group size	Child:staff ratio	Group size	Preservice requirements	Ongoing hours	Preservice requirements in ECE & administration	Ongoing hours
AK	5:1	NR	10:1	NR	None	15	12 College credits in ECE	15
AL	6:1	6	20:1	20	12 hours training in child care & development	12	124 hours training in child care, 20 hours training in administration & 12 months experience	24
AR	6:1	NR	15:1	NR	None	10	None	10
AZ	5:1/11:2	NR	15:1		None	12	60 hours of workshop training in ECE & 2 years experience	12
CA	4:1	NR	12:1	NR	6 post secondary semester or equivalent quarter units in ECE	0	12 semester units in ECE; 3 units in administration & 4 years experience	0
CO	5:1	10	12:1	24	None	9	24 semester hours in ECE & 2 years experience	9
CT	4:1	8	10:1	20	None	1% hrs worked	CDA credential & 1080 hours experience	1% hrs worked
DC	4:1	8	10:1	20	CDA credential & experience	0	2 or more years of college, including courses in ECE or related field & experience	0
DE	4:1	NR	15:1	NR	60 hours training in ECE & 1 year experience	15	CDA credential & 2 years experience	15
FL	4:1	NR	20:1	NR	40 clock hours ECE training	8	40 clock hours ECE training	8
GA	6:1	12	18:1	36	10 clock hours of child care training within first year of employment	10	None	10
HI	4:1	8	16:1	NR	CDA credential & 1 year experience	0	CDA & 4 years experience	0
IA	4:1	NR	12:1	NR	None	10	CDA or 1 year diploma in child development from community college or technical school & 1 course in business administration or 12 contact hours in administrative training	10
ID	6:1	NR	12:1	NR	None	4	None	4
IL	4:1	12	10:1	20	CDA or CCP credential	15	CDA or CCP credential, 12 semester hours in ECE, & 2 years of experience	15
IN	4:1	8	12:1	NR	None	12	Associate's degree in ECE & 3 years experiece in direct service to children	12
KS	3:1	9	12:1	24	CDA credential & 1 year experience	10	CDA credential & 1 year experience	5
KY	5:1	10	14:1	28	None	12	None	12
LA	5:1	10	15:1	15	None	0	30 clock hours of ECE training & 1 years experience	0
MA	3:1/7:2	7	10:1	20	3 credit course in child development & 9 months experience	20	14 college credits in ECE, 2 credits in child care administration & 42 months experience	20
MD	3:1	6	10:1	20	90 clock hours in ECE & 1 year experience	3	90 clock hours in ECE	6
ME	4:1	12	10:1	30	None	24	CDA credential	24
MI	4:1	NR	12:1	NR	None	0	CDA credential & 12 semester hours in child-related topics	0
MN	4:1	8	10:1	20	CDA credential & 1560 hours experience	2% of hours worked	90 clock hours in child development, human relations, or staff supervision & 1040 hours of supervisory experience	2% of hours worked
MO	4:1	8	10:1	NR	None	12	12 semester hours in child-related courses, & 2 years experience	12
MS	5:1	10	16:1	20	None	15	CDA credential or OCY Child Care Director's Credential & 2 years experience	15
MT	4:1	NR	10:1	NR	8 hours ECE training in first year	0	None	0
NC	5:1	10	20:1	25	None	20	NC Early Childhood Administrative Credential or equivalent	20
ND	4:1	8	10:1	20	None	13	CDA credential & 1 year experience	13
NE	4:1	NR	12:1	NR	None	12	None	12

states based on a state's per capita income, the number of children under age five, and the number of children receiving free or reduced-price lunches through the National School Lunch Program. Highlights of the law include:

- States must use 70% of grant funds to assist families in paying for care.
- At least 4% of funds must be used to improve availability and quality of child care.

TABLE 3.8

State child care licensing regulations, 2001 [CONTINUED]

| State | Infants (9 months) | | Four-year-olds | | Center teacher ECE training requirements (lowest alternative) | | Center director ECE & administrative training requirements (lowest alternative) | |
	Child:staff ratio	Group size	Child:staff ratio	Group size	Preservice requirements	Ongoing hours	Preservice requirements in ECE & administration	Ongoing hours
NH	4:1	12	12:1	24	Completion of 2-year vocational child care course	6	CDA credential & 4,000 hours experience	6
NJ	4:1	20	12:1	20	Certified Child Care Professional Certificate	8	None	12
NM	6:1	NR	12:1	NR	None	24	CDA, CPC, NAC, or Master Certificate & 2 years experience	24
NV	6:1	NR	13:1	NR	3 hours ECE training in first 6 months	12	12 semester hours in child-related topics	12
NY	4:1	8	8:1	21	None	15	Associate's degee in ECE/related field (with plan of study leading to Bachelor's degree) 2 years full-time teaching experience, & 2 years supervising experience	15
OH	5:1	12	14:1	28	None	15	CDA credential and 2 years experience	0
OK	4:1	8	15:1	30	None	12	None	20
OR	4:1	8	10:1	20	None	15	None	15
PA	4:1	8	10:1	20	None	6	Associate's degree that includes 30 ECE credits & 4 years experience	6
RI	4:1	8	10:1	20	Bachelor's degree in any field & must meet standards for RI Early Childhood Certificate	20	6 college courses in ECE and/or child development and 5 years experience	20
SC	6:1	NR	18:1	NR	10 clock hours training 1st year	15	15 clock hours training 1st year	20
SD	5:1	20	10:1	20	None	20	None	20
TN	5:1	10	15:1	20	None	6	None	12
TX	4:1/10:2	10	20:1	35	8 hours ECE training	15	CDA credential, 6 credits in business management & 2 years experience	20
UT	4:1	8	15:1	30	None	20	CDA, CCP, or NAC credential	20
VA	4:1	NR	12:1	NR	None	8	CDA credential & 2 years experience	0
VT	4:1	8	10:1	20	12 credits in topics related to ECE & 3 years experience	12	12 credits in topics related to ECE & 3 years experience	9
WA	4:1	8	10:1	20	20 hours approved tranning	10	CDA credential & 2 years experience	10
WI	4:1	8	13:1	24	2 non-credit dept.-approved ECE courses, 80 days experience	25	2 non-credit dept.-approved ECE courses, 10 hours training in administration if no previous training & 80 days experience	25
WV	4:1	NR	12:1	NR	None	Unspecified	CDA credential & 1 year experience	Unspecified
WY	4:1	10	12:1	30	None	30 every 2 years	CDA or CCP & 1 year experience with age served	30 every 2 years

Abbreviations: CCP = Certified child care professional credential
CDA = Child development associate credential
CEU = Continuing education unit
ECE = Early childhood education, child development or child-related field
NAC = National administrators credential
NR = Not regulated
Note: States often list a set of required preservice training alternatives. If a state has requirements for experience, high school completion, age, or training not specified in early childhood, we define it as "None."

SOURCE: Sheri Azer, et al, "2001 State Child Care Licensing Regulations at a Glance," in "Regulation of Child Care," *Early Childhood Research and Policy Briefs,* vol. 2, no. 1, Winter 2002, http://www.fpg.unc.edu/~ncedl/PDFs/RegBrief.pdf (accessed August 24, 2004)

• Working parents qualify for assistance if they have children under the age of thirteen and family income is no more than 85% of the state's median income.

Head Start

Perhaps the best-known and most successful government-funded child-care program is Head Start, a federal program begun in 1965 under the Administration for Children and Families of the U.S. Department of Health and Human Services. The free program provides early education, health care, social services, and free meals to preschool children in families whose incomes are below the poverty line or who receive public assistance. Head Start operates in every state, and in fiscal year 2002 it served 912,345 children. The Children's Defense Fund reported in *Key Facts: Essential Information about Child Care, Early Education and School-Age Care* (2003) that the program has been shown to provide many benefits, including a greater likelihood that children would do well in school and graduate from high school.

Tax Credits

The Federal Dependent Care Tax Credit helps families by allowing them to claim an income tax credit for part of their child-care expenses for children under the age of thirteen that enabled parents to work outside the home. The credit is on a sliding scale, ranging from 20% to 35% of qualified expenses; therefore, lower-income families receive slightly larger credits. In 2003 parents could claim up to $3,000 in qualified expenses for one child or $6,000 for two or more children.

Family Leave

In 1993 Congress enacted the Family and Medical Leave Act (FMLA; PL 103-3), requiring employers with fifty or more employees to give unpaid time off—twelve weeks in any twelve-month period—to employees to care for newborn or newly adopted children, sick family members, or for personal illness. The employee must be returned to the same position—or one equivalent in pay, benefits, and other terms of employment—and must receive uninterrupted health benefits. The U.S. Department of Labor reported that prior to this legislation fewer than 25% of all workers received family leave benefits and most of those who did worked in establishments of more than one hundred employees.

Jane Waldfogel reported in "Family and Medical Leave: Evidence from the 2000 Surveys" (*Monthly Labor Review,* September 2001) that in 2000 17.9% percent of FMLA leave takers took their leave to care for a newborn, newly adopted, or newly placed foster child; 9.8% used it to care for a sick child; and 7.8% used it as maternity or disability time. Of all employees covered by the FMLA with children eighteen months or younger, 45.1% of men and 75.8% of women had taken an FMLA leave in the previous eighteen months.

EMPLOYER INVOLVEMENT

Employers are increasingly providing family leave beyond the requirements of the FMLA as well as provid-

FIGURE 3.3

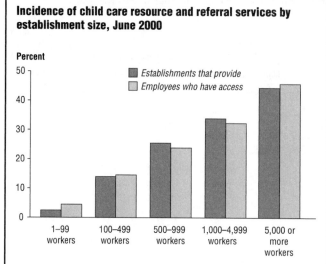

Incidence of child care resource and referral services by establishment size, June 2000

SOURCE: "Chart B. Incidence of Child Care Resources and Referral Services by Establishment Size, June 2000," in *Pilot Survey on the Incidence of Child Care Resource and Referral Services in June 2000,* Report 946, U.S. Bureau of Labor Statistics, November 2000, http://www.bls.gov/ncs/ocs/sp/ncrp0002.pdf (accessed August 24, 2004)

ing assistance to employees in finding child care. Employers have found that providing such benefits can pay off in increased productivity, worker recruitment and retention, and community goodwill. According to *Pilot Survey on the Incidence of Child Care Resource and Referral Services in June 2000* (Bureau of Labor Statistics, November 2000), 13.8% of workers in private industry, as well as in state and local government, had access to child-care resource and referral services. Most often these services were provided to employees by outside resources rather than directly by their employers. People working for large establishments (employing five thousand or more workers) fare best in access to child-care resources. (See Figure 3.3.)

CHAPTER 4
CHILDREN, TEENS, AND MONEY

FAMILY INCOME

Almost all children are financially dependent upon their parents, with their financial condition directly dependent on how much their parents earn. The U.S. Census Bureau reports that real income rose throughout the 1990s and then declined from 2001 to 2003. The median (half were higher and half were lower) household income in 2003 was $43,318. For married-couple families it was $62,405—down slightly from the previous year (Carmen DeNavas-Walt, Bernadette D. Proctor, and Robert J. Mills, U.S. Census Bureau, Current Population Reports, P60–226, *Income, Poverty, and Health Insurance Coverage in the United States: 2003*, U.S. Government Printing Office, Washington, DC, 2004).

Single-parent families, particularly those headed by single mothers, fared worse than other households. Families with female heads-of-household and no husband present had a 2003 median income of $29,307, while male-headed households with no wife present had a median income of $41,959.

Median income varied greatly by race and ethnic group in 2003. Asians had the highest median income, at $55,262, followed by non-Hispanic whites at $47,777. The median income for Hispanics in 2003 was $32,997, while for African-Americans it was approximately $29,689.

CHILDREN IN POVERTY

Children are the largest group of America's poor. In 1975 they replaced the elderly as the poorest age group. (See Figure 4.1.) In 2002 the poverty rate for all children younger than eighteen years of age was 16.7%—about 12.1 million children. In 2002 children under eighteen years old made up one quarter (25.5%) of the population of the United States, but over one third (35.1%) of the people living below the poverty line. Children under the age of six are particularly vulnerable to poverty. In 2002 the poverty rate for families with children under six was

18.5%, higher than the overall rate of child poverty. Among children under six living with a single mother, almost half (48.6%) were in poverty.

While the child poverty rate declined from 1994 to 2000, the rate of children living in poor (100% of poverty line or below) and low-income families (100–200% of poverty line) began to rise again in 2000. (See Figure 4.2.) And the majority of both African-American children (58%) and Latino children (62%) lived in low-income or poor families in 2002. (See Figure 4.3.)

The Children's Defense Fund reported in *The State of Children in America's Union: A 2002 Action Guide to Leave No Child Behind* (Washington, DC, 2002) that the United States ranks twelfth among industrialized nations in the percentage of children living in poverty, and seventeenth in "efforts to lift children out of poverty." The organization contends that an American child is born into poverty every forty-three seconds, and that one in every three children will be poor at some point in his or her childhood.

FORMS OF AID TO CHILDREN

Welfare Reform, Aid to Families with Dependent Children (AFDC), and Temporary Assistance for Needy Families (TANF)

Many programs exist in the United States to assist families and children living with economic hardship. Some of these programs are federally run, and others are run at the state level. In many cases the programs are mandated at the federal level and administered by the states, which can make tracking them complicated.

In 1996 the U.S. Congress enacted the Personal Responsibility and Work Opportunity Reconciliation Act (PL 104–193) to reform the welfare system. The primary goal of the legislation was to get as many people as possible into the paid labor force and off welfare rolls. The law set limits on how long welfare recipients could receive

FIGURE 4.1

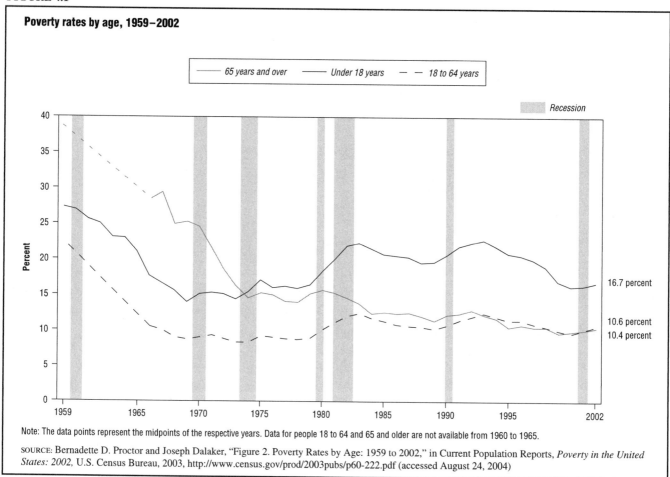

Poverty rates by age, 1959–2002

Note: The data points represent the midpoints of the respective years. Data for people 18 to 64 and 65 and older are not available from 1960 to 1965.

SOURCE: Bernadette D. Proctor and Joseph Dalaker, "Figure 2. Poverty Rates by Age: 1959 to 2002," in Current Population Reports, *Poverty in the United States: 2002,* U.S. Census Bureau, 2003, http://www.census.gov/prod/2003pubs/p60-222.pdf (accessed August 24, 2004)

FIGURE 4.2

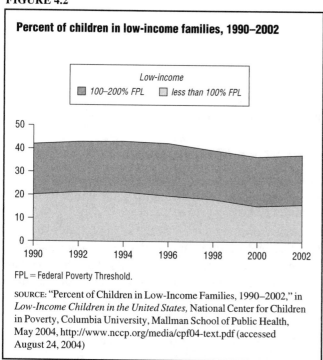

Percent of children in low-income families, 1990–2002

FPL = Federal Poverty Threshold.

SOURCE: "Percent of Children in Low-Income Families, 1990–2002," in *Low-Income Children in the United States,* National Center for Children in Poverty, Columbia University, Mallman School of Public Health, May 2004, http://www.nccp.org/media/cpf04-text.pdf (accessed August 24, 2004)

FIGURE 4.3

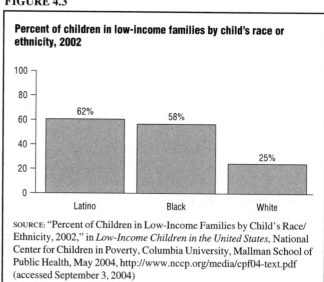

Percent of children in low-income families by child's race or ethnicity, 2002

SOURCE: "Percent of Children in Low-Income Families by Child's Race/ Ethnicity, 2002," in *Low-Income Children in the United States,* National Center for Children in Poverty, Columbia University, Mallman School of Public Health, May 2004, http://www.nccp.org/media/cpf04-text.pdf (accessed September 3, 2004)

assistance, encouraging them to seek gainful employment. Aid to Families with Dependent Children (AFDC), a guaranteed assistance program for low-income families, was eliminated and replaced with the Temporary Assistance for Needy Families (TANF) program. Under TANF, states receive a fixed amount from the federal government based on what they spent on welfare programs in 1994 without regard to subsequent changes in need. TANF frees the states from many federal constraints on how they manage the funds. The program reduced the federal wel-

TABLE 4.1

Total number of families and recipients of Temporary Assistance for Needy Families (TANF), September 1996 and September 2003

	TANF families			TANF recipients		
	Total families 4th qtr FY03	Change from September 1996 to Sep-03		Total recipients 4th qtr FY03	Change from September 1996 to Sep-03	
State	3-Sep	Sep-96 families	% change	3-Sep	Sep-96 recipients	% change
Alabama	19,228	40,708	−52.80%	45,528	99,818	−54.40%
Alaska	4,909	12,319	−60.20%	13,650	36,033	−62.10%
Arizona	51,336	61,787	−16.90%	121,271	167,410	−27.60%
Arkansas	10,745	22,109	−51.40%	24,469	56,470	−56.70%
California	449,275	870,343	−48.40%	1,099,695	2,550,032	−56.90%
Colorado	14,210	33,554	−57.70%	37,114	93,282	−60.20%
Connecticut	20,967	57,103	−63.30%	43,844	158,454	−72.30%
Delaware	5,699	10,474	−45.60%	12,951	23,743	−45.50%
Dist. of Col.	16,825	25,139	−33.10%	42,980	68,858	−37.60%
Florida	58,555	200,292	−70.80%	121,921	531,485	−77.10%
Georgia	56,496	120,914	−53.30%	134,819	323,471	−58.30%
Guam	3,072	2,254	36.30%	10,783	8,364	28.90%
Hawaii	9,367	21,887	−57.20%	24,384	66,510	−63.30%
Idaho	1,727	8,393	−79.40%	3,175	21,142	−85.00%
Illinois	34,688	217,815	−84.10%	87,545	635,538	−86.20%
Indiana	51,711	49,747	3.90%	135,339	131,775	2.70%
Iowa	20,135	31,088	−35.20%	52,528	84,556	−37.90%
Kansas	15,859	23,386	−32.20%	41,288	62,466	−33.90%
Kentucky	35,252	70,442	−50.00%	77,697	169,822	−54.20%
Louisiana	23,069	66,542	−65.30%	58,504	225,498	−74.10%
Maine	9,196	19,745	−53.40%	28,195	53,205	−47.00%
Maryland	25,678	68,931	−62.70%	61,168	189,342	−67.70%
Massachusetts	50,875	84,333	−39.70%	112,810	225,439	−50.00%
Michigan	78,549	167,529	−53.10%	210,154	494,991	−57.50%
Minnesota	36,096	57,248	−36.90%	93,508	167,362	−44.10%
Mississippi	19,722	45,223	−56.40%	45,182	120,626	−62.50%
Missouri	41,494	79,100	−47.50%	102,031	219,651	−53.50%
Montana	5,465	9,812	−44.30%	15,017	28,299	−46.90%
Nebraska	11,049	14,379	−23.20%	27,533	38,914	−29.20%
Nevada	9,547	13,210	−27.70%	22,874	32,803	−30.30%
New Hampshire	6,077	8,915	−31.80%	14,044	22,340	−37.10%
New Jersey	43,656	100,806	−56.70%	105,702	269,632	−60.80%
New Mexico	17,421	32,974	−47.20%	45,885	98,427	−53.40%
New York	145,627	412,720	−64.70%	331,144	1,127,888	−70.60%
North Carolina	39,201	107,483	−63.50%	80,956	263,093	−69.20%
North Dakota	3,336	4,668	−28.50%	8,667	12,748	−32.00%
Ohio	85,008	201,945	−57.90%	188,226	541,055	−65.20%
Oklahoma	15,154	35,299	−57.10%	37,169	94,239	−60.60%
Oregon	18,093	28,525	−36.60%	41,302	74,320	−44.40%
Pennsylvania	84,288	180,123	−53.20%	220,136	509,430	−56.80%
Puerto Rico	18,601	49,511	−62.40%	52,295	149,944	−65.10%
Rhode Island	12,961	20,489	−36.70%	34,187	55,953	−38.90%
South Carolina	19,266	42,906	−55.10%	46,281	110,837	−58.20%
South Dakota	2,690	5,698	−52.80%	5,919	15,384	−61.50%
Tennessee	72,345	96,206	−24.80%	191,652	251,717	−23.90%
Texas	117,532	238,757	−50.80%	281,765	638,119	−55.80%
Utah	8,944	14,044	−36.30%	22,944	38,564	−40.50%
Vermont	4,815	8,680	−44.50%	12,243	24,045	−49.10%
Virgin Islands	526	1,348	−61.00%	1,591	4,808	−66.90%
Virginia	8,225	60,455	−86.40%	23,527	148,529	−84.20%
Washington	53,534	96,801	−44.70%	131,721	266,591	−50.60%
West Virginia	16,405	37,595	−56.40%	41,750	84,911	−50.80%
Wisconsin	21,708	49,932	−56.50%	52,280	142,746	−63.40%
Wyoming	388	4,343	−91.10%	694	11,783	−94.10%
U.S. totals	**2,006,597**	**4,346,029**	**−53.80%**	**4,880,037**	**12042462**	**−59.50%**

SOURCE: Adapted from "Temporary Assistance for Needy Families: Total Number of Families and Recipients, July–September 2003," in *Welfare Rolls Drop Again*, U.S. Department of Health and Human Services, March 30, 2004, http://www.acf.hhs.gov/news/press/2004/TANF_TOTFAM_4th2003.htm (accessed August 24, 2004)

fare commitment by $55 billion. Total TANF expenditures for fiscal year 2002 were $23.4 billion.

Since the inception of TANF, the number of welfare cases has declined. The total number of welfare recipients fell from 14.4 million in March 1994 to 5.3 million in September 2001,

a drop of 63%. Between September and December 2001, due in part to the terrorist attacks of September 11, 2001, AFDC/TANF recipient rolls increased by two hundred thousand. At the end of 2001 there were 5.5 million participants. But by September 2003 the number of recipients had once again declined, to about 4.9 million. (See Table 4.1.)

When welfare caseloads are counted by the number of recipient families instead of individual recipients, the same pattern of decline is seen. Participating families peaked at 5.1 million in March 1994. At the end of 2001 there were 2.1 million families enrolled, a 59% decrease. By September 2003 there were only two million families enrolled. (See Table 4.1.) This represents the largest welfare caseload decrease in history, the smallest number of people on welfare since 1968, and the lowest percentage of the population on welfare since 1965. The strong economy and job market during the 1990s played a role in reducing caseloads.

Under TANF each state decides what categories of children receive aid. AFDC required states to aid all families with children eligible under federal rules unless their income was above state-set limits. TANF, on the other hand, requires that a recipient work in exchange for time-limited assistance. Because of this requirement, the number of working recipients reached an all-time high of 34% in 2000, compared with less than 7% in 1992.

Despite such improvements, welfare reform has been attacked for its coercive aspects. The new standards set a number of ineligibility rules. For example, states are not permitted to use TANF to aid unwed mothers under the age of eighteen unless they live in an adult-supervised setting and, if not already a high school graduate, attend school. Mothers are in most cases barred from receiving TANF assistance unless they are willing to name the fathers of their children. And Congress used the welfare law to launch a campaign against "illegitimacy"—and not only among TANF recipients. In both 2000 and 2001 the Department of Health and Human Services offered an award ($100 million in 2000 and $75 million in 2001) to states that had the greatest decrease in their ratio of births to unmarried mothers to total births without an increase in abortion rates.

CHARACTERISTICS OF TANF RECIPIENTS. One of the primary goals of the welfare reform laws enacted in the mid-1990s was to help people receiving public assistance get back into the paid labor force. A count of how many current and former welfare recipients are employed is, therefore, an important measure of the success of welfare reforms. Analysis shows that the employment rate of current and former TANF recipients has increased significantly. In fiscal year 2001 working recipients accounted for 26.7% of adult TANF recipients, compared with 11.3% in fiscal year 1996 (*Indicators of Welfare Dependence, Annual Report to Congress,* U.S. Department of Health and Human Services, 2003).

Consequently, income levels of TANF recipients also rose. Average monthly earnings of employed adult TANF recipients increased from $466 in fiscal year 1996 to $533 in 1998, $598 in 1999, $668 in 2000, and $686 in 2001—an increase of 47% between 1996 and 2001.

According to the U.S. Department of Health and Human Services, the average number of people in a TANF family was 2.6 in 2001, down from an average of 2.8 in 1996. Almost half (44.8%) of TANF families in 2001 included one child recipient, 28.5% included two child recipients, and 24.7% included three or more child recipients. Two-thirds (66.9%) of these families were headed by a single adult. Only 11.7% of recipients were married.

The average monthly benefit per TANF recipient in 2001 was $137, down from a high of $221 (in 2001 dollars) in 1978 under the AFDC program. The average monthly benefit per family was $351, down from a high of $766 (in 2001 dollars) in 1969. (See Table 4.2.) Benefits included cash assistance, food stamps, and health insurance under Medicaid.

Earned Income Tax Credit

The Earned Income Tax Credit (EITC), originally approved by Congress in 1975, reduces the amount of taxes owed by working people with low incomes and can result in a tax refund. To receive the EIC for 2003, a single person with no children must have had an adjusted gross income of no more than $11,230, with one child no more than $29,666, and with two or more children no more than $33,692. The adjusted gross income levels were $1,000 higher for married couples filing jointly. The maximum credit in 2003 was $2,547 for a family with one child and $4,204 for a family with two or more children. The maximum credit for those without qualifying children was $382.

In 2004 employees with at least one child living with them could file an Earned Income Credit Advance Payment Certificate with an employer to receive the advance EITC payments. The employer paid part of the credit to the employee in advance throughout the year, and the taxpayer could claim the rest when filing a 2004 federal tax return.

The Special Supplemental Nutrition Program for Women, Infants, and Children

The Special Supplemental Nutrition Program for Women, Infants, and Children (WIC) provides food assistance and nutritional screening for low-income pregnant and postpartum women and their infants and children under the age of five. Congress appropriated almost $5 billion for WIC in fiscal year 2004. Participants must have an income below 185% of the poverty level and be nutritionally at risk. The 2004–05 eligibility guidelines stated that a family of one could earn up to $1,436 a month and still qualify for WIC. A family of four could earn $2,907 a month and participate in WIC.

Recipients receive food items or vouchers for purchases of certain items in retail stores. The WIC program is federally funded but administered by state and local health agencies. In April 2002 about eight million women

TABLE 4.2

Trends in average monthly payment for Aid to Families with Dependent Children (AFDC) and Temporary Assistance for Needy Families (TANF), 1962–2001

Fiscal year	Monthly benefit per recipient		Average number of persons per family	Monthly benefit per family (not reduced by child support)		Weighted average[1] maximum benefit (per 3-person family)	
	Current dollars	2001 dollars		Current dollars	2001 dollars	Current dollars	2001 dollars
1962	$31	$168	3.9	$121	$634	NA	NA
1963	31	166	4	126	650	NA	NA
1964	32	167	4.1	131	670	NA	NA
1965	34	174	4.2	140	705	NA	NA
1966	35	178	4.2	146	716	NA	NA
1967	36	179	4.1	150	716	NA	NA
1968	40	188	4.1	162	746	NA	NA
1969	43	198	4	173	766	186[2]	854
1970	46	200	3.9	178	753	194[2]	848
1971	48	200	3.8	180	730	201[2]	840
1972	51	207	3.6	187	732	205[2]	828
1973	53	205	3.5	187	701	213[2]	824
1974	57	202	3.4	194	670	229[2]	816
1975	63	206	3.3	209	658	243	791
1976	71	216	3.2	226	665	257	782
1977	78	220	3.1	241	662	271	768
1978	83	221	3	249	644	284	756
1979	87	213	2.9	257	609	301	735
1980	94	207	2.9	274	583	320	703
1981	96	192	2.9	277	536	326	651
1982	103	192	2.9	300	543	331	617
1983	106	190	2.9	311	537	336	600
1984	110	189	2.9	321	534	352	602
1985	112	186	2.9	329	527	369	610
1986	115	186	2.9	339	529	383	618
1987	123	193	2.9	359	546	393	617
1988	127	192	2.9	370	541	404	609
1989	131	189	2.9	381	531	412	593
1990	135	185	2.9	389	516	421	577
1991	135	176	2.9	388	490	425	554
1992	136	172	2.9	389	477	419	530
1993	131	161	2.8	373	444	414	509
1994	134	160	2.8	376	437	420	497
1995	134	157	2.8	376	425	418	487
1996	135	152	2.8	374	410	422	478
1997[3]	130	144	2.8	362	405	420	464
1998	130	142	2.7	358	406	432	469
1999	133	142	2.7	357	439	452	481
2000	133	138	2.6	349	428	453	468
2001	137	137	2.6	351	351	456	456

[1]The maximum benefit for a 3-person family in each state is weighted by that state's share of total AFDC families.
[2]Estimated based on the weighted average benefit for a 4-person family.
[3]The Personal Responsibility and Work Opportunity Reconciliation Act of 1996 repealed the AFDC program as of July 1, 1997 and replaced it with the Temporary Assistance to Needy Families (TANF) program.
Note: AFDC benefit amounts have not been reduced by child support collections. Constant dollar adjustments to 2001 level were made using a CPI-U-X1 fiscal-year price index.

SOURCE: "Table TANF 6. Trends in AFDC/TANF Average Monthly Payments, 1962–2001," in *Indicators of Welfare Dependence, Annual Report to Congress,* U.S. Department of Health and Human Services, 2003, http://aspe.hhs.gov/hsp/indicators03/index.htm (accessed August 24, 2004)

and their children participated in WIC, an increase of 2% since April 2000 (*WIC Participant and Program Characteristics, 2002*, U.S. Department of Agriculture, Food and Nutrition Service, September 2003). About two-thirds (75.8%) were infants and children. Two-thirds of WIC participants were at or below the poverty line.

The Food Stamp Program

The food stamp program, administered by the U.S. Department of Agriculture (USDA), provides low-income households with online electronic benefit cards that can be used at most grocery stores much like debit cards in place of cash. Food stamps are intended to ensure that recipients

have access to a nutritious diet. They are available to households that have a gross monthly income of no more than 130% of the poverty line and a net monthly income at or below the poverty line. Almost all households that received food stamp benefits in 2002 lived in poverty.

The amount of money a family receives on their benefit card is based on the USDA's estimate of how much it costs to provide households with nutritious, low-cost meals. This estimate changes yearly to reflect inflation. In fiscal year 2002 the maximum monthly benefit for a family of four was $452, while the average monthly benefit for all households was $173. Food stamp households containing children received an average of $254 in benefits per

TABLE 4.3

Average values of selected characteristics of food stamp households, 2002

Households with:	Average values			
	Gross monthly income (dollars)	Net monthly income (dollars)	Monthly food stamp benefit (dollars)	Household size (persons)
Total	**633**	**355**	**173**	**2.3**
Children	747	436	254	3.3
Single-adult household	676	381	247	3.1
Male adult	681	387	223	2.9
Female adult	676	381	249	3.1
Multiple-adult household	1022	649	298	4.4
Married head household	1057	667	299	4.5
Other multiple-adult household	945	610	295	4.3
Children only	512	253	190	2.2
Elderly	646	368	64	1.3
Living alone	589	316	50	1.0
Not living alone	876	582	121	2.4
Disabled	739	454	106	2.0
Living alone	596	311	50	1.0
Not living alone	942	657	187	3.3
Other households*	198	67	128	1.1
Single-person household	174	53	122	1.0
Multi-person household	472	219	201	2.2
Single-person households	460	229	73	1.0

*Households not containing children, elderly persons, or disabled persons.

SOURCE: Randy Rosso and Melissa Faux, "Table 3.4. Average Values of Selected Characteristics by Household Composition, Fiscal Year 2002," in *Characteristics of Food Stamp Households: Fiscal Year 2002,* Report No. FSP-03-CHAR02, U.S. Department of Agriculture, Food and Nutrition Service, Office of Analysis, Nutrition and Evaluation, 2003, http://www.fns.usda.gov/oane/MENU/Published/FSP/FILES/Participation/2002Characteristics.pdf (accessed August 24, 2004)

month, in part because households with children tended to be larger (3.3 people) than households in general (2.3 people). (See Table 4.3.)

The majority of households that received food stamps in 2002 contained children—54.1%, or 4.4 million households. Two-thirds of these households (34.5%) were headed by a single parent, usually a single mother (32.8%) (*Characteristics of Food Stamp Households: Fiscal Year 2002*, U.S. Department of Agriculture, Food and Nutrition Service, Office of Analysis, Nutrition and Evaluation, 2003).

Supplemental Security Income (SSI)

The SSI program was enacted in Public Law 92–603 on October 30, 1972, to provide a minimum income for blind or disabled individuals. For children to qualify for SSI, their parents must meet the income requirements, they must be neither married nor the head of a household, must be under the age of eighteen (or under the age of twenty-two if a full-time student), and must meet the SSI definition of disabled. Children are considered disabled if they have "marked and severe functional limitations" because of a physical or mental impairment. Many of these children are automatically eligible for food stamps and Medicaid coverage.

In 1974 70,900 disabled and blind children received SSI benefits, representing 1.8% of all recipients. The pro-

gram has since expanded to include a greater proportion of disabled children. In 1996 the number of children receiving benefits peaked at 955,174, or 14.4% of all SSI recipients, and then dropped to 846,784 in December 2000. (See Table 4.4.) In December 2002 914,821 children received SSI payments averaging $487.73 per month. These children made up 13.5% of SSI recipients in 2002. By July 2004 the maximum monthly payment per child was $564.

Other Forms of Assistance

The federal government spends billions of dollars on behalf of low-income children. Most services are spread over several major income-tested programs (meaning the family income cannot exceed a certain limit). Many programs are for noncash assistance. These include Medicaid, subsidized housing, and free or reduced-price school lunch and breakfast programs.

The National School Lunch Program provides millions of children with nutritious food each day. Children whose families earn no more than 185% of the poverty level are eligible for reduced price school lunches; children whose families earn no more than 130% of the poverty level are eligible for free school lunches. In fiscal year 2003 the U.S. government spent $6.3 billion for the National School Lunch Program and another $1.7 billion on the school breakfast program. In that year 28.4 million

TABLE 4.4

Supplemental Security Income (SSI) recipients by age, December 1974–2002

Year	Total	Under age 18		Aged 18–64		Aged 65 or older	
		Number	Percentage of total	Number	Percentage of total	Number	Percentage of total
1974	3,996,064	70,900	1.8	1,503,155	37.6	2,422,009	60.6
1975	4,314,275	107,026	2.5	1,699,394	39.4	2,507,855	58.1
1976	4,235,939	125,412	3.0	1,713,594	40.5	2,396,933	56.6
1977	4,237,692	147,355	3.5	1,736,879	41.0	2,353,458	55.5
1978	4,216,925	165,899	3.9	1,747,126	41.4	2,303,900	54.6
1979	4,149,575	177,306	4.3	1,726,553	41.6	2,245,716	54.1
1980	4,142,017	190,394	4.6	1,730,847	41.8	2,220,776	53.6
1981	4,018,875	194,890	4.8	1,702,895	42.4	2,121,090	52.8
1982	3,857,590	191,570	5.0	1,655,279	42.9	2,010,741	52.1
1983	3,901,497	198,323	5.1	1,699,774	43.6	2,003,400	51.3
1984	4,029,333	211,587	5.3	1,780,459	44.2	2,037,287	50.6
1985	4,138,021	227,384	5.5	1,879,168	45.4	2,031,469	49.1
1986	4,269,184	241,198	5.6	2,010,458	47.1	2,017,528	47.3
1987	4,384,999	250,902	5.7	2,118,710	48.3	2,015,387	46.0
1988	4,463,869	255,135	5.7	2,202,714	49.3	2,006,020	44.9
1989	4,593,059	264,890	5.8	2,301,926	50.1	2,026,243	44.1
1990	4,817,127	308,589	6.4	2,449,897	50.9	2,058,641	42.7
1991	5,118,470	397,162	7.8	2,641,524	51.6	2,079,784	40.6
1992	5,566,189	556,470	10.0	2,910,016	52.3	2,099,703	37.7
1993	5,984,330	722,678	12.1	3,148,413	52.6	2,113,239	35.3
1994	6,295,786	841,474	13.4	3,335,255	53.0	2,119,057	33.7
1995	6,514,134	917,048	14.1	3,482,256	53.5	2,114,830	32.5
1996	6,613,718	955,174	14.4	3,568,393	54.0	2,090,151	31.6
1997	6,494,985	879,828	13.5	3,561,625	54.8	2,053,532	31.6
1998	6,566,069	887,066	13.5	3,646,020	55.5	2,032,983	31.0
1999	6,556,634	847,063	12.9	3,690,970	56.3	2,018,601	30.8
2000	6,601,686	846,784	12.8	3,744,022	56.7	2,010,880	30.5
2001	6,688,489	881,836	13.2	3,811,494	57.0	1,995,159	29.8
2002	6,787,857	914,821	13.5	3,877,752	57.1	1,995,284	29.4

SOURCE: "Table 3. Recipients by Age, December 1974–2002," in *Supplemental Security Income Annual Statistical Report, 2002,* U.S. Social Security Administration, 2003, http://www.ssa.gov/policy/docs/statcomps/ssi_asr/2002/ssi_asr02.pdf (accessed August 24, 2004)

children took part in the school lunch program, up from 26.9 million in 1999. (See Table 4.5.)

CHILD SUPPORT

Who Receives Child Support?

Children living in single-parent families are far more likely to be poor than children living in two-parent households, and the number of children living with only one parent—usually the mother—is increasing. According to a report by the U.S. Census Bureau (*Custodial Mothers and Fathers and Their Child Support: 2001,* 2003), in spring 2002 13.4 million parents had custody of 21.5 million children under the age of twenty-one whose other parent lived elsewhere. Mothers accounted for 84.4% of all custodial parents; 15.6% of custodial parents were fathers. These proportions have not changed significantly since 1994.

More than half (59.1%) of the 13.4 million custodial parents in April 2002 had a child support agreement with the other parent. Most of these agreements required child support payments from the noncustodial parent. In 2001 74% of custodial parents due support received at least some payments. Almost half (44.8%) received all the payments they were due, up from only a little more than a

third (36.9%) in 1993. (See Figure 4.4.) Noncustodial parents who had visitation rights to their children were more likely to pay child support (77.1%) than parents who did not (55.8%).

Receipt of child support payments made a significant difference in the household incomes of single-parent families. In 2001 the average family income of custodial parents who received child support was $29,008. In contrast, custodial parents who either had no child support agreements or had agreements but received only part or none of the amount due had an average family income of $24,055 and $23,571, respectively. (See Table 4.6.)

Government Assistance in Obtaining Child Support

Inadequate financial support from noncustodial parents contributes to the high incidence of poverty among children living in single-parent families. When custodial parents are not paid the child support due them, their families suffer financially and often must turn to public welfare. Government agencies, therefore, have an interest in recovering child support from delinquent parents.

In 1975 Congress established the Child Support Enforcement program (CSE), a collaborative effort among local, state, and federal agencies, to ensure that children received financial support from both parents.

TABLE 4.5

National School Lunch Program, total participation, 1999–2003

Data as of June 24, 2004

State/territory	Fiscal year 1999	Fiscal year 2000	Fiscal year 2001	Fiscal year 2002	Fiscal year 2003
					Preliminary
Alabama	540,810	541,403	542,346	545,747	549,312
Alaska	49,882	50,421	52,310	52,807	52,962
Arizona	443,495	446,697	470,420	489,637	517,944
Arkansas	310,741	311,943	312,901	315,263	317,850
California	2,537,539	2,566,924	2,613,904	2,659,390	2,732,026
Colorado	318,809	320,778	321,516	325,715	327,775
Connecticut	258,521	265,095	272,008	280,212	283,625
Delaware	70,267	71,546	71,670	73,803	75,377
Dist. of Columbia	47,255	47,203	50,990	50,349	47,961
Florida	1,307,102	1,322,452	1,342,800	1,369,013	1,397,558
Georgia	1,054,226	1,065,362	1,083,434	1,112,375	1,129,514
Guam	14,141	13,401	13,779	15,849	17,408
Hawaii	145,914	143,108	140,739	135,219	131,954
Idaho	141,624	142,779	143,895	147,111	148,927
Illinois	1,035,129	1,057,807	1,071,930	1,090,013	1,098,525
Indiana	613,022	622,399	630,733	643,464	663,592
Iowa	381,877	382,630	380,864	380,099	380,864
Kansas	307,285	308,414	312,712	316,260	317,481
Kentucky	496,734	499,368	499,733	508,526	511,470
Louisiana	652,265	646,083	634,852	632,139	626,153
Maine	105,813	106,983	107,012	107,618	103,773
Maryland	386,356	392,414	403,446	426,838	435,790
Massachusetts	520,478	528,225	538,639	541,981	541,767
Michigan	780,189	802,805	816,753	826,252	842,600
Minnesota	566,210	562,471	570,852	576,121	577,211
Mississippi	400,699	397,111	398,513	397,076	394,883
Missouri	583,973	586,760	591,502	622,416	603,434
Montana	80,974	79,000	77,912	77,649	77,621
Nebraska	217,617	220,042	219,261	221,491	222,865
Nevada	108,417	113,726	120,947	130,314	136,859
New Hampshire	100,808	103,961	105,864	107,514	115,808
New Jersey	567,684	585,571	588,152	599,548	604,595
New Mexico	193,935	192,374	195,228	198,166	201,272
New York	1,773,276	1,789,676	1,777,983	1,792,804	1,789,181
North Carolina	815,517	821,586	834,328	843,699	863,206
North Dakota	81,979	80,367	79,384	77,833	77,230
Ohio	986,279	995,968	999,069	1,012,719	1,022,307
Oklahoma	371,286	374,309	373,613	377,357	382,662
Oregon	266,428	266,059	266,988	274,337	275,713
Pennsylvania	1,007,162	1,013,043	1,024,563	1,041,254	1,057,855
Puerto Rico	397,160	397,842	386,977	399,236	392,900
Rhode Island	61,014	63,304	64,589	68,802	82,161
South Carolina	473,096	470,932	468,866	469,483	466,834
South Dakota	104,266	104,646	104,717	103,480	103,592
Tennessee	609,197	621,630	621,187	636,692	635,613
Texas	2,392,448	2,450,504	2,494,054	2,582,527	2,671,907
Utah	266,892	269,491	273,112	278,500	283,627
Vermont	52,048	51,970	52,724	53,713	54,356
Virgin Islands	17,232	16,116	15,135	15,440	15,450
Virginia	651,242	665,276	669,890	678,369	687,945
Washington	457,640	465,968	473,725	488,104	495,458
West Virginia	204,129	201,588	196,138	195,950	204,626
Wisconsin	530,915	536,099	545,827	552,574	561,176
Wyoming	53,399	51,688	49,806	49,889	49,485
Dept. of Defense	33,934	34,176	36,239	36,990	33,488
Total	**26,946,327**	**27,239,490**	**27,506,537**	**28,005,726**	**28,393,529**

Participation data are nine-month averages; summer months (June–August) are excluded. Participation is based on average daily meals divided by an attendance factor of 0.927. Department of Defense activity represents children of armed forces personnel attending schools overseas. Data are subject to revision.

SOURCE: "National School Lunch Program: Total Participation," U.S. Department of Agriculture, Food and Nutrition Service, June 24, 2004, http://www.fns.usda.gov/pd/slfypart.htm (accessed August 24, 2004)

Under the Child Support Recovery Act of 1992, noncustodial parents delinquent on child support due in another state can be prosecuted. CSE services are automatically provided to families receiving assistance under the Temporary Assistance for Needy Families (TANF) program; any support collected usually reimburses the state and federal governments for TANF payments made to the family. Child support services also are available for a small application fee to families not receiving TANF.

Provisions in the Personal Responsibility and Work Opportunity Reconciliation Act of 1996 (PL 104–193) strengthened and improved child support collection activities. The law established a National Directory of New Hires to track parents across state lines, made the process for establishing paternity faster and easier, and enacted tough new penalties for delinquent parents, including expanded wage garnishment and suspension or revocation of driver's licenses. The law also requires single-mother TANF applicants to disclose the paternity of their children and to assign any child support payments to the state. These efforts have paid off; in fiscal year 2003 CSE handled more than 15.9 million cases and collected more than $25 billion, up 5.2% from the previous year (*Child Support Enforcement FY 2003 Preliminary Data Report*, Department of Health and Human Services, Administration for Children and Families, June 2004).

Interstate Child Support

Child-support awards in which the noncustodial parent lives in a state different from the custodial parent are among the most difficult to enforce. In 2001 the government estimated that 30% of all child support cases involved more than one state. Custodial parents in interstate cases are less likely to receive payments than those in in-state cases, even though about the same proportion are awarded child support.

THE COST OF RAISING A CHILD

USDA Estimates

Since the 1960s the Family Economics Research Group of the U.S. Department of Agriculture (USDA) has provided estimates on the cost of rearing a child. The estimates are calculated per child in a household with two children and are categorized by the age of the child using different family income levels. (See Table 4.7 and Table 4.8.) Attorneys and judges use these estimates in determining child-support awards in divorce cases as well as cases involving the wrongful death of a parent. Public officials use the estimates to determine payments for the support of children in foster care and for subsidies to adoptive families. Financial planners and consumer educators use them in helping people determine their life insurance needs.

Income Levels

Estimated annual family expenditures for a child vary widely depending upon the income level of the household. The estimated amount a family will spend on a child also

FIGURE 4.4

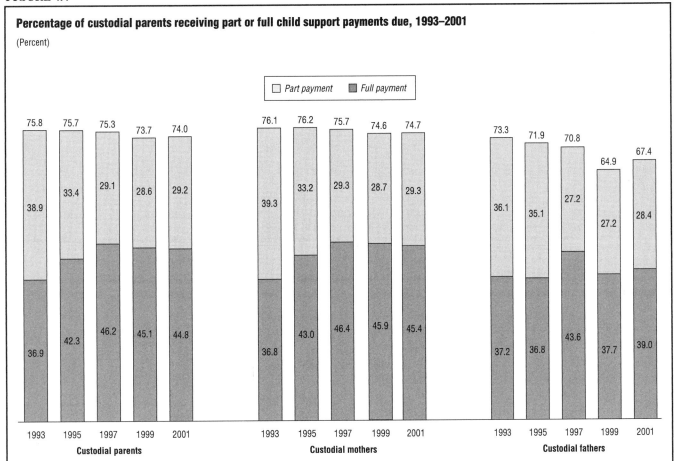

Percentage of custodial parents receiving part or full child support payments due, 1993–2001

(Percent)

☐ Part payment   ▨ Full payment

Custodial parents

1993	1995	1997	1999	2001
75.8	75.7	75.3	73.7	74.0
38.9	33.4	29.1	28.6	29.2
36.9	42.3	46.2	45.1	44.8

Custodial mothers

1993	1995	1997	1999	2001
76.1	76.2	75.7	74.6	74.7
39.3	33.2	29.3	28.7	29.3
36.8	43.0	46.4	45.9	45.4

Custodial fathers

1993	1995	1997	1999	2001
73.3	71.9	70.8	64.9	67.4
36.1	35.1	27.2	27.2	28.4
37.2	36.8	43.6	37.7	39.0

SOURCE: Timothy S. Grall, "Figure 5. Custodial Parents Receiving Part, or Full Child Support Payments Due: 1993–2001," in *Custodial Mothers and Fathers and Their Child Support: 2001,* Current Population Reports, U.S. Census Bureau, 2003, http://www.census.gov/prod/2003pubs/p60-225.pdf (accessed August 24, 2004)

tends to increase as the child ages. The USDA estimates that in 2003 married-couple households earning less than $40,700 a year spent between $6,820 on very young children and $7,770 on fifteen- to seventeen-year-olds. (See Table 4.7.) Estimates for middle-income, married-couple families range from $9,510 for infants and young toddlers to $10,560 for fifteen- to seventeen-year-olds. Estimates for married-couple families with incomes above $68,400 ranged from $14,140 to $15,350, depending on the age of the child.

Estimated annual expenditures for single-parent families earning less than $40,700 a year were slightly less than those of two-parent families, most likely because their average incomes were lower ($17,000 for single-parent families and $25,400 for two-parent families). The USDA estimates that in 2003 these single parents will spend an annual average of $5,770 to $7,960, depending on the age of the child. (See Table 4.8.) The USDA estimates that those single-parent families earning $40,700 or more will spend $13,060 to $15,620 per child, slightly more than the middle-income, two-parent families.

Although the USDA projected that in 2003 the highest-income households would spend about twice the amount

on their children than the lowest-income households, this difference varies by the type of expense. For example, the estimated food expenditure for children ages fifteen to seventeen in the highest-income husband-wife families was $2,630, compared with $1,850 in the lowest-income group. (See Table 4.7.) However, the estimated annual expense for education and child care for children ages fifteen to seventeen in these high-income families ($1,670) was almost four times that for a child the same age in the lowest-income families ($450). These variations among income groups by type of expense held true for single-parent households as well. (See Table 4.8.)

Age of Child

The 2003 estimates of family expenditures on a child generally increased with the child's age, except for housing, education, and child care. (See Table 4.7 and Table 4.8.) Households with young children are more likely to have recently purchased homes at higher prices and, until recently, with higher interest rates, explaining the higher housing estimates. Estimates for education, child care, and related expenses were also highest for preschoolers (under the age of six) in all income groups. Many women with

TABLE 4.6

Average income and child support received by custodial parents, by selected characteristics, 2001

(In 2001 dollars)

	Supposed to receive child support in 2001				
	Received payments		Did not receive payments	Child support not awarded
	Total money income	Child support income	Total money income	
Custodial parents	29,008	4,274	23,571	24,055
Custodial mothers	28,258	4,274	21,835	19,339
Custodial fathers	36,255	4,273	35,348	39,396
Custodial parents below poverty	7,571	3,041	6,832	6,113
Custodial mothers below poverty	7,604	3,078	6,755	6,089
Custodial fathers below poverty	7,189	2,622	7,492	6,287

SOURCE: Adapted from Timothy S. Grall, "Table 5. Mean Total Money Income of People and Child Support Received by Custodial Parents by Selected Characteristics and Sex: 2001," in *Custodial Mothers and Fathers and Their Child Support: 2001,* Current Population Reports, U.S. Census Bureau, 2003, http://www.census.gov/hhes/www/childsupport/chldsu01.pdf (accessed August 24, 2004)

TABLE 4.7

Estimated annual expenditures on a child by husband–wife families, 2003

Age of child	Total	Housing	Food	Transportation	Clothing	Health care	Child care and education	Miscellaneous*
			Before-tax income: Less than $40,700 (average=$25,400)					
0–2	$6,820	$2,620	$950	$800	$350	$500	$950	$650
3–5	6,970	2,580	1,050	770	340	480	1,080	670
6–8	7,040	2,500	1,360	900	380	550	640	710
9–11	6,990	2,250	1,620	970	420	600	390	740
12–14	7,840	2,510	1,710	1,100	710	610	270	930
15–17	7,770	2,030	1,850	1,480	630	650	450	680
Total	$130,290	$43,470	$25,620	$18,060	$8,490	$10,170	$11,340	$13,140
			Before-tax income: $40,700 to $68,400 (average=$54,100)					
0–2	$9,510	$3,540	$1,130	$1,190	$410	$660	$1,570	$1,010
3–5	9,780	3,510	1,310	1,160	400	630	1,740	1,030
6–8	9,730	3,420	1,670	1,290	450	720	1,110	1,070
9–11	9,600	3,180	1,960	1,360	490	780	730	1,100
12–14	10,350	3,440	1,980	1,490	830	790	530	1,290
15–17	10,560	2,950	2,200	1,880	740	830	920	1,040
Total	$178,590	$60,120	$30,750	$25,110	$9,960	$13,230	$19,800	$19,620
			Before-tax income: More than $68,400 (average=$102,400)					
0–2	$14,140	$5,620	$1,500	$1,660	$540	$760	$2,370	$1,690
3–5	14,470	5,590	1,700	1,630	530	730	2,580	1,710
6–8	14,240	5,500	2,050	1,760	580	830	1,770	1,750
9–11	14,040	5,260	2,380	1,840	630	900	1,240	1,790
12–14	14,850	5,520	2,500	1,960	1,050	900	950	1,970
15–17	15,350	5,040	2,630	2,380	950	950	1,670	1,730
Total	$261,270	$97,590	$38,280	$33,690	$12,840	$15,210	$31,740	$31,920

Notes: Estimates are based on 1990–92 Consumer Expenditure Survey data updated to 2003 dollars using the Consumer Price Index. For each age category, the expense estimates represent average child-rearing expenditures for each age (e.g., the expense for the 3–5 age category, on average, applies to the 3-year-old, the 4-year-old, or the 5-year-old). The figures represent estimated expenses on the younger child in a two-child family. Estimates are about the same for the older child, so to calculate expenses for two children, figures should be summed for the appropriate age categories. To estimate expenses for an only child, multiply the total expense for the appropriate age category by 1.24. To estimate expenses for each child in a family with three or more children, multiply the total expense for each appropriate age category by 0.77. For expenses on all children in a family, these totals should be summed.
*Miscellaneous expenses include personal care items, entertainment, and reading materials.

SOURCE: Mark Lino, "Table ES1. Estimate Annual Expenditures on a Child by Husband-Wife Families, Overall United States, 2003," in *Expenditures on Children by Families, 2003 Annual Report,* Miscellaneous Publication No. 1528-2003, Center for Nutrition Policy and Promotion, U.S. Department of Agriculture, 2004, http://www.usda.gov/cnpp/Crc/crc2003.pdf (accessed August 24, 2004)

children this age are in the labor force and must pay for child care. Once the child enters school, the cost decreases. And as a school-age child grows up, the need for after-school and summer care also decreases. The estimates do not include expenses related to college attendance, which typically do not occur until the child is at least eighteen.

Future Costs

The USDA also estimated the cost of raising a child born in 2003 who will reach the age of seventeen in the year 2020, incorporating an average annual inflation rate of 3.1% (the average annual inflation rate over the previous twenty years). Total family expenses for raising a

TABLE 4.8

Estimated annual expenditures on a child by single-parent families, 2003

Age of child	Total	Housing	Food	Transportation	Clothing	Health care	Child care and education	Miscellaneous*
			Before-tax income: Less than $40,700 (average=$17,000)					
0–2	$5,700	$2,350	$1,050	$740	$320	$240	$600	$400
3–5	6,440	2,670	1,100	650	330	360	810	520
6–8	7,230	2,830	1,390	760	390	420	740	700
9–11	6,710	2,720	1,610	540	400	530	350	560
12–14	7,210	2,730	1,620	630	670	570	450	540
15–17	7,960	2,890	1,760	990	790	560	340	630
Total	**$123,750**	**$48,570**	**$25,590**	**$12,930**	**$8,700**	**$8,040**	**$9,870**	**$10,050**
			Before-tax income: $40,700 or more (average=$61,700)					
0–2	$13,060	$5,050	$1,620	$2,270	$450	$560	$1,470	$1,640
3–5	14,080	5,370	1,710	2,180	470	750	1,840	1,760
6–8	14,930	5,540	2,050	2,280	540	860	1,720	1,940
9–11	14,350	5,430	2,470	2,070	550	1,030	1,000	1,800
12–14	15,210	5,430	2,420	2,160	900	1,090	1,430	1,780
15–17	15,620	5,600	2,560	2,330	1,030	1,070	1,160	1,870
Total	**$261,750**	**$97,260**	**$38,490**	**$39,870**	**$11,820**	**$16,080**	**$25,860**	**$32,370**

Notes: Estimates are based on 1990–92 Consumer Expenditure Survey data updated to 2003 dollars using the Consumer Price Index. For each age category, the expense estimates represent average child-rearing expenditures for each age (e.g., the expense for the 3–5 age category, on average, applies to the 3-year-old, the 4-year-old, or the 5-year-old). The figures represent estimated expenses on the younger child in a single-parent, two-child family. For estimated expenses on the older child, multiply the total expense for the appropriate age category by 0.93. To estimate expenses for two children, the expenses on the younger child and older child after adjusting the expense on the older child downward should be summed for the appropriate age categories. To estimate expenses for an only child, multiply the total expense for the appropriate age category by 1.35. To estimate expenses for each child in a family with three or more children, multiply the total expense for each appropriate age category by 0.72 after adjusting the expenses on the older children downward. For expenses on all children in a family, these totals should be summed.
*Miscellaneous expenses include personal care items, entertainment, and reading materials.

SOURCE: Mark Lino,"Table 7. Estimated Annual Expenditures on a Child by Single-Parent Families, Overall United States, 2003," in *Expenditures on Children by Families, 2003 Annual Report,* Miscellaneous Publication No. 1528-2003, Center for Nutrition Policy and Promotion, U.S. Department of Agriculture, 2004, http://www.usda.gov/cnpp/Crc/crc2003.pdf (accessed August 24, 2004)

child through the age of seventeen years are estimated to be $172,370 for the lowest-income group, $235,670 for the middle-income group, and $344,250 for highest-income group. (See Table 4.9.)

TEENS AS CONSUMERS

By the last decades of the twentieth century, teens had a big influence on the economy—from affecting major family purchases to buying groceries. A Rand Youth poll estimated that in 1997 24.8 million teens spent $82 billion. According to Teenage Research Unlimited, by 2003 teens spent $175 billion annually, most of it from parents, gifts, and jobs (Teenage Research Unlimited Press Release, "New Book Helps Marketers in 'Getting Wiser to Teens,'" June 14, 2004, http://www.teenresearch.com/PRview.cfm?edit_id=214 [accessed July 15, 2004]).

TEEN EMPLOYMENT

The U.S. Bureau of Labor Statistics (BLS) reported that in June 2004 8.1 million people ages sixteen to nineteen, or about half of the population that age (50.2%), were employed or looking for work (*The Employment Situation: June 2004*). The unemployment rate in this age group was 19.9%. Employment rates among the young are highest during the summer months, when many full-time students are out of school. However, a January 2003

BLS press release ("Employment Experience of Youths during the School Year and Summer") noted that "most teenage students who worked during the summer also worked during the school year."

The rate of teens in the labor force was correlated with family income; as a household's income rises, the likelihood that a teen within the household will work also rises. In March 2002 only 17% of teens ages fifteen to seventeen from families with a household income of less than $15,000 were in the labor force, compared with 28% of teens from families with a household income of more than $50,000. (See Figure 4.5.)

The Jobs Teens Hold

According to the January 2003 BLS press release, the top occupations for youths employed during the 1999–2000 school year varied by age and gender. For boys ages sixteen to eighteen, cashier and cook jobs ranked in the top five jobs for both the school year and the summer. Girls in the same age group tended to work as cashiers, at food counters, in retail sales, and in restaurants.

Most teens are employed as hourly workers. In 1998 the average amount earned by employed teens between the ages of fifteen and seventeen was $5.57 (*Report on the Youth Labor Force,* U.S. Department of Labor, Bureau of Labor Statistics, Washington, DC, June 2000). In 2003 9.9% of

TABLE 4.9

Estimated annual expenditures on children born in 2003, by income group

Year	Age	Income group		
		Lowest	Middle	Highest
2003	<1	$6,820	$9,510	$14,140
2004	1	7,030	9,800	14,580
2005	2	7,250	10,110	15,030
2006	3	7,640	10,720	15,860
2007	4	7,880	11,050	16,350
2008	5	8,120	11,390	16,860
2009	6	8,460	11,690	17,100
2010	7	8,720	12,050	17,630
2011	8	8,990	12,420	18,180
2012	9	9,200	12,640	18,480
2013	10	9,490	13,030	19,050
2014	11	9,780	13,430	19,640
2015	12	11,310	14,930	21,420
2016	13	11,660	15,390	22,080
2017	14	12,020	15,870	22,770
2018	15	12,280	16,690	24,270
2019	16	12,660	17,210	25,020
2020	17	13,060	17,740	25,790
Total		$172,370	$235,670	$344,250

Note: Estimates are for the younger child in husband-wife families with two children.

SOURCE: Mark Lino, "Table 12. Estimated Annual Expenditures on Children Born in 2003, by Income Group, Overall United States," in *Expenditures on Children by Families, 2003 Annual Report,* Miscellaneous Publication No. 1528-2003, Center for Nutrition Policy and Promotion, U.S. Department of Agriculture, 2004, http://www.usda.gov/cnpp/Crc/crc2003.pdf (accessed August 24, 2004)

teenagers earned the minimum hourly wage of $5.15 or less (*Characteristics of Minimum Wage Workers: 2003*, U.S. Department of Labor, Bureau of Labor Statistics, May 10, 2004, http://www.bls.gov/cps/minwage2003.htm [accessed July 15, 2004]).

How Does Working Affect Academic Achievement?

A September/October 2001 article in the *Journal of Educational Research* (Kimberly J. Quirk et al., "Employment during High School and Student Achievement") presented the results of a longitudinal study examining the effects of high-school student employment on academic achievement. The researchers concluded that "working displayed a moderate, significant, and negative effect on high school grades." However, smaller amounts of work (twelve hours or less per week) seemed to slightly improve grades. The researchers also found that the lower a student's grades were, the more likely he or she was to get a job.

A 2000 report by the U.S. Department of Labor ("The Relationship of Youth Employment to Future Educational Attainment and Labor Market Experience," in *Report on the Youth Labor Force*) found a correlation between teen employment and future college education. More than half of adults who had worked one to twenty hours per week as sixteen- and seventeen-year-olds were more likely than other adults to have completed at least some college edu-

FIGURE 4.5

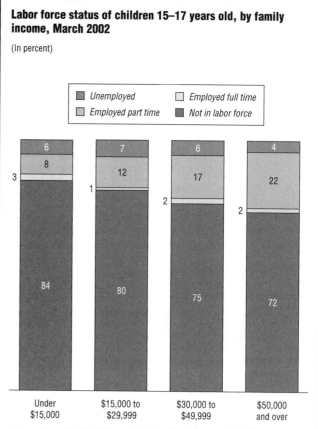

Labor force status of children 15–17 years old, by family income, March 2002

(In percent)

SOURCE: Jason Fields, "Figure 4. Labor Force Status of Children 15 to 17 Years Old by Family Income, March 2002," in *Children's Living Arrangements and Characteristics: March 2002*, P20–547, U.S. Census Bureau: June 2003, http://www.census.gov/prod/2003pubs/p20-547.pdf (accessed August 24, 2004)

cation by age thirty. In contrast, less than half of adults who had not worked at all or who had worked more than twenty hours per week had completed some college education. The findings suggested that working a limited number of hours in the junior and senior years of high school has a positive effect on educational attainment.

Working Teens and Trouble

In November 1998 a committee of the National Research Council and the Institute of Medicine issued a report that warned about the dangers of teenage employment. The national panel of scientists said that young people who worked more than twenty hours a week, regardless of their economic background, were less likely to finish high school and more likely to use drugs and run into trouble with the police.

Risky behaviors may also increase with teen employment. A Centers for Disease Control and Prevention Youth Behavior Risk Survey, reported in the *Journal of Child and Family Studies* (Robert F. Valois et al., "Association between Employment and Sexual Risk-Taking Behaviors among Public High School Adolescents," June 1998), demonstrated a link between employment and sexual risk-taking for both genders and all races. Students working more than ten hours per week were more likely to have sexually transmitted diseases or unintended pregnancies than other teens.

CHAPTER 5
HEALTH AND SAFETY

LIFE EXPECTANCY

In the early twenty-first century America's young people could look forward to living longer than the generations before them had. The average life expectancy for both sexes of all races born in 2001 was 77.2 years, although individual expectations varied considerably according to race and gender. (See Table 5.1.) Average life expectancy for white males born in 2001 was seventy-five years, up from 66.5 in 1950. The average life expectancy for African-American males born in 2001 was 68.6 years, up from 59.1 in 1950. Average life expectancy for white females born in 2001 was 80.2 years, up from 72.2 in 1950, while the average life expectancy for African-American females born in 2001 was 75.5 years, up from 62.9 in 1950.

While the life expectancy for whites and African-Americans differs at birth, statistics show that the gap narrows with age. (See Figure 5.1.) By age sixty-five there is a difference of approximately two years between life expectancies of whites and African-Americans. By age seventy-five there is almost no difference. This may be because African-Americans have a higher rate of deaths from accidents or injuries in their younger years. Women of both races have a slightly longer life expectancy than men do.

INFANT MORTALITY

The National Center for Health Statistics (NCHS) defines the infant mortality rate as the number of deaths of babies younger than one year per one thousand live births. Neonatal deaths occur within twenty-eight days after birth and post-neonatal deaths twenty-eight to 365 days after birth. The U.S. infant mortality rate declined from 165 per one thousand live births in 1900 to a record low of 6.8 per one thousand live births in 2001. (See Table 5.2.) In *Health, United States, 2003*, the Centers for Disease Control and Prevention (CDC) noted that several factors—including improved access to health care, advances in neonatal medi-

cine, and educational campaigns—contributed to the overall decline in infant mortality in the twentieth century.

Unfortunately, not all racial and ethnic groups have reached that record-low infant mortality rate. In 2001 the infant mortality rate for white infants was 5.7 deaths per one thousand live births, less than half the rate of 13.3 for African-American infants. Rates for Native American/ Alaska Native, Hispanic, and Asian/Pacific Islander babies were 9.7, 5.4, and 4.7, respectively. The infant mortality rate for Native Americans/Alaska Natives went up from the previous year. (See Table 5.2.)

The National Center for Health Statistics listed the ten leading causes of infant mortality in the United States in 2002. (See Table 5.3.) Birth defects were the primary cause of infant mortality (140.7 deaths per one hundred thousand live births). Premature delivery or low birth weight was the second leading cause of infant mortality (114.4). Sudden Infant Death Syndrome (SIDS) (50.6), complications of pregnancy (42.9), complications in the placenta or umbilical cord (25.3), respiratory distress (23.8), accidents (22.2), bacterial sepsis (18.3), circulatory system diseases (16.1), and intrauterine hypoxia/birth asphyxia (14.4) completed the list.

Although infant mortality rates are decreasing for the African-American population, the CDC reported that infant mortality rates in 2002 were more than twice as high for African-American infants than for non-Hispanic white infants. (See Table 5.4.) Premature birth/low birth weight was the leading cause of death for African-American infants (310.9 per one thousand live births) and was particularly high compared with the rate for white infants (135 per one thousand live births). For unknown reasons, African-American infants are also at a much higher risk of SIDS than white infants.

Sudden Infant Death Syndrome (SIDS)

Sudden Infant Death Syndrome (SIDS; sometimes called crib death), the unexplained death of a previously

TABLE 5.1

Life expectancy at birth according to race and sex, selected years 1900–2001

[Data are based on death certificates]

Specified age and year	All races			White			Black or African American[1]		
	Both sexes	Male	Female	Both sexes	Male	Female	Both sexes	Male	Female
At birth	Remaining life expectancy in years								
1900[2,3]	47.3	46.3	48.3	47.6	46.6	48.7	33.0	32.5	33.5
1950[3]	68.2	65.6	71.1	69.1	66.5	72.2	60.8	59.1	62.9
1960[3]	69.7	66.6	73.1	70.6	67.4	74.1	63.6	61.1	66.3
1970	70.8	67.1	74.7	71.7	68.0	75.6	64.1	60.0	68.3
1980	73.7	70.0	77.4	74.4	70.7	78.1	68.1	63.8	72.5
1985	74.7	71.1	78.2	75.3	71.8	78.7	69.3	65.0	73.4
1990	75.4	71.8	78.8	76.1	72.7	79.4	69.1	64.5	73.6
1991	75.5	72.0	78.9	76.3	72.9	79.6	69.3	64.6	73.8
1992	75.8	72.3	79.1	76.5	73.2	79.8	69.6	65.0	73.9
1993	75.5	72.2	78.8	76.3	73.1	79.5	69.2	64.6	73.7
1994	75.7	72.4	79.0	76.5	73.3	79.6	69.5	64.9	73.9
1995	75.8	72.5	78.9	76.5	73.4	79.6	69.6	65.2	73.9
1996	76.1	73.1	79.1	76.8	73.9	79.7	70.2	66.1	74.2
1997	76.5	73.6	79.4	77.1	74.3	79.9	71.1	67.2	74.7
1998	76.7	73.8	79.5	77.3	74.5	80.0	71.3	67.6	74.8
1999	76.7	73.9	79.4	77.3	74.6	79.9	71.4	67.8	74.7
2000[4]	77.0	74.3	79.7	77.6	74.9	80.1	71.9	68.3	75.2
2001[5]	77.2	74.4	79.8	77.7	75.0	80.2	72.2	68.6	75.5

[1]Data shown for 1900–60 are for the nonwhite population.
[2]Death registration area only. The death registration area increased from 10 states and the District of Columbia in 1900 to the coterminous United States in 1933.
[3]Includes deaths of persons who were not residents of the 50 states and the District of Columbia.
[4]Life expectancies (LEs) for 2000 were revised and may differ from those shown previously. LEs for 2000 were computed using population counts from Census 2000 and replace LEs for 2000 using 1990-based postcensal estimates.
[5]Life expectancies for 2001 were computed using 2000-based postcensal estimates.
Notes: Populations used for computing life expectancy and other life table values for 1991–1999 are postcensal estimates of U.S. resident population, based on the 1990 census.

SOURCE: Adapted from "Table 27. Life Expectancy at Birth, at 65 Years of Age, and at 75 Years of Age, according to Race and Sex: United States, Selected Years 1900–2001," in *Health, United States, 2003,* Centers for Disease Control and Prevention, National Center for Health Statistics, 2003, http://www.cdc.gov/nchs/data/hus/tables/2003/03hus027.pdf (accessed September 3, 2004)

healthy infant, was the third leading cause of infant mortality in the United States in 2002 and the leading cause of death of infants one month to one year of age. In 1992 the American Academy of Pediatrics recommended that babies sleep on their backs to reduce the risk of SIDS and launched its "Back to Sleep" campaign to educate parents. It had been a long-held belief that the best position for babies to sleep was on their stomachs. The American SIDS Institute reported that the Back to Sleep campaign had resulted in the reduction of SIDS cases by 52% between 1990 and 2000. Other risk factors for SIDS include maternal use of drugs or tobacco during pregnancy, low birth weight, and poor prenatal care.

STUDIES ON THE CAUSES OF AND RISK FACTORS FOR SIDS. A number of recent studies have considered the possible causes of and risk factors for SIDS. One study, ongoing since 1985, conducted by Dr. Hannah Kinney of Harvard Medical School in Boston, Massachusetts, found a brain defect believed to affect breathing in babies who died of SIDS ("SIDS Risk Prevention Research Begins to Define Physical Abnormalities in Brainstem, Points to Possible Diagnostic/Screening Tools," *PR Newswire,* October 18, 1999). Researchers suggest that as carbon dioxide levels rise and oxygen levels fall during sleep, the brains of some babies do not get the signal to regulate

breathing or blood pressure accordingly to make up for the change. This condition is particularly dangerous for infants sleeping on their stomachs or on soft bedding. According to a May 2002 article in *Clinical Psychiatry News* ("Brainstem Abnormality May Be Culprit in SIDS Subset: Maternal Smoking Tied to Abnormality"), the study had shifted its focus to maternal cigarette smoking in the first trimester of pregnancy as a possible cause of the brain abnormality.

FETAL ALCOHOL SYNDROME (FAS)

Alcohol consumption by pregnant women can cause Fetal Alcohol Syndrome (FAS), a birth defect characterized by a low birth weight, facial abnormalities such as small eye openings, growth retardation, and central nervous system deficits, including learning and development disabilities. The condition is a lifelong, disabling condition that puts those children affected at risk for secondary conditions, such as mental health problems, criminal behavior, alcohol and drug abuse, and inappropriate sexual behavior. Not all children affected by prenatal alcohol use are born with the full syndrome, but they may only have selected abnormalities.

According to the CDC, estimates of the prevalence of FAS vary from 0.2 to 1.5 per one thousand births. Other

TABLE 5.2

Infant mortality rate among selected groups by race and Hispanic origin of mother, selected years 1983–2001

(Data are based on linked birth and death certificates for infants)

Race and Hispanic origin of mother	1983[2]	1985[2]	1990[2]	1995[3]	1998[3]	1999[3]	2000[3]	2001[3]
	Infant[4] deaths per 1,000 live births							
All mothers	10.9	10.4	8.9	7.6	7.2	7.0	6.9	6.8
White	9.3	8.9	7.3	6.3	6.0	5.8	5.7	5.7
Black or African American	19.2	18.6	16.9	14.6	13.8	14.0	13.5	13.3
American Indian or Alaska Native	15.2	13.1	13.1	9.0	9.3	9.3	8.3	9.7
Asian or Pacific Islander	8.3	7.8	6.6	5.3	5.5	4.8	4.9	4.7
Chinese	9.5	5.8	4.3	3.8	4.0	2.9	3.5	3.2
Japanese	5.6[1]	6.0[1]	5.5[1]	5.3[1]	3.4[1]	3.5[1]	4.5[1]	4.0[1]
Filipino	8.4	7.7	6.0	5.6	6.2	5.8	5.7	5.5
Hawaiian	11.2	9.9[1]	8.0[1]	6.5[1]	9.9	7.0[1]	9.0	7.3[1]
Other Asian or Pacific Islander	8.1	8.5	7.4	5.5	5.7	5.1	4.8	4.8
Hispanic or Latino[5,6]	9.5	8.8	7.5	6.3	5.8	5.7	5.6	5.4
Mexican	9.1	8.5	7.2	6.0	5.6	5.5	5.4	5.2
Puerto Rican	12.9	11.2	9.9	8.9	7.8	8.3	8.2	8.5
Cuban	7.5	8.5	7.2	5.3	3.7[1]	4.6	4.6	4.2
Central and South American	8.5	8.0	6.8	5.5	5.3	4.7	4.6	5.0
Other and unknown Hispanic or Latino	10.6	9.5	8.0	7.4	6.5	7.2	6.9	6.0
Not Hispanic or Latino:								
White[6]	9.2	8.6	7.2	6.3	6.0	5.8	5.7	5.7
Black or African American[6]	19.1	18.3	16.9	14.7	13.9	14.1	13.6	13.5
	Neonatal[4] deaths per 1,000 live births							
All mothers	7.1	6.8	5.7	4.9	4.8	4.7	4.6	4.5
White	6.1	5.8	4.6	4.1	4.0	3.9	3.8	3.8
Black or African American	12.5	12.3	11.1	9.6	9.4	9.5	9.1	8.9
American Indian or Alaska Native	7.5	6.1	6.1	4.0	5.0	5.0	4.4	4.2
Asian or Pacific Islander	5.2	4.8	3.9	3.4	3.9	3.2	3.4	3.1
Chinese	5.5	3.3	2.3	2.3	2.7	1.8	2.5	1.9
Japanese	3.7[1]	3.1[1]	3.5[1]	3.3[1]	2.5[1]	2.8[1]	2.6[1]	2.5[1]
Filipino	5.6	5.1	3.5	3.4	4.6	3.9	4.1	4.0
Hawaiian	7.0[1]	5.7[1]	4.3[1]	4.0[1]	7.2[1]	4.9[1]	6.2[1]	3.6[1]
Other Asian or Pacific Islander	5.0	5.4	4.4	3.7	3.9	3.3	3.4	3.2
Hispanic or Latino[5,6]	6.2	5.7	4.8	4.1	3.9	3.9	3.8	3.6
Mexican	5.9	5.4	4.5	3.9	3.7	3.7	3.6	3.5
Puerto Rican	8.7	7.6	6.9	6.1	5.2	5.9	5.8	6.0
Cuban	5.0[1]	6.2	5.3	3.6[1]	2.7[1]	3.5[1]	3.2[1]	2.5[1]
Central and South American	5.8	5.6	4.4	3.7	3.6	3.3	3.3	3.4
Other and unknown Hispanic or Latino	6.4	5.6	5.0	4.8	4.5	4.8	4.6	3.9
Not Hispanic or Latino:								
White[6]	5.9	5.6	4.5	4.0	3.9	3.8	3.8	3.8
Black or African American[6]	12.0	11.9	11.0	9.6	9.4	9.6	9.2	9.0

[1]Estimates are considered unreliable. Rates preceded by an asterisk are based on fewer than 50 events. Rates not shown are based on fewer than 20 events.
[2]Rates based on unweighted birth cohort data.
[3]Rates based on a period file using weighted data.
[4]Infant (under 1 year of age) and neonatal (under 28 days).
[5]Persons of Hispanic origin may be of any race.
[6]Prior to 1995, data shown only for states with an Hispanic-origin item on their birth certificates.
Notes: The race groups white, black, American Indian or Alaska Native, and Asian or Pacific Islander include persons of Hispanic and non-Hispanic origin. National linked files do not exist for 1992–94.

SOURCE: Adapted from "Table 19 (page 1 of 2). Infant, Neonatal, Postneonatal Mortality Rates, according to Detailed Race and Hispanic Origin of Mother: United States, Selected Years 1983–2001," in *Health: United States, 2003,* Centers for Disease Control and Prevention, National Center for Health Statistics, 2003, http://www.cdc.gov/nchs/data/hus/tables/2003/03hus019.pdf (accessed September 3, 2004)

alcohol-related birth defects are thought to occur three times as often as FAS. As many as 130,000 pregnant women each year drink alcohol at levels known to put their babies at risk for alcohol-related birth defects.

MORTALITY AMONG CHILDREN

In the second half of the twentieth century, childhood death rates declined dramatically. The majority of childhood deaths are from injuries and violence. While death rates for all ages decreased, the largest declines were among children.

In 2001 three of the leading causes of childhood death were unintentional injuries, congenital anomalies (birth defects), and malignant neoplasms (cancers). (See Table 5.5.) The remaining deaths were spread across a variety of diseases, including heart disease, pneumonia, influenza, HIV/AIDS, homicide, and suicide.

Motor Vehicle Injuries

Although motor vehicle fatalities decreased by 25% between 1982 and 2000 for fifteen- to twenty-year-olds,

FIGURE 5.1

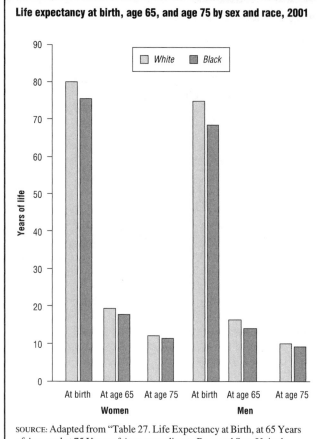

Life expectancy at birth, age 65, and age 75 by sex and race, 2001

SOURCE: Adapted from "Table 27. Life Expectancy at Birth, at 65 Years of Age, and at 75 Years of Age, according to Race and Sex: United States, Selected Years 1900–2001," in *Health, United States, 2003,* Centers for Disease Control and Prevention, National Center for Health Statistics, 2003, http://www.cdc.gov/nchs/data/hus/tables/2003/03hus027.pdf (accessed September 3, 2004)

TABLE 5.3

Ten leading causes of infant mortality by race and Hispanic origin, 2002

	Rate per 100,000 live births
Birth defects	140.7
Preterm/low birth weight	114.4
SIDS	50.6
Maternal pregnancy complications	42.9
Placenta, cord complications	25.3
Respiratory distress	23.8
Accidents	22.2
Bacterial sepsis	18.3
Circulatory system diseases	16.1
Intrauterine hypoxia/birth asphyxia	14.4

SOURCE: Adapted from "Table 8. Infant Deaths and Infant Mortality Rates for the 10 Leading Causes of Infant Death, by Race and Hispanic Origin: United States, Preliminary 2002," in "Deaths: Preliminary Data for 2002," *National Vital Statistics Report,* vol. 52, no. 13, February 11, 2004, http://www.cdc.gov/nchs/data/nvsr/nvsr52/nvsr52_13.pdf (accessed September 3, 2004)

traffic accidents were still the leading cause of death for that age group in 2002. That year, 3,827 young people were killed in traffic accidents. Many of those killed had been drinking alcohol and were not wearing their seat belts.

Suicide

In 2001 suicide was the fifth leading cause of death among people five to fourteen years old and the third leading cause of death in fifteen- to twenty-four-year-olds. (See Table 5.5.) In 2001 white males ages fifteen to nineteen had twice the suicide rate (fourteen per one hundred thousand) of African-American males (7.3 per one hundred thousand) or Hispanic male youth (7.8 per one hundred thousand). Among females ages fifteen to nineteen, the rate for whites (2.9 per one hundred thousand) was considerably higher than that for Hispanics (2.5 per one hundred thousand) or African-Americans (1.3 per one hundred thousand) (*National Vital Statistics Reports*, vol. 52, no. 9, November 7, 2003).

The 2003 *Youth Risk Behavior Survey* questioned high school students regarding their thoughts about suicide. Almost one in six students surveyed (16.9%)

claimed that they had thought about attempting suicide in the previous twelve months. (See Table 5.6.) Although the suicide death rate was much higher among males than females, females (21.3%) were more likely to have considered suicide than males (12.8%). Of all students, 16.5% (18.9% of females and 14.1% of males) had made a specific plan to attempt suicide, 8.5% of students (11.5% of females and 5.4% of males) claimed they had attempted suicide in the previous year, and 2.9% of high school students (3.2% of females and 2.4% of males) said they had suffered injuries from the attempt that required medical attention. These numbers reflect the fact that females of all ages tend to choose less fatal methods of attempting suicide, such as overdosing and cutting veins, than males, who tend to choose more deadly methods, such as shooting or hanging.

The likelihood that a child will commit suicide increases with the presence of certain factors in his or her profile. Among the factors whose presence may indicate heightened risk are depression, substance abuse, behavioral disorders, accessibility of handguns, and a tendency toward perfectionism. The suicide rate among male homosexual teens is believed to be extremely high. A 2002 study corroborated previous estimates that 20% to 42% of teens and young men who have sex with other males attempt suicide (Gary Remafedi, "Suicidality in a Venue-Based Sample of Young Men Who Have Sex with Men," *Journal of Adolescent Health*, vol. 31, October 2002).

HIV/AIDS

Acquired Immune Deficiency Syndrome (AIDS) was identified as a new disease in 1981, and, according to the CDC, an estimated 886,575 cases had been diagnosed in the United States through 2002. AIDS is caused by the human immunodeficiency virus (HIV), which weakens the victim's immune system, making it vulnerable to other

TABLE 5.4

Infant mortality rates for the 10 leading causes of infant death, by race and Hispanic origin, 2002

Rank[1]	Non-Hispanic white	Number	Rate per 100,000 live births
—	All causes	13,542	587.9
1	Congenital malformations, deformations and chromosomal abnormalities	3,110	135.0
2	Disorders related to short gestation and low birth weight, not elsewhere classified	1,811	8.6
3	Sudden infant death syndrome	1,112	48.3
4	Newborn affected by maternal complications of pregnancy	821	35.6
5	Newborn affected by complications of placenta, cord and membranes	493	21.4
6	Respiratory distress of newborn	446	19.4
7	Accidents (unintentional injuries)	437	19.0
8	Bacterial sepsis of newborn	361	15.7
9	Diseases of the circulatory system	320	13.9
10	Intrauterinehypoxia and birth asphyxia	311	13.5
—	All other causes	4,321	187.6
	Total black[2]		
—	All causes	8,380	1,419.0
1	Disorders related to short gestation and low birth weight, not elsewhere classified	1,836	310.9
2	Congenital malformations, deformations and chromosomal abnormalities	1,023	173.2
3	Sudden infant death syndrome	603	102.1
4	Newborn affected by maternal complications of pregnancy	575	97.3
5	Respiratory distress of newborn	336	57.0
6	Newborn affected by complications of placenta, cord and membranes	315	53.3
7	Accidents (unintentional injuries)	303	51.4
8	Bacterial sepsis of newborn	231	39.1
9	Diseases of the circulatory system	189	32.1
10	Intrauterinehypoxia and birth asphyxia	147	24.8
—	All other causes	2,822	477.8

— Category not applicable.
[1]Rank based on number of deaths.
[2]Race and Hispanic origin are reported separately on both the birth and death certificate. Data for persons of Hispanic origin are included in the data for each race group, according to the decedent's reported race.

SOURCE: Adapted from "Table 8. Infant Deaths and Infant Mortality Rates for the 10 Leading Causes of Infant Death, by Race and Hispanic Origin: United States, Preliminary 2002," in "Deaths: Preliminary Data for 2002," *National Vital Statistics Report*, vol. 52, no. 13, February 11, 2004, http://www.cdc.gov/nchs/data/nvsr/nvsr52/nvsr52_13.pdf (accessed September 16, 2004)

opportunistic infections. Young children with AIDS usually have the virus transmitted to them either by an infected parent or through contaminated transfusions of blood or blood products. Adolescents who are exploring their sexuality or experimenting with drugs are also vulnerable to HIV infection, which can be spread through sexual intercourse without the use of a condom or through shared hypodermic needles.

In adults the most common opportunistic infections of AIDS are Kaposi's sarcoma—a rare skin cancer—and *pneumocystis carinii* pneumonia. In infants and children a failure to thrive and unusually severe bacterial infections characterize the disease. With the exception of *pneumocystis carinii* pneumonia, children with symptomatic HIV infection seldom develop opportunistic infections as adults do. More often they are plagued by recurrent bacterial infections, persistent oral thrush (a common fungal infection of the mouth or throat), and chronic and recurrent diarrhea. They may also suffer from enlarged lymph nodes, chronic pneumonia, developmental delays, and neurological abnormalities.

HOW MANY ARE INFECTED? As of December 2002 the CDC reported a cumulative total of 9,300 AIDS cases in children under the age of thirteen since record-keeping

began in 1981. (See Table 5.7.) African-American children made up the overwhelming majority with 5,476 cases, followed by Hispanic children (2,111 cases), non-Hispanic white children (1,606 cases), Asian/Pacific Islanders (59 cases), and Native American/Alaska Natives (31 cases). By the end of 2002, 5,315 children ages fourteen and under had died from the disease.

MEANS OF TRANSMITTAL. Most babies of HIV-infected mothers do not develop HIV. HIV-positive mothers can reduce the risk of transmission by taking antiretroviral drugs during the last two trimesters of pregnancy and during labor; giving birth by caesarean section; giving the infant a short course of antiretroviral drugs after birth; and not breast feeding. With these interventions, the transmission rate can be reduced to as low as 2%.

The overwhelming majority of children with AIDS, however, contracted it from mothers either infected with HIV or at risk for AIDS (93%). (See Table 5.7.) Other means of transmission were a blood transfusion contaminated with the virus and regular receipt of blood products because of a hemophilia/coagulation disorder.

ADOLESCENTS WITH AIDS. The number of AIDS cases among adolescents is comparatively low. The CDC reported that, as of December 31, 2002, 5,108 adolescents ages

TABLE 5.5

Leading causes of death and numbers of deaths, by age, 1980 and 2001

(Data are based on death certificates)

Age and rank order	1980 Cause of death	Deaths	2001* Cause of death	Deaths
1–4 years				
—	All causes	8,187	All causes	5,107
1	Unintentional injuries	3,313	Unintentional injuries	1,714
2	Congenital anomalies	1,026	Congenital malformations, deformations and chromosomal abnormalities	557
3	Malignant neoplasms	573	Malignant neoplasms	420
4	Diseases of heart	338	Homicide	415
5	Homicide	319	Diseases of heart	225
6	Pneumonia and influenza	267	Influenza and pneumonia	112
7	Meningitis	223	Septicemia	108
8	Meningococcal infection	110	Certain conditions originating in the perinatal period	72
9	Certain conditions originating in the perinatal period	84	In situ neoplasms, benign neoplasms and neoplasms of uncertain or unknown behavior	58
10	Septicemia	71	Cerebrovascular diseases	54
5–14 years				
—	All causes	10,689	All causes	7,095
1	Unintentional injuries	5,224	Unintentional injuries	2,836
2	Malignant neoplasms	1,497	Malignant neoplasms	1,008
3	Congenital anomalies	561	Congenital malformations, deformations and chromosomal abnormalities	376
4	Homicide	415	Homicide	326
5	Diseases of heart	330	Suicide	279
6	Pneumonia and influenza	194	Diseases of heart	272
7	Suicide	142	In situ neoplasms, benign neoplasms and neoplasms of uncertain or unknown behavior	105
8	Benign neoplasms	104	Chronic lower respiratory diseases	104
9	Cerebrovascular diseases	95	Influenza and pneumonia	92
10	Chronic obstructive pulmonary diseases	85	Cerebrovascular diseases	80
15–24 years				
—	All causes	49,027	All causes	32,252
1	Unintentional injuries	26,206	Unintentional injuries	14,41 1
2	Homicide	6,537	Homicide	5,297
3	Suicide	5,239	Suicide	3,971
4	Malignant neoplasms	2,683	Malignant neoplasms	1,704
5	Diseases of heart	1,223	Diseases of heart	999
6	Congenital anomalies	600	Congenital malformations, deformations and chromosomal abnormalities	505
7	Cerebrovas cular diseases	418	Human immunodeficiency virus (HIV) disease	225
8	Pneumonia and influenza	348	Cerebrovascular diseases	196
9	Chronic obstructive pulmonary diseases	141	Influenza and pneumonia	181
10	Anemias	133	Chronic lower respiratory diseases	171

— Category not applicable.

*Figures for homicide and suicide include September 11, 2001 related deaths for which death certificates were filed as of October 24, 2002.

SOURCE: Adapted from "Table 32. Leading Causes of Death and Numbers of Deaths, according to Age: United States, 1980 and 2001," in *Health: United States, 2003*, Centers for Disease Control and Prevention, National Center for Health Statistics, 2003, http://www.cdc.gov/nchs/data/hus/tables/2003/03hus032.pdf (accessed September 16, 2004)

thirteen to nineteen had been diagnosed with AIDS since the beginning of the epidemic in the early 1980s. But because of the lengthy incubation period between the time of infection and the onset of symptoms, it is highly probable that many people who develop AIDS in their early twenties became infected with HIV in their teenage years.

HEALTH CARE

Immunizations

The proportion of preschool-age children immunized against communicable and potentially dangerous childhood diseases—including diphtheria, tetanus, and pertussis (whooping cough), known collectively as DTP; polio; and measles—dropped during the 1980s but rose significantly during the 1990s. By 2002 82% had received four doses of DTP, 90% had received three doses of poliovirus vaccine, 93% had received *haemophilus influenzae* type b vaccine (Hib), 92% had received measles vaccines, 90% had received three doses of hepatitis B vaccine, and 81% had received varicella (chickenpox) vaccine. More than three quarters of these children received the vaccinations in combined series. Children living below the poverty line and African-American children are slightly less likely than the general child population to be immunized. (See Table 5.8.)

In 1994 the U.S. Department of Health and Human Services (HHS) implemented the Vaccines for Children (VFC) program, which provides free or low-cost vaccines

TABLE 5.6

Percentage of high school students who felt sad or hopeless, who seriously considered attempting suicide, who made a suicide plan, and who attempted suicide, by sex, race, ethnicity, and grade, 2003

Category	Felt sad or hopeless*			Seriously considered attempting suicide[†]			Made a suicide plan[†]			Attempted suicide[†¶]			Suicide attempt required medical attention		
	Female %	Male %	Total %	Female %	Male %	Total %	Female %	Male %	Total %	Female %	Male %	Total %	Female %	Male %	Total %
Race/ethnicity															
White[§]	33.3	19.6	26.2	21.2	12.0	16.5	18.6	13.9	16.2	10.3	3.7	6.9	2.4	1.1	1.7
Black[§]	30.8	21.7	26.3	14.7	10.3	12.5	12.4	8.4	10.4	9.0	7.7	8.4	2.2	5.2	3.7
Hispanic	44.9	25.9	35.4	23.4	12.9	18.1	20.7	14.6	17.6	15.0	6.1	10.6	5.7	4.2	5.0
Grade															
9	35.7	21.0	28.0	22.2	11.9	16.9	20.9	14.8	17.7	14.7	5.8	10.1	3.9	3.1	3.5
10	36.9	22.7	29.7	23.8	13.2	18.3	19.5	13.1	16.3	12.7	5.5	9.1	3.2	2.1	2.6
11	35.9	22.1	28.9	20.0	12.9	16.4	17.9	14.4	16.2	10.0	4.6	7.3	2.9	2.0	2.4
12	32.6	22.0	27.4	18.0	13.2	15.5	16.2	13.7	14.9	6.9	5.2	6.1	2.2	1.8	2.1
Total	35.5	21.9	28.6	21.3	12.8	16.9	18.9	14.1	16.5	11.5	5.4	8.5	3.2	2.4	2.9

* Felt so sad or hopeless almost every day for ≥2 weeks in a row that they stopped doing some usual activities.
† During the 12 months preceding the survey.
§ Non-Hispanic.
¶ One or more times.

SOURCE: Adapted from "Table 16. Percentage of High School Students Who Felt Sad or Hopeless, Who Seriously Considered Attempting Suicide, and Who Made a Suicide Plan, by Sex, Race/Ethnicity, and Grade," and "Table 18. Percentage of High School Students Who Actually Attempted Suicide and Whose Suicide Attempt Required Medical Attention, by Sex, Race/Ethnicity, and Grade," in "Youth Risk Behavior Surveillance—United States, 2003," *Centers for Disease Control and Prevention Surveillance Summaries: Morbidity and Mortality Weekly Report,* vol. 53, no. SS–02, May 21, 2004, http://www.cdc.gov/mmwr/PDF/SS/SS5302.pdf (accessed September 16, 2004)

to children at participating private and public health-care provider sites. Eligible children, including children on Medicaid, children without insurance or whose insurance does not cover vaccinations, and Native American or Alaskan Native children can receive the vaccinations through their primary care physician. Children not covered under the program but whose parents cannot afford vaccinations can receive free vaccines at public clinics under local programs. According to the CDC, in fiscal year 2003 the VFC program spent $975 million on vaccines. The program served about 41% of the childhood population in 2002.

The World Health Organization reported in *State of the World's Vaccines and Immunizations,* Geneva, Switzerland, 2002) that developed nations, including the United States, generally have among the highest immunization rates in the world. Global immunization rates for DTP hovered around 70% from the mid-1990s through 2001. Immunization rates for the developed world for the same time period were ten to twenty percentage points higher. Only about 50% of children in Sub-Saharan Africa received the DTP immunizations, the lowest rate in the world.

Physician Visits

Children's health depends upon access to and usage of medical care. Based on household interviews of a sample of the civilian noninstitutionalized population, the National Center for Health Statistics found that in 2001 54.6% of children under age eighteen visited the doctor between one and three times, 26.1% saw the doctor between four and nine times, and 7.6% saw the doctor ten or more times.

(See Table 5.9.) But 11.6% of children did not see a doctor at all. Poor children have less access to health care than nonpoor children. In 2001 only 78.3% of children from poor families were treated in a doctor's office, compared with 86% of children from nonpoor families.

HEALTH INSURANCE

Coverage Levels

According to the U.S. Census Bureau, 11.4% of American children—8.4 million—had no health insurance coverage in 2003. Factors affecting children's access to coverage included their age, race and ethnicity, and family's economic status. Children between the ages of twelve and seventeen were less likely to receive coverage than those under twelve (12.7% versus 10.6%). Poor children were more likely to be uninsured than their wealthier counterparts (19.2% versus 11.4%), and those of Hispanic origin were the least likely racial or ethnic group to receive health insurance coverage, with 21% of them being uninsured. Uninsured rates for other racial and ethnic groups were 7.4% for non-Hispanic white children, 12.4% for Asian-American children, and 14.5% for African-American children (U.S. Bureau of the Census, *Income, Poverty, and Health Insurance Coverage in the United States: 2003,* 2004). The National Center for Health Statistics estimates that 13.7% of all children were uninsured for at least part of 2003 (Robin A. Cohen and Zakia Coriaty-Nelson, *Health Insurance Coverage: Estimates from the National Health Interview Survey, 2003,* June 30, 2004, http://www.cdc.gov/nchs/nhis.htm [accessed July 30, 2004]).

TABLE 5.7

Diagnoses of AIDS in children younger than 13, by year of diagnosis and exposure category, 1998–2002

	Year of diagnosis					Cumulative through 2002
	1998	1999	2000	2001	2002	
Race/ethnicity						
White, not Hispanic	33	19	13	16	7	1,606
Black, not Hispanic	156	129	85	70	58	5,476
Hispanic	47	33	18	22	24	2,111
Asian/Pacific Islander	0	1	2	2	1	59
American Indian/Alaska Native	1	0	0	0	0	31
Exposure category						
Hemophilia coagulation disorder	0	0	0	0	0	236
Mother with, or at risk for, HIV infection	236	181	115	106	90	8,629
Injection drug use	46	43	20	13	9	3,309
Sex with injection drug user	31	24	15	5	5	1,526
Sex with bisexual male	6	6	2	3	4	202
Sex with person with hemophilia	1	2	0	1	0	35
Sex with HIV-infected transfusion recipien	1	0	0	0	0	26
Sex with HIV-infected person, risk not specified	62	50	36	32	32	1,453
Receipt of blood transfusion, blood components, or tissue	0	1	2	2	3	159
Has HIV infection, risk not specified	89	55	40	50	37	1,920
Receipt of blood transfusion, blood components, or tissue	1	0	1	0	1	390
Other/risk not reported or identified	0	2	2	3	0	45
Total[b]	**238**	**183**	**118**	**110**	**92**	**9,300**

Note: These numbers do not represent actual cases in persons with a diagnosis of AIDS. Rather, these numbers are point estimates of cases diagnosed that have been adjusted for reporting delays and for redistribution of cases in persons initially reported without an identified risk. The estimates have not been adjusted for incomplete reporting.
[a]Includes children with a diagnosis of AIDS, from the beginning of the epidemic through 2002.
[b]Includes children of unknown or multiple race. Cumulative total includes 17 children of unknown or multiple race. Because column totals were calculated independently of the values for the subpopulations, the values in each column may not sum to the column total.

SOURCE: "Table 4. Estimated Numbers of Diagnoses of AIDS in Children <13 Years of Age, by Year of Diagnosis and Exposure Category, 1998–2002," in *HIV/AIDS Surveillance Report,* vol. 14, Centers for Disease Control and Prevention, 2003, http://www.cdc.gov/hiv/stats/hasr1402/ table4.htm (accessed September 3, 2004)

In 2002 government programs, such as Medicare, Medicaid, and military insurance, covered 27% of all children. Forty-four percent of African-American children and 40% of Hispanic children had government insurance, compared with only 18% of white, non-Hispanic children.

Child health insurance coverage increased among all age groups, races, and ethnicities from 1998 to 2002 by about 3%. (See Table 5.10.) In a December 31, 2002, press release ("HHS Issues New Report Showing More American Children Received Health Insurance in Early 2002," National Center for Health Statistics), Health and Human Services Secretary Tommy G. Thompson attributed ongoing increases to a push to provide more government coverage, particularly under the State Children's Health Insurance Program (SCHIP). This trend, however, may be leveling off. The National Center for Health Statistics stated that the decrease in uninsured children from 2002 to 2003 was not statistically significant, and the U.S. Census Bureau reported no change in the number of covered children from 2002 to 2003. (See Figure 5.2.)

Medicaid Coverage

In 2002 Medicaid covered 23.9% of children younger than eighteen. (See Figure 5.3.) More than two out of five African-American children (41.2%) and 37.3% of Hispanic children were covered by Medicaid, compared with

15.5% of non-Hispanic white children, and 18.1% of Asian children. In 2000 51% of all those served by Medicaid were children.

To remain in the Medicaid program, families must have their eligibility reassessed at least every six months. If family income or other circumstances change even slightly, the family can lose its eligibility for the Medicaid program, disrupting health care coverage.

The State Children's Health Insurance Program (SCHIP)

From the late 1980s through the mid-1990s, the numbers of uninsured American children rose as coverage rates for employer-sponsored health insurance declined, even though the proportion of children covered by Medicaid also rose. In 1997, as part of the Balanced Budget Act, Congress created the State Children's Health Insurance Program (SCHIP) to expand health insurance to children whose families earned too much money to be eligible for Medicaid but not enough money to pay for private insurance. SCHIP provides funding to states to insure children, offering three alternatives: states may use SCHIP funds to establish separate coverage programs, expand their Medicaid coverage, or use a combination of both. By September 1999 all fifty states had SCHIP plans in place. By September 4, 2003, the program had been expanded to enroll even more children at higher income levels.

TABLE 5.8

Percentage of children vaccinated for selected diseases, by poverty status, race, and Hispanic origin, 1996–2002

Characteristic	Total							Below poverty							At or above poverty						
	1996	1997	1998	1999	2000	2001	2002	1996	1997	1998	1999	2000	2001	2002	1996	1997	1998	1999	2000	2001	2002
Total																					
Combined series (4:3:1:3)[a]	76	76	79	78	76	77	78	69	71	74	73	71	72	72	80	79	82	81	78	79	79
Combined series (4:3:1)[b]	78	78	81	80	78	79	79	72	72	76	75	72	73	73	81	80	83	82	79	80	80
DTP (4 doses or more)[c]	81	82	84	83	82	82	82	74	76	80	79	76	77	75	84	84	86	85	84	84	84
Polio (3 doses or more)	91	91	91	90	90	89	90	88	89	90	87	87	87	88	92	92	92	91	90	90	91
Measles-containing (MCV)[d]	91	90	92	92	91	91	92	87	86	90	90	89	89	90	92	92	93	92	91	92	92
Hib (3 doses or more)[e]	91	93	93	94	93	93	93	87	90	91	91	89	90	90	93	94	95	95	95	94	94
Hepatitis B (3 doses or more)[f]	82	84	87	88	90	89	90	78	81	85	87	87	87	88	83	85	88	89	91	90	90
Varicella[g]	12	26	43	58	68	76	81	5	17	41	55	64	74	79	15	29	44	58	69	77	81
White, non-Hispanic																					
Combined series (4:3:1:3)[a]	79	79	82	81	79	79	80	68	72	77	76	73	71	72	80	80	83	82	80	80	81
Combined series (4:3:1)[b]	80	80	83	82	80	80	81	70	73	79	77	74	72	73	82	82	84	83	81	81	82
DTP (4 doses or more)[c]	83	84	87	86	84	84	84	72	76	82	81	78	75	75	85	85	88	86	85	85	86
Polio (3 doses or more)	92	92	92	90	91	90	91	88	90	91	88	88	87	88	93	92	93	91	91	91	92
Measles-containing (MCV)[d]	91	91	93	92	92	92	93	85	84	90	90	88	87	91	93	93	94	93	92	92	93
Hib (3 doses or more)[e]	93	94	95	95	95	94	94	87	90	92	93	92	89	88	94	95	96	95	95	95	95
Hepatitis B (3 doses or more)[f]	82	85	88	89	91	90	91	76	80	87	88	88	86	86	83	85	88	89	92	90	92
Varicella[g]	15	28	42	56	66	75	79	6	17	38	51	58	67	75	16	29	43	57	68	76	80
Black, non-Hispanic																					
Combined series (4:3:1:3)[a]	74	73	73	74	71	71	71	69	71	72	72	69	69	68	79	77	74	77	72	74	72
Combined series (4:3:1)[b]	77	74	74	75	72	73	72	73	72	74	74	70	71	69	81	78	76	78	73	75	73
DTP (4 doses or more)[c]	79	77	77	79	76	76	76	74	76	77	78	75	74	74	83	80	79	83	78	78	77
Polio (3 doses or more)	90	89	88	87	87	85	87	87	89	88	86	85	84	87	93	91	87	88	85	86	87
Measles-containing (MCV)[d]	90	89	89	90	88	89	90	88	87	89	90	88	88	90	91	91	90	91	87	90	90
Hib (3 doses or more)[e]	89	91	90	92	93	90	92	86	91	90	91	92	87	88	93	94	90	94	93	91	94
Hepatitis B (3 doses or more)[f]	82	82	84	87	89	85	88	78	82	86	86	89	85	89	85	84	83	90	90	85	88
Varicella[g]	9	21	42	58	67	75	83	N/A	16	40	57	60	71	80	13	27	44	60	72	77	84
Hispanic[h]																					
Combined series (4:3:1:3)[a]	71	73	75	75	73	77	76	68	70	73	73	70	73	75	73	77	79	78	74	79	76
Combined series (4:3:1)[b]	74	75	77	77	75	79	77	71	71	76	76	73	76	76	75	77	80	80	75	80	77
DTP (4 doses or more)[c]	77	78	81	80	79	83	79	74	75	79	78	76	79	78	78	81	83	82	80	83	80
Polio (3 doses or more)	89	90	89	89	88	91	90	88	88	90	89	88	90	89	90	90	90	90	87	91	91
Measles-containing (MCV)[d]	88	88	91	90	90	92	91	87	85	90	90	90	91	91	89	90	92	91	90	93	89
Hib (3 doses or more)[e]	89	90	92	92	91	93	92	87	89	92	91	88	91	93	90	92	94	95	93	94	92
Hepatitis B (3 doses or more)[f]	81	81	86	89	88	90	90	80	79	83	87	87	88	89	81	84	88	88	90	91	89
Varicella[g]	8	22	47	61	70	80	82	6	18	44	59	70	81	82	11	25	49	62	70	82	81

— = not available

Note: ( ) is the NIS Web site's footnote.

[a]The 4:3:1:3 combined series consists of 4 (or more) doses of diphtheria and tetanus toxoids and pertussis vaccine (DTP), 3 (or more) doses of polio vaccine, 1 (or more) dose of a measles-containing vaccine (MCV), and 3 (or more) doses of Haemophilus influenzae type b (Hib) vaccine.

[b]The 4:3:1 combined series consists of 4 (or more) doses of diphtheria and tetanus toxoids and pertussis vaccine (DTP), 3 (or more) doses of polio vaccine, and 1 (or more) dose of a measles containing vaccine (MCV).

[c]Four or more doses of any diphtheria and tetanus toxoids and pertussis vaccines including diphtheria and tetanus toxoids, and any acellular pertussis vaccine (DTP/DTaP/DT).

[d]One or more doses of measles-mumps-rubella vaccine; previous reports of vaccination coverage were for measles-containing vaccine (MCV). Immunization providers respondents were asked about measles-containing vaccine, including MMR (measles mumps rubella) vaccines.

[e](Three or more doses of) Haemophilus influenzae type b (Hib) vaccine.

[f]The percentage of children 19 to 35 months of age who received 3 (or more) doses of hepatitis B vaccine was low in 1994, because universal infant vaccination with a 3-dose series was not recommended until November 1991.

[g](One or more doses of varicella at or after child's first birthday, unadjusted for history of varicella illness). Recommended in July 1996. Administered on or after the first birthday, unadjusted for history of varicella illness (chicken pox).

[h]Persons of Hispanic origin may be of any race.

SOURCE: "Childhood Immunization: Percentage of Children Ages 19 to 35 Months Vaccinated for Selected Diseases by Poverty Status, Race, and Hispanic Origin, 1996–2002," in America's Children in Brief: Key National Indicators of Well-Being, 2004, Federal Interagency Forum on Child and Family Statistics, 2004, http://www.childstats.gov/ac2003/tbl.asp?iid=123&id=4&indcode=HEALTH4 (accessed August 24, 2004)

TABLE 5.9

Health care visits to doctor's offices, emergency departments, and home visits over a 12-month period, according to selected characteristics, selected years, 1997–2001

(Data are based on household interviews of a sample of the civilian noninstitutionalized population)

	Number of health care visits[1]											
	None			1–3 visits			4–9 visits			10 or more visits		
Characteristic	1997	1999	2001	1997	1999	2001	1997	1999	2001	1997	1999	2001
	Percent distribution											
All persons[2,3]	16.5	17.5	16.5	46.2	45.8	45.8	23.6	23.3	24.4	13.7	13.4	13.3
Age												
Under 18 years	11.8	12.4	11.6	54.1	54.4	54.6	25.2	25.0	26.1	8.9	8.2	7.6
Under 6 years	5.0	5.9	5.5	44.9	45.9	45.8	37.0	36.8	37.9	13.0	11.3	10.8
6–17 years	15.3	15.5	14.6	58.7	58.5	58.9	19.3	19.4	20.5	6.8	6.7	6.1
18–44 years	21.7	24.2	23.3	46.7	45.8	46.1	19.0	17.8	18.9	12.6	12.3	11.8
18–24 years	22.0	24.8	25.4	46.8	46.1	44.7	20.0	17.8	19.5	11.2	11.4	10.5
25–44 years	21.6	24.0	22.6	46.7	45.7	46.5	18.7	17.8	18.7	13.0	12.6	12.2
45–64 years	16.9	16.9	15.6	42.9	42.4	42.9	24.7	25.0	25.7	15.5	15.7	15.9
45–54 years	17.9	18.4	17.1	43.9	43.2	44.9	23.4	22.8	23.6	14.8	15.7	14.4
55–64 years	15.3	14.7	13.3	41.3	41.1	39.6	26.7	28.4	28.9	16.7	15.8	18.2
65 years and over	8.9	7.9	7.1	34.7	34.3	32.3	32.5	34.1	35.6	23.8	23.7	25.0
65–74 years	9.8	8.6	8.1	36.9	36.9	35.8	31.6	33.2	33.5	21.6	21.3	22.6
75 years and over	7.7	7.2	5.8	31.8	31.1	28.2	33.8	35.1	38.1	26.6	26.6	27.9
Sex[3]												
Male	21.3	23.1	21.3	47.1	45.5	46.5	20.6	20.6	21.6	11.0	10.8	10.7
Female	11.8	12.0	11.9	45.4	46.1	45.1	26.5	25.9	27.1	16.3	15.9	15.9
Race[3,4]												
White only	16.0	16.9	15.9	46.1	45.7	45.7	23.9	23.8	24.8	14.0	13.6	13.5
Black or African American only	16.8	18.4	16.4	46.1	46.2	46.4	23.2	21.9	24.0	13.9	13.5	13.2
American Indian and Alaska Native only	17.1	20.6	*21.4	38.0	34.3	36.4	24.2	27.8	25.4	20.7	17.2	16.9
Asian only	22.8	23.1	20.8	49.1	47.3	48.3	19.7	19.4	22.3	8.3	10.2	8.6
Native Hawaiian and Other Pacific Islander only	—	*	*	—	*	*	—	*	*	—	*	*
2 or more races	—	15.2	18.0	—	40.8	41.2	—	22.2	23.5	—	21.8	17.3
Hispanic Origin and race[3,4]												
Hispanic or Latino	24.9	26.2	27.0	42.3	44.3	40.2	20.3	19.2	20.7	12.5	10.3	12.0
Mexican	28.9	30.2	31.4	40.8	43.0	39.2	18.5	18.2	19.6	11.8	8.7	9.8
Not Hispanic or Latino	15.4	16.2	15.0	46.7	46.0	46.5	24.0	23.9	25.0	13.9	13.9	13.5
White only	14.7	15.5	14.3	46.6	46.0	46.4	24.4	24.5	25.4	14.3	14.1	13.9
Black or African American only	16.9	18.4	16.4	46.1	46.2	46.4	23.1	21.9	24.0	13.8	13.5	13.1
Respondent-assessed health status[3]												
Fair or poor	7.8	9.8	9.0	23.3	25.9	22.1	29.0	24.3	27.7	39.9	40.1	41.3
Good to excellent	17.2	18.1	17.3	48.4	47.7	48.0	23.3	23.2	24.3	11.1	11.0	10.5
Poverty status[3,5]												
Poor	20.3	21.5	21.7	37.1	39.2	37.2	22.7	21.3	23.4	19.9	18.0	17.7
Near poor	19.9	22.2	20.4	42.8	41.6	41.4	21.8	21.5	22.9	15.5	14.7	15.3
Nonpoor	14.0	14.9	14.0	48.0	47.0	47.4	25.0	25.0	25.8	13.0	13.1	12.8
Hispanic origin and race and poverty status[3,4,5]												
Hispanic or Latino:												
Poor	30.6	31.2	34.3	33.8	38.2	32.7	20.0	18.7	18.1	15.6	11.8	14.9
Near poor	29.1	30.2	28.9	39.0	42.1	39.3	20.9	17.5	20.2	11.0	10.1	11.6
Nonpoor	18.7	21.0	19.9	48.6	46.8	44.6	20.3	21.9	24.7	12.3	10.2	10.8
Not Hispanic or Latino:												
White only:	16.3	17.2	16.2	37.7	38.9	38.7	24.0	23.3	26.4	22.1	20.7	18.8
Poor	17.1	19.8	17.1	43.7	40.8	41.3	22.3	23.3	24.1	17.0	16.1	17.6
Near poor	13.2	14.0	13.1	47.6	46.9	47.5	25.7	25.5	26.1	13.4	13.6	13.3
Nonpoor												
Black or African American only:												
Poor	17.8	18.0	17.3	37.4	39.9	38.1	23.3	23.1	24.0	21.5	19.0	20.5
Near poor	18.9	19.9	18.1	43.0	44.0	44.9	23.4	20.5	23.4	14.7	15.6	13.6
Nonpoor	15.6	16.3	14.6	50.5	48.2	47.4	23.3	23.7	26.6	10.6	11.8	11.4

According to the Centers for Medicare and Medicaid Services, in the first quarter of fiscal year 2004 about 4.1 million children were enrolled in SCHIP.

HEALTH OF HOMELESS CHILDREN

The Urban Institute suggests that as many as 2% of American children are homeless in the course of one year. Doctor Catherine Karr, in *Homeless Children: What Every*

Health Care Provider Should Know (National Health Care for the Homeless Council, December 29, 2003, http://www.nhchc.org/Children/index.htm [accessed July 28, 2004]), argues that these children suffer from frequent health problems. They are seen in emergency rooms and hospitalized more often than other poor children. The often crowded and unsanitary conditions they live in lead to a higher rate of infectious diseases, like upper respiratory infections, diarrhea, and scabies. Homeless children live in

TABLE 5.9

Health care visits to doctor's offices, emergency departments, and home visits over a 12-month period, according to selected characteristics, selected years, 1997–2001 [CONTINUED]

(Data are based on household interviews of a sample of the civilian noninstitutionalized population)

	Number of health care visits[1]											
	None			1–3 visits			4–9 visits			10 or more visits		
Characteristic	1997	1999	2001	1997	1999	2001	1997	1999	2001	1997	1999	2001
	Percent distribution											
Health insurance status[6,7]												
Under 65 years of age:												
Insured	14.3	15.4	14.1	49.0	48.6	49.1	23.6	23.2	24.2	13.1	12.7	12.6
Private	14.7	15.9	14.4	50.6	49.9	50.6	23.1	22.9	24.0	11.6	11.3	11.0
Medicaid	9.8	10.7	10.4	35.5	35.6	35.4	26.5	26.0	26.3	28.2	27.6	27.8
Uninsured	33.7	37.3	37.5	42.8	41.6	41.4	15.3	13.2	14.6	8.2	7.9	6.5
65 years of age and over:												
Medicare HMO	8.9	5.7	5.0	35.8	34.2	30.0	33.1	34.6	41.1	22.3	25.5	23.9
Private	7.3	6.7	5.5	35.9	34.9	34.6	34.0	34.9	35.2	22.7	23.5	24.8
Medicaid	9.3	*7.3	6.1	19.2	21.4	18.7	27.9	34.8	31.6	43.7	36.5	43.5
Medicare fee-for-service only	15.5	14.0	14.1	34.0	35.8	30.5	28.1	31.0	34.2	22.4	19.2	21.2
Poverty status and health insurance status[5,6,7]												
Under 65 years of age:												
Poor:												
Insured	13.7	14.6	14.0	38.8	41.4	41.1	24.5	23.2	24.9	22.9	20.7	20.0
Uninsured	36.7	39.8	43.2	38.8	39.3	34.6	14.9	12.6	15.3	9.5	8.3	6.9
Near poor:												
Insured	15.6	17.0	15.8	45.5	44.9	44.7	22.3	22.6	22.7	16.6	15.5	16.8
Uninsured	34.5	38.0	35.3	41.8	40.2	40.9	15.6	13.4	16.6	8.1	8.4	7.2
Nonpoor:												
Insured	13.4	14.7	13.6	50.3	49.1	49.8	24.2	24.2	25.0	12.1	12.0	11.6
Uninsured	29.1	32.9	31.9	45.4	43.7	46.0	17.0	14.6	15.5	8.4	8.8	6.6
Geographic region[3]												
Northeast	13.2	12.8	11.8	45.9	46.4	47.2	26.0	25.6	26.6	14.9	15.2	14.3
Midwest	15.9	16.2	14.9	47.7	46.7	47.2	22.8	23.8	24.0	13.6	13.3	13.9
South	17.2	18.9	17.7	46.1	45.5	45.2	23.3	22.5	24.4	13.5	13.2	12.8
West	19.1	20.9	20.5	44.8	44.8	44.1	22.8	21.9	22.8	13.3	12.4	12.7
Location of residence[3]												
Within MSA[8]	16.2	17.4	16.4	46.4	45.9	45.7	23.7	23.4	24.6	13.7	13.2	13.2
Outside MSA[8]	17.3	17.7	16.7	45.4	45.1	46.1	23.3	22.9	23.6	13.9	14.4	13.6

*Estimates are considered unreliable.

— Data not available.

[1]This table presents a summary measure of ambulatory and home health care visits during a 12-month period.

[2]Includes all other races not shown separately, unknown poverty status, and unknown health insurance status.

[3]Estimates are age adjusted to the year 2000 standard population using six age groups: Under 18 years, 18–44 years, 45–54 years, 55–64 years, 65–74 years, and 75 years and over.

[4]The race groups, white, black, American Indian and Alaska Native (AI/AN), Asian, Native Hawaiian and Other Pacific Islander, and 2 or more races, include persons of Hispanic and non-Hispanic origin. Persons of Hispanic origin may be of any race. Starting with data year 1999 race-specific estimates are tabulated according to 1997 Standards for Federal data on Race and Ethnicity and are not strictly comparable with estimates for earlier years. The five single race categories plus multiple race categories shown in the table conform to 1997 Standards. The 1999 race-specific estimates are for persons who reported only one racial group; the category "2 or more races" includes persons who reported more than one racial group. Prior to data year 1999, data were tabulated according to 1977 Standards with four racial groups and the category "Asian only" included Native Hawaiian and Other Pacific Islander. Estimates for single race categories prior to 1999 included persons who reported one race or, if they reported more than one race, identified one race as best representing their race. The effect of the 1997 Standard on the 1999 estimates can be seen by comparing 1999 data tabulated according to the two Standards: Age-adjusted estimates based on the 1977 Standard of the percent of persons with a specified number of health care contacts are: (no visits) identical for white and black persons; 0.1 percentage points higher for AI/AN persons; 0.4 percentage points lower for Asian and Pacific Islander persons; (1–3 visits) identical for white persons; 0.1 percentage points lower for black persons; 1.3 percentage points higher for AI/AN persons; 0.1 percentage points lower for Asian and Pacific Islander persons; (4–9 visits) identical for white persons; 0.2 percentage points higher for black persons; 2.2 percentage points lower for AI/AN persons; 0.4 percentage points higher for Asian and Pacific Islander persons; (10 or more visits) identical for white and black persons; 0.9 percentage points higher for AI/AN persons; and 0.1 percentage points higher for Asian and Pacific Islander persons than estimates based on the 1997 Standards.

[5]Poor persons are defined as below the poverty threshold. Near poor persons have incomes of 100 percent to less than 200 percent of poverty threshold. Nonpoor persons have incomes of 200 percent or greater than the poverty threshold. Poverty status was unknown for 20 percent of persons in the sample in 1997, 25 percent in 1998, 28 percent in 1999, 27 percent in 2000, and 28 percent in 2001.

[6]Estimates for persons under 65 years of age are age adjusted to the year 2000 standard using four age groups: Under 18 years, 18–44 years, years, and 55–64 years of age. Estimates for persons 65 years of age and over are age adjusted to the year 2000 standard using two age groups: 65–74 years and 75 years and over.

[7]Health insurance categories are mutually exclusive. Persons who reported both Medical and private coverage are classified as having private coverage. Persons 65 years of age and over who reported Medicare HMO (health maintenance organization) and some other type of health insurance coverage are classified as having Medicare HMO. Starting in 1997 Medical includes state-sponsored health plans and State Children's Health Insurance Program (SCHIP). The category "insured" also includes military, other State, and Medicare coverage.

[8]MSA is a metropolitan statistical area.

Notes: Some numbers is this table for health insurance estimates were revised and differ from previous editions of *Health, United States*. In 1997 the National Health Interview Survey questionnaire was redesigned. Data for additional years are available.

SOURCE: "Table 70. Health Care Visits to Doctors' Offices, Emergency Departments, and Home Visits within the Past 12 Months, according to Selected Characteristics, Selected Years 1997–2001," in *Health: United States, 2003,* Centers for Disease Control and Prevention, National Center for Health Statistics, 2003, http://www.cdc.gov/nchs/data/hus/tables/2003/03hus070.pdf (accessed September 3, 2004)

less structured and often unsafe environments, leaving them more vulnerable to accidents and injury. They tend not to have access to nutritious food, and are often malnourished or obese. Homeless children tend to lag behind their housed peers developmentally, and school-age homeless children often have academic problems. The greater likelihood that

TABLE 5.10

Percentage of children under age 18 covered by health insurance, by type of insurance, age, race, and Hispanic origin, 1987–2002

Characteristic	1987	1988	1989	1990	1991	1992	1993	1994	1995	1996	1997	1998	1999[b]	2000[b]	2001[b]	2002
All health insurance																
Total	**87**	**87**	**87**	**87**	**87**	**87**	**86**	**86**	**86**	**85**	**85**	**85**	**87**	**88**	**88**	**88**
Age																
Ages 0–5	88	87	87	89	89	89	88	86	87	86	86	84	87	89	89	89
Ages 6–11	87	87	87	87	88	88	87	87	87	85	86	85	88	88	89	89
Ages 12–17	86	86	86	85	85	85	83	85	86	84	83	84	87	87	87	87
Race and Hispanic origin																
White, non-Hispanic	90	90	90	90	90	90	89	89	90	89	89	89	92	93	93	92
Black	83	84	84	85	85	86	84	83	85	81	81	80	84	86	86	86
Hispanic[c]	72	71	70	72	73	75	74	72	73	71	71	70	74	75	76	77
Private health insurance[d]																
Total	**74**	**74**	**74**	**71**	**70**	**69**	**67**	**66**	**66**	**66**	**67**	**68**	**70**	**70**	**68**	**67**
Age																
Ages 0–5	72	71	71	68	66	65	63	60	60	62	63	64	66	66	64	63
Ages 6–11	74	74	75	73	71	71	70	67	67	67	68	68	70	70	69	68
Ages 12–17	75	76	76	73	72	71	69	70	71	70	69	70	73	73	72	71
Race and Hispanic origin																
White, non-Hispanic	83	83	83	81	80	80	78	77	78	78	78	79	81	81	80	79
Black	49	50	52	49	45	46	46	43	44	45	48	47	52	53	52	50
Hispanic[c]	48	48	48	45	43	42	42	38	38	40	42	43	46	45	44	43
Government health insurance[d]																
Total	**19**	**19**	**19**	**22**	**24**	**25**	**27**	**26**	**26**	**25**	**23**	**23**	**23**	**24**	**26**	**27**
Age																
Ages 0–5	22	23	24	28	30	33	35	33	33	31	29	27	27	29	31	32
Ages 6–11	19	18	18	20	22	23	25	25	26	25	23	23	23	25	26	27
Ages 12–17	16	16	15	18	19	19	20	20	21	19	19	19	19	20	20	22
Race and Hispanic origin																
White, non-Hispanic	12	13	13	15	16	17	19	18	18	18	17	16	16	17	17	18
Black	42	42	41	45	48	49	50	48	49	45	40	42	40	42	42	44
Hispanic[c]	28	27	27	32	37	38	41	38	39	35	34	31	33	35	37	40

[a]Children are considered to be covered by health insurance if they had government or private coverage at any time during the year. Some children are covered by both types of insurance; hence, the sum of government and private is greater than the total.

[b]Estimates beginning in 1999 include follow-up questions to verify health insurance status and use the Census 2000-based weights. Estimates for 1999 through 2001 are not directly comparable with earlier years, before the verification questions were added.

[c]Persons of Hispanic origin may be of any race.

[d]Government health insurance for children consists mostly of Medicaid, but also includes Medicare, the State Children's Health Insurance Programs (SCHIP), and Civilian Health and Medical Care Program of the Uniformed Services (CHAMPUS/Tricare).

SOURCE: "Access to Health Care: Percentage of Children under Age 18 Covered by Health Insurance by Type of Insurance, Age, Race, and Hispanic Origin, 1987–2002," in *America's Children in Brief: Key National Indicators of Well-Being, 2004*, Federal Interagency Forum on Child and Family Statistics, 2004, http://www.childstats.gov/ac2003/tbl.asp?iid=118&id=3&indcode=ECON5A (accessed August 24, 2004)

FIGURE 5.2

Percent of children under 18 years of age who lacked health insurance coverage when interviewed, for at least part of the year, or for more than a year, 1997–2003

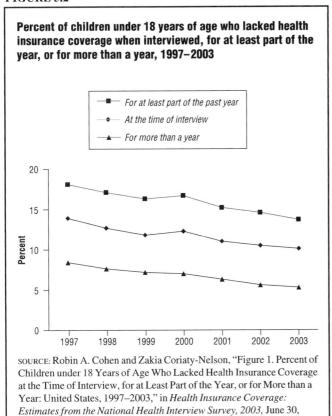

SOURCE: Robin A. Cohen and Zakia Coriaty-Nelson, "Figure 1. Percent of Children under 18 Years of Age Who Lacked Health Insurance Coverage at the Time of Interview, for at Least Part of the Year, or for More than a Year: United States, 1997–2003," in *Health Insurance Coverage: Estimates from the National Health Interview Survey, 2003,* June 30, 2004, http://www.cdc.gov/nchs/nhis.htm (accessed July 30, 2004)

FIGURE 5.3

Children covered by Medicaid, by race and ethnicity, 2002

(In percent)

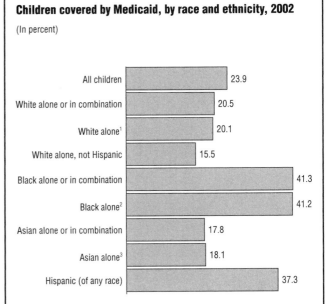

[1]The 2003 CPS asked respondents to choose one or more races. White alone refers to people who reported white and did not report any other race category. The use of this single-race population does not imply that it is the preferred method of presenting or analyzing data. The Census Bureau uses a variety of approaches. About 2.6 percent of people reported more than one race in 2000.
[2]Black alone refers to people who reported Black or African American and did not report any other race category.
[3]Asian alone refers to people who reported Asian and did not report any other race category.

SOURCE: Robert J. Mills and Shailesh Bhandari, "Figure 5. Children Covered by Medicaid by Race and Ethnicity: 2002," in *Health Insurance Coverage in the United States: 2002,* Current Population Reports, P60–223, U.S. Census Bureau, September 2003, http://www.census.gov/prod/2003pubs/p60-224.pdf (accessed September 3, 2004)

homeless children come from families plagued by mental illness, drug use, and domestic violence negatively impacts their own mental health. Homelessness results in serious negative consequences for children's health.

OVERWEIGHT AND OBESE CHILDREN

The increasing numbers of overweight and obese Americans has become a national concern. The percentage of overweight children and adolescents has grown significantly since the 1970s. Between 1976 and 1980 6.2% of boys and 6% of girls ages six to eleven years were overweight. (See Table 5.11.) From 1999 to 2002 those percentages had almost tripled for boys (16.9%) and more than doubled for girls (14.7%). An even more alarming upward trend was seen in the rates of overweight adolescents; 3.7% of boys and 5.7% of girls ages twelve to eighteen were overweight in the period from 1976 to 1980, but 17.5% of adolescent boys and 13.8% of adolescent girls were overweight between 1999 and 2002. The proportion of overweight children overall between the ages of six and eighteen almost tripled between 1976 and 2002.

Percentages of overweight children vary by race and ethnicity. In 2002 non-Hispanic white adolescents were less likely to be overweight (14.8%) than were non-Hispanic African-American (23.7%) and Mexican-American adolescents (21.5%). White children aged 6–11 were also less

likely to be overweight (13.5%) than Mexican-American (21.8%) or African-American children (19.8%).

Medical professionals are concerned about this trend, because overweight children are at increased risk for premature death in adulthood, as well as for many chronic diseases, including coronary heart disease, hypertension, diabetes mellitus (type 2), gallbladder disease, respiratory disease, some cancers, and arthritis. Type 2 diabetes, previously considered an adult disease, has increased dramatically in children and adolescents. Being overweight or obese also can lead to poor self-esteem and depression in children. According to the CDC, in 2003 15.4% of high school students were at risk for becoming overweight and 13.5% were already overweight (*Youth Risk Behavior Surveillance—United States, 2003*). (See Table 5.12.)

Weight problems in children are thought to be caused by lack of physical activity, unhealthy eating habits, or a combination of these factors, with genetics and lifestyle playing important roles in determining a child's weight. Television watching and playing computer and video games also contribute to inactive lifestyles of children. According to the 2003 *Youth Risk Behavior Surveillance*, 38.2% of high school students spent three or more hours

TABLE 5.11

Percentage of children 6–18 who are overweight, by gender, race, and Hispanic origin, selected years 1976–2002

	Total			Male			Female		
	1976–1980	1988–1994	1999–2002	1976–1980	1988–1994	1999–2002	1976–1980	1988–1994	1999–2002
Children ages 6–18									
Total[a]	**5.7**	**11.2**	**16**	**5.5**	**11.8**	**17.2**	**5.8**	**10.6**	**14.8**
Race and Hispanic origin									
White, non-Hispanic	4.9	10.5	13.2	4.7	11.3	14.3	5.1	9.6	12.1
Black, non-Hispanic	8.2	14	20.7	5.8[b]	11.5	18.4	10.7	16.5	23.2
Mexican American	—	15.4	23.1	—	16.1	26.9	—	14.7	19
Children ages 6–11									
Total[a]	**6.1**	**11.3**	**15.8**	**6.2**	**11.6**	**16.9**	**6**	**11**	**14.7**
Race and Hispanic origin									
White, non-Hispanic	5.6	10.2	13.5	6.1	10.7	14	5.2	9.8	13.1
Black, non-Hispanic	9	14.6	19.8	6.8[b]	12.3	17	11.2	17	22.8
Mexican American	16.4	21.8	-17.5	26.5	-15.3	17.1			
Children ages 12–18									
Total[a]	**4.7**	**11.1**	**16.2**	**3.7**	**12**	**17.5**	**5.7**	**10.2**	**14.8**
Race and Hispanic origin									
White, non-Hispanic	4.3	10.8	12.9	3.6	12	14.7	5	9.5	11.1
Black, non-Hispanic	7.5	13.3	21.8	*10.7	19.9	10.3	16	23.7	21.5
Mexican American	—	—	14.2	24.6	—	14.4	27.3	-14	21.5

— = not available

* = Estimates are considered unreliable (relative standard error greater than 40 percent)

[a]Totals include data for racial/ethnic groups not shown separately.

[b]Estimates are unstable because they are based on a small number of persons (relative standard error greater than 30 percent).

Note: Overweight is defined as body mass index (BMI) at or above the 95th percentile of the 2000 Centers for Disease Control and Prevention BMI-for-age growth charts (http://www.cdc.gov/growthcharts). BMI is calculated as weight in kilograms divided by the square of height in meters.

SOURCE: "Table HEALTH3. Percentage of Children Ages 6 to 18 Who Are Overweight by Gender, Race, and Hispanic Origin, 1976–1980, 1988–1994, and 1999–2002," in "Federal Interagency Forum on Child and Family Statistics," *America's Children in Brief: Key National Indicators of Well-Being, 2004*, Federal Interagency Forum on Child and Family Statistics, U.S. Government Printing Office, 2004, http://childstats.gov/ac2004/tables/health3.asp (accessed September 16, 2004)

TABLE 5.12

Percentage of high school students who had or thought they had a problem with weight, by demographic characteristics, 2003

Category	At risk for becoming overweight[a]			Overweight[b]			Described themselves as overweight			Were trying to lose weight		
	Female	Male	Total	Female	Male	Total	Female	Male	Total	Female	Male	Total
	%	%	%	%	%	%	%	%	%	%	%	%
Race/ethnicity												
White[c]	13.8	14.3	**14.1**	7.8	16.2	**12.2**	38.5	23.5	**30.8**	62.6	27.9	**44.8**
Black[c]	21.2	15.5	**18.3**	15.6	19.5	**17.6**	26.4	17.9	**22.3**	46.7	22.7	**34.7**
Hispanic	15.7	19.0	**17.3**	11.8	21.7	**16.8**	36.1	27.1	**31.6**	61.7	37.4	**49.4**
Grade												
9	15.6	15.3	**15.4**	11.2	19.0	**15.3**	33.1	22.6	**27.7**	54.1	31.2	**42.2**
10	15.3	14.7	**15.0**	9.3	17.9	**13.7**	36.1	23.2	**29.6**	62.2	28.3	**45.1**
11	16.9	16.6	**16.8**	8.6	17.0	**12.9**	36.9	24.3	**30.5**	60.4	28.3	**44.1**
12	13.2	15.6	**14.4**	8.0	14.7	**11.4**	38.7	24.1	**31.4**	61.7	28.0	**44.6**
Total	**15.3**	**15.5**	**15.4**	**9.4**	**17.4**	**13.5**	**36.1**	**23.5**	**29.6**	**59.3**	**29.1**	**43.8**

[a]Students who were ≥85th percentile but <95th percentile for body mass index, by age and sex, based on reference data.
[b]Students who were ≥95th percentile for body mass index, by age and sex, based on reference data.
[c]Non-Hispanic

SOURCE: Adapted from "Table 58. Percentage of High School Students Who Were at Risk for Becoming or Were Overweight, by Sex, Race/Ethnicity, and Grade," and "Table 60. Percentage of High School Students Who Described Themselves as Slightly or Very Overweight and Who Were Trying to Lose Weight, by Sex, Race/Ethnicity, and Grade," in "Youth Risk Behavior Surveillance—United States, 2003," *Centers for Disease Control and Prevention Surveillance Summaries: Morbidity and Mortality Weekly Report,* vol. 53, no. SS–02, May 21, 2004, http://www.cdc.gov/mmwr/PDF/SS/SS5302.pdf (accessed September 3, 2004)

per school day watching television, often not getting a sufficient amount of physical exercise as a consequence.

Physical Activity

Physical activity patterns established during youth may extend into adulthood and affect the risk of illnesses such as coronary heart disease, diabetes, and cancer. Mental health experts correlate increased physical activity with improved mental health and overall improvement in life satisfaction. The CDC's *Youth Risk Behavior Surveillance—United States, 2003* reported that the percentage of students in high school who participated in vigorous physical activity, exercise, and physical education classes varied. (See Table 5.13.) Almost three out of four males engaged in sufficient vigorous physical activity (70%), but only slightly more than half of high school females did (55%). White students were somewhat more likely to engage in vigorous activity (65.2%) than African-American (54.8%) or Hispanic students (59.3%). Rigorous activity among high school students also generally declined with age.

ASTHMA

The July 2003 American Lung Association fact sheet "Asthma in Children" reported that asthma was the leading chronic illness in children. Childhood asthma was the third leading cause of hospitalization among children younger than fifteen, and caused 14.6 million missed days of school in 2002. A National Center for Health Statistics (NCHS) survey found that in 2001 8.7% of children from infancy to seventeen years, or 6.3 million, suffered from asthma. The American Lung Association estimated that

TABLE 5.13

High school participation in physical activity, by demographic characteristics, 2003

Category	Participated in sufficient vigorous physical activity[a]			Participated in sufficient moderate physical activity[b]		
	Female	Male	Total	Female	Male	Total
	%	%	%	%	%	%
Race/ethnicity						
White[c]	58.1	71.9	65.2	23.3	28.9	26.2
Black[c]	44.9	65.0	54.8	17.5	25.8	21.7
Hispanic	51.8	66.7	59.3	20.6	23.3	22.0
Grade						
9	63.6	73.1	68.5	22.3	28.3	25.4
10	58.2	71.5	64.9	25.3	26.2	25.7
11	49.4	70.4	60.1	20.0	28.1	24.2
12	46.4	63.7	55.0	20.0	26.3	23.2
Total	**55.0**	**70.0**	**62.6**	**22.1**	**27.2**	**24.7**

[a]Exercised or participated in physical activities that made students sweat and breathe hard for ≥20 minutes on ≥3 of the 7 days preceding the survey (e.g., basketball, soccer, running, swimming laps, fast bicycling, fast dancing, or similar aerobic activities).
[b]Physical activities that did not make students sweat and breathe hard for ≥30 minutes on ≥5 of the 7 days preceding the survey (e.g., fast walking, slow bicycling, skating, pushing a lawn mower, or mopping floors).
[c]Non-Hispanic.

SOURCE: "Table 50. Percentage of High School Students Who Participated in Sufficient Vigorous Physical Activity and Sufficient Moderate Physical Activity, by Sex, Race/Ethnicity, and Grade," in "Youth Risk Behavior Surveillance—United States, 2003," *Centers for Disease Control and Prevention Surveillance Summaries: Morbidity and Mortality Weekly Report,* vol. 53, no. SS–02, May 21, 2004, http://www.cdc.gov/mmwr/PDF/SS/SS5302.pdf (accessed September 4, 2003)

up to a million asthmatic children are exposed to second-hand smoke, worsening their condition. In 2000 223 children died from complications of asthma.

A study published in the August 2002 issue of *Pediatrics* ("Residential Exposures Associated with Asthma in

U.S. Children") concluded from a 1988 to 1994 survey that a higher percentage of African-American children (8.9%) than white children (5.2%) have asthma. Experts suggest that because a higher number of African-Americans than other racial and ethnic groups lack health insurance and live in poverty they are more likely to postpone treatment and rely on emergency room care rather than preventive medications and treatment. A 2003 University of Rochester Medical Center Study found that white children with asthma were 1.7 to two times more likely than African-American children to use medication to prevent sudden asthma attacks (Pediatric Academic Societies, News Release, "Race Plays Role in Children's Care in Emergency Department," released May 3, 2004, http://www.newswise.com/articles/view/504300 [accessed August 3, 2004]).

HUNGER

Food insecurity is defined as the lack of access to enough food to meet basic needs. According to the U.S. Department of Agriculture, in 2002 88.9% of U.S. households were food secure (*Household Food Security in the United States, 2002*). However, the remaining twelve million U.S. households (11.1%) experienced food insecurity at some time during the year. A higher percentage of children than adults were food insecure (18.1% and 10.5%, respectively), and almost one out of every hundred children were hungry on one or more days during the year. Households with incomes below the poverty line, households with children headed by a single woman, and African-American and Hispanic households were the most likely to experience food insecurity.

Households that are experiencing food insecurity tend to go through a sequence of steps as food insecurity increases: first, families begin to worry about having enough food, then they begin to decrease other necessities, then they reduce the quality and quantity of all household members' diets, then decrease the frequency of meals and quantity of adult members' food, and finally they decrease the frequency of meals and the quantity of children's food.

Emergency Food Assistance

Second Harvest, the nation's largest charitable hunger-relief organization, reported that in 2001 23.3 million Americans sought emergency food assistance. According to the USDA, in 2002 3% of all households used food pantries and 0.5% ate meals in emergency food centers (soup kitchens). A family with children headed by a single woman was most likely to receive this kind of food assistance. A December 2003 study by the U.S. Conference of Mayors and Sodexho (*Hunger and Homelessness Survey: A Status Report on Hunger and Homelessness in America's Cities 2003*) found that requests for emergency food

assistance increased by 17% throughout 2002, continuing a rapid increase in these requests; the 2002 requests had increased 19% over those in 2001. More than half (59%) of the people who requested food assistance were members of families with children. An average of 14% of the demand for such assistance was unmet. The most frequent reasons for hunger cited by city officials were unemployment, low-paying jobs, high housing and medical costs, homelessness, substance abuse and mental health problems, reduced public benefits, high childcare costs, and the weakening of the economy.

LEAD POISONING

Lead exposure comes primarily from leaded paints that have worn off or been scraped from older homes. Lead is also found in lead plumbing and emitted by factory smokestacks. Because they have smaller bodies and are growing, children suffer the effects of lead exposure more acutely than adults do. Lead poisoning causes nervous system disorders, reduction in intelligence, fatigue, inhibited infant growth, and hearing loss. Toxic levels of lead in a parent can also affect unborn children.

According to the CDC fact sheet "About Childhood Lead Poisoning," in 2000 approximately 434,000 children in the United States between the ages of one and five, or about 2.2% of all children in that age group, had blood lead levels greater than the CDC's recommended level of ten micrograms per deciliter of blood. This number has dropped substantially from 1976 to 1980, when 88.2% of children under age five showed high blood lead levels. Although children from all social and economic levels can be affected by lead poisoning, children in families with low incomes, those who live in older, deteriorated housing, and African-American and Hispanic children are at higher risk. Paint produced prior to 1978 frequently contained lead, so federal legislation now requires owners to disclose any information they may have about lead-based paint before renting or selling a home built earlier than 1978.

MENTAL HEALTH ISSUES IN YOUNG PEOPLE

Marital Conflict and Divorce

Marital conflict hurts children whether it results in the breakup of marriages or not. Nearly all the studies on children of divorce have focused on the period after the parents separated. But some recent studies suggest that the negative effects children experience may not come so much from divorce itself as from marital discord between parents prior to divorce. In fact, some research suggests that many problems reported with troubled teens not only began during the marriage but may have contributed to the breakup of the marriage. Children raised in discord and marital instability often experience a variety of social, emotional, and psychological problems.

TABLE 5.14

Percentage of high school students who engaged in healthy and unhealthy behaviors associated with weight control[1], by sex, race, ethnicity, and grade, 2003

Category	Ate less food, fewer calories, or foods low in fat to lose weight or to keep from gaining weight			Exercised to lose weight or to keep from gaining weight			Went without eating for ≥24 hours to lose weight or to keep from gaining weight			Took diet pills, powders, or liquids to lose weight[3] or to keep from gaining weight			Vomited or took laxatives to lose weight or to keep from gaining weight		
	Female %	Male %	Total %	Female %	Male %	Total %	Female %	Male %	Total %	Female %	Male %	Total %	Female %	Male %	Total %
Race/ethnicity															
White[2]	61.1	29.1	44.6	69.6	48.1	58.5	18.4	7.1	12.5	13.0	6.8	9.8	8.5	2.7	5.5
Black[2]	39.0	21.8	30.5	49.2	46.1	47.5	14.5	10.5	12.5	5.1	4.9	5.0	5.6	5.0	5.3
Hispanic	54.9	33.7	44.2	64.1	53.7	58.9	18.2	9.2	13.7	11.7	9.2	10.5	9.7	5.1	7.4
Grade															
9	53.0	28.8	40.4	65.7	50.2	57.6	18.8	10.7	14.6	9.2	7.0	8.0	7.9	4.6	6.2
10	58.1	27.8	42.7	68.9	49.8	59.2	18.5	7.0	12.7	10.9	5.8	8.3	9.3	3.5	6.4
11	56.4	29.4	42.8	64.5	49.4	56.8	19.6	8.2	13.8	12.6	7.7	10.1	8.3	2.6	5.7
12	57.9	29.8	43.7	63.2	46.4	54.6	15.7	6.9	11.2	13.0	8.5	10.8	7.3	3.8	5.5
Total	**56.2**	**28.9**	**42.2**	**65.7**	**49.0**	**57.1**	**18.3**	**8.5**	**13.3**	**11.3**	**7.1**	**9.2**	**8.4**	**3.7**	**6.0**

[1]During the 30 days preceding the survey
[2]Non-Hispanic
[3]Without a doctor's advice

SOURCE: Adapted from "Table 62. Percentage of High School Students Who Engaged in Healthy Behaviors Associated with Weight Control to Lose Weight or to Keep from Gaining Weight, by Sex, Race/Ethnicity, and Grade," and "Table 64. Percentage of High School Students Who Engaged in Unhealthy Behaviors Associated with Weight Control, by Sex, Race/Ethnicity, and Grade," in "Youth Risk Behavior Surveillance—United States, 2003," *Centers for Disease Control and Prevention Surveillance Summaries: Morbidity and Mortality Weekly Report,* vol. 53, no. SS–02, May 21, 2004, http://www.cdc.gov/mmwr/PDF/SS/SS5302 .pdf (accessed September 3, 2004)

Divorce can cause stressful situations for children in several ways. One or both parents may have to move to a new home, removing the children from family and friends who could have given them support. Custody issues can generate hostility between parents. And if one or both parents remarry, children are faced with yet another adjustment in their living arrangements.

Eating Disorders

While young people who are overweight increase their risk for certain diseases in adulthood, an over-emphasis on thinness during childhood may contribute to eating disorders such as anorexia nervosa (extreme and often fatal weight loss) and bulimia ("binging and purging"). Girls are both more likely to have a distorted view of their weight and more likely to have eating disorders than boys.

The CDC reported that although 13.5% of students were overweight, a much higher proportion thought they were overweight (29.6%) (*Youth Risk Behavior Survey, 2003*). (See Table 5.12.) Girls (36.1%) are much more likely than boys (23.5%) to believe they are overweight. White (30.8%) and Hispanic (31.6%) youths are more likely than African-American youths (22.3%) to think of themselves as overweight.

In 2003 nearly half (43.8%) of high school students nationwide were trying to lose weight by a variety of methods. (See Table 5.12.) Six percent of high school students had taken laxatives or induced vomiting to lose weight, 13.3% went without eating for twenty-four hours or more, and 9.2% took diet pills. (See Table 5.14.) Hispanic and

white students were more likely to resort to these unhealthy behaviors than African-American students. Many more females than males engaged in risky weight-loss methods.

Well over half of high school females dieted or exercised to lose weight (56.2% and 65.7%, respectively); among males, only 28.9% dieted and 49% exercised to lose weight. (See Table 5.14.) Once again, among females these behaviors varied by race: far more white and Hispanic female students engaged in these weight loss activities than did African-American female students.

Hyperactivity (ADHD)

Attention Deficit Hyperactivity Disorder (ADHD) is one of the most common psychiatric disorders to appear in childhood. No one knows what causes ADHD, although recent research reported by the National Institute of Mental Health has found a link between a person's ability to pay attention and the body's use of glucose in the brain. Symptoms include restlessness, inability to concentrate, aggressiveness, and impulsivity; lack of treatment can lead to problems in school, at work, and in making friends. The National Institute of Mental Health estimated that 4.1% of youths ages nine to seventeen are affected in any six-month period by ADHD. Boys are two or three times more likely to be affected by ADHD than girls. Ritalin, a stimulant, is frequently used to treat hyperactive children.

DRUGS, ALCOHOL, AND SMOKING

Drug Use

Few factors negatively influence the health and well-being of young people more than the use of drugs, alcohol, and tobacco. *Monitoring the Future* (MTF), a long-term study on the use of drugs, alcohol, and tobacco conducted by the University of Michigan's Institute for Social Research, annually surveys eighth, tenth, and twelfth graders on their use of these substances. According to the institute's *Overview of Key Findings 2003*, the percentage of high school students who have ever tried any illicit drug either remained steady or decreased slightly from the mid-1990s to 2003. This plateau followed sharp increases during the early 1990s. The survey showed a decrease in the use of LSD, tranquilizers, amphetamines, and methamphetamines in 2002 and 2003. The use of heroin, other narcotics, crack, cocaine, and hallucinogens other than LSD remained steady. Only inhalants showed signs of increasing use, and then only among eighth graders. Still, half (51%) of American youths have tried an illicit drug by the time they leave high school.

Each year MTF asks twelfth graders, "How much do you think people risk harming themselves by using the following drugs?" The results show that from 1975 to 2003 the majority of students consistently perceived cocaine, LSD, and heroin as high-risk drugs in terms of overdose, addiction, and death. According to the MTF report in 2004, marijuana remained the only drug that barely half of all twelfth graders (54.9%) surveyed in 2003 believed had high-risk factors if used regularly. Between 1975 and 2003 83–90% of high school seniors reported that they could easily obtain marijuana, more than any other drug.

Table 5.15 shows reported drug and alcohol use by twelfth graders in 2003, according to the MTF. Alcohol remained teenagers' drug of choice; 70.1% of high school seniors had used alcohol in the twelve months prior to the survey and 47.5% had used alcohol in the prior thirty days. Marijuana was a distant second; 34.9% of twelfth graders had used marijuana in the prior twelve months and 21.2% had used it in the prior thirty days. The 2003 *Youth Risk Behavior Survey* found that 40.2% of high school students reported they had tried marijuana, and 22.4% reported they had used it at least once in the thirty days before the survey. (See Table 5.16.)

Alcohol Use Still High

Alcohol use remains high among high school students. Although there was some decline in drinking among students in the 1980s, it remained generally stable among young people between 1993 and 2003.

The 2003 *Youth Risk Behavior Survey* found that nationwide 74.9% of all high school students had had at least one alcoholic drink in their lifetime, 44.9% had taken a drink in the thirty days prior to the survey, and 28.3% had had five or more drinks on one occasion at least once in the thirty days prior to the survey. (See Table 5.16.) African-American youth were less likely than

TABLE 5.15

Reported drug and alcohol use during 12-month period and 30-day period, by high school seniors, 2003

	Used in past 12 months	Used in past 30 days
Marijuana/Hashish	34.9	21.2
Inhalants	3.9	1.5
PCP	1.3	0.6
MDMA (Ecstasy)	4.5	1.3
Cocaine	4.8	2.1
Crack	2.2	0.9
Heroin	0.8	0.4
Other Narcotics	9.3	4.1
Amphetamines	9.9	5
Methamphetamine	3.2	1.7
Sedatives (Barbituates)	6	2.9
Tranquilizers	6.7	2.8
Alcohol	70.1	47.5
Steroids	2.1	1.3

SOURCE: Adapted from "Table 2. Trends in Annual and 30-Day Prevalence of Use of Various Drugs for Eighth, Tenth, and Twelfth Graders," in *Monitoring the Future: National Results on Adolescent Drug Use, Overview of Key Findings, 2003*, NIH Publication No. 04-5506, National Institute on Drug Abuse, 2004, http://www.monitoringthefuture.org/data/03data/pr03t2.pdf (accessed September 16, 2004)

either white or Hispanic high schoolers to have ever had a drink, to have had a drink in the previous thirty days, or to engage in episodic heavy drinking.

TEENAGE DRINKING AND DRIVING. According to *Determine Why There Are Fewer Young Alcohol-Impaired Drivers* by the National Highway Traffic Safety Administration (September 2001), traffic fatalities linked to teenage drinking fell from 1982 to 1993 and remained fairly steady from 1993 to 1998. This decline was due in large part to stricter enforcement of drinking age laws and driving while intoxicated (DWI) or driving under the influence (DUI) laws. Motor vehicle crashes were the leading cause of death among fifteen- to twenty-year-olds in 2002. In that year 24% of all young drivers ages fifteen to twenty who were killed in crashes were intoxicated.

The 2003 *Youth Risk Behavior Survey* found that in the month before the survey, 12.1% of students reported they had driven a vehicle after drinking alcohol. (See Table 5.17.) Males (15%) were more likely than females (8.9%) to drive after drinking. Another 30.2% admitted they had ridden with a driver who had been drinking. Females were slightly more likely to ride with a driver who had been drinking (31.1%) than were males (29.2%).

Tobacco

Most states prohibit the sale of cigarettes to anyone under eighteen but the laws are often ignored and may carry no penalties for youths who buy cigarettes or smoke in public. According to the American Lung Association, nearly six thousand children start smoking each day, and 4.5 million adolescents are smokers. The *Youth Risk Behavior Survey* reported that in 2003

TABLE 5.16

Percentage of high school students who drank alcohol and used marijuana, by sex, race, ethnicity, and grade, 2003

Category	Lifetime alcohol use*			Current alcohol use†			Episodic heavy drinking§			Lifetime marijuana use‡			Current marijuana use△△		
	Female %	Male %	Total %	Female %	Male %	Total %	Female %	Male %	Total %	Female %	Male %	Total %	Female %	Male %	Total %
Race/ethnicity															
White**¶	76.6	74.3	75.4	48.4	45.9	47.1	31.5	32.1	31.8	38.9	40.5	39.8	19.9	23.3	21.7
Black**¶	74.0	68.6	71.4	37.0	37.5	37.4	12.7	17.9	15.3	37.6	49.0	43.3	18.1	29.8	23.9
Hispanic	81.4	77.5	79.5	48.4	42.7	45.6	29.8	27.9	28.9	38.5	46.7	42.7	20.4	27.1	23.8
Grade															
9	66.2	64.0	65.0	38.5	33.9	36.2	20.9	18.8	19.8	28.1	33.1	30.7	17.2	19.6	18.5
10	76.5	74.9	75.7	44.9	42.2	43.5	27.2	27.7	27.4	36.4	44.2	40.4	18.2	25.7	22.0
11	80.9	76.4	78.6	46.8	47.3	47.0	29.4	34.1	31.8	43.5	45.4	44.5	20.9	27.3	24.1
12	83.3	82.6	83.0	55.5	56.0	55.9	34.5	39.5	37.2	44.9	51.7	48.5	21.3	30.0	25.8
Total	**76.1**	**73.7**	**74.9**	**45.8**	**43.8**	**44.9**	**27.5**	**29.0**	**28.3**	**37.6**	**42.7**	**40.2**	**19.3**	**25.1**	**22.4**

*Ever had one or more drinks of alcohol on ≥1 day.
† Drank one or more drinks of alcohol on ≥1 of the 30 days preceding the survey.
§ Drank ≥5 drinks of alcohol in a row on ≥1 of the 30 days preceding the survey.
¶ 95% confidence interval.
** Non-Hispanic.
‡ Used marijuana one or more times during their lifetime.
△△Used marijuana one or more times during the 30 days preceding the survey.

SOURCE: Adapted from "Table 26. Percentage of High School Students Who Drank Alcohol, by Sex, Race/Ethnicity, and Grade," and "Table 28. Percentage of High School Students Who Used Marijuana, by Sex, Race/Ethnicity, and Grade," in "Youth Risk Behavior Surveillance—United States, 2003," *Centers for Disease Control and Prevention Surveillance Summaries: Morbidity and Mortality Weekly Report*, vol. 53, no. SS-02, May 21, 2004, http://www.cdc.gov/mmwr/PDF/SS/SS5302.pdf (accessed September 16, 2004)

TABLE 5.17

Percentage of high school students who rode with a driver who had been drinking alcohol and who drove after drinking alcohol, by sex, race, ethnicity, and grade, 2003

Category	Rode with a driver who had been drinking alcohol*			Drove after drinking alcohol*		
	Female %	Male %	Total %	Female %	Male %	Total %
Race/ethnicity						
White§	29.8	27.3	28.5	10.3	15.2	12.9
Black§	29.8	31.8	30.9	4.6	13.4	9.1
Hispanic	40.0	32.8	36.4	8.6	14.9	11.7
Grade						
9	30.2	26.4	28.2	5.1	7.2	6.2
10	31.0	27.6	29.3	6.9	11.3	9.2
11	30.7	30.3	30.5	11.1	19.5	15.3
12	32.6	34.0	33.3	13.6	25.6	19.8
Total	**31.1**	**29.2**	**30.2**	**8.9**	**15.0**	**12.1**

*In a car or other vehicle one or more times during the 30 days preceding the survey.
§Non-Hispanic.

SOURCE: Adapted from "Table 4. Percentage of High School Students Who Rode with a Driver Who Had Been Drinking Alcohol and Who Drove after Drinking Alcohol, by Sex, Race/Ethnicity, and Grade," in "Youth Risk Behavior Surveillance—United States, 2003," *Centers for Disease Control and Prevention Surveillance Summaries: Morbidity and Mortality Weekly Report*, vol. 53, no. SS-02, May 21, 2004,http://www.cdc.gov/mmwr/PDF/SS/SS5302.pdf (accessed September 16, 2004)

21.9% of high school students had smoked at least one cigarette in the month prior to the survey and 9.7% had smoked at least twenty days in the past month. (See Table 5.18.) The percentage of female and male heavy smokers was almost equal: 2.4% of female adolescents and 3.6% of male adolescents smoked more than ten cigarettes per day.

Teens say they smoke for a variety of reasons—they "just like it," "it's a social thing," and many young women who are worried about their weight report that they smoke because "it burns calories." Many of them report they have seen their parents smoke. A 1995 Los Angeles study, "The Influence of Parental Smoking on Youth Smoking: Is the Recent Downplaying Justified?" by Mike Males of the University of California at Irvine, found that parental smoking is a significant influence on youth smoking, especially among boys and among youth who began smoking at a young age.

SMOKELESS TOBACCO. Smokeless tobacco use—chewing tobacco, snuff, or dip—among adolescents is a predominantly white male activity, according to the 2003 *Youth Risk Behavior Survey.* Of high school students, 11% of males and 2.2% of females had used smokeless tobacco at least once in the thirty days preceding the survey; 7.6% of white and 3% of African-American students had used smokeless tobacco in that time. White male students had the highest proportion of users (13.3%); only 4.1% of African-American males and 6.1% of Hispanic males used smokeless tobacco.

SECONDHAND SMOKE AND CHILDREN. The Environmental Protection Agency reported that environmental tobacco smoke (ETS) is a major hazard for children, whose respiratory, immune, and other systems are not as well developed as those of adults. According to the EPA's Web site, secondhand or passive smoke—smoke produced by other people's cigarettes—increases the number of attacks and severity of symptoms in children with asthma and can even cause asthma in preschool-age children.

TABLE 5.18

Percentage of high school students who used tobacco, by sex, race, ethnicity, and grade, 2003

Category	Lifetime cigarette use* Female %	Male %	Total %	Lifetime daily cigarette use† Female %	Male %	Total %	Current cigarette use§ Female %	Male %	Total %	Current frequent cigarette use‡ Female %	Male %	Total %	Smoked >10 cigarettes/day** Female %	Male %	Total %	Purchased cigarettes at a store or gas station** Female %	Male %	Total %
Race/Ethnicity																		
White¶	58.7	57.4	58.1	20.9	17.1	18.9	26.6	23.3	24.9	13.2	10.4	11.8	3.1	3.6	3.4	12.0	24.1	17.5
Black¶	56.9	59.8	58.4	5.2	10.9	8.2	10.8	19.3	15.1	3.1	7.9	5.5	0.8	2.1	1.4	23.7	20.9	21.8
Hispanic	59.8	63.9	61.9	9.1	12.2	10.7	17.7	19.1	18.4	4.4	6.6	5.5	1.4	2.0	1.7	19.2	27.2	23.8
Grade																		
9	50.9	53.0	52.0	11.6	11.4	11.5	18.9	16.0	17.4	6.9	5.7	6.3	1.3	2.4	1.9	10.4	13.8	12.0
10	57.7	59.0	58.3	15.8	14.3	15.0	21.9	21.7	21.8	9.0	9.5	9.2	2.4	2.4	2.4	7.8	19.3	13.6
11	59.8	60.1	60.0	18.4	17.8	18.1	24.0	23.2	23.6	11.8	10.5	11.2	3.1	3.5	3.3	21.2	34.5	27.9
12	65.9	64.7	65.4	18.3	21.0	19.8	23.3	29.0	26.2	11.4	14.5	13.1	2.6	6.8	4.8	18.9	33.6	26.1
Total	**58.1**	**58.7**	**58.4**	**15.6**	**15.7**	**15.8**	**21.9**	**21.8**	**21.9**	**9.7**	**9.6**	**9.7**	**2.4**	**3.6**	**3.1**	**13.8**	**24.2**	**18.9**

*Ever tried cigarette smoking, even one or two puffs.
†Ever smoked one or more cigarettes every day for 30 days.
§Smoked cigarettes on ≥1 of the 30 days preceding the survey.
¶Non-Hispanic.
‡Smoked cigarettes on >20 of the 30 days preceding the survey.
**Smoked >10 cigarettes per day on the days they smoked during the 30 days preceding the survey.
††Among the 20.8% of students who were aged <18 years who smoked cigarettes on ≥1 of the 30 days preceding the survey.
§§During the 30 days preceding the survey.

SOURCE: Adapted from "Table 20. Percentage of High School Students Who Smoked Cigarettes, by Sex, Race/Ethnicity, and Grade," and "Table 22. Percentage of High School Students Who Smoked Cigarettes and Who Purchased Cigarettes in a Store or Gas Station, by Sex, Race/Ethnicity, and Grade," in "Youth Risk Behavior Surveillance—United States, 2003," *Centers for Disease Control and Prevention Surveillance Summaries: Morbidity and Mortality Weekly Report*, vol. 53, no. SS-02, May 21, 2004, http://www.cdc.gov/mmwr/PDF/SS/SS5302.pdf (accessed September 16, 2004)

According to the agency, secondhand smoke causes between 150,000 and 300,000 lower respiratory tract infections each year in children under eighteen months of age, and those infections result in between 7,500 and 15,000 hospitalizations each year. Passive smoking can also cause middle-ear disease and reduction in lung function in children, and is considered a risk factor in SIDS. The 2000 National Youth Tobacco Survey, a survey of more than 35,000 students in grades six through twelve conducted by the American Legacy Foundation, found that 42.1% of the students surveyed lived in homes where others smoked, and 69.7% were exposed to others who smoked outside the home.

"Not My Kid"

Recent surveys show that parental denial of their children's substance use is rampant among baby boomer parents. According to the Partnership for a Drug-Free America (*Partnership Attitude Tracking Study: Parents, 2002*), teens reported smoking marijuana three times more often than their parents reported they had. Almost all parents surveyed (91%) said they had talked to their children about the dangers of drugs. About half of parents (48%) agreed with the statement, "My child and I regularly sit down together and have open discussions about important issues like drugs," but only 19% of teens agreed. By 2003 the percentage of teens who reported their parents frequently talked to them about the risks of drugs decreased further.

Experts contend the key for parents who want to prevent their children's experimentation from turning into abuse is to stop sending ambivalent messages about drug use and not to abuse substances themselves. Nonetheless, even if parents strongly oppose drugs, do not abuse them, and talk to their child about the danger of drug abuse, children may still choose to use drugs.

CHILD ABUSE AND NEGLECT

It is impossible to determine how many children suffer abuse. All observers can do is count the number of reported cases—which include only those known to public authorities—or they can survey families, in which case parents may deny or downplay abuse. As a result, most estimates of child abuse are generally considered low. The National Child Abuse and Neglect Data System (NCANDS) and its annual report, *Child Maltreatment,* is the primary source of national information on abused and neglected children that has been reported to state child protective services agencies.

In 2002 1.8 million referrals alleging child abuse or neglect of more than three million children were sent to state child protective services agencies. Approximately 896,000 children were found to be victims of child maltreatment. Reports most often came from professional

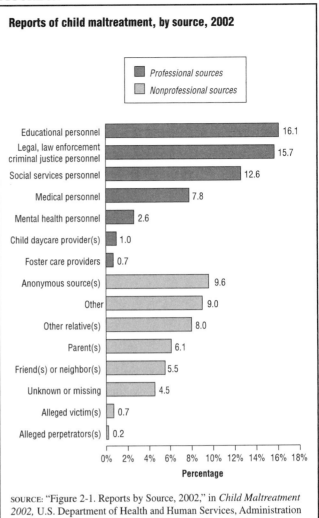

FIGURE 5.4

Reports of child maltreatment, by source, 2002

SOURCE: "Figure 2-1. Reports by Source, 2002," in *Child Maltreatment 2002,* U.S. Department of Health and Human Services, Administration for Children, Youth and Families, 2004, http://www.acf.hhs.gov/programs/cb/publications/cm02/cm02.pdf (accessed September 16, 2004)

sources, such as educators, the legal system, social service employees, and medical professionals, and less often from nonprofessional sources, such as relatives, friends, neighbors, parents, the victims themselves, and a small percentage of perpetrators. (See Figure 5.4.)

In 2002 60.5% of reported victims suffered neglect; 18.6% were physically abused; 9.9% were sexually abused; and 6.5% were emotionally or psychologically maltreated. (Figure 5.5 shows victimization rates for each group per one thousand children.) The highest rate of victims was among children three years or younger (sixteen per one thousand), followed by children four to seven years of age (13.7 per one thousand). (See Figure 5.6.) The rate of occurrence decreased as the child's age increased.

The most tragic result of child maltreatment is death. In 2002 an estimated fourteen hundred children died as a result of abuse or neglect. Children in the youngest age groups were most likely to die of maltreatment; three-quarters of the children who died were three years old or younger.

FIGURE 5.5

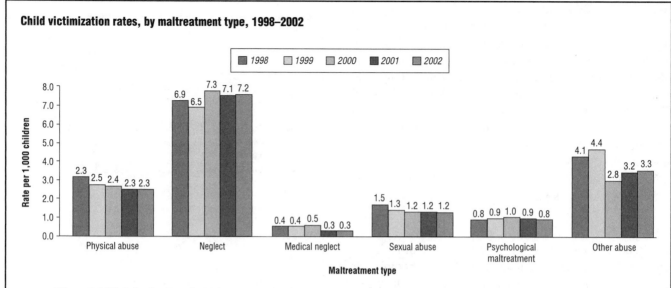

Child victimization rates, by maltreatment type, 1998–2002

SOURCE: "Figure 3-3. Victimization Rates by Maltreatment Type, 1998–2002," in *Child Maltreatment 2002,* U.S. Department of Health and Human Services, Administration for Children, Youth and Families, 2004, http://www.acf.hhs.gov/programs/cb/publications/cm02/cm02.pdf (accessed September 16, 2004)

The largest group of abusers were mothers acting alone (40.3%) followed by fathers acting alone (19.1%). (See Figure 5.7.) Abuse of children was overwhelmingly perpetrated by parents; only 13% of perpetrators were not parents.

MISSING CHILDREN

In the 1980s, as a result of several prominent abductions and tragedies, the media focused public attention on the problem of missing children. Citizens became concerned and demanded action to address what appeared to be a national crisis. Attempting to discover the nature and dimension of the problem, Congress passed the 1984 Missing Children's Assistance Act (PL 98–473). The legislation mandated the Office of Juvenile Justice and Delinquency Prevention (OJJDP) to conduct national incidence studies to determine the number of juveniles who were "victims of abduction by strangers" and the number of children who were victims of "parental kidnapping." The result was the National Incidence Studies of Missing, Abducted, Runaway, and Thrownaway Children (NISMART), the first of which was conducted in 1988, with the results published in 1990. The second, more recent NISMART was conducted mainly in 1999, with many of the data published in a series of October 2002 reports.

Family Abductions

According to *Children Abducted by Family Members: National Estimates and Characteristics* (Heather Hammer et al., OJJDP, Washington, DC, October 2002), a family abduction is "the taking or keeping of a child by a family member in violation of a custody order, a decree, or other legitimate custodial rights, where the taking or keeping involved some element of concealment, flight, or intent to

FIGURE 5.6

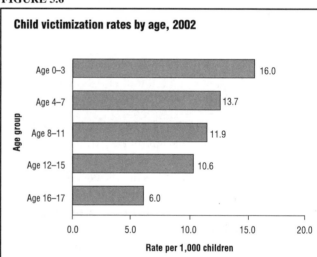

Child victimization rates by age, 2002

SOURCE: "Figure 3-4. Victimization Rates by Age Group, 2002," in *Child Maltreatment 2002*, U.S. Department of Health and Human Services, Administration for Children, Youth and Families, 2004, http://www.acf.hhs.gov/programs/cb/publications/cm02/cm02.pdf (accessed September 16, 2004)

deprive a lawful custodian indefinitely of custodial privileges." In 1999 203,900 children were victims of a family abduction. About half of these (53%) were abducted by biological fathers, and 25% by biological mothers. Most family-abducted children were not missing for long— 46% were gone less than a week, and only 21% were away a month or more. Nearly half (42%) were abducted from a single-parent family. At the time the survey was done, 91% of the children had been returned, 6% had been located but not returned, and less than 1% had not been located or returned (there was no information on outcomes for 2% of cases).

FIGURE 5.7

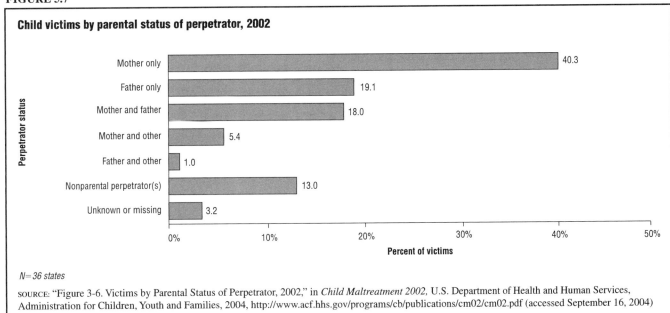

Child victims by parental status of perpetrator, 2002

Perpetrator status	Percent of victims
Mother only	40.3
Father only	19.1
Mother and father	18.0
Mother and other	5.4
Father and other	1.0
Nonparental perpetrator(s)	13.0
Unknown or missing	3.2

N= 36 states

SOURCE: "Figure 3-6. Victims by Parental Status of Perpetrator, 2002," in *Child Maltreatment 2002*, U.S. Department of Health and Human Services, Administration for Children, Youth and Families, 2004, http://www.acf.hhs.gov/programs/cb/publications/cm02/cm02.pdf (accessed September 16, 2004)

Nonfamily Abductions

Although far fewer children are abducted by strangers than by family members, the consequences are often far worse. Violence, the use of force or weapons, sexual assault, and murder are more prevalent in nonfamily abductions. According to *Nonfamily Abducted Children: National Estimates and Characteristics* (David Finkelhor et al., OJJDP, Washington, DC, October 2002), 58,200 children were abducted by nonfamily members in 1999. Nearly half (46%) of these were sexually assaulted by their abductors. Only 115 of the abductions were "stereotypical kidnappings," in which a child was abducted by a slight acquaintance or stranger, detained overnight, transported fifty miles or more, held for ransom or with intention to keep permanently, or killed. Most nonfamily abducted children (59%) were 15–17 years old and 65% were female. The perpetrators were strangers 37% of the time and were three times as likely to be male as female. Most perpetrators (67%) were ages thirteen to twenty-nine. Most nonfamily abducted children (91%) were away for twenty-four hours or less, and 99% returned alive. The remaining 1% were either killed or had not been located at the time of the survey.

Runaways and Thrownaways

According to the OJJDP (Heather Hammer et al., *Runaway/Thrownaway Children: National Estimates and Characteristics*, Washington, DC, October 2002), runaways are children who meet at least one of the following criteria:

• A child who leaves home without permission and stays away overnight

• A child fourteen years old (or older and mentally incompetent) who is away from home who chooses not to come home when expected to and who stays away overnight

• A child fifteen years old or older who is away from home who chooses not to come home and stays away two nights

In the 1970s the label "throwaways" or "thrownaways" was given by researchers to juveniles who were made to leave home or were abandoned. A thrownaway child meets one of the following criteria:

• A child who is asked or told to leave home by a parent or other household adult, with no adequate alternative care arranged for the child by a household adult, and who is out of the household overnight

• A child who is away from home who is prevented from returning home by a parent or other household adult, with no adequate alternative care arranged for by a household adult, and who is out of the household overnight

The OJJDP now combines its estimates of runaways and thrownaways. In 1999 1.7 million youths had a runaway/thrownaway episode. The runaway episode was thought to indicate that 1.2 million of these children were endangered in the following ways:

• The child had been physically or sexually abused at home in the year prior to the episode or was afraid of abuse upon return (21%).

• The child was substance dependent (19%).

• The child was thirteen years old or younger (18%).

• The child was in the company of someone known to be abusing drugs (18%).

• The child was using hard drugs (17%).

Most runaway/thrownaway youth (68%) were fifteen years old or older; half were females and half were males. Most runaways (77%) were away less than one week, and more than 99% returned. An estimated 38,600 of the runaways were at risk of sexual endangerment—assault, attempted assault, or prostitution—while away from home.

CHAPTER 6
GETTING AN EDUCATION

Despite the controversies surrounding the quality and direction of American education, the United States remains one of the most highly educated nations in the world. According to the *Digest of Education Statistics* (U.S. Department of Education), in fall 2002 69.2 million Americans were enrolled students in elementary and secondary schools and colleges. (See Table 6.1.) An additional 4.3 million were teachers and faculty at these institutions, and 4.8 million were employed as administrative and support staff.

THE COST OF PUBLIC EDUCATION

The average annual expenditure per student in the public school system in constant 2001–02 dollars more than doubled between 1970 and 2002, from $3,849 per pupil in 1969–70 to $8,048 per pupil during the 2001–02 school year. (See Figure 6.1.) Each year, when the federal budget is determined in Washington, D.C., the battle over the education budget is fierce. Public school officials and teachers stress the importance of investing in the public education system, arguing that more money will provide more teachers, educational materials, and—eventually—a better education. They point to school buildings in need of repair and classes that meet in hallways and other cramped areas because of a lack of space. Opponents of increasing public school funding say that more money does not create a better education—better teachers do. To support their argument they point to the increase in spending per pupil while some measurements of academic achievement remain low.

THE VOUCHER CONTROVERSY

Many people believe that problems like large class sizes, poor teacher training, and lack of computers and supplies in many public schools are unsolvable within the current public school system. One solution proposed in the early 1990s was the school voucher system: the govern- ment would provide a certain amount of money each year to parents in the form of a voucher to enroll their children at the school of their choice, either public or private. School vouchers have since become a highly polarized issue, with strong opinions both for and against the idea.

The National Education Association (NEA), a union of teachers and one of the larger unions in the country, immediately objected to school vouchers, arguing that voucher programs divert money from the public education system and make the current problems worse. The union also argued that giving money to parents who choose to send their child to a religious or parochial school is unconstitutional.

Supporters of the measure claim that parents should be able to choose the best educational environment for their children. They also argue that vouchers would give all people, not just the wealthy or middle class, the opportunity for a better education for their children in private schools. Most importantly, supporters believe that making the educational system a "free market" enterprise, in which parents could choose which school their children would attend, would force the public educational system to provide a higher standard of education in order to compete.

George W. Bush was elected president of the United States in 2000. Throughout his campaign Bush called for national education reform, including the possible use of vouchers. During the legislative process of getting the No Child Left Behind Act (PL 107–110) (NCLB) through the U.S. Congress, Bush agreed to drop the voucher provisions from the legislation, recognizing that debate on the vouchers issue could prevent the bill from being passed. On January 8, 2002, the No Child Left Behind Act became law without specific provisions for a nationwide voucher program.

Frustrated at the national level, supporters of vouchers turned to state and local governments. Programs launched in Wisconsin, Florida, and Ohio provided stu-

TABLE 6.1

Estimated number of participants in elementary and secondary education and in higher education, fall 2002

[In millions]

Participants	All levels (elementary, secondary, and degree-granting)	Elementary and secondary schools			Degree-granting institutions		
		Total	Public	Private	Total	Public	Private
1	2	3	4	5	6	7	8
Total	78.3	60.3	53.7	6.6	18.0	13.6	4.4
Enrollment	69.2	53.6	47.6	6.0	15.6	12.0	3.6
Teachers and faculty	4.3	3.5	3.1	0.4	0.8	0.5	0.2
Other professional administrative and support staff	4.8	3.2	2.9	0.3	1.6	1.1	0.5

Note: Includes enrollments in local public school systems and in most private schools (religiously affiliated and nonsectarian). Excludes subcollegiate departments of institutions of higher education and federal schools. Elementary and secondary includes most kindergarten and some nursery school enrollment. Excludes preprimary enrollment in schools that do not offer first grade or above. Degree-granting institutions include full-time and part-time students enrolled in degree-credit and nondegree-credit programs in universities, other 4-year colleges, and 2-year colleges that participated in Title IV federal financial aid programs. Data for teachers and other staff in public and private elementary and secondary schools and colleges and universities are reported in terms of full-time equivalents. Detail may not sum to totals due to rounding.

SOURCE: "Table 1. Projected Number of Participants in Educational Institutions, by Level and Control of Institution: Fall 2002," in *Digest of Education Statistics, 2002,* National Center for Education Statistics, 2003, http://nces.ed.gov/programs/digest/d02/tables/PDF/table1.pdf (accessed September 16, 2004)

FIGURE 6.1

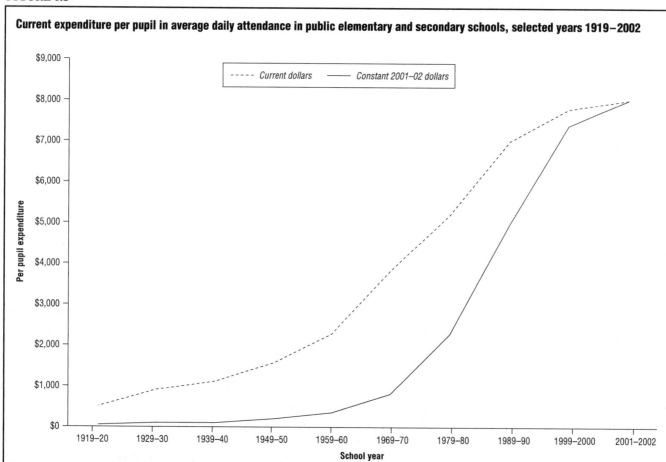

Current expenditure per pupil in average daily attendance in public elementary and secondary schools, selected years 1919–2002

SOURCE: Adapted from "Table 166. Total and Current Expenditure per Pupil in Public Elementary and Secondary Schools: 1919–20 to 2001–2002," in *Digest of Education Statistics, 2002,* National Center for Education Statistics, 2003, http://nces.ed.gov/programs/digest/d02/tables/dt166.asp (accessed September 16, 2004)

dents in some overcrowded or poorly performing schools with vouchers that could be used for private tuition. All of these programs were met with court challenges. A land-

mark decision came on June 27, 2002, when the U.S. Supreme Court upheld the use of public money for religious school tuition in Cleveland, Ohio, calling the city's

FIGURE 6.2

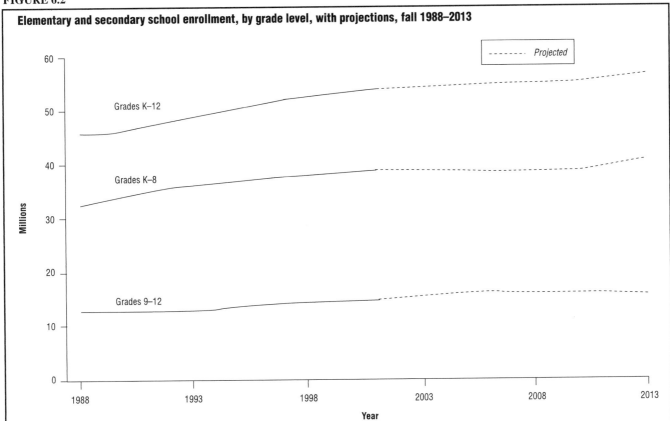

Elementary and secondary school enrollment, by grade level, with projections, fall 1988–2013

SOURCE: Debra E. Gerald and William J. Hussar, "Figure 2. Enrollment in Elementary and Secondary Schools, by Grade Level, with Projections: Fall 1988 to Fall 2013," in *Projections of Education Statistics,* National Center for Education Statistics, October 2003, http://nces.ed.gov/programs/projections/figures/figure_02.asp (accessed September 16, 2004)

voucher plan "a program of true private choice." In spring 2004 eleven states had school voucher programs functioning in selected areas or statewide: Florida, Iowa, Colorado, Arizona, Pennsylvania, Vermont, Maine, Illinois, Minnesota, Ohio, and Wisconsin.

Public School Choice—No Child Left Behind and Charter Schools

In lieu of a voucher program, the No Child Left Behind Act offered a public school choice program. Parents of students enrolled in "failing" public schools were allowed to move their children to a better-performing public or charter school. Local school districts were required to provide this choice and also provide students with transportation to the alternative school.

Public charter schools are funded by government money and run by a group under an agreement, or charter, with the state that exempts it from many state or local regulations that govern most public schools. In return for these exemptions and funding, the school must meet certain standards. In 2001–02 thirty-nine states allowed charter schools, with 2,348 in operation. Although charter schools served less than 1% of public elementary and secondary students in 2001–02, the idea has been increasing in popularity since Minnesota passed the first charter

school law in 1991. The No Child Left Behind Act authorized $300 million to help local communities and states fund charter schools, as well as $150 million to encourage innovative approaches to funding charter school construction and infrastructure needs.

PREPRIMARY, ELEMENTARY, AND SECONDARY ENROLLMENT

Preprimary, elementary, and secondary school enrollments reflect the number of births over a specified period. Because of the baby boom following World War II, school enrollment grew rapidly during the 1950s and 1960s when those children reached school age. Elementary enrollment reached a then-record high in 1969, as did high school enrollment in 1971.

In the late 1960s the birth rate began to decline, resulting in a steadily falling school enrollment. An "echo effect" occurred in the late 1970s and early 1980s when those born during the baby boom began their own families. This echo effect triggered an increase in school enrollment starting in the mid-1980s. In 1985 public elementary and secondary school enrollment increased for the first time since 1971 and continued to increase, reaching 49.5 million in 2002 and projected to reach 49.7 million by 2013. (See Figure 6.2.)

TABLE 6.2

Enrollment of 3- to 5-year-old children in preprimary programs, by level and control of program and by attendance, 1965–2001

[In thousands]

Year and age	Total population, 3 to 5 years old	Enrollment by level and control						Enrollment by attendance		
		Total	Percent enrolled	Nursery school		Kindergarten		Full-day	Part-day	Percent full-day
				Public	Private	Public	Private			
1	2	3	4	5	6	7	8	9	10	11
1965	12,549	3,407	27.1	127	393	2,291	596	—	—	—
1970	10,949	4,104	37.5	332	762	2,498	511	698	3,405	17.0
1975	10,185	4,955	48.7	570	1,174	2,682	528	1,295	3,659	26.1
1980	9,284	4,878	52.5	628	1,353	2,438	459	1,551	3,327	31.8
1985	10,733	5,865	54.6	846	1,631	2,847	541	2,144	3,722	36.6
1986	10,866	5,971	55.0	829	1,715	2,859	567	2,241	3,730	37.5
1987	10,872	5,931	54.6	819	1,736	2,842	534	2,090	3,841	35.2
1988	10,993	5,978	54.4	851	1,770	2,875	481	2,044	3,935	34.2
1989	11,039	6,026	4.6	930	1,894	2,704	497	2,238	3,789	37.1
1990	11,207	6,659	59.4	1,199	2,180	2,772	509	2,577	4,082	38.7
1991	11,370	6,334	55.7	996	1,828	2,967	543	2,408	3,926	38.0
1992	11,545	6,402	55.5	1,073	1,783	2,995	550	2,410	3,992	37.6
1993	11,954	6,581	55.1	1,205	1,779	3,020	577	2,642	3,939	40.1
1994[1]	12,328	7,514	61.0	1,848	2,314	2,819	534	3,468	4,046	46.2
1995[1]	12,518	7,739	61.8	1,950	2,381	2,800	608	3,689	4,051	47.7
1996[1]	12,378	7,580	61.2	1,830	2,317	2,853	580	3,562	4,019	47.0
1997[1]	12,121	7,860	64.9	2,207	2,231	2,847	575	3,922	3,939	49.9
1998[1]	12,078	7,788	64.5	2,213	2,299	2,674	602	3,959	3,829	50.8
1999[1]	11,920	7,844	65.8	2,209	2,298	2,777	560	4,154	3,690	53.0
2000[1]	11,858	7,592	64.0	2,146	2,180	2,701	565	4,008	3,584	52.8
2001[1]	11,899	7,602	63.9	2,164	2,201	2,724	512	3,940	3,662	51.8

—Not available.

[1]Data collected using new procedures. May not be comparable with figures prior to 1994.

Note: Data are based on sample surveys of the civilian noninstitutional population. Although cells with fewer than 75,000 children are subject to wide sampling variation, they are included in the table to permit various types of aggregations. Detail may not sum to totals due to rounding.

SOURCE: Adapted from "Table 43. Enrollment of 3- to 5-Year-Old Children in Preprimary Programs, by Level and Control of Program and by Attendance Status: October 1965 to October 2001," in *Digest of Education Statistics, 2002,* National Center for Education Statistics, 2003, http://nces.ed.gov/programs/digest/d02/tables/PDF/table43.pdf (accessed September 16, 2004)

Preprimary Growth

Participating in early childhood programs such as nursery school, Head Start, pre-kindergarten, and kindergarten helps prepare children for the academic challenges of first grade. In contrast to the declining elementary and secondary school enrollment between 1970 and 1980, preprimary enrollment showed substantial growth, increasing from 4.1 million in 1970 to 4.9 million in 1980. (See Table 6.2 and Figure 6.3.) According to the Census Bureau, enrollment had grown to eight million by 2002.

Not only did the numbers of children enrolled in early childhood programs increase, but the percentage of three- to five-year-olds enrolled also increased substantially between 1965 and 2001. In 1965, 27.1% of three- to five-year-olds were enrolled in nursery school or kindergarten; by 2001 63.9% were enrolled. (See Table 6.2.)

Although programs like Head Start and other locally funded preschool programs are available to children in low-income families, preprimary school attendance is still generally linked to parental income and educational achievement levels. According to data presented in the NCES publication *The Condition of Education 2002*, 46.7% of three- to five-year-olds from households with an income below the poverty level in 2001 were enrolled in preprimary programs. (See Table 6.3.) That same year 59.1% of children ages three to five whose families were at or above the poverty level were enrolled in preprimary programs.

Preschool enrollment rates also increased with a mother's educational level. In 2001 the enrollment rate of children whose mothers had not earned a high school diploma was only 38.3%. (See Table 6.3.) The enrollment rate of children whose mothers had a high school diploma or equivalent was 47.1%. The majority of three- to five-year-olds whose mothers had attended some college were enrolled in preprimary programs; 62% of children whose mothers had attended some college were enrolled, and 69.5% of children whose mothers had a bachelor's degree or higher were enrolled. These numbers likely reflect three things: women with higher educational levels were more likely to continue working after becoming mothers, they were better able to pay for these programs, and they valued the educational benefits of preprimary programs for their children.

HEAD START. The Head Start program, established as part of the Economic Opportunity Act of 1964 (PL 88–452),

FIGURE 6.3

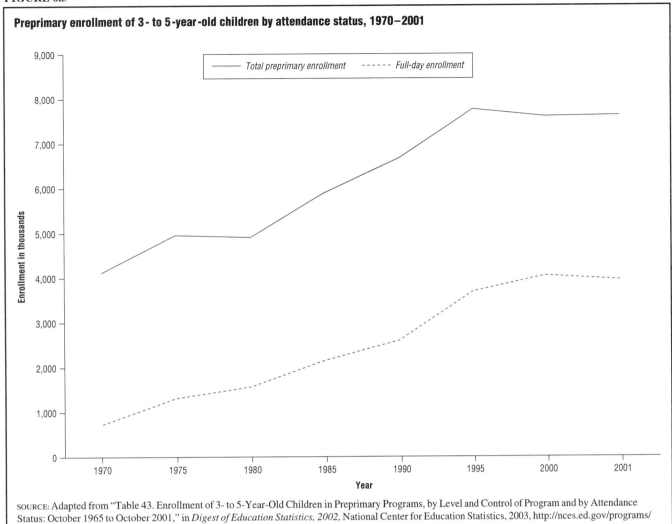

Preprimary enrollment of 3- to 5-year-old children by attendance status, 1970–2001

SOURCE: Adapted from "Table 43. Enrollment of 3- to 5-Year-Old Children in Preprimary Programs, by Level and Control of Program and by Attendance Status: October 1965 to October 2001," in *Digest of Education Statistics, 2002,* National Center for Education Statistics, 2003, http://nces.ed.gov/programs/digest/d02/tables/PDF/table43.pdf (accessed September 16, 2004)

is one of the most durable and successful federal programs for low-income and at-risk children. Directed by the Administration for Children and Families (ACF), Head Start is designed to help improve the social competence, learning skills, health, and nutrition of low-income children so they can begin school on a more level footing with children from higher income families. Regulations require that 90% of children enrolled in Head Start be from low-income households.

In 2003 909,608 children were served by Head Start programs. Of these children, 31.5% were African-American, 30.6% were Hispanic, 27.6% were white, 3.2% were Native American, and 2.9% were Asian/Pacific Islander. Most participating children were three and four years old (34% and 53%, respectively). A significant portion (12.5%) were disabled—children with mental retardation, health impairments, visual handicaps, hearing impairments, emotional disturbance, speech and language impairments, orthopedic handicaps, and learning disabilities.

The average cost per child for Head Start in 2003 was $7,092. Between its inception in 1965 and 2003, Head Start provided services to more than twenty-two million children and their families. The appropriation for Head Start in fiscal year 2004 was $6.8 billion. Despite these expenditures, according to the Children's Defense Fund 2003 Head Start basic fact sheet, Head Start served only three out of five poor children who were eligible because the program has always been underfunded.

Elementary and Secondary Enrollment

The Census Bureau reported that in 2002 33.1 million students were enrolled in kindergarten through eighth grade and 16.4 million in high school. (See Figure 6.2.) Most (88.5%) attended public schools. Total public school enrollment rose 15.7% from 1990 to 2001 after falling in the 1970s and early 1980s because of a decline in the school-age population.

EDUCATIONAL ATTAINMENT AND EARNINGS

The educational attainment of the U.S. population has risen steadily since the 1940s. In 2003 84.6% of adults

TABLE 6.3

Percent of children ages 3–5 years old enrolled in center-based early childhood care and education programs, by child and family characteristics, 1991 and 2001

Characteristic	1991	2001
Total[1]	52.8	56.4
Age		
3 years	42.3	43.0
4 years	60.4	66.2
5 years	63.9	72.8
Sex		
Male	52.4	53.6
Female	53.2	59.2
Race/ethnicity		
White	54.0	59.0
Black	58.3	63.7
Hispanic	38.8	39.8
Poverty status		
Below poverty	44.2	46.7
At or above poverty	55.7	59.1
Poverty status and race/ethnicity		
Below poverty		
White	41.0	46.1
Black	55.4	60.1
Hispanic	34.4	36.2
At or above poverty		
White	56.4	60.8
Black	61.8	66.2
Hispanic	42.2	42.4
Family type		
Two parents	53.7	56.5
One or no parent	49.7	56.1
Mother's education		
Less than high school	31.5	38.3
High school diploma or equivalent	45.8	47.1
Some college, including vocational/technical	60.2	62.0
Bachelor's degree or higher	71.9	69.5
Mother's employment status		
Worked 35 hours or more per week	59.3	62.9
Worked less than 35 hours per week	58.0	61.4
Looking for work	43.2	46.9
Not in labor force	45.3	46.8

[1]Children from racial/ethnic groups other than white, black, and Hispanic are included in the totals but not shown separately.
Note: Estimates are based on children who had not entered kindergarten. Center-based programs include day care centers, Head Start, preschool, nursery school, prekindergarten, and other early childhood programs. Children without mothers in the home are not included in estimates concerning mother's education or mother's employment status.

SOURCE: Adapted from "Table 1-1. Percent of Children Ages 3–5 Who Were Enrolled in Center-Based Early Childhood Care and Education Programs, by Child and Family Characteristics: Selected Years 1991–2001," in *The Condition of Education 2002,* National Center for Education Statistics, 2002, http://nces.ed.gov/programs/coe/2002/section1/tables/t01_1.asp (accessed September 16, 2004)

FIGURE 6.4

Educational attainment of the population 25 years and over, by age, 1947–2003

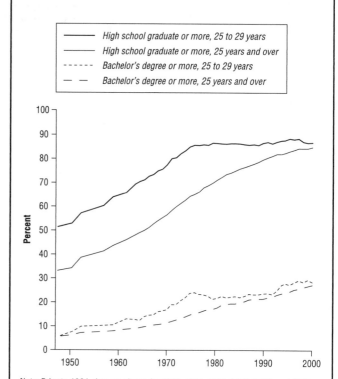

Note: Prior to 1964, data are shown for 1947, 1950, 1952, 1957, 1959, and 1962.

SOURCE: Nicole Stoops, "Figure 1. Educational Attainment of the Population 25 Years and over by Age: 1947 to 2003," in *Educational Attainment in the United States: 2003,* Current Population Reports, P20–550, U.S. Census Bureau, June 2004, http://www.census.gov/prod/2004pubs/p20-550.pdf (accessed September 16, 2004)

older than twenty-five had graduated from high school—the highest number ever. More than one in four (27.2%) had earned a bachelor's degree or more. (See Figure 6.4.)

The level of educational attainment has traditionally been higher for men than for women. In 2003, however, for the second year in a row, the high school graduation rate for women ages twenty-five and over (85%) exceeded that of men (84.1%). (See Table 6.4.) The 2002 difference was the first statistically significant one in high school graduation rates between men and women since 1989. In 2003 28.9% of men and 25.7% of women had obtained bachelor's degrees or higher. Although college attainment had increased since 1990 for both men and women, women were narrowing the gap and making faster gains then men.

Educational attainment also varied by race and ethnic origin. Non-Hispanic whites were most likely to complete high school (89.4%), followed by Asians (87.6%), African-Americans (80%), and Hispanics (57%). (See Table 6.4 and Figure 6.5.) Asians were by far the most likely to be college graduates (49.8%), followed by non-Hispanic whites (30%), African-Americans (17.3%), and Hispanics (11.4%).

Earning levels rise with increased education. For people ages eighteen or older who had not finished high school the average annual income in 2002 was $18,826. (See Table 6.5.) High school graduates earned an average income of $27,280, and people with some college or an associate degree earned an average income of $31,046. The incomes of college graduates increased with the level of the degree earned. People with a bachelor's degree had mean earnings of $51,194, while holders of advanced degrees earned an average of $72,824.

These averages differed considerably by gender and race or ethnicity. On average, women earned sixty-two cents for every dollar men earned. (See Table 6.5.) The most highly educated women earned the least compared to their male counterparts—fifty-six cents for every dollar

TABLE 6.4

Educational attainment of the population 25 years and over, by age, sex, race, ethnicity, nativity, marital status, and region, 2003

Characteristic	Number of people (in thousands)	High school graduate or more Percent	Some college or more Percent	Bachelor's degree or more Percent
Population 25 years and over	185,183	84.6	52.5	27.2
Age group:				
25 to 29 years	18,721	86.5	57.4	28.4
30 to 34 years	20,521	87.6	58.6	31.5
35 to 39 years	21,284	87.6	56.5	29.8
40 to 44 years	22,790	88.4	56.5	29.1
45 to 49 years	21,420	89.3	57.4	29.9
50 to 54 years	18,814	88.7	58.9	31.1
55 to 59 years	15,470	86.9	55.1	29.0
60 to 64 years	11,930	83.0	47.3	24.5
65 to 69 years	9,438	76.9	39.1	19.6
70 to 74 years	8,673	72.8	36.4	18.5
75 years and over	16,123	67.5	32.4	15.4
Sex:				
Men	88,597	84.1	53.2	28.9
Women	96,586	85.0	51.9	25.7
Race and origin:				
White alone	153,188	85.1	52.9	27.6
Non-Hispanic white alone	133,488	89.4	56.4	30.0
Black alone	20,527	80.0	44.7	17.3
Asian alone	7,691	87.6	67.4	49.8
Hispanic (of any race)	21,189	57.0	29.6	11.4
Nativity:				
Native	158,128	87.5	54.2	27.2
Foreign born	27,055	67.2	42.7	27.2
Marital status:				
Never married	28,694	84.9	54.8	29.0
Married spouse present	113,748	87.0	55.9	30.5
Married spouse absent	7,389	72.5	38.2	16.1
Separated	4,447	74.5	38.6	13.8
Widowed	13,970	67.2	30.3	12.5
Divorced	21,382	86.5	50.9	21.0
Region:				
Northeast	36,182	85.7	50.7	30.3
Midwest	41,728	87.8	52.5	26.0
South	66,071	82.2	50.1	25.3
West	41,202	84.0	58.1	28.7

SOURCE: Nicole Stoops, "Table A. Summary Measures of the Educational Attainment of the Population 25 Years and Over: 2003," in *Educational Attainment in the United States: 2003,* Current Population Reports, P20–550, U.S. Census Bureau, June 2004, http://www.census.gov/prod/2004pubs/p20-550.pdf (accessed September 16, 2004)

the men earned. The disparity between races and ethnic groups was not as pronounced. Annual earnings for high school graduates ranged from $28,756 for non-Hispanic whites to $22,823 for African-Americans. For college graduates earnings ranged from $40,949 for Hispanics to $53,185 for non-Hispanic whites.

PRIVATE SCHOOLS

Enrollment in public schools far surpasses enrollment in private schools. The National Center for Education Statistics (NCES) projects that total elementary and secondary school enrollment will continue to rise, reaching 55.9 million in 2012. (See Figure 6.2.) During this same period total private school enrollment is expected to rise from 6.2 million in 2001 to 6.6 million in 2013.

NCES statistics show that more than three-quarters (77.4%) of private school students in 1999–2000 were white. African-American students made up only 9.4% of private school students; 8.3% were Hispanic; and 4.5% were Asian/Pacific Islander. Most private schools (95.6%) were coeducational, and close to equal percentages of boys (50.7%) and girls (49.3%) attended.

Catholic Schools

According to the NCES report *Private School Universe Survey: 1999–2000* (August 2001), the most recent report available, 29.8% of all private schools in 1999–2000 were Catholic, and 48.6% of private school students attended Catholic schools. Economic and social changes have caused a decline in Catholic school enrollment and in the number of Catholic schools. In 1985 there were 9,220 Catholic schools in the United States; by 2002 there were only 8,114. Many closures took place in inner cities where financial difficulties made closings necessary. Between 1982 and 1999 Catholic school enrollment in elementary

TABLE 6.5

Average earnings by educational attainment, sex, race, and Hispanic origin for all workers, age 18 and over, 2002

Characteristic	Total	Not a high school graduate	High school graduate	Some college or associate's degree	Bachelor's degree	Advanced degree
Total	$36,308	$18,826	$27,280	$31,046	$51,194	$72,824
Men	$44,310	$22,091	$32,673	$38,377	$63,503	$90,761
Women	$27,271	$13,459	$21,141	$23,905	$37,909	$50,756
White alone	$37,376	$19,264	$28,145	$31,878	$52,479	$73,870
Non-Hispanic white alone	$39,220	$19,423	$28,756	$32,318	$53,185	$74,122
Black alone	$28,179	$16,516	$22,823	$27,626	$42,285	$59,944
Asian alone	$40,793	$16,746	$24,900	$27,340	$46,628	$72,852
Hispanic (of any race)	$25,824	$18,981	$24,163	$27,757	$40,949	$67,679

SOURCE: Nicole Stoops, "Table C. Average Earnings in 2002 by Educational Attainment, Sex, Race, and Hispanic Origin for All Workers, 18 Years and Over," in *Educational Attainment in the United States: 2003,* Current Population Reports, P20–550, U.S. Census Bureau, June 2004, http://www.census.gov/prod/2004pubs/p20-550.pdf (accessed September 16, 2004)

and secondary schools dropped from three million to 2.5 million, but rose again to 2.6 million in 2002.

Other Religious and Nonreligious Private Schools

The other types of private schools are non-Catholic religious schools and nonreligious (nonsectarian) schools. According to the NCES report, non-Catholic religious schools made up 48.6% of all private schools in 1999–2000 and enrolled 35.7% of all private school students. Nonsectarian schools enrolled only 15.7% of private school students in 21.6% of private schools.

COMPULSORY ATTENDANCE

In 2000 all U.S. states required students to attend school through at least age sixteen. (See Table 6.6.) Most industrialized Western nations require children to attend school for about ten years. According to the *Digest of Education Statistics 2001,* the countries requiring the most years of schooling were the Netherlands (ages five through eighteen), Germany and Belgium (both ages six through eighteen), Kazakhstan (ages six through seventeen), and the United Kingdom (ages five through sixteen).

DROPPING OUT

Dropout Rates

"Status" dropouts are sixteen- to twenty-four-year-olds who have not finished high school and are not enrolled in school. The U.S. Department of Education reports that status dropout rates decreased from 1960 (27.2%) through 2002 (10.7%). In 2001 10.7% of sixteen- to twenty-four-year-olds had dropped out of high school. The Hispanic status dropout rate was considerably higher, at 27%, than that of non-Hispanic African-Americans (10.9%) or non-Hispanic whites (7.3%).

Dropout rates also fluctuate greatly according to family income. In 2000 20.7% of people ages sixteen to twenty-four from families who had the lowest incomes (bottom 25%) had dropped out of school, nearly six times the

dropout rates of sixteen- to twenty-four-year-olds whose families had the highest incomes (3.5%). (See Figure 6.6.)

Status dropout rates are consistently lower for women than for men regardless of race or ethnicity. This has been the case since 1977. (See Table 6.7.) In 2001 the status dropout rate for young women ages sixteen to twenty-four was 9.3%. Males of the same age in 2001 had a status dropout rate of 12.2%.

Returning to School or Getting an Alternative Diploma (GED)

The decision to drop out of high school does not necessarily mean the end of a young person's education. Many former students return to school to get their diploma or take the test necessary to obtain an alternative credential or degree, such as a General Equivalency Diploma (GED). In 2001 648,000 GEDs were issued. Many young people who earn their GED then go on to get a college education.

THE NATIONAL EDUCATION GOALS PANEL

Because of concern that American youth were falling behind young people in other industrialized countries in educational achievement, the National Education Goals Panel was created in 1989 to oversee the progress of six national goals adopted by the states in a 1990 meeting of governors. The panel set these goals to be achieved by 2000:

1. All children in America will start school ready to learn.

2. The high school graduation rate will increase to at least 90%.

3. Students will leave grades four, eight, and twelve having demonstrated competency in English, mathematics, science, history, and geography.

4. American students will be first in the world in science and mathematics achievement.

5. Every adult American will be literate and possess the knowledge and skills necessary to compete in a global economy and exercise the rights and responsibilities of citizenship.

FIGURE 6.5

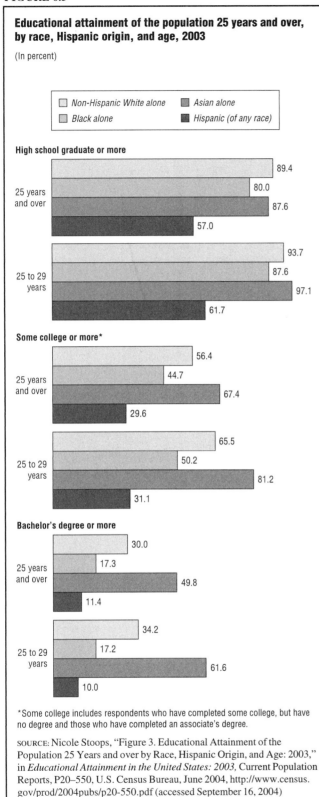

Educational attainment of the population 25 years and over, by race, Hispanic origin, and age, 2003

(In percent)

Legend:
- Non-Hispanic White alone
- Black alone
- Asian alone
- Hispanic (of any race)

High school graduate or more

25 years and over
- 89.4
- 80.0
- 87.6
- 57.0

25 to 29 years
- 93.7
- 87.6
- 97.1
- 61.7

Some college or more*

25 years and over
- 56.4
- 44.7
- 67.4
- 29.6

25 to 29 years
- 65.5
- 50.2
- 81.2
- 31.1

Bachelor's degree or more

25 years and over
- 30.0
- 17.3
- 49.8
- 11.4

25 to 29 years
- 34.2
- 17.2
- 61.6
- 10.0

*Some college includes respondents who have completed some college, but have no degree and those who have completed an associate's degree.

SOURCE: Nicole Stoops, "Figure 3. Educational Attainment of the Population 25 Years and over by Race, Hispanic Origin, and Age: 2003," in *Educational Attainment in the United States: 2003,* Current Population Reports, P20–550, U.S. Census Bureau, June 2004, http://www.census.gov/prod/2004pubs/p20-550.pdf (accessed September 16, 2004)

6. Every school in America will be free of drugs and violence and offer a disciplined environment conducive to learning.

Expressing the nation's continued concern, Congress passed the Goals 2000: Educate America Act (PL 103–227)

in 1994. The act reemphasized the National Education Goals and added two more goals for teacher and parental involvement:

1. The nation's teaching force will have access to programs for continued improvement of their professional skills.

2. Every school will promote partnerships to increase parental involvement and participation in the social, emotional, and academic growth of children.

Progress of the Goals

In its last completed progress report in 1999, the National Education Goals Panel noted advances in the following areas:

- The proportion of infants born with health risks declined.

- The percentage of two-year-olds fully immunized increased.

- The percentage of families reading and telling stories to their children increased.

- The gap in preschool attendance between high- and low-income families decreased.

- The percentages of students proficient in reading rose in grade eight, of students proficient in mathematics rose in grades four, eight, and twelve, and the proportion of college degrees awarded in mathematics and science increased for all students—including minorities and female.

- The percentage of students who reported being threatened or injured at school decreased.

Areas the National Education Goals Panel reported as disappointing were:

- The percentage of secondary school teachers with a degree in their main teaching assignment declined.

- The percentage of students reporting illicit drug use increased.

- The percentage of students reporting that someone offered to sell or give them drugs at school increased.

- The percentage of public school teachers reporting they were threatened or injured at school increased.

- There was a higher percentage of disruptions in classrooms of secondary school teachers.

The Decommissioning of the National Education Goals Panel

Although the original authorization of the National Education Goals Panel was set for the decade 1990–2000, a 1999 task force on the future of the panel and goals recommended it be reauthorized. However, the passage of

TABLE 6.6

Ages for compulsory school attendance; special education services for students; policies for kindergarten programs; and year-round schools, by state, 1997 and 2000

State	Compulsory attendance, 2000	Compulsory special education services, 1997 [1]	Year-round schools, 2000		Provision of kindergarten education, 2000			
			Has policy on year-round schools	Has districts with year-round schools	School districts required to offer		Attendance required	
					Half day	Full day	Half day	Full day
1	2	3	4	5	6	7	8	9
Alabama	7 to 16	6 to 21		X		X		X
Alaska	7 to 16	3 to 22		X				
Arizona	[2]6 to 16	3 to 22	X	X	X		X	
Arkansas	[3]5 to 17	5 to 21	X	X		X		X
California	[4]6 to 18	Birth to 21	X	X	X			
Colorado	–	3 to 21		X				
Connecticut	7 to 16	[5]Under 21			X			
Delaware	[6]5 to 16	3 to 20			X			
District of Columbia	–	–	–	–	–	X		X
Florida	6 to 18	–	X	X		X		X
Georgia	6 to 16	[5]Under 21		X		X		
Hawaii	6 to 18	Under 20	X	X				
Idaho	7 to 16	3 to 21		X				
Illinois	7 to 16	3 to 21	X	X	[7]X			
Indiana	7 to 16	3 to 22		X	X			
Iowa	[8]6 to 16	Under 21	X	X	[7]X			
Kansas	[9]7 to 18	(10)						
Kentucky	[11]6 to 16	Under 21	X	X	X			
Louisiana	7 to 17	3 to 21		X				
Maine	7 to 17	[12]5 to 19		X				
Maryland	5 to 16	Under 21		X	X		X	
Massachusetts	6 to 16	3 to 21		X	X			
Michigan	6 to 16	Under 26						
Minnesota	[13]7 to 18	Under 22	X	X	[7]X			
Mississippi	6 to 17	Birth to 20				X		
Missouri	7 to 16	Under 21		X	[7]X			
Montana	[14]7 to 16	3 to 18			X			
Nebraska	7 to 16	Birth to 21						
Nevada	7 to 17	Under 22	X	X	X			
New Hampshire	6 to 16	3 to 21						
New Jersey	6 to 16	5 to 21		X				
New Mexico	5 to 18	(15)		X	X		X	
New York	[16]6 to 16	Under 21						
North Carolina	7 to 16	5 to 20	X	X		X		
North Dakota	7 to 16	[17]3 to 20				[18]X		
Ohio	6 to 18	Under 22		X	[7]X		X	
Oklahoma	5 to 18	[19]3 and up	X	X	X		X	
Oregon	7 to 18	3 to 21	X	X	X			
Pennsylvania	8 to 17	6 to 21	X	X	X			
Rhode Island	6 to 16	3 to 21		X	X		X	
South Carolina	5 to 16	3 to 21		X		X		X
South Dakota	6 to 16	Under 21				[18]X		
Tennessee	6 to 17	3 to 21		X	X		X	
Texas	6 to 18	[20]3 to 21	X	X		[18]X	X	
Utah	6 to 18	3 to 22	X	X	X		X	

the No Child Left Behind Act in January 2002 repealed the panel's authorization, and it officially shut down in early 2002.

NO CHILD LEFT BEHIND ACT

With the passage of the No Child Left Behind Act (NCLB) in early 2002, sweeping changes were made to the laws defining and regulating the federal government's role in kindergarten through grade twelve education. The law is based on four basic education reform principles. The four principles, as described on the government's No Child Left Behind Web site (http://www.NoChildLeftBehind.gov/next/overview/index.html) are:

• Stronger accountability for results

• Increased flexibility and local control

• Expanded options for parents

• An emphasis on teaching methods that have been proven to work

Accountability

Under No Child Left Behind (NCLB), schools are required to demonstrate "adequate yearly progress" toward statewide proficiency goals, including closing the achievement gap between advantaged and disadvantaged

TABLE 6.6

Ages for compulsory school attendance; special education services for students; policies for kindergarten programs; and year-round schools, by state, 1997 and 2000 [CONTINUED]

State	Compulsory attendance, 2000	Compulsory special education services, 1997[1]	Year-round schools, 2000		Provision of kindergarten education, 2000			
			Has policy on year-round schools	Has districts with year-round schools	School districts required to offer		Attendance required	
					Half day	Full day	Half day	Full day
1	2	3	4	5	6	7	8	9
Vermont	7 to 16	3 to 21				[18]X		
Virginia	5 to 18	2 to 21		X		[18]X		X
Washington	[13]8 to 18	[21]3 to 21		X				
West Virginia	6 to 16	5 to 21	X	X		X		X
Wisconsin	6 to 18	Under 21		X	X			
Wyoming	[2]6 to 16	3 to 21		X	X			

[1]Most states have an upper age limit whereby education is provided up to a certain age or completion of secondary school, whichever comes first.
[2]Ages 6 to 16 or 10th grade completion.
[3]Must have turned 17 by October 1.
[4]At least 16 and have graduated high school or passed California High School Proficiency Exam (CHSPE) and obtained parental permission.
[5]Under 21 or until child graduates from high school.
[6]Must have turned 5 by August 31.
[7]State requires either half-day or full-day program.
[8]Must have turned 16 by September 15.
[9]Eligible for waiver at 16.
[10]School age, to be determined in accordance with rules and regulations adopted by the state board.
[11]Must have turned 6 by October 1.
[12]Must be 5 before October 1, and not 20 before start of school year, assistance in providing coordination of services from birth to age 6.
[13]Eligible for waiver.
[14]Age 16 and completion of eighth grade.
[15]School-age unless otherwise provided by law.
[16]Age 16 and completion of school year.
[17]Must not be 21 by September 1.
[18]State requires both half-day and full-day program.
[19]Children from birth through two are eligible for additional services. Eligibility for special education services cease upon completion of a secondary education program, no age limit.
[20]For visually and auditorily impaired individuals under 21.
[21]Student may complete school year if 21st birthday occurs while attending school.
– Data not available.
Note: The Education of the Handicapped Act (EHA) Amendments of 1986 make it mandatory for all states receiving EHA funds to serve all 3- to 18-year-old disabled children.

SOURCE: "Table 150. Ages for Compulsory School Attendance, Special Education Services for Students, Policies for Year-Round Schools and Kindergarten Programs, by State: 1997 and 2000," in *Digest of Education Statistics, 2002,* National Center for Education Statistics, 2003, http://nces.ed.gov/programs/digest/d02/tables/PDF/table150.pdf (accessed September 16, 2004)

students. Those schools that do not demonstrate progress face corrective action and restructuring measures. Progress reports are public, so parents can stay informed about their school and school district. Schools that are making or exceeding adequate yearly progress are eligible for awards.

The accountability outlined under No Child Left Behind is measured through standards testing. Under NCLB, states are required to establish strong academic standards and test students annually to see how they are meeting them. The requirement for annual testing will be phased in over a six-year period. During the 2002–03 school year, students in grades three to five, six to nine, and ten to twelve were tested in math and reading. Beginning in school year 2005–06, testing will expand to all students in grades three to eight. General science achievement testing will be fully implemented two years later, in the 2007–08 school year. NCLB linked federal financing of schools to the results of these mandated tests.

The provisions of this law related to testing are the subject of much debate. Advocates see testing as a means

of raising expectations and helping guarantee that all children are held to the same high standards. They argue that many young people have passed through school without acquiring the basic reading and math skills needed in society and especially in the information-oriented economy. Critics of testing say classroom experiences become limited to the need to teach students with the test in mind—and what is tested is only a sample of what kids should know. Further, critics claim that standards exams tend to test for those things most easily measured and not the critical thinking skills students need to develop.

PROFICIENCY TESTING. The testing requirements of the NCLB will be debated for some time to come as states grapple with the best means of implementing them. Standardized tests have, however, been around for some time. A look at the changes in proficiency test scores over time is one way to gauge the performance of the education system.

In *Condition of Education, 2004,* the National Center for Education Statistics lists test results for a series of years. The percentage of both fourth- and eighth-graders who tested proficient in reading rose from 29% of both

FIGURE 6.6

Percent of high school dropouts (status dropouts) among persons 16 to 24 years old by income level, 1970–2000

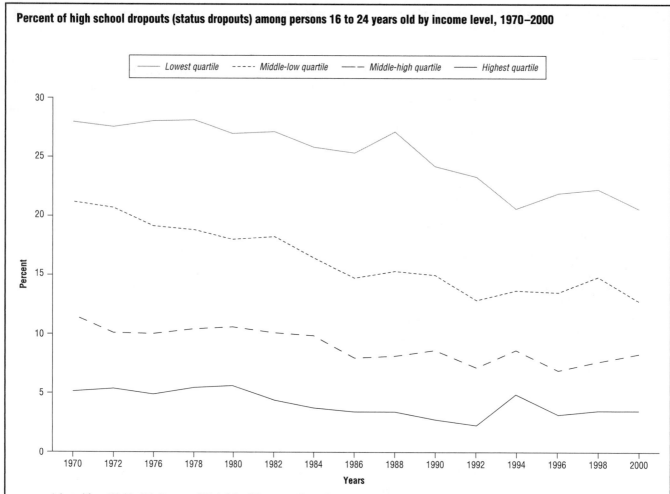

SOURCE: Adapted from "Table 109. Percent of High School Dropouts (Status Dropouts) among Persons 16 to 24 Years Old, by Income Level, and Distribution of Dropouts by Labor Force Status and Education Attainment: October 1970 to October 2001," in *Digest of Education Statistics, 2002,* National Center for Education Statistics, 2003, http://nces.ed.gov/programs/digest/d01/dt109.asp (accessed September 16, 2004)

groups in 1992 to 31% of fourth-graders and 32% of eighth-graders in 2003. The percentage of fourth-graders at or above proficiency in mathematics rose from 13% in 1992 to 32% in 2003; the percentage of eighth-graders at proficiency rose from 15% in 1992 to 29% in 2003.

Despite these positive results, the public's opinion of school performance has dropped. The National Center for Education Statistics' publication *Digest of Education Statistics: 2002* presents data on the grades that the public gives to schools nationally. Based on a scale of A=4, B=3, C=2, D=1, and F=0, the average grade given by adults to schools in 1985 was 2.14. In 2001 the average grade had dropped to 2.01. When adults with children in the school system were asked to rate their school, they gave a grade of 2.20 in 1985 and a grade of 2.04 in 2001, higher than the scores given by the general adult population but also declining over the period.

Another way to evaluate the educational system in the United States is to compare it with the systems of other industrialized countries. In May 2003 the National Center for Education Statistics published a study entitled *Compar-* *ative Indicators of Education in the United States and Other G-8 Countries: 2002.* The study was designed to compare the U.S. education system with the systems in seven other highly industrialized nations: Canada, France, Germany, Italy, Japan, the Russian Federation, and the United Kingdom. Eighth-grade students in the United States had a mean mathematics achievement score of 502, below that of Japan (579), Canada (531), and the Russian Federation (526), but higher than that of the other countries for which this measure was reported—England (496) and Italy (479). The score for mean science achievement obtained by students in the United States was (515), higher than the score for Italy (493), but below all the other countries for which this measure was reported. Fifteen-year-olds in the United States scored the same on the reading literacy scale (504) as students in France, Italy, Germany, Japan, and the United Kingdom, but below those in Canada.

Flexibility

The No Child Left Behind Act gave states and local school districts more control over the federal funding they

TABLE 6.7

Percentage of high school dropouts (status dropouts) among persons 16–24 years old, by sex, race, and ethnicity, 1960–2001

Year	Total				Men				Women			
	All races	White, non-Hispanic	Black, non-Hispanic	Hispanic origin	All races	White, non-Hispanic	Black, non-Hispanic	Hispanic origin	All races	White, non-Hispanic	Black, non-Hispanic	Hispanic origin
1	2	3	4	5	6	7	8	9	10	11	12	13
1960[1]	27.2	—	—	—	27.8	—	—	—	26.7	—	—	—
1967[2]	17.0	15.4	28.6	—	16.5	14.7	30.6	—	17.3	16.1	26.9	—
1968[2]	16.2	14.7	27.4	—	15.8	14.4	27.1	—	16.5	15.0	27.6	—
1969[2]	15.2	13.6	26.7	—	14.3	12.6	26.9	—	16.0	14.6	26.7	—
1970[2]	15.0	13.2	27.9	—	14.2	12.2	29.4	—	15.7	14.1	26.6	—
1971[2]	14.7	13.4	23.7	—	14.2	12.6	25.5	—	15.2	14.2	22.1	—
1972	14.6	12.3	21.3	34.3	14.1	11.6	22.3	33.7	15.1	12.8	20.5	34.8
1973	14.1	11.6	22.2	33.5	13.7	11.5	21.5	30.4	14.5	11.8	22.8	36.4
1974	14.3	11.9	21.2	33.0	14.2	12.0	20.1	33.8	14.3	11.8	22.1	32.2
1975	13.9	11.4	22.9	29.2	13.3	11.0	23.0	26.7	14.5	11.8	22.9	31.6
1976	14.1	12.0	20.5	31.4	14.1	12.1	21.2	30.3	14.2	11.8	19.9	32.3
1977	14.1	11.9	19.8	33.0	14.5	12.6	19.5	31.6	13.8	11.2	20.0	34.3
1978	14.2	11.9	20.2	33.3	14.6	12.2	22.5	33.6	13.9	11.6	18.3	33.1
1979	14.6	12.0	21.1	33.8	15.0	12.6	22.4	33.0	14.2	11.5	20.0	34.5
1980	14.1	11.4	19.1	35.2	15.1	12.3	20.8	37.2	13.1	10.5	17.7	33.2
1981	13.9	11.3	18.4	33.2	15.1	12.5	19.9	36.0	12.8	10.2	17.1	30.4
1982	13.9	11.4	18.4	31.7	14.5	12.0	21.2	30.5	13.3	10.8	15.9	32.8
1983	13.7	11.1	18.0	31.6	14.9	12.2	19.9	34.3	12.5	10.1	16.2	29.1
1984	13.1	11.0	15.5	29.8	14.0	11.9	16.8	30.6	12.3	10.1	14.3	29.0
1985	12.6	10.4	15.2	27.6	13.4	11.1	16.1	29.9	11.8	9.8	14.3	25.2
1986	12.2	9.7	14.2	30.1	13.1	10.3	15.0	32.8	11.4	9.1	13.5	27.2
1987	12.6	10.4	14.1	28.6	13.2	10.8	15.0	29.1	12.1	10.0	13.3	28.1
1988	12.9	9.6	14.5	35.8	13.5	10.3	15.0	36.0	12.2	8.9	14.0	35.4
1989	12.6	9.4	13.9	33.0	13.6	10.3	14.9	34.4	11.7	8.5	13.0	31.6
1990	12.1	9.0	13.2	32.4	12.3	9.3	11.9	34.3	11.8	8.7	14.4	30.3
1991	12.5	8.9	13.6	35.3	13.0	8.9	13.5	39.2	11.9	8.9	13.7	31.1
1992[3]	11.0	7.7	13.7	29.4	11.3	8.0	12.5	32.1	10.7	7.4	14.8	26.6
1993[3]	11.0	7.9	13.6	27.5	11.2	8.2	12.6	28.1	10.9	7.6	14.4	26.9
1994[3]	11.4	7.7	12.6	30.0	12.3	8.0	14.1	31.6	10.6	7.5	11.3	28.1
1995[3]	12.0	8.6	12.1	30.0	12.2	9.0	11.1	30.0	11.7	8.2	12.9	30.0
1996[3]	11.1	7.3	13.0	29.4	11.4	7.3	13.5	30.3	10.9	7.3	12.5	28.3
1997[3]	11.0	7.6	13.4	25.3	11.9	8.5	13.3	27.0	10.1	6.7	13.5	23.4
1998[3]	11.8	7.7	13.8	29.5	13.3	8.6	15.5	33.5	10.3	6.9	12.2	25.0
1999[3]	11.2	7.3	12.6	28.6	11.9	7.7	12.1	31.0	10.5	6.9	13.0	26.0
2000[3]	10.9	6.9	13.1	27.8	12.0	7.0	15.3	31.8	9.9	6.9	11.1	23.5
2001[3]	10.7	7.3	10.9	27.0	12.2	7.9	13.0	31.6	9.3	6.7	9.0	22.1

—Not available.

[1]Based on the April 1960 decennial census.

[2]White and black include persons of Hispanic origin.

[3]Because of changes in data collection procedures, data may not be comparable with figures for earlier years.

Note: "Status" dropouts are 16- to 24-year-olds who are not enrolled in school and who have not completed a high school program regardless of when they left school. People who have received GED credentials are counted as high school completers. All data except for 1960 are based on October counts. Data are based upon sample surveys of the civilian noninstitutionalized population.

SOURCE: "Table 108. Percent of High School Dropouts (Status Dropouts) among Persons 16 to 24 Years Old, by Sex and Race/Ethnicity: April 1960 to October 2001," in *Digest of Education Statistics, 2002,* National Center for Education Statistics, 2003, http://nces.ed.gov/programs/digest/d02/tables/dt108.asp (accessed September 16, 2004)

receive for education. Up to half of all non-Title I federal education funding can be allocated by states to whichever programs they wish. Federal programs were also simplified and consolidated under the law, so receiving funding is easier.

Parental Options

No Child Left Behind provided that parents of students attending failing schools would be provided with the opportunity and transportation to send their child to an alternative public or charter school. If the parent chose to keep their child in a failing school, federal Title I funds would be available for supplemental services such as tutoring and summer school, run by either nonsectarian or faith-based organizations. The creation and use of charter schools were expanded under NCLB.

Proven Educational Methods

No Child Left Behind attached federal funding to programs that had already been shown to help children learn.

Emphasis was placed on the Reading First initiative, more than tripling funding for reading programs from $300 million in fiscal year 2001 to a proposed $1.1 billion in fiscal year 2005. In addition, a new Early Reading First program was established to support literacy skills among preschool-age children to try to meet President George W. Bush's goal of every child being able to read by the third grade. Teacher quality programs received $2.8 billion in fiscal year 2001 for hiring new teachers, increasing teacher salaries, and improving teacher training and development; President Bush proposed $2.9 billion for teacher professional development in fiscal year 2005.

STUDENTS WITH DISABILITIES

In 1976 the U.S. Congress passed the Education of the Handicapped Act (PL 94–142, superseded by PL 98–199), which required schools to develop programs for disabled children. Formerly, parents of many disabled students had few options other than institutionalization or nursing care. The Education of the Handicapped Act required that disabled children be put in the "least restrictive environment," which led to increased efforts to educate them in regular classrooms (known as mainstreaming).

The law defined "handicapped" children as those who are mentally retarded, hard of hearing or deaf, orthopedically impaired, speech- and language-impaired, visually impaired, seriously emotionally disturbed or otherwise health-impaired. It also includes children with specific learning disabilities who require special education and related services.

In 1990 the Individuals with Disabilities Education Act (PL 101–476) (IDEA) was passed. This was a reauthorization and expansion of the earlier Education of the Handicapped Act. It added autism and traumatic brain injury to the list of disabilities covered by the law, and amendments added in 1992 and 1997 increased coverage for infants and toddlers and for children with attention deficit disorder (ADD) and attention deficit hyperactivity disorder (ADHD). The law required public school systems to develop an Individualized Education Program (IEP) for each disabled child, reflecting the needs of individual students.

In February 2001 President Bush announced the New Freedom Initiative, designed to give people with disabilities more opportunities in various arenas, including education. In the overview report describing the initiative, President Bush noted he would seek to increase funding for IDEA and place stress on both the "Reading First" and "Early Reading First" programs. He proposed an $11 billion budget for IDEA in fiscal year 2005.

Special Education Programs

As a result of legislation that enforces their rights, increased numbers of disabled children have been served in public schools. Between 1976 and 2001 the proportion of students who participated in federal education programs for children with disabilities increased from 8.3% to 13.3%. (See Table 6.8.) In 2001 the highest proportion of students needed services for specific learning disabilities (6%), followed by students who needed help with speech or language impairments (2.3%) and students who were mentally retarded (1.3%). According to the Office of Special Education Programs 2002 Annual Report, six hundred thousand preschoolers received early intervention services annually, and 5.8 million children six to twelve years old with disabilities received special education services in 2001.

HOMELESS CHILDREN

Homelessness harms children in many ways, including hindering their ability to attend and succeed in school. Homeless children have difficulty with transportation to school, maintaining necessary documents, and attaining privacy needed for homework, sleep, and interaction with parents in a shelter. Experts report that homeless children—compared with children who are poor but housed—miss more days of school, more often repeat a grade, and are more often put into special education classes.

The McKinney-Vento Homeless Assistance Act of 1987 (PL 100–77) required in Title VII, subtitle B, that each state provide "free, appropriate, public education" to homeless youth. The law further required that all states develop a plan to address the denial of access to education to homeless children.

The McKinney-Vento Homeless Education Assistance Improvements Act of 2001 went further to address inequities that affect homeless children in the public school system. New guidance for states and school systems released by the Department of Education in April 2003 noted the main differences between the old and new programs:

- Homeless children may no longer be segregated in a separate program on the basis of their homeless status.

- Schools must immediately enroll homeless students even if they are missing some of the documentation normally required.

- Upon parental request, states and school districts must provide transportation for homeless children to the school they attended before they became homeless.

- School districts must designate a local liaison for homeless children and youths.

HOMESCHOOLING

A number of parents, unhappy with public schools, teach their children at home. In 1990 the Home School Legal Defense Association (which provides legal assistance to home-school families) estimated that about

TABLE 6.8

Number of children with disabilities who were served by federal programs, as a percentage of total public K–12 enrollment, by type of disability, 1976–77 to 2000–01

Type of disability	1976–77	1980–81	1988–89	1989–90	1990–91	1991–92	1992–93	1993–94	1994–95	1995–96	1996–97	1997–98	1998–99	1999–2000	2000–01
1	2	3	4	5	6	7	8	9	10	11	12	13	14	15	16
						Number served as a percent of total enrollment[2]									
All disabilities	8.32	10.14	11.27	11.42	11.55	11.75	11.94	12.21	12.19	12.43	12.56	12.80	13.01	13.21	13.33
Specific learning disabilities	1.80	3.58	4.94	5.05	5.17	5.31	5.49	5.54	5.64	5.75	5.81	5.91	5.99	6.04	6.02
Speech or language impairments	2.94	2.86	2.40	2.40	2.39	2.37	2.32	2.33	2.30	2.28	2.29	2.29	2.29	2.30	2.30
Mental retardation	2.17	2.03	1.39	1.35	1.30	1.28	1.21	1.23	1.26	1.27	1.27	1.28	1.28	1.28	1.27
Emotional disturbance	0.64	0.85	0.93	0.94	0.95	0.95	0.95	0.97	0.98	0.98	0.98	0.99	1.00	1.00	
Hearing impairments	0.20	0.19	0.14	0.14	0.14	0.14	0.14	0.15	0.15	0.15	0.15	0.15	0.15	0.15	0.15
Orthopedic impairments	0.20	0.14	0.12	0.12	0.12	0.12	0.12	0.13	0.14	0.14	0.14	0.15	0.15	0.15	0.15
Other health impairments	0.32	0.24	0.12	0.13	0.13	0.14	0.15	0.19	0.24	0.30	0.35	0.41	0.47	0.54	0.62
Visual impairments	0.09	0.08	0.05	0.05	0.06	0.06	0.05	0.06	0.05	0.06	0.05	0.05	0.06	0.06	0.05
Multiple disabilities	—	0.17	0.21	0.21	0.23	0.23	0.24	0.25	0.20	0.21	0.21	0.23	0.23	0.24	0.26
Deaf-blindness	—	0.01	[3]	[3]	[3]	[3]	[3]	[3]	[3]	[3]	[3]	[3]	[5]	[5]	
Autism and traumatic brain injury	—	—	—	—	—	0.01	0.04	0.06	0.07	0.09	0.10	0.12	0.14	0.17	0.20
Developmental delay	—	—	—	—	—	—	—	—	—	—	—	0.01	0.03	0.04	0.06
Preschool disabled[1]	—	—	0.97	1.03	1.07	1.15	1.23	1.33	1.18	1.21	1.21	1.22	1.22	1.24	1.25

—Not available.

[1]Includes preschool children 3–5 years served under Chapter I and IDEA (Individuals with Disabilities Education Act), Part B. Prior to 1987–88, these students were included in the counts by disability condition. Beginning in 1987–88, states were no longer required to report preschool children (0–5 years) by disability condition.

[2]Based on the enrollment in public schools, kindergarten through 12th grade, including a relatively small number of prekindergarten students.

[3]Less than 0.005 percent.

Note: Counts are based on reports from the 50 states and District of Columbia only (i.e., figures from outlying areas are not included). Increases since 1987–88 are due in part to new legislation enacted fall 1986, which mandates public school special education services for all disabled children ages 3 through 5. Some data have been revised from previously published figures. Detail may not sum to totals due to rounding.

SOURCE: Adapted from "Table 52. Children 3 to 21 Years Old Served in Federally Supported Programs for the Disabled, by Type of Disability: 1976–77 to 2000–01," in *Digest of Education Statistics, 2002,* National Center for Education Statistics, 2003, http://nces.ed.gov/programs/digest/d02/tables/PDF/table52.pdf (accessed September 16, 2004)

474,000 children were being taught at home. According to data from the National Center for Education Statistics, approximately 850,000, or 1.7% of school-age children, were being homeschooled in the spring of 1999. By 2003 that number had risen to 1.1 million students, or 2.2% of school-age children (National Center for Education Statistics, "1.1 Million Homeschooled Students in the United States in 2003," Issue Brief NCES 2004-115, July 2004, http://nces.ed.gov/pubs2004/2004115.pdf [accessed August 3, 2004]).

Parents choose to homeschool their children for a variety of reasons. Almost a third (31%) of the homeschooling parents surveyed in the National Household Education Survey said the most important reason they chose to homeschool was concern about the environment of the other schools. Another 30% said they chose to homeschool to provide religious or moral instruction. The third most common reason parents gave for homeschooling was dissatisfaction with the academic instruction available at other schools (16%). (See Figure 6.7.)

States have differing requirements for parents who teach their children at home ("FAQ about Home Education Regulation," March 2002). Some states, such as Colorado and New Jersey, give parents the right to educate their children as they see fit, and impose only minor con-trols or none at all. Other states have more strict regulations. Opponents of homeschooling argue that parents may not be qualified to be teachers, but proponents believe that parents can gain teaching skills through experience, just as other teachers do.

ISSUES AFFECTING EDUCATION

Violence in the Classroom

April 20, 1999, marks the date of the worst school shooting in U.S. history. Two students at Columbine High School in Littleton, Colorado, shot and killed thirteen fellow students and teachers before turning their guns on themselves. Parents worried about how safe their schools really were, and schools have implemented a number of safety measures to deal with violence and crime at school. According to *Indicators of School Crime and Safety,* in the 1999–2000 school year 2% of public schools required students to pass through a metal detector each day, while 8% used random metal detector tests and 21% conducted drug sweeps. Nearly one-quarter (23%) reported the daily on-campus presence of police officers or security personnel, and 15% used video surveillance. More than half (59%) reported having a school violence prevention program. Critics of increased surveillance in schools contend that bullying, stalking, and harassment present the real

FIGURE 6.7

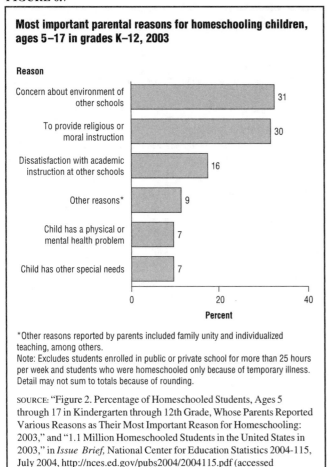

Most important parental reasons for homeschooling children, ages 5–17 in grades K–12, 2003

Reason

Concern about environment of other schools	31
To provide religious or moral instruction	30
Dissatisfaction with academic instruction at other schools	16
Other reasons*	9
Child has a physical or mental health problem	7
Child has other special needs	7

Percent

*Other reasons reported by parents included family unity and individualized teaching, among others.
Note: Excludes students enrolled in public or private school for more than 25 hours per week and students who were homeschooled only because of temporary illness. Detail may not sum to totals because of rounding.

SOURCE: "Figure 2. Percentage of Homeschooled Students, Ages 5 through 17 in Kindergarten through 12th Grade, Whose Parents Reported Various Reasons as Their Most Important Reason for Homeschooling: 2003," and "1.1 Million Homeschooled Students in the United States in 2003," in *Issue Brief,* National Center for Education Statistics 2004-115, July 2004, http://nces.ed.gov/pubs2004/2004115.pdf (accessed September 16, 2004)

risk to students and believe that stronger counseling and early-intervention programs are urgently needed.

A 2002 joint report by the National Center for Education Statistics (NCES) and the Bureau of Justice Statistics (BJS) (*Indicators of School Crime and Safety*) reported mixed results of efforts to decrease violence in schools. The report found that between 1992 and 2000 violent crime in schools had actually decreased from earlier years, but, despite the decline, seven hundred thousand violent crimes still occurred in schools in 2000. The percentage of high school students who had been threatened or injured with a weapon while at school remained relatively constant between 1993 and 2001.

The Condition of School Facilities

Education experts and members of Congress recognize that the quality of the learning environment affects the education children receive. In 1996 the U.S. General Accounting Office (GAO) reported in *School Facilities— America's Schools Report Differing Conditions* that the presence of "decent facilities" in schools—including buildings that are structurally safe and have fire safety measures, adequate exits, safe drinking water, proper

sewage disposal systems, and good lighting—was crucial to provide a high-quality learning environment. This finding was confirmed in a November 2002 report (*Do School Facilities Affect Academic Outcomes?*) by Mark Schneider and the National Clearinghouse for Educational Facilities.

Serious problems with school facilities continue to surface. According to the NCES report *Condition of America's Public School Facilities: 1999* (2000), many schools were in need of major repairs. Three-quarters of schools reported a need to spend some money on repairs, renovations, and modernizations to put buildings into good overall condition. Fifty percent of schools reported that at least one building feature was in less than adequate condition. Approximately eleven million students were enrolled in schools reporting at least one type of on-site building feature in less than adequate condition. Of these students, about 3.5 million attended schools where at least one type of building feature was in poor condition or needed to be replaced. Approximately one-fifth of schools indicated less than adequate conditions for life safety features (20%), roofs (22%), and electric power (22%), and about a quarter of schools reported less than adequate conditions for plumbing (25%) and exterior walls, finishes, windows, and doors (24%). Heating, ventilation, and air conditioning systems were reported to be in less than adequate condition at 29% of schools. Schools with the highest concentration of poverty were more likely to report at least one unsatisfactory environmental condition than those with the lowest concentration of poverty (55% compared with 38%).

COLLEGE ENTRANCE EXAMINATIONS

Most students who wish to enter colleges and universities in the United States must take either the SAT (once known as the Scholastic Aptitude Test, then the Scholastic Assessment Test, now simply the SAT I) or the American College Test (ACT) as part of their admission requirements. The ACT is a curriculum-based achievement test, measuring proficiency in reading, math, English, and science, while the SAT is the primary admissions test to measure a student's mathematical and verbal reasoning ability in a way intended to assess readiness for college. Students who take these tests usually plan to continue their education beyond high school; therefore, these tests do not profile all high school students.

More Are Taking SAT and ACT Exams, with Mixed Results

The number of students who take both the SAT and the ACT has grown steadily. In 2003 1.5 million students took the SAT. This represented an increase of 33.8% over the number who took the test in 1975 (996,000). The number of students taking the ACT increased over the same period, from 714,000 in 1975 to 1.2 million in 2003, an increase of 40.5%. College admissions officers reported significant increases in the number of applicants as well, despite the declining number of high school graduates since 1980 (Tim Goral, "Intelligent Admissions: With College Applications Reaching Record Levels, IHEs Are Using Technology to Work Smarter and More Efficiently," *University Business,* March 2003). Students were either applying to a larger number of schools or, as the increased numbers taking the SAT and ACT suggested, more high school graduates were pursuing a college education.

Performance on the SAT is measured on a scale of two hundred to eight hundred for each of two sections, with the established average score being around five hundred for each. According to *2003 College-Bound Seniors,* a report from the College Board Summary Reporting Service, over the period from 1972 to 2003, average verbal scores on the SAT declined from 537 to 507. The results for the math portion of the SAT, however, dropped and then rebounded over the same period, from 509 in 1972 to 519 in 2003. Average ACT scores also improved; in 1970 the average composite ACT score was 19.9, and in 2003 the average composite score was 20.8.

Characteristics of Test Takers

GENDER. More women than men took the tests in 2003—53.6% of those who took the SAT and 56% taking the ACT were women. More women than men have taken the SAT since the 1970s as well. Men scored higher on both the verbal and the math portions of the SAT test in 2003 (average scores of 512 and 537, respectively) compared with women (503 in each section) (*2003 Profile of College-Bound Seniors,* College Entrance Examination Board, 2003). The average composite ACT score was 21 for males and 20.8 for females. Women scored higher than men on the English and reading sections of the ACT, while men scored higher on the mathematics and science sections (National Data Release, ACT, August 20, 2003, http://act.org/news/releases/2003/8-20-03.html).

PLANNED AREAS OF STUDY AND FUTURE CAREERS. The favorite intended areas of study or future career choice among those who took the SAT in order of preference were health-related (16%), business (13%), and social science/history (10%) (*2003 Profile of College-Bound Seniors*). Areas in which students taking the ACT hoped to pursue future studies were similar to those reported for takers of the SAT. But in an August 20, 2003, press release from ACT—"College-Bound Students' Academic Skills at Odds with Career Plans"— Richard L. Ferguson, ACT's chief executive officer, stated that while the top planned college major was health sciences, only a quarter (25%) of ACT test-takers reached the college readiness benchmark on the science test.

RACIAL AND ETHNIC DIFFERENCES. Despite improvements in the scores of minority students, they lagged behind those of white students. In 2003 whites scored a

mean of 529 on verbal and 534 on math on the SAT. African-Americans scored an average of 431 on verbal and 426 on math, the lowest average scores of any racial or ethnic group. Mexican-Americans scored an average of 448 on verbal and 457 on math; Puerto Ricans scored 456 on verbal and 453 on math; and other Hispanics scored 457 on verbal and 464 on math. Native Americans and Alaska Natives scored 480 on verbal and 482 on math, and Asians and Pacific Islanders scored an average of 508 on verbal and 575 on math (*2003 Profile of College-Bound Seniors*).

Although average scores for all racial and ethnic groups except for Asians fell below scores of whites, the College Board reported some progress from 1992 to 2002. During that period average scores for African-Americans increased by ten points, scores for American Indians/Alaska Natives by nineteen points, and scores for Asians/Pacific Islanders by thirty-two points. While scores of Puerto Rican students showed a jump of twenty-six points, scores for other students of Hispanic origin generally showed no change ("Strong SAT Math Score Gains for Almost All Racial/Ethnic Groups between 1993 and 2003," *2003 Profile of College-Bound Seniors*). However, the College Board noted that gaps between high school grade-point averages of white and nonwhite students actually increased between 1993 and 2003 ("Most Gaps between High School GPAs of White and Nonwhite Students Have Increased," *2003 Profile of College-Bound Seniors*).

According to the ACT's Web site (http://www.act.org/news/releases/2003/8-20-03.html [accessed January 17, 2005]), results on the ACT in 2003 showed that African-American students scored an average of 16.9, Native Americans/Alaska Natives scored an average of 18.7, non-Hispanic whites scored an average of 21.7, and Asian-Americans scored an average of 21.8. Puerto Ricans earned an average score of 19, while Mexican-Americans earned an average of 18.2. In "ACT Scores Hold Steady in 2003," Richard L. Ferguson noted, "Our research has shown that far too many African-American students are not being adequately prepared for college. They are less likely than others to take rigorous, college-preparatory courses, and they often don't receive the information and guidance they need to properly plan for college." ACT data showed that fewer minority test-takers had taken the core college-preparatory coursework, and that groups that had taken more core coursework, such as non-Hispanic whites and Asian-Americans, tended to score higher on the ACT.

Controversy over the SAT

In the late twentieth and early twenty-first centuries, the SAT came under fire. One of the most notable critics of the SAT was University of California President Richard Atkinson, who argued that the test did not add much information to the overall picture of a student's academic performance. Atkinson believed the SAT II tests, which test knowledge in specific subject areas, were a more useful tool for college admissions officers than the SAT I.

In response to Atkinson's criticisms, the College Board announced numerous changes to the SAT. Changes implemented in 1994 included non-multiple-choice questions in the math section; the removal of antonyms and a greater emphasis on reading in the verbal section; and permitting the use of calculators during testing. March 2005 changes included an expansion of the math section to cover Algebra II as well as Algebra I and Geometry; the addition of a new writing section containing grammar questions and an essay; and a change in name for the verbal section to critical reading and the removal of analogies from that section.

HIGHER EDUCATION—OFF TO COLLEGE

Formal schooling beyond high school increasingly is being viewed as a necessity, not only to a young person's development but also to his or her economic success. President Bill Clinton, in his 1997 State of the Union address, spoke of the goal of making two years of college education "standard" for all American young people, much like high school had been considered in the past, and a four-year degree possible for anyone who desired it. Many parents consider helping their children attend college to be an important financial responsibility.

Enrollment

Enrollment in institutions of higher education is expected to rise through 2013, due not only to large numbers of children of baby boomers approaching college age but also to the increasing numbers of people of all ages seeking advanced learning. Enrollment in degree-granting postsecondary institutions stood at 15.3 million in 2000 and is expected to reach 18.2 million by 2013. (See Figure 6.8.)

College Costs

Paying for a college education, even at public four-year institutions, now ranks as one of the most costly investments for American families. In 2001–02 the average annual in-state cost at a four-year public college, including tuition and room and board, was $9,199. For one year at a private four-year college in 2002 the average cost for tuition and room and board was $22,968. (See Table 6.9.)

Nationwide the average tuition in 2001–02 (not including room and board) for full-time, resident undergraduate students at public four-year colleges was $3,746. (See Table 6.9.) Tuition at four-year public colleges varied widely among states—from $2,388 in Utah to $7,470 in Vermont. Most states with the highest tuition were in the

FIGURE 6.8

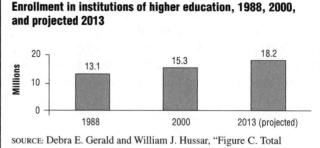

Enrollment in institutions of higher education, 1988, 2000, and projected 2013

SOURCE: Debra E. Gerald and William J. Hussar, "Figure C. Total Enrollment in Degree–Granting Institutions, with Middle Alternative Projections: Selected Years," in *Projections of Education Statistics,* National Center for Education Statistics, October 2003, http://nces.ed .gov/programs/projections/ch_2.asp (accessed September 16, 2004)

Northeast and most with the lowest tuition were in the South and West.

Private schools also raised tuition and room and board fees in an effort to meet their financial obligations. Average tuition in a private four-year college in 2001–02 was $16,287, up from $15,470 in 2000–01. (See Table 6.9.) The average tuition in such institutions varied greatly by state, from a low in Utah of $4,014 to a high in Massachusetts of $21,526.

Financial Assistance for Students

During the 1999–2000 academic year, the last year for which national data were available, more than half (55%) of about 16.5 million undergraduates enrolled in postsecondary institutions received some type of financial aid from federal, state, institutional, or other sources to meet their educational expenses. About 39% of undergraduates received some form of federal aid, and 14% of undergraduates received state aid. More than one in ten students (13.6%) received grants (which do not have to be paid back), 5% took out loans (which do have to be paid back), 2.7% received state merit grants, and 3% were on work-study programs (*Digest of Education Statistics,* chap. 3-A, National Center for Education Statistics, Washington, DC, 2003). Federal assistance that goes directly to students includes Pell Grants (the annual maximum was increased to $4,050 for the 2004–05 award year), the Stafford Student Loan Program (a maximum loan of $17,125 for four years of study for dependent undergraduate students), and Supplemental Education Opportunity Grants (which can range from $100 to $5,000 per year).

During 1999–2000, 75% of dependent undergraduates whose family income was below $30,000 received financial aid (Lutz Berkner et al., *Student Financing of Undergraduate Education: 1999–2000,* National Center for Education Statistics, Washington, DC, July 2002). About 37% of undergraduates in this income category received aid with no loans, and 38% received aid that

TABLE 6.9

Average undergraduate tuition, fees, and room and board rates paid by full-time equivalent students in degree-granting institutions, by control of institution and by state, 2000–01 and 2001–02

State or other area	Public 4-year, 2000–01		Public 4-year, 2001–02[1]				Private 4-year, 2000–01		Private 4-year, 2001–02[1]				Public 2-year, tuition only (in-state)	
	Total	Tuition and required fees (in-state)	Total	Tuition and required fees (in-state)	Room	Board	Total	Tuition and required fees	Total	Tuition and required fees	Room	Board	2000–01	2001–02[1]
1	2	3	4	5	6	7	8	9	10	11	12	13	14	15
United States	$8,653	$3,501	$9,199	$3,746	$2,811	$2,642	$21,856	$15,470	$22,968	$16,287	$3,571	$3,111	$1,333	$1,379
Alabama	7,349	2,987	7,654	3,245	2,321	2,088	14,136	9,334	15,269	10,229	2,415	2,626	1,672	1,990
Alaska	8,390	2,941	9,258	3,065	3,035	3,157	14,656	9,381	15,675	9,852	2,440	3,382	1,674	1,717
Arizona	7,874	2,346	8,222	2,488	2,719	3,015	15,109	9,322	14,510	9,759	2,616	2,135	924	962
Arkansas	6,797	3,011	7,302	3,387	2,036	1,879	13,377	9,109	14,414	9,952	1,988	2,474	1,158	1,314
California	9,590	2,566	10,320	2,730	3,830	3,760	24,679	17,219	26,203	18,399	4,269	3,535	315	315
Colorado	8,362	2,980	8,808	3,159	2,663	2,987	23,129	15,445	24,351	16,245	3,725	4,380	1,655	1,685
Connecticut	10,521	4,553	11,058	4,772	3,406	2,880	27,737	20,056	29,065	21,075	4,780	3,209	1,868	1,889
Delaware	10,283	4,789	10,889	5,065	3,082	2,742	13,936	8,415	14,698	8,755	3,146	2,798	1,680	1,800
District of Columbia	†	2,070	†	2,070	†	†	26,933	19,186	28,310	20,093	5,090	3,126	†	†
Florida	7,947	2,366	8,361	2,555	3,138	2,667	19,870	13,805	20,978	14,708	3,316	2,954	1,438	1,494
Georgia	7,463	2,699	7,915	2,838	2,730	2,346	19,951	13,770	21,124	14,555	3,763	2,806	1,260	1,293
Hawaii	8,272	2,968	7,987	3,051	2,376	2,560	16,078	8,000	16,627	8,777	3,477	4,373	1,066	1,067
Idaho	6,765	2,628	7,163	2,860	1,993	2,310	17,793	13,664	10,163	5,326	1,862	2,976	1,316	1,410
Illinois	9,532	4,178	10,194	4,567	2,653	2,974	21,784	15,317	22,844	16,194	3,726	2,924	1,532	1,569
Indiana	9,239	3,786	9,783	4,002	2,821	2,960	21,378	16,078	22,545	16,973	2,823	2,749	2,108	2,121
Iowa	7,587	3,157	8,253	3,470	2,512	2,271	19,414	14,630	20,341	15,383	2,289	2,670	2,141	2,362
Kansas	6,654	2,642	6,987	2,700	2,056	2,231	15,670	11,206	16,653	11,987	2,058	2,608	1,378	1,441
Kentucky	6,923	2,898	7,370	3,194	2,131	2,045	14,644	10,176	15,710	10,972	2,261	2,477	1,342	1,561
Louisiana	6,329	2,783	6,689	2,865	1,895	1,929	21,937	15,591	23,050	16,539	3,469	3,042	935	1,009
Maine	9,371	4,267	10,259	4,804	2,716	2,739	22,690	16,450	24,132	17,619	3,214	3,299	2,594	2,642
Maryland	10,834	4,772	11,385	4,973	3,553	2,859	25,670	18,621	27,108	19,652	4,185	3,271	2,301	2,244
Massachusetts	9,207	4,003	9,370	3,999	2,926	2,445	28,666	20,566	29,970	21,526	4,696	3,749	1,894	1,946
Michigan	9,825	4,615	10,565	5,054	2,679	2,832	16,011	11,155	17,046	11,802	2,527	2,717	1,743	1,780
Minnesota	8,127	4,009	9,080	4,494	2,463	2,122	21,332	16,243	22,420	16,986	2,716	2,717	2,507	2,746
Mississippi	7,195	2,969	7,599	3,410	2,252	1,937	13,767	9,659	14,203	10,004	2,047	2,151	1,138	1,362
Missouri	8,203	3,879	8,672	4,111	2,587	1,975	17,886	12,600	18,787	13,218	2,860	2,710	1,472	1,498
Montana	7,615	3,079	8,309	3,467	2,177	2,665	14,454	9,631	15,929	9,926	3,104	2,899	2,004	2,159
Nebraska	7,355	3,101	7,731	3,228	2,105	2,398	16,093	11,619	18,837	14,074	2,386	2,377	1,421	1,498
Nevada	8,247	2,344	8,570	2,437	3,523	2,610	17,835	11,465	19,719	13,510	3,230	2,979	1,369	1,410
New Hampshire	11,720	6,458	12,348	6,728	3,457	2,163	25,184	18,261	26,482	19,186	4,121	3,175	3,933	4,324
New Jersey	12,007	5,609	12,854	6,078	4,034	2,741	23,738	16,680	25,203	17,403	4,113	3,687	2,295	2,236
New Mexico	7,086	2,627	7,587	2,838	2,252	2,497	19,011	14,062	20,508	14,499	3,121	2,888	876	921
New York	10,260	4,063	10,777	4,140	3,637	2,999	25,178	17,433	26,509	18,357	4,697	3,455	2,562	2,584
North Carolina	7,076	2,298	7,667	2,646	2,650	2,371	20,185	14,274	21,024	15,110	2,852	3,062	896	1,014
North Dakota	6,418	2,942	6,843	3,130	1,405	2,308	11,399	8,026	11,840	8,362	1,520	1,959	1,902	2,090
Ohio	10,451	4,742	11,179	5,142	3,188	2,849	20,983	15,419	22,134	16,259	2,945	2,929	2,292	2,373
Oklahoma	6,022	2,259	6,296	2,373	1,744	2,178	15,307	10,587	16,492	11,405	2,343	2,744	1,253	1,214
Oregon	9,394	3,646	10,063	3,862	3,191	3,010	23,123	17,533	24,428	18,308	3,090	3,030	1,637	1,722
Pennsylvania	11,091	5,917	11,861	6,316	2,955	2,590	24,737	17,821	26,002	18,796	3,833	3,373	2,287	2,369
Rhode Island	11,095	4,506	11,610	4,708	3,677	3,225	26,073	18,320	27,192	19,177	4,068	3,946	1,806	1,854
South Carolina	9,096	4,701	10,077	5,502	2,485	2,089	17,518	12,713	18,435	13,429	2,511	2,495	1,467	1,787
South Dakota	6,975	3,484	7,469	3,692	1,504	2,273	15,335	11,194	15,935	11,796	1,907	2,232	2,857	2,964
Tennessee	7,658	2,950	7,781	3,340	2,111	2,330	18,128	12,922	19,143	13,682	2,918	2,543	1,441	1,652
Texas	7,614	2,785	8,062	2,975	2,659	2,428	16,890	11,865	18,185	12,728	2,724	2,733	929	981
Utah	6,598	2,226	7,393	2,388	2,002	3,004	8,600	3,754	8,992	4,014	2,445	2,533	1,571	1,679
Vermont	12,847	7,142	13,450	7,470	3,700	2,280	22,454	15,740	23,205	16,407	3,659	3,140	3,004	3,148
Virginia	8,751	3,723	8,988	3,775	2,796	2,417	18,499	13,118	19,541	13,892	2,786	2,863	1,132	1,131
Washington	8,909	3,600	9,986	3,788	2,862	3,337	21,505	15,874	22,612	16,638	3,038	2,936	1,758	1,885
West Virginia	7,290	2,551	7,625	2,645	2,421	2,559	18,285	12,999	18,329	13,136	2,406	2,787	1,661	1,661
Wisconsin	7,396	3,417	7,786	3,691	2,265	1,829	20,317	15,032	21,330	15,907	2,836	2,587	2,262	2,310
Wyoming	7,017	2,575	7,421	2,807	2,012	2,602	†	†	†	†	†	†	1,440	1,490

†Not applicable.

[1]Preliminary data based on fall 2000 enrollments.

Note: Data are for the entire academic year and are average charges. Tuition and fees were weighted by the number of full-time-equivalent undergraduates in 2000, but are not adjusted to reflect student residency. Room and board are based on full-time students. Data revised from previously published figures. Detail may not sum to totals due to rounding.

SOURCE: "Table 313. Average Undergraduate Tuition and Fees and Room and Board Rates Paid by Full-Time-Equivalent Students in Degree-Granting Institutions, by Control of Institution and by State: 2000–01 and 2001–02," in *Digest of Education Statistics, 2002,* National Center for Education Statistics, 2003, http://nces.ed.gov/programs/digest/d02/tables/PDF/table313.pdf (accessed September 14, 2004)

included loans. About 57% of dependent undergraduates whose family income was in the $30,000–$80,000 range received financial aid—about 20% received aid with no loans and 37% received aid that included loans. About 48% of dependent undergraduates whose family income was more than $80,000 received financial aid; 20% received aid with no loans, and 28% received aid that included loans.

CHAPTER 7

TEEN SEXUALITY AND PREGNANCY

EARLY SEXUAL ACTIVITY

The Centers for Disease Control and Prevention (CDC) reported in its 2003 *Youth Risk Behavior Survey* that almost half of high school students (46.7%) had had sexual intercourse, down from the 54% who were reported as sexually active in 1991. (See Table 7.1 and Figure 7.1.) Almost one in seven (14.2%) had had sex with four or more partners. Girls (45.3%) were slightly less likely than boys (48%) to have had intercourse, and African-American students (67.3%) were more likely than Hispanics (51.4%) or white students (41.8%) to be sexually active.

The proportion of students who had intercourse rose with age; 27.9% of ninth graders, 43.1% of tenth graders, 53.1% of eleventh graders, and 62.3% of twelfth graders had had intercourse at the time of the survey. (See Table 7.1.) Many youth were sexually active before age thirteen; 7.4% had had intercourse at age twelve or younger.

Risk Factors for Early Sexual Activity

In "Early Adolescent Sexual Activity: A Developmental Study," Les B. Whitbeck and his colleagues noted that "the main predictors of early intercourse were age, association with delinquent peers, alcohol use, opportunity, and sexually permissive attitudes" (*Journal of Marriage and the Family,* November 1999). Family conflict has also been linked to early sexual activity among poor urban African-American adolescents (Cami K. McBride et al., "Individual and Familial Influences on the Onset of Sexual Intercourse among Urban African American Adolescents," *Journal of Consulting and Clinical Psychology,* February 2003). Another study of poor African-American children found that those who reported high levels of monitoring from parents were less likely to have sex before adolescence (at age ten or earlier) and had lower rates of sexual initiation in their teen years as well (D. Romer et al., "Parental Influences on Adolescent Sexual Behavior in High Poverty Settings," *Archives of Pediatrics and Adoles-*

cent Medicine, 1999). A 2004 study of inner-city seventh graders found that peer norms about refraining from sex were strongly correlated with seventh and eighth graders abstaining; drug or alcohol use, on the other hand, increased the risk of early sexual activity (John S. Santelli et al., "Initiation of Sexual Intercourse among Middle School Adolescents: The Influence of Psychosocial Factors," *Journal of Adolescent Health,* vol. 34, March 2004).

Reasons Given for Not Delaying Sex

A number of studies have reported that both sexes consider social pressure the major factor in engaging in early sexual activity. Peer pressure and a belief that "everyone is doing it" have often been cited as explanations. But a recent study found that most female adolescents (78% of the studied group) felt that they had been "too young" at their first sexual experience (Sian Cotton et al., "Adolescent Girls' Perceptions of the Timing of Their Sexual Initiation: 'Too Young' or 'Just Right'?" *Journal of Adolescent Health,* vol. 34, May 2004).

Figure 7.2 shows that in the 1990s both adults and teens overestimated the percent of teens who were sexually experienced by age fifteen. In addition, some more recent research has challenged the theory that social pressure is the strongest influence on teenagers' sexual decisions. A survey commissioned by Students Against Destructive Decisions (SADD) and the Liberty Mutual Group in January 2002 (*Teens Today*) asked students in grades six through twelve what factors had most influenced their decisions about sexuality. The most common reasons teenagers gave were to feel good, to have fun, and to please one's partner. The most commonly mentioned reasons not to have sex were fear of pregnancy, fear of sexually transmitted diseases, and not being in a relationship or in love.

The Media and Teen Concepts of Sexuality

In February 2003 the Kaiser Family Foundation released the results of its latest biennial study of sexual

TABLE 7.1

Percentage of high school students who engaged in sexual behaviors, by sex, race, ethnicity, and grade, 2003

	Ever had sexual intercourse			Had first sexual intercourse before age 13 years			Had ≥4 sex partners during lifetime		
Category	Female %	Male %	Total %	Female %	Male %	Total %	Female %	Male %	Total %
Race/ethnicity									
White*	43.0	40.5	**41.8**	3.4	5.0	**4.2**	10.1	11.5	**10.8**
Black*	60.9	73.8	**67.3**	6.9	31.8	**19.0**	16.3	41.7	**28.8**
Hispanic	46.4	56.8	**51.4**	5.2	11.6	**8.3**	11.2	20.5	**15.7**
Grade									
9	27.9	37.3	**32.8**	5.3	13.2	**9.3**	6.4	14.2	**10.4**
10	43.1	45.1	**44.1**	5.7	11.2	**8.5**	8.8	16.4	**12.6**
11	53.1	53.4	**53.2**	3.2	7.5	**5.4**	13.4	18.6	**16.0**
12	62.3	60.7	**61.6**	1.9	8.8	**5.5**	17.9	22.2	**20.3**
Total	**45.3**	**48.0**	**46.7**	**4.2**	**10.4**	**7.4**	**11.2**	**17.5**	**14.4**

	Currently sexually active			Condom use during last sexual intercourse			Birth control pill use before last sexual intercourse		
Category	Female %	Male %	Total %	Female %	Male %	Total %	Female %	Male %	Total %
Race/ethnicity									
White*	33.1	28.5	**30.8**	56.5	69.0	**62.5**	26.5	17.3	**22.3**
Black*	44.2	54.0	**49.0**	63.6	81.2	**72.8**	11.7	4.4	**7.9**
Hispanic	35.8	38.5	**37.1**	52.3	62.5	**57.4**	12.1	10.3	**11.2**
Grade									
9	18.3	24.0	**21.2**	66.1	71.2	**69.0**	11.6	6.6	**8.7**
10	31.2	30.0	**30.6**	66.4	71.8	**69.0**	13.5	11.8	**12.7**
11	42.9	39.2	**41.1**	55.5	66.7	**60.8**	24.1	14.8	**19.6**
12	51.0	46.5	**48.9**	48.5	67.0	**57.4**	27.2	17.5	**22.6**
Total	**34.6**	**33.8**	**34.3**	**57.4**	**68.8**	**63.0**	**20.6**	**13.1**	**17.0**

*Non-Hispanic.

SOURCE: Adapted from "Table 42. Percentage of High School Students Who Engaged in Sexual Behaviors, by Sex, Race/Ethnicity, and Grade," and "Table 44. Percentage of High School Students Who Were Currently Sexually Active and Who Used a Condom during or Birth Control Pills before Last Sexual Intercourse, by Sex, Race/Ethnicity, and Grade," in "Youth Risk Behavior Surveillance–United States, 2003," *Centers for Disease Control and Prevention Surveillance Summaries: Morbidity and Mortality Weekly Report,* vol. 53, no. SS–02, May 21, 2004, http://www.cdc.gov/mmwr/PDF/SS/SS5302.pdf (accessed September 16, 2004)

messages on television (Dale Kunkel et al., *Sex on TV 3: Content and Context*). Of the twenty shows most popular with teenagers during the 2000–01 television season, five out of every six episodes (83%) included some sexual content, as compared with the average of 64% for television programs overall. One-fifth (20%) of the episodes reviewed included a portrayal of sexual intercourse, but nearly half (45%) of those included a reference to sexual risk or responsibility. The study's authors noted that while "the effect of viewing sexual content is not thought to be direct and powerful, with a single exposure to a particular program leading a viewer to think or act in any given way," television clearly does influence teenagers' decisions about sex, or their "sexual socialization."

Sexual Activity and Substance Use

Over the years, a number of studies have suggested a link between substance use and sexual activity. Researchers have found that both sexual activity and a history of multiple partners correlated with some use of drugs, alcohol, and cigarettes. However, the 2003 *Youth Risk Behavior Survey* found that among sexually active students, only one-fourth (25.4%) reported they had used alcohol or drugs at the time of their last sexual experience. (See Table 7.2.) Males (29.8%) were more likely than females (21%) to report this behavior; African-Americans (19.5%) were somewhat less likely than Hispanics (24.1%) or whites (26.8%) to report using alcohol or drugs during sexual activity.

A 2002 report in the *Journal of Adolescent Health* (J. Guo et al., "Developmental Relationships between Adolescent Substance Use and Risky Sexual Behavior in Young Adulthood," vol. 31, no. 4) noted a link between adolescent binge drinking and marijuana use and risky sexual behavior. Young people who used marijuana or binge drank in high school were more likely at age twenty-one to have had more sexual partners and to use condoms inconsistently.

In *Substance Abuse and Risky Sexual Behavior* (February 2002), the Kaiser Family Foundation reported on a

FIGURE 7.1

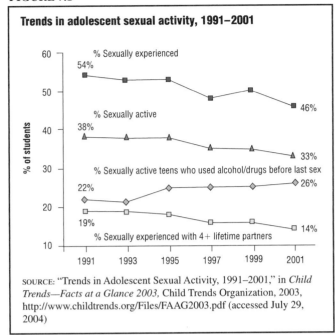

Trends in adolescent sexual activity, 1991–2001

SOURCE: "Trends in Adolescent Sexual Activity, 1991–2001," in *Child Trends—Facts at a Glance 2003,* Child Trends Organization, 2003, http://www.childtrends.org/Files/FAAG2003.pdf (accessed July 29, 2004)

FIGURE 7.2

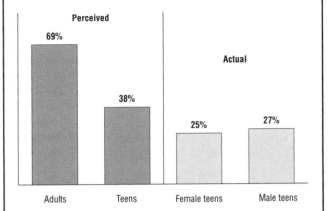

Perceived versus real age at first sex (age at which people become "sexually experienced"), 1990s

(Percent who were believed to have had sex by age 15 years and percent of teens who were actually sexually experienced by that age)

These data are reported in the source listed below. Two Kaiser Family Foundation surveys were the basis for the data on adult and teen perceptions. Data on actual sexual experience are from two U.S. Department of Health and Human Services surveys, the National Survey of Family Growth and the National Survey of Adolescent Males.

SOURCE: "Perceived vs. Real Age at First Sex among Parents and Teens in the 1990s," in *Child Trends—Facts at a Glance 2001,* Child Trends Organization, August 2001, http://www.childtrends.org/Files/FAAG2001.pdf (accessed August 6, 2004)

survey of almost a thousand teens and young adults from November 2001 through January 2002. More than a quarter (29%) of sexually active fifteen- to seventeen-year-olds surveyed said that alcohol or drugs had influenced their sexual decisions. (See Figure 7.3.) More than one in ten (12%) sexually active fifteen-year-year-olds reported having had unprotected sex while under the influence of drugs or alcohol. Two out of five of these (41%) said their peers drank or used drugs before having sex "a lot" of the time.

VOLUNTARY AND NONVOLUNTARY EXPERIENCES. The 1995 National Survey of Family Growth asked women whether their first sexual experience was voluntary. Nearly one out of every ten women ages fifteen to twenty-four (9%) reported that their first premarital intercourse was nonvoluntary (reported as either "not voluntary" or "rape"). The first experience for 24% of females who had sexual intercourse by age fourteen was described as not voluntary, compared with 10% of women whose first sexual experience occurred at nineteen to twenty-four years of age (*Family Planning Perspectives*, January/February 1998). Frequently these girls were coerced into having unwanted relations by a date. Other girls were raped, either by an acquaintance or a family member.

Additionally, in a study of four thousand high school students, almost a third of the girls (30.2%) and a tenth of the boys (9.3%) reported having been sexually abused. Sexually abused females were twice as likely to engage in early sexual intercourse and other risky sexual behaviors as girls who had not been abused (A. Raj et al., "The Relationship between Sexual Abuse and Sexual Risk among High School Students: Findings from the 1997 Massachusetts Youth Risk Behavior Survey," *Maternal and Child*

Health Journal, vol. 4, 2000). A study published in 2004 corroborated evidence of the increased sexual risks taken by sexually abused youth (Elizabeth M. Saewyc et al., "Teenage Pregnancy and Associated Risk Behaviors among Sexually Abused Adolescents," *Perspectives on Sexual and Reproductive Health*, vol. 26, May/June 2004).

Moreover, according to Child Trends, a Washington, D.C.-based nonprofit research organization dedicated to improving the lives of children, early sexual initiation for teenage girls has been linked to a higher risk of becoming the victim of rape or sexual assault at some later time during their adolescence. The October 1997 publication *Facts at a Glance* indicated that more than half (54%) of females fourteen or younger at first sexual intercourse reported experiencing nonvoluntary sex at some point during their teen years. Early sexual initiation has also been linked to domestic violence and verbal abuse later in life (Vaughn I. Rickert, "The Relationship among Demographics, Reproductive Characteristics, and Intimate Partner Violence," *American Journal of Obstetrics and Gynecology,* October 2002) and to depression and low self-esteem (B. C. Miller, B. H. Monson, and M. C. Norton, "The Effects of Forced Sexual Intercourse on White Female Adolescents," *Child Abuse and Neglect,* vol. 19, 1995).

CONTRACEPTIVE USE

Too Few Use Contraceptives

In its 2003 *Youth Risk Behavior Survey* the CDC found that almost two-thirds of sexually active teenagers (63%)

TABLE 7.2

Percentage of high school students who had drunk alcohol or used drugs before last sexual intercourse[1]; were ever pregnant or got someone pregnant; and were taught about AIDS/HIV in school, by sex, race, ethnicity, and grade, 2003

Category	Alcohol or drug use before last sexual intercourse			Had been pregnant or gotten someone pregnant			Taught in school about AIDS or HIV infection		
	Female %	Male %	Total %	Female %	Male %	Total %	Female %	Male %	Total %
Race/ethnicity									
White[2]	23.6	30.5	**26.8**	2.8	1.7	**2.3**	90.6	90.1	**90.3**
Black[2]	14.6	23.8	**19.5**	10.4	7.6	**9.1**	87.5	82.5	**85.1**
Hispanic	18.8	29.5	**24.1**	7.3	5.2	**6.4**	83.9	82.8	**83.4**
Grade									
9	23.9	24.7	**24.4**	2.3	2.8	**2.6**	85.4	83.2	**84.3**
10	23.1	30.5	**26.8**	5.0	3.6	**4.3**	90.5	88.0	**89.2**
11	21.0	28.8	**24.7**	5.3	3.2	**4.3**	89.7	88.9	**89.3**
12	17.6	33.5	**25.2**	7.6	4.7	**6.2**	90.3	90.3	**90.3**
Total	**21.0**	**29.8**	**25.4**	**4.9**	**3.5**	**4.2**	**88.7**	**87.2**	**87.9**

[1]Among currently sexually active students.
[2]Non-Hispanic.

SOURCE: "Table 46. Percentage of High School Students Who Had Drunk Alcohol or Used Drugs before Last Sexual Intercourse; Were Ever Pregnant or Got Someone Pregnant; and Were Taught about Acquired Immunodeficiency Syndrome (AIDS) or Human Immunodeficiency Virus (HIV) Infection in School, by Sex, Race/Ethnicity, and Grade," in "Youth Risk Behavior Surveillance—United States, 2003," *Centers for Disease Control and Prevention Surveillance Summaries: Morbidity and Mortality Weekly Report,* vol. 53, no. SS-02, May 21, 2004, http://www.cdc.gov/mmwr/PDF/SS/SS5302.pdf (accessed September 16, 2004)

reported that they or their partners used condoms during their last sexual intercourse, up from 46.2% in 1991, when the CDC began tracking condom use. (See Table 7.1.) Young African-Americans reported the highest condom use (72.8%) among sexually active youth, up from 48% in 1991. Hispanic students reported the lowest rate of condom use (57.4%), but this was still significantly higher than the 1991 rate of 37.4%. Males (68.8%) were significantly more likely than females (57.4%) to report condom use. The use of condoms decreased from the ninth grade (69%) to the twelfth grade (57.4%), a period during which the frequency of sexual intercourse increased.

Among sexually active students nationwide in 2003, 17% reported they or their partners used birth control pills ("the Pill") prior to their last sexual intercourse. (See Table 7.1.) More white students (22.3%) reported using birth control pills than either Hispanic (11.2%) or African-American students (7.9%). This disparity may be due to the need for a prescription for birth control pills; white students tend to have greater access to medical care than minority students do. Birth control pill use increased between ninth (8.7%) and twelfth grade (22.6%).

A Decade of Tracking Teen Condom Use

CDC researchers noted in 2002 that an increase in condom use among teenagers at last intercourse from 1991 to 2001 was mirrored by a decrease in the percentages of high school students who had ever had intercourse or who had had multiple sex partners. Such safer sexual behaviors in turn corresponded to a decrease in gonorrhea, pregnancy, and birth rates among adolescents. The

FIGURE 7.3

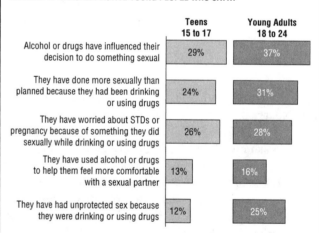

Percent of 15- to 17-year-old adolescents reporting risky sexual behavior while drinking or using drugs, 2002

PERCENT OF SEXUALLY ACTIVE YOUNG PEOPLE WHO SAY...

	Teens 15 to 17	Young Adults 18 to 24
Alcohol or drugs have influenced their decision to do something sexual	29%	37%
They have done more sexually than planned because they had been drinking or using drugs	24%	31%
They have worried about STDs or pregnancy because of something they did sexually while drinking or using drugs	26%	28%
They have used alcohol or drugs to help them feel more comfortable with a sexual partner	13%	16%
They have had unprotected sex because they were drinking or using drugs	12%	25%

SOURCE: "Substance Use and Risky Sexual Activity," (#3214), in *Sexual Activity and Substance Use among Youth,* The Henry J. Kaiser Family Foundation, February 2002, http://www.kff.org/youthhivstds/loader. cfm?url=/commonspot/security/getfile.cfm&PageID = 14907 (accessed September 16, 2004). This information is reprinted with permission from the Henry J. Kaiser Family Foundation. The Kaiser Family Foundation, based in Menlo Park, California, is a nonprofit, independent national healthcare philanthropy and is not associated with Kaiser Permanente or Kaiser Industries.

CDC added that these "improvements in health outcomes probably resulted from the combined efforts of parents and families, schools, community organizations that serve young persons, healthcare providers, religious organiza-

FIGURE 7.4

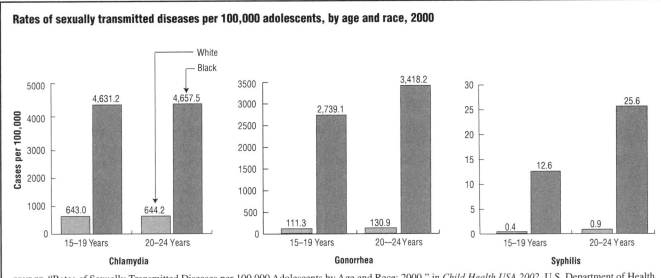

Rates of sexually transmitted diseases per 100,000 adolescents, by age and race, 2000

SOURCE: "Rates of Sexually Transmitted Diseases per 100,000 Adolescents by Age and Race: 2000," in *Child Health USA 2002*, U.S. Department of Health and Human Services, Maternal and Child Health Bureau, November 2002, http://www.mchb.hrsa.gov/chusa02/main_pages/page_37.htm (accessed September 16, 2004)

tions, the media, and government agencies to reduce sexual risks among young persons."

Reasons for Use or Nonuse

Research indicates that adolescents' attitudes and beliefs about condoms determine whether or not they will use them. In 2000 the Henry J. Kaiser Family Foundation joined together with *Seventeen* magazine on a campaign called *SexSmarts,* which was designed "to provide young people with information and resources on sexual health issues." As part of the program, a survey of 519 teens ages twelve to seventeen was conducted in September 2000 on safe sex, including condoms and the Pill. Students were asked how important various factors were in choosing a method of birth control or protection. The three highest-ranking factors were pregnancy prevention (92%), HIV/AIDS and sexually transmitted disease prevention (88%), and "what my partner wants to use" (83%).

The survey also showed that teens did not completely understand the importance of using condoms consistently to avoid sexually transmitted diseases including HIV/AIDS. Eleven percent agreed with the statement "having sex without a condom every now and then is not that big of a deal," and 9% believed that "if you don't have a lot of partners you don't need to use condoms." More than one in five teens (22%) and one in four teenage females (25%) agreed with the statement "condoms break so often they are not worth using."

SEXUALLY TRANSMITTED DISEASES

Adolescents and young adults have a higher risk of acquiring sexually transmitted diseases (STDs) than older adults. Female adolescents may have an increased suscep-

tibility to chlamydia, a bacterial infection that can cause pelvic inflammatory disease and is a contributing factor in the transmission of HIV. In 2002 chlamydia was the most common sexually transmitted disease among adolescents. It was also more common in adolescents than in any other age group, with 2,619.1 cases among every one hundred thousand fifteen- to nineteen-year-old girls. This group also had the highest rates of gonorrhea infection, although the rate of gonorrhea among fifteen- to nineteen-year-olds had decreased from 542.4 per one hundred thousand in 1998 to 476.4 per one hundred thousand in 2002. Syphilis was far less common in teens, with only 2.3 cases per one hundred thousand reported in 2000. As Figure 7.4 shows, African-American non-Hispanic teens had much higher rates of STDs than white non-Hispanic teens.

A 2004 study emphasized that half of all new HIV infections in the United States are diagnosed in people under twenty-five years old (Kathleen J. Sikkema et al., "HIV Risk Behavior among Ethnically Diverse Adolescents Living in Low-Income Housing Developments," *Journal of Adolescent Health,* vol. 35, 2004). Most of these young people become infected through sexual activity. The authors found that the risk of HIV infection was highest among older adolescents who believed their partners did not see a need to practice safer sex and among teens who abused drugs and alcohol. The researchers suggested that study results could be used to design prevention programs for those adolescents most at risk.

Another 2004 study in *Archives of Pediatrics and Adolescent Medicine* tested whether parental involvement had any impact on rates of STDs among low-income African-American adolescent girls (J. A. Bettinger et al., "Does Parental Involvement Predict New Sexually Transmitted Diseases in Female Adolescents?"). Researchers found that when these high-risk teens perceived their parents as exercising a high degree of supervision over their activities, they had lower rates of both gonorrhea and chlamydia infection.

TEEN CHILDBEARING TRENDS

The 2003 *Youth Risk Behavior Survey* found that 4.2% of students had been pregnant or had gotten someone pregnant. (See Table 7.1.) African-Americans (9.1%) were more likely than Hispanics (6.4%) or whites (2.3%) to have been pregnant or gotten someone pregnant. Pregnancy reports increased with grade level, with 2.6% of ninth graders and 6.2% of twelfth graders reporting having been pregnant or gotten someone pregnant.

Teen Birth Rate Falling

The National Center for Health Statistics (NCHS) reported that birth rates among American girls aged fifteen to nineteen dropped from 61.8 per one thousand girls in 1991 to 43 per one thousand in 2002. (See Figure 7.5.) A 2004 report, "Can Changes in Sexual Behaviors among High School Students Explain the Decline in Teen Pregnancy Rates in the 1990s?" in the *Journal of Adolescent Health* (August 2004), found that both later ages at first intercourse and improved contraceptive practice contributed equally to the decline in pregnancy rates over the period.

Available data by race show that the greatest percentage decline in births between 1991 and 2002 was among African-American teens ages fifteen to nineteen, down from 118.2 births per one thousand in 1991 to 68.3 in 2002, although the 2002 rate remains high. (See Figure 7.6.) The Hispanic rate in that age group in 2002 was even higher (83.4 births per one thousand), even though it had declined from the 1991 rate of 104.6. Non-Hispanic white teens fifteen to nineteen years old had a birth rate of 28.5 in 2002, down from 43.4 in 1991. The rate for Native American teens dropped from 84.1 in 1991 to 53.8 in 2002, and for Asian/Pacific Islander teens, from 27.3 in 1991 to 18.3 in 2002.

Trends in Marital and Nonmarital Births

According to the CDC, the number of marital births (babies born to parents married to each other) dropped dramatically during the 1980s, while the number of nonmarital (out-of-wedlock) births rose steadily to a record high of 44.1 per one thousand unmarried women in 2000. That rate dropped to 43.7 births per one thousand unmarried women in 2002.

The rate of nonmarital births among teens has risen dramatically. In 1960 15.3 babies were born to every one thousand unmarried fifteen- to nineteen-year-olds. In 1994 that rate had risen to 46.9 births per one thousand before declining to 35.4 in 2002. However, births to unmarried teens have risen even more sharply when taken

FIGURE 7.5

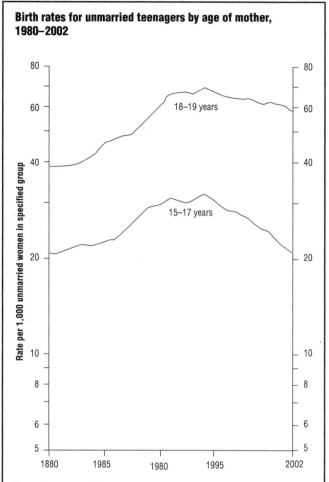

Birth rates for unmarried teenagers by age of mother, 1980–2002

Notes: Rates are plotted on a log scale. Rates for 1991–2001 have been revised and may differ from those previously published.

SOURCE: Adapted from "Figure 6. Birth Rates for Unmarried Women, by Age of Mother: United States, 1980–2002," in *Births: Final Data for 2002,* National Vital Statistics Reports, vol. 52, no. 10, National Center for Health Statistics, 2002, http://www.cdc.gov/nchs/data/nvsr/nvsr52/nvsr52_10.pdf (accessed September 16, 2004)

as a percentage of all births to teenage women. Among teenage mothers fifteen to nineteen years old, the proportion of nonmarital births rose from 14.8% of all teen births in 1960 to 80% in 2002. Since the mid-1980s the majority of births to teens at every age have occurred outside of marriage.

Health Consequences for Teen Mothers and Their Children

Teenage mothers and their babies face more health risks than older women and their children. Teenagers who become pregnant are more likely than older women to be anemic and malnourished and to suffer from pregnancy-induced hypertension and eclampsia (a life-threatening condition that sometimes results in convulsions and/or coma). An immature pelvis can cause prolonged or difficult labor, possibly resulting in bladder or bowel damage to the mother, infant brain damage, or even death of moth-

FIGURE 7.6

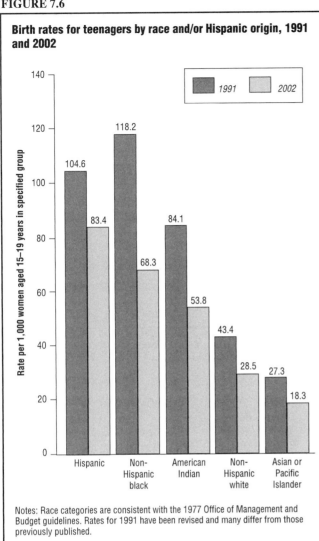

Birth rates for teenagers by race and/or Hispanic origin, 1991 and 2002

Notes: Race categories are consistent with the 1977 Office of Management and Budget guidelines. Rates for 1991 have been revised and many differ from those previously published.

SOURCE: "Figure 1. Birth Rates for Teenagers by Race and/or Hispanic Origin for 1991 and 2002," in *Births: Final Data for 2002,* National Vital Statistics Reports, vol. 52, no. 10, National Center for Health Statistics, 2002, http://www.cdc.gov/nchs/data/nvsr/nvsr52/nvsr52_10.pdf (accessed September 16, 2004)

One," *Perspectives on Sexual and Reproductive Health,* vol. 35, January–February 2003).

Consequences of Early Motherhood

Few teenage mothers are ready for the emotional, psychological, and financial responsibilities and challenges of parenthood. Becoming a parent at a young age usually cuts short a teenage mother's education, limiting her ability to support herself and her child. According to an article in *Family Planning Perspectives* (Sandra L. Hofferth, "The Effects of Early Childbearing on Schooling Over Time," November–December 2001), women who gave birth as teens in the early 1990s had only a 65% probability of graduating from high school, and only a 29% probability of completing some college. Another *Family Planning Perspectives* report in the same issue (Susheela Singh et al., "Socioeconomic Disadvantage and Adolescent Women's Sexual and Reproductive Behavior: The Case of Five Developed Countries") noted that 40% of American women ages twenty to twenty-four who gave birth before age twenty had an income of less than 149% of the federal poverty guideline.

In 1996 President Bill Clinton signed into law the Personal Responsibility and Work Opportunity Reconciliation Act (PL 104–193), which abolished the sixty-year-old Aid to Families with Dependent Children (AFDC) program and created the Temporary Assistance for Needy Families (TANF) block grant program. In order to be eligible for TANF benefits, unmarried minor parents are required to remain in high school or its equivalent and to live with a parent or in an adult-supervised setting. One provision in the law allows for the creation of second-chance homes for teen parents and their children. These homes require that all residents either enroll in school or participate in a job-training program. They also provide parenting and life-skills classes, as well as counseling and support services.

er and/or child. CDC data show that in nearly one-third of live births to women under twenty in 1997, the mother received delayed (30.2%) or no (2.1%) prenatal care. Poor prenatal care can increase the risk of undetected complications of pregnancy that can lead to illness and/or death.

While most health risks are similar for children born to teenage and older mothers, teenage mothers may have a higher prevalence of certain risk factors. According to the CDC, for example, teenagers had the highest rates of smoking during pregnancy (17.5% for those ages fifteen to nineteen) of all pregnant women (12.3% among all ages) over the period 1990–99, and smokers were nearly twice as likely to have low-birthweight babies as nonsmokers. Researchers have also found that babies born to adolescents have a greater risk of dying between one and twelve months after birth (M. Klitsch, "Youngest Mothers' Infants Have Greatly Elevated Risk of Dying by Age

ADOLESCENT AND NONADOLESCENT FATHERS

Adolescent fathers were more likely than their childless peers to perform poorly in school, to drop out, to have few financial resources, and to have poor employment prospects. They were more likely than teen mothers to have more than one child and less likely to have an ongoing relationship with the mother of the first child.

In 2002 fifteen- to nineteen-year-old males had a birth rate of 17.4 per one thousand males in the age group, down from a high of 24.7 in 1991. This rate was substantially lower than the rate for teenage girls of 43 per one thousand. The rate was higher for African-American teens (33.3) than for white teens (14.8). The data suggest that many teen mothers had older partners (*National Vital Statistics Reports,* vol. 52, no. 10, December 17, 2003). In "Adolescent Pregnancy—Current Trends and Issues:

1998" (*Pediatrics*, 1999), the American Academy of Pediatrics Committee on Adolescence reported that nearly two-thirds of teen mothers had partners older than twenty. In its publication *2003 Facts at a Glance*, the organization Child Trends reported that 38% of births to mothers age eighteen and younger were to fathers four or more years older than the mother. In some cases teen mothers have been sexually abused by their older partners.

Such studies have alerted officials who design programs for the prevention of pregnancy and STDs to the need to pay attention not only to preadolescent and adolescent males, but also to older males who are partners of teenage girls. Because these men are typically out of the public school system, officials agree that programs must be broader in scope.

TEEN ABORTION

According to an article in *Perspectives on Sexual and Reproductive Health,* 1,313,300 legal induced abortions were performed in 2000, representing an 11% reduction in the abortion rate since 1994. About 18.6% of those legal abortions were performed on women under the age of twenty. (See Table 7.3.) Although the number of abortions for U.S. teens rose from 1975 to 1980, the number has decreased dramatically since 1988. (See Figure 7.7.)

In 2000 the overall abortion ratio (number of abortions per one thousand live births) was 232. The younger the pregnant woman, the higher the abortion ratio. (See Figure 7.8.) Although less than 1% of all abortions were obtained by teenagers younger than fifteen years of age, their abortion ratio (708 per one thousand live births) was the highest. This finding shows that while the actual number of abortions in this age group was small, a significantly large proportion of adolescents younger than fifteen who got pregnant chose abortion. Women ages fifteen to nineteen and women over age forty had the next highest ratios of abortions to live births. Since not all states require reporting the age of women who obtain legal abortions, however, complete data for adolescents are not available.

States have varying laws on parental involvement in minors' abortion decisions. According to the Alan Guttmacher Institute, as of July 1, 2004, seventeen states and the District of Columbia required no parental involvement in minors' abortions. Thirty-three states required some parental involvement; nineteen required parental consent and fourteen required parental notification. All of these states except Utah have an alternative judicial process for minors seeking an abortion.

HOMOSEXUALITY

Just the Facts about Sexual Orientation and Youth, a pamphlet for school personnel put together by several organizations, including the American Academy of Pediatrics,

FIGURE 7.7

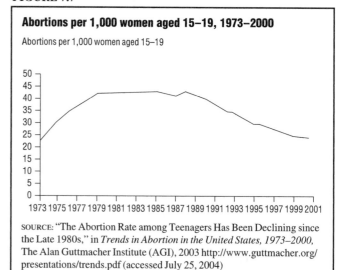

Abortions per 1,000 women aged 15–19, 1973–2000

Abortions per 1,000 women aged 15–19

SOURCE: "The Abortion Rate among Teenagers Has Been Declining since the Late 1980s," in *Trends in Abortion in the United States, 1973–2000,* The Alan Guttmacher Institute (AGI), 2003 http://www.guttmacher.org/presentations/trends.pdf (accessed July 25, 2004)

FIGURE 7.8

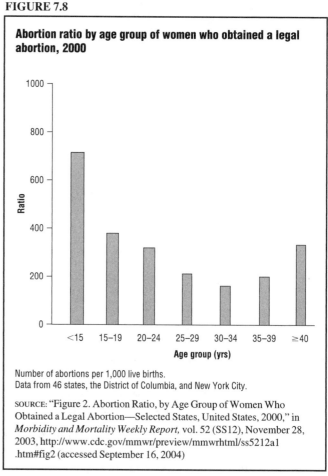

Abortion ratio by age group of women who obtained a legal abortion, 2000

Number of abortions per 1,000 live births.
Data from 46 states, the District of Columbia, and New York City.

SOURCE: "Figure 2. Abortion Ratio, by Age Group of Women Who Obtained a Legal Abortion—Selected States, United States, 2000," in *Morbidity and Mortality Weekly Report,* vol. 52 (SS12), November 28, 2003, http://www.cdc.gov/mmwr/preview/mmwrhtml/ss5212a1.htm#fig2 (accessed September 16, 2004)

the American Psychological Association, and the National Education Association, stressed that sexual orientation is one aspect of the identity of adolescents—not a mental disorder. According to the publication, sexual orientation is developed across a lifetime and along a continuum; in other words, teens are not necessarily simply homosexual or heterosexual, but may feel varying degrees of attraction to people of both genders. The pamphlet stressed that gay, les-

TABLE 7.3

Percentage distribution of women obtaining abortions, by demographic characteristics, 1994 and 2000

Characteristic	Women having abortions		Women aged 15–44, 2000	Abortion rate*			Pregnancies, 2000	
	2000	1994	2000	2000	1994	% change	Rate†	% ending in abortion
Total	100.0	100.0	100.0	21	24	−11	87	25
Age								
<15	0.7	1.2	u	u	u	u	u	u
15–19	18.6	20.6	16.0	25	34‡	−27	72	34
15–17	6.5	8.8	9.5	15	24‡	−39	42	35
18–19	12.0	11.5	6.5	39	48‡	−18	119	33
20–24	33.0	32.8	15.1	47	52	−9	159	29
25–29	23.1	21.4	15.6	32	32	0	153	21
30–34	13.5	14.4	16.5	17	18	−5	112	16
35–39	8.1	7.5	18.5	9	10	3	50	19
≥40§	3.1	2.3	18.4	4	3	10	11	31
Marital status								
Married	17.0	18.4	47.7	8	9	−14	99	8.
Previously married**	15.6	17.1	11.5	29	32	−11	67	43
Never-married	67.3	64.4	40.8	35	41	−14	79	45
Cohabiting‡‡								
Yes	30.7	20.5	18.7	55	57	−3	u	u
No	69.3	79.5	81.3	29	36	−20	u	u
No. of live births								
0	39.1	45.4	42.8	19	26	−25	81	24
1	27.4	24.7	18.0	32	33	−2	151	22
≥2	33.5	29.9	39.2	18	18	2	64	28
Residence								
Metropolitan	88.0	88.5	78.8	24	27	−11	u	u
Nonmetropolitan	12.0	11.5	21.2	12	13	−10	u	u
Poverty status‡‡								
<100%	26.6	25.4	12.8	44	36§§	25	133	33
100–199%	30.8	24.4	17.5	38	31§§	23	115	33
200–299%	18.0	18.9	17.9	21	25§§	−13	87	24
≥300%	24.6	31.3	51.8	10	16§§	−39	66	15
Medicaid coverage								
Yes	24.2	26.5	9.0	57	50	14	u	u
No	75.8	73.5	91.0	18	20	−12	u	u
Race/ethnicity								
Non-Hispanic								
White	40.9	48.0	68.2	13	16	−20	73	18
Black	31.7	30.0	13.7	49	54	−8	115	43
Asian/Pacific Islander	6.4	4.4	4.4	31	28	11	88	35
Native American	0.9	1.2	0.9	u	u	u	u	u
Hispanic	2.1	16.5*†	12.8	33	37*†	−10	132	25
Education*‡								
Not H.S. graduate	12.7	12.0	11.2	23	22	7	85	27
H.S. graduate/GED	30.3	30.4	30.9	20	20	1	73	27
Some college	40.6	40.3	32.5	26	29	−12	68	38
College graduate	16.4	17.3	25.5	13	19	−30	63	21
Religion*§								
Protestant	42.8	37.4	51.0	18	17	10	u	u
Catholic	27.4	31.3	27.5	22	25	−13	u	u
Other	7.6	7.6	5.4	31	30	2	u	u
None	22.2	23.7	16.2	30	46	−35	u	u

*Number of abortions per 1,000 women in relevant subgroup.
†Sum of births and abortions per 1,000 women aged 15–44.
‡Differs from previously published figures, which were based on state abortion reports.
§Denominator is women aged 40–44.
**Includes separated women.
††Based on single women only.
‡‡Percentage of federal poverty level.
§§Previously published AGI estimates of abortion rates by poverty status (reference 1) were inaccurate because of a programming error.
*†Previously published for Hispanics (references 1 and 7) have been adjusted according to state abortion reports.
*‡Limited to women older than 19.
*§Limited to women older than 17. u=unavailable.

SOURCE: Rachel K. Jones, Jacqueline E. Darroch, and Stanley K. Henshaw, "Table 1. Percentage Distribution of Women Obtaining Abortions in 2000 and 1994, and of All U.S. Women Aged 15–44 in 2000; Estimated Abortion Rates for 2000 and 1994, and Percentage Change in the Rate between the Two Years; and Pregnancy Rate and Proportion of Pregnancies Ending in Abortion in 2000—All by Selected Characteristics at Outcome," reproduced with the permission of The Alan Guttmacher Institute from "Patterns in the Socioeconomic Characteristics of Women Obtaining Abortions in 2000–02," *Perspectives on Sexual and Reproductive Health,* New York, AGI, vol. 34, no. 5, September/October 2002, p. 228, http://www.guttmacher.org/pubs/journals/3422602.pdf (accessed September 16, 2004

bian, and bisexual adolescents face prejudice and discrimination that negatively affect their educational experiences and emotional and physical health. Their legitimate fear of being hurt as a result of disclosing their sexuality often leads to a feeling of isolation. All of these factors account for lesbian, gay, and bisexual adolescents' higher rates of emotional distress, suicide attempts, risky sexual behavior, and substance use. The authors stress the need for school personnel to be as open and accepting as possible in order to support these adolescents.

STD AND PREGNANCY PREVENTION PROGRAMS FOR TEENS

Abstinence

In response to the growing concern about out-of-wedlock births and the threat of AIDS, several national youth organizations and religious groups began campaigns in the early and mid-1990s to encourage teens to sign an abstinence pledge—a promise to abstain from sexual activity until marriage. In January 2001 researchers at Columbia and Yale universities released a study finding that by 1995 2.5 million teens (10% of adolescent boys and 16% of girls) had taken a "virginity pledge" ("Virginity Pledge Helps Teens Delay Sexual Activity," National Institutes of Health News Release, January 5, 2001). The analysis showed that, on average, teens who took the pledge delayed having sex about one-third longer than teens who had not pledged. However, the effectiveness of pledging depended on the student's age. Among teens aged eighteen and older, pledging had no effect. Among sixteen and seventeen year olds, pledgers delayed sex about eighteen months longer than those who did not pledge. Among the youngest teens, the effect of pledging depended on the social environment of the teen's school.

The 2003 *Youth Risk Behavior Survey* found that 65.7% of high school students—65.4% of females and 66.2% of males—claimed to be sexually inactive at the time of the survey (no sexual intercourse during the three months prior to the survey). (See Table 7.1.) The rate of inactivity was higher among younger students (78.8% of ninth graders and 51.1% of twelfth graders). More white students (69.2%) were sexually inactive than Hispanic (62.9%) or African-American students (51%).

The administration of President George W. Bush placed a new stress on abstinence among teens. According to the February 2002 White House report *Working toward Independence,* an overview of President Bush's suggested plan for welfare reform, "the goal of Federal policy should be to emphasize abstinence as the only certain way to avoid both unintended pregnancies and STDs." As of July 15, 2003, sixty-two Adolescent Family Life abstinence education programs were funded by the Department of Health and Human Services. The directorship of the programs was transferred to the Administration for

Children and Families Family and Youth Services Bureau on June 9, 2004. In fiscal year 2004 $33 million was available for making grants to provide abstinence education to adolescents.

Sex and STD/HIV Education in Schools

As of July 1, 2004, thirty-eight states and the District of Columbia required schools to provide education on HIV/AIDS and other STDs. (See Table 7.4.) Thirty-six of these states and the District of Columbia allowed parents to remove their children from sex education classes. Twenty-two states and the District of Columbia required schools to provide education on sexuality in addition to HIV/AIDS and STD education. Twelve states did not have laws requiring schools to provide sex or STD/HIV education. Twenty-one states required schools to stress the importance of abstinence in STD and HIV/AIDS education; nine states required abstinence to be covered. (Michigan passed a law in June 2004 that abstinence must be not only covered, but stressed, effective in 2005.) Seventeen states required schools to teach students about contraception, but none required that it be stressed.

The CDC reported that, as of December 31, 2002, 5,108 adolescents thirteen to nineteen years of age had been diagnosed with AIDS since the beginning of the epidemic. In addition, because of the long dormancy period of the virus (an average of ten years), many people who are diagnosed in their twenties were infected during their adolescent years. According to *Child Health USA 2002,* about 58% of adolescent AIDS cases were males and 42% were females. Most males contracted the virus through homosexual activities, clotting products (for hemophilia), or blood transfusions. Most females contracted the virus through heterosexual contact or IV drug use (either their own drug use or drug use by their partners).

In 2000 the Henry J. Kaiser Family Foundation conducted a survey of teens on topics related to HIV and AIDS. The survey found that about one in five teens (21%) was either not sure if there was an AIDS cure or believed there was one. Most adolescents knew sharing IV needles (92%) and having unprotected sex (91%) increases the risk of infection, but smaller numbers were aware of the risk from unprotected oral sex (69%) or from partners with another STD (41%). Only half (51%) knew there were drug treatments available that could lengthen an AIDS patient's life. When asked how much they had learned about AIDS/HIV in school, 78% of students responded either "some" or "a lot." Still, more than half of the teens wanted more information about how to protect themselves from HIV infection (57%) and where to go to get tested for HIV (55%).

According to the *Youth Risk Behavior Survey* report of 1997, 91.5% of all students were taught about AIDS or HIV in school that year. A slightly lower percentage of stu-

TABLE 7.4

State sex and STD/HIV education policy, July 2004

State	Sex education Mandated	If taught, content required Abstinence	Contraception	STD/HIV education Mandated	If taught, content required Abstinence	Contraception	Parental role Consent required	Opt-out permitted
Alabama		Stress	Cover	X	Stress	Cover		X*
Alaska	X			X				
Arizona		Stress			Stress		X^a	X^a
Arkansas		Stress			Stress			
California		Cover	Cover	X	Stress	Cover		X
Colorado								X
Connecticut		Cover		X				X
Delaware	X	Cover	Cover	X	Cover	Cover		
Dist. of Columbia	X		Cover	X				X
Florida	X	Cover		X				X
Georgia	X	Cover		X	Cover			X
Hawaii	X	Stress	Cover	X	Stress	Cover		
Idaho								X
Illinois	X	Stress	Cover^a	X	Cover			X
Indiana		Stress		X	Stress			
Iowa	X			X				X
Kansas	X			X				X
Kentucky	X	Cover		X	Cover			
Louisiana		Stress			Stress			X
Maine	X	Stress	Cover	X	Stress	Cover		X
Maryland	X	Stress	Cover	X	Stress	Cover		X*
Massachusetts								X
Michigan		Cover		X	Cover			X
Minnesota	X	Stress		X	Cover			X
Mississippi^c		Stress			Stress			X
Missouri		Stress	Cover	X	Stress	Cover		X
Montana								X†
Nebraska								
Nevada	X						X	
New Hampshire				X				
New Jersey	X	Stress		X	Stress			X*
New Mexico				X	Stress	Cover		
New York				X	Stress	Cover		X^a
North Carolina	X	Stress		X	Stress			X
North Dakota				X				
Ohio				X	Stress			X
Oklahoma		Stress		X	Cover	Cover		X
Oregon		Stress	Cover	X	Stress	Cover		X
Pennsylvania				X	Stress			X*,†
Rhode Island	X	Stress	Cover	X	Stress	Cover		X
South Carolina	X	Stress	Cover	X	Stress	Cover		X
South Dakota^d								
Tennessee	X	Stress		X	Stress			X
Texas		Stress			Stress			X
Utah^◊	X	Stress		X	Stress		X	
Vermont	X	Cover	Cover	X	Cover	Cover		X*
Virginia		Cover	Cover		Cover	Cover		X
Washington				X	Stress	Cover		X
West Virginia	X	Stress	Cover	X	Stress	Cover		X
Wisconsin				X				
Wyoming	X			X				
Total in effect	**22 + DC**	**21 Stress 9 Cover**	**14 + DC Cover**	**38 + DC**	**25 Stress 9 Cover**	**17 Cover**	**3**	**36 + DC**

*Parents' removal of student must be based on religious or moral beliefs.
^a In AZ, MT, NY and PA, opt-out is only permitted for STD education, including instruction on HIV/AIDS; in AZ, parental consent is required only for sex education.
^b IL has a broad law mandating comprehensive health education, including abstinence instruction; a more specific second law requires a school district that elects to provide the specific sex education package to stress abstinence and cover contraception.
^c Localities may override state requirements for sex education topics, including abstinence; state prohibits including material that "contradicts the required components."
^d Abstinence is taught within state-mandated character education.
^e State prohibits teachers from responding to students' spontaneous questions in ways that conflict with the law's requirements.

SOURCE: "State Sex and STD/HIV Education Policy," in *State Policies in Brief,* The Alan Guttmacher Institute (AGI), 2004, http://www.guttmacher.org/statecenter/spibs/spib_SE.pdf (accessed July 25, 2004)

dents (87.9%) reported in 2003 that they had learned about the disease in school. As HIV/AIDS is increasingly common among young people, the declining percentages of students who learn about the disease in school is problematic.

CHAPTER 8
JUVENILE CRIME AND VICTIMIZATION

For some young people, growing up can be troubling. While their peers are playing football, going to proms, and making plans for adulthood, a certain percentage of juveniles, for whatever reason, have brushes with the law. Each state has its own definition of the term juvenile: most states put the upper age limit at seventeen years old, although some states set it as low as fourteen. In reporting national crime statistics, the Federal Bureau of Investigation (FBI) considers people under eighteen to be juveniles. The FBI often breaks its juvenile crime statistics down into age-based subcategories, such as sixteen or older and fifteen or younger, to demonstrate how juvenile offenses vary with age.

ARRESTS

According to Howard N. Snyder's "Juvenile Arrests 2001" (*Juvenile Justice Bulletin,* U.S. Department of Justice, Office of Juvenile Justice and Delinquency Prevention, December 2003), in 2001 there were an estimated 2.3 million arrests of people under age eighteen. (See Table 8.1.) Juveniles made up 17% of all arrests and 15% of violent crime arrests. Property crimes—burglary, larceny-theft, motor vehicle theft, and arson—accounted for 21.6% of juvenile arrests; drug or liquor law violations accounted for 15%; violent crimes accounted for 4.2% of arrests; and the rest were for a wide variety of offenses including fraud, vandalism, prostitution, offenses against family and children, and vagrancy.

Beginning in the late 1980s and peaking in 1994, there was considerable growth in the number of arrests of juveniles for violent crimes. (See Figure 8.1.) After 1994 the number began to decline, falling 44% between 1994 and 2001. The 2001 juvenile violent crime arrest rate was the lowest it had been since 1983. The juvenile arrest rate for murder fell 70% between its peak in 1993 and 2001.

In 2000 juvenile arrests for property crimes were at the lowest level in more than two decades. (See Figure 8.2.)

Among property crimes committed by juveniles, larceny-theft (which includes things like shoplifting, theft from motor vehicles, and bicycle theft) was the most common offense.

Arrests by Gender

Among youths under the age of nineteen, far more males than females are arrested for most types of juvenile crimes. In 2001 28% of all juvenile arrests involved females. (See Table 8.1.) Detailed arrest data available for 2002 show that 150,845 males and 98,016 females under eighteen years old were arrested for larceny-theft; 26,958 males and 5,586 females under eighteen were arrested for motor vehicle theft; 54,915 males and 6,928 females under eighteen were arrested for burglary; and 15,858 males and 2,961 females under eighteen were arrested for receiving, buying, or possessing stolen property. (See Table 8.2 and Table 8.3.) However, more females than males were arrested for running away (54,010 females versus 36,339 males), prostitution, and commercialized vice (729 females versus 366 males).

Girls ages thirteen to fifteen were involved in approximately one-third (33.1%) of all arrests of juveniles in that age group in 2002, and 26% of all arrests of juveniles ages sixteen to seventeen were girls. (See Table 8.2 and Table 8.3.) Between 1980 and 2001 the rate of arrests of juvenile females increased more than the rate for males, particularly for violent crimes. (See Figure 8.3.) The change in arrest rates between 1980 and 2001 for aggravated assault (113% versus 22%), simple assault (257% versus 109%), and weapons law violations (140% versus 16%) were all much higher for females than males.

Arrests by Race/Ethnicity

Table 8.4 shows arrest trends from 1980 to 2001 by offense and race. Asian and Pacific Islander juveniles had the lowest arrest rates in all offense categories. African-American youths accounted for a disproportionate share of juvenile arrests.

TABLE 8.1

Number of juveniles arrested, by gender, age group, and type of offense, 2001

Most serious offense	2001 estimated number of juvenile arrests	Percent of total juvenile arrests		Percent change		
		Female	Under age 15	1992–2001	1997–2001	2000–2001
Total	**2,273,500**	**28%**	**32%**	**−3%**	**−20%**	**−4%**
Crime Index total	587,900	29	37	−31	−28	−5
Violent Crime Index	96,500	18	33	−21	−21	−2
Murder and nonnegligent manslaughter	1,400	10	12	−62	−47	−2
Forcible rape	4,600	1	38	−24	−14	−1
Robbery	25,600	9	24	−32	−35	−4
Aggravated assault	64,900	23	37	−14	−13	−1
Property Crime Index	491,400	31	38	−32	−29	−6
Burglary	90,300	12	38	−40	−30	−6
Larceny-theft	343,600	39	39	−27	−30	−6
Motor vehicle theft	48,200	17	25	−51	−26	−2
Arson	9,300	12	64	−7	−9	8
Nonindex						
Other assaults	239,000	32	43	30	−2	2
Forgery and counterfeiting	5,800	36	11	−27	−26	−8
Fraud	8,900	33	16	−5	−18	−9
Embezzlement	1,800	44	7	152	24	−10
Stolen property (buying, receiving, possessing)	26,800	17	27	−45	−37	−6
Vandalism	105,300	13	44	−29	−22	−7
Weapons (carrying, possessing, etc.)	37,500	11	34	−35	−26	0
Prostitution and commercialized vice	1,400	69	15	−8	−5	15
Sex offense (except forcible rape and prostitution)	18,000	8	54	−10	6	1
Drug abuse violations	202,500	15	17	121	−7	0
Gambling	1,400	3	13	−53	−47	−17
Offenses against the family and children	9,600	37	37	109	−11	6
Driving under the influence	20,300	18	5	35	5	−3
Liquor law violations	138,100	32	10	21	−9	−11
Drunkenness	20,400	21	13	4	−21	−10
Disorderly conduct	171,700	30	40	34	−21	1
Vagrancy	2,300	19	25	−37	−24	−10
All other offenses (except traffic)	397,200	26	28	27	−13	−3
Suspicion	1,300	36	33	−53	−42	9
Curfew and loitering	142,900	31	28	34	−29	−13
Runaways	133,300	59	38	−25	−30	−6

- In 2001, there were an estimated 1,400 juvenile arrests for murder. Between 1997 and 2001, juvenile arrests for murder fell 47%.
- Females accounted for 23% of juvenile arrests for aggravated assault and 32% of juvenile arrests for other assaults (i.e., simple assaults and intimidations) in 2001. Females were involved in 59% of all arrests for running away from home and 31% of arrests for curfew and loitering law violations.
- Between 1992 and 2001, there were substantial declines in juvenile arrests for murder (62%), motor vehicle theft (51%), and burglary (40%) and major increases in juvenile arrests for drug abuse violations (121%).

Note: Detail may not add to totals because of rounding.

SOURCE: Howard N. Snyder, " The number of juvenile arrests in 2001—2.3 million—was 4% below the 2000 level and 20% below the 1997 level," in "Juvenile Arrests 2001," *Juvenile Justice Bulletin*, U.S. Department of Justice, Office of Justice Programs, Office of Juvenile Justice and Delinquency Prevention, December 2003, http://www.ncjrs.org/pdffiles1/ojjdp/201370.pdf (accessed September 16, 2004)

DELINQUENCY COURT CASES

For statistical purposes, the Office of Juvenile Justice and Delinquency Prevention (OJJDP) divides juvenile crimes into two general categories: delinquency offenses (acts that are illegal regardless of the age of the perpetrator) and status offenses (acts that are illegal only for minors, such as truancy, running away, curfew violations, ungovernability, and underage drinking).

Since the 1980s the justice system has implemented a variety of "tough-on-crime" policies, from which juvenile offenders are not exempt. When a juvenile is arrested and charged with a violation of criminal law, he or she becomes a delinquency case. When counting delinquency cases, one case can include more than one charge. For example, a youth brought in one time but on three different robbery charges is counted as one case. According to the OJJDP, juvenile courts handled an estimated 1.7 million delinquency cases in 1998 (the most recent year for which these statistics are available), a 44% increase over the 1989 caseload. In the same time period property offenses increased 11%, offenses against persons increased 88%, public order offenses increased 73%, and drug law violations increased 148%. Between 1994 and 1998 significant decreases occurred in several areas, including aggravated assault (22%), criminal homicide (36%), robbery (23%), and motor vehicle theft (28%).

Delinquency and Detention

Juvenile courts hear delinquency cases referred to them from law enforcement agencies, social service agen-

FIGURE 8.1

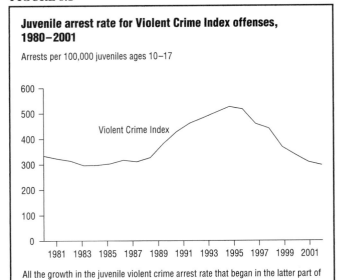

Juvenile arrest rate for Violent Crime Index offenses, 1980–2001

Arrests per 100,000 juveniles ages 10–17

All the growth in the juvenile violent crime arrest rate that began in the latter part of the 1980s was erased by 2001.

SOURCE: Howard N. Snyder, "The Juvenile Violent Crime Index Arrest Rate in 2001 Was at Its Lowest Level since 1983—44% below the Peak Year of 1994," in "Juvenile Arrests 2001," *Juvenile Justice Bulletin,* U.S. Department of Justice, Office of Justice Programs, Office of Juvenile Justice and Delinquency Prevention, December 2003, http://www.ncjrs .org/pdffiles1/ojjdp/201370.pdf (accessed September 16, 2004)

FIGURE 8.2

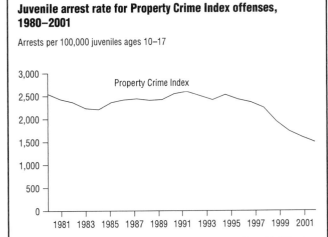

Juvenile arrest rate for Property Crime Index offenses, 1980–2001

Arrests per 100,000 juveniles ages 10–17

The relatively stable juvenile arrest rate trend between 1980 and the mid-1990s for Property Crime Index offenses stands in stark contrast to the Violent Crime Index arrest rate trend.

SOURCE: Howard N. Snyder, "After Years of Relative Stability, the Juvenile Arrest Rate for Property Crime Index Offenses Began a Decline in the Mid–1990s that Continued through 2001," in "Juvenile Arrests 2001," *Juvenile Justice Bulletin,* U.S. Department of Justice, Office of Justice Programs, Office of Juvenile Justice and Delinquency Prevention, December 2003, http://www.ncjrs.org/pdffiles1/ojjdp/201370.pdf (accessed September 16, 2004)

cies, schools, parents, probation officers, and victims. In 1997 (the most recent year of data available), law enforcement agencies accounted for 85% of all referrals.

One of the first decisions made in processing a delinquency case is whether the juvenile should be held in a detention facility between referral to the court and case disposition (the time a decision is reached). Detention may be necessary to protect the community from the juvenile, to ensure the juvenile's safety, to have the juvenile evaluated, or to ensure future court appearances. Between 1985 and 2000 the number of delinquency cases involving detention increased 41% (up by 95,200 cases). (See Figure 8.4.) Youths were held in detention facilities at some point between referral and disposition in 20% of all delinquency cases in 2000. In 2000 cases involving property were the least likely to result in detention (16%), while those involving crimes against a person were most likely to result in detention (24%). In the same year African-American youths (25%) were more likely than white youths (18%) to be held in detention.

Delinquency Case Processing

There is no national uniform procedure for processing juvenile delinquency cases, but cases generally follow similar paths. They are first screened by an intake department—the court, a state department of social services, or a prosecutor's office. A case may be handled either formally or informally.

When a case is to be handled formally, a petition must first be filed with the court (the offender is officially charged with the offense). The court is asked for either an adjudicatory hearing (where a judge alone rules on the case) or waiver hearing (the juvenile court judge is asked to decide if the case should be waived to a criminal court where the youth will be tried as an adult).

A case is handled informally if the intake officer decides it will be resolved either by dismissing it for lack of evidence, referring it to a social services agency, imposing a fine or some form of restitution, or through informal probation.

Between 1985 and 2000 the number of delinquency cases that were handled formally increased 81%, although the delinquency caseload rose only 43%. In 2000 there were 36% more formal than informal delinquency cases. (See Figure 8.5.)

ADJUDICATION AND DISPOSITION. If a youth is adjudicated delinquent, the juvenile court judge then makes a dispositional decision (imposes a sentence) that could include commitment to a residential facility, probation, referral to another agency or treatment program, fines, restitution, or community service. In 2000 formal probation was the most common outcome, ordered in 63% of adjudicated cases, an increase of 108% since 1985. (See Figure 8.6.) Almost one in four delinquents (24%) were sent to residential facilities, a 49% increase since 1985. Another 11% received other dispositions (sentences), including fines and restitution such as community service or enrollment in a nonresidential treatment or counseling program.

TABLE 8.2

Female arrests for ages 21 and under, by age, 2002

(10,372 agencies; 2002 estimated population 205,122,185)

Offense charged	Total all ages	Ages under 15	Ages under 18	Ages 18 and over	Under 10	10–12	13–14	15	16	17	18	19	20	21
Total	2,260,066	160,919	469,999	1,790,067	3,747	32,255	124,917	98,894	108,824	101,362	100,865	104,101	97,688	83,776
Percent distribution[1]	100.0	7.1	20.8	79.2	0.2	1.4	5.5	4.4	4.8	4.5	4.5	4.6	4.3	3.7
Murder and nonnegligent manslaughter	1,092	17	101	991	0	4	13	18	27	39	39	44	56	54
Forcible rape	278	56	109	169	6	15	35	18	19	16	10	9	13	10
Robbery	7,973	480	1,583	6,390	8	68	404	334	363	406	479	454	405	402
Aggravated assault	68,532	3,960	10,461	58,071	87	848	3,025	2,083	2,301	2,117	2,186	2,347	2,505	2,567
Burglary	27,330	2,856	6,928	20,402	121	732	2,003	1,380	1,308	1,384	1,570	1,464	1,189	1,057
Larceny-theft	312,735	37,151	98,016	214,719	865	9,041	27,245	19,186	21,348	20,331	18,101	14,984	12,539	10,735
Motor vehicle theft	17,724	1,768	5,586	12,138	4	173	1,591	1,482	1,323	1,013	993	904	785	716
Arson	1,802	427	666	1,136	35	143	249	108	75	56	41	44	40	39
Violent crime[2]	77,875	4,513	12,254	65,621	101	935	3,477	2,453	2,710	2,578	2,714	2,854	2,979	3,033
Percent distribution[1]	100.0	5.8	15.7	84.3	0.1	1.2	4.5	3.1	3.5	3.3	3.5	3.7	3.8	3.9
Property crime[3]	359,591	42,202	111,196	248,395	1,025	10,089	31,088	22,156	24,054	22,784	20,705	17,396	14,553	12,547
Percent distribution[1]	100.0	11.7	30.9	69.1	0.3	2.8	8.6	6.2	6.7	6.3	5.8	4.8	4.0	3.5
Crime Index[4]	437,466	46,715	123,450	314,016	1,126	11,024	34,565	24,609	26,764	25,362	23,419	20,250	17,532	15,580
Percent distribution[1]	100.0	10.7	28.2	71.8	0.3	2.5	7.9	5.6	6.1	5.8	5.4	4.6	4.0	3.6
Other assaults	220,114	22,873	54,250	165,864	454	5,512	16,907	10,980	10,961	9,436	7,987	7,988	7,973	7,929
Forgery and counterfeiting	33,323	156	1,303	32,020	14	34	108	154	337	656	1,248	1,563	1,694	1,642
Fraud	105,191	401	2,111	103,080	44	70	287	294	530	886	2,289	3,610	4,183	4,144
Embezzlement	6,676	28	415	6,261	0	10	18	20	127	240	435	453	406	354
Stolen property; buying, receiving, possessing	16,322	953	2,961	13,361	20	169	764	563	698	747	883	903	857	748
Vandalism	32,976	4,635	10,291	22,685	271	1,322	3,042	1,805	1,942	1,909	1,707	1,568	1,308	1,332
Weapons; carrying, possessing, etc.	9,553	1,167	2,786	6,767	23	290	854	608	547	464	406	411	353	365
Prostitution and commercialized vice	38,631	94	729	37,902	0	6	88	127	180	328	1,261	1,353	1,275	1,297
Sex offenses (except forcible rape and prostitution)	5,599	661	1,276	4,323	46	166	449	257	202	156	247	253	211	237
Drug abuse violations	199,361	4,837	21,500	177,861	48	639	4,150	4,075	5,584	7,004	9,806	10,148	9,728	8,435
Gambling	776	8	33	743	0	5	3	6	7	12	17	35	25	17
Offenses against the family and children	23,960	996	2,576	21,384	136	234	626	571	528	481	537	624	711	859
Driving under the influence	177,607	116	2,944	174,663	20	6	90	141	786	1,901	4,219	5,577	6,009	8,557
Liquor laws	114,980	4,920	35,765	79,215	40	383	4,497	6,463	10,351	14,031	20,121	20,339	15,757	2,243
Drunkenness	57,835	629	2,922	54,913	13	47	569	555	682	1,056	1,772	1,808	1,721	2,111
Disorderly conduct	118,132	18,075	41,875	76,257	247	3,998	13,830	9,055	8,200	6,545	5,112	4,612	4,407	4,334
Vagrancy	3,520	116	357	3,163	1	14	101	79	65	97	106	96	101	117
All other offenses (except traffic)	570,186	23,267	75,828	494,358	675	3,942	18,650	16,555	18,219	17,787	19,233	22,450	23,384	23,42
Suspicion	1,567	77	336	1,231	1	12	64	66	78	115	60	60	53	48
Curfew and loitering law violations	32,281	10,071	32,281	—	131	1,638	8,302	7,857	8,690	5,663	—	—	—	—
Runaways	54,010	20,124	54,010	—	437	2,734	16,953	14,054	13,346	6,486	—	—	—	—

[1]Because of rounding, the percentages may not add to 100.0.

[2]Violent crimes are offenses of murder, forcible rape, robbery, and aggravated assault.

[3]Property crimes are offenses of burglary, larceny-theft, motor vehicle theft, and arson.

[4]Includes arson.

SOURCE: Adapted from "Table 40. Arrests, Females, by Age, 2002," in *Crime in the United States, 2002*, U.S. Department of Justice, Federal Bureau of investigation, 2003, http://www.fbi.gov/ucr/cius_02/pdf/4sectionfour.pdf (accessed September 16, 2004)

TABLE 8.3

Male arrests for ages 21 and under, by age, 2002

(10,372 agencies; 2002 estimated population 205,122,185)

Offense charged	Total all ages	Ages under 15	Ages under 18	Ages 18 and over	Under 10	10–12	13–14	15	16	17	18	19	20	21
Total	7,559,435	349,307	1,154,193	6,405,242	16,157	87,842	245,308	207,784	273,085	324,017	377,971	398,150	374,598	342,014
Percent distribution[1]	100.0	4.6	15.3	84.7	0.2	1.2	3.2	2.7	3.6	4.3	5.0	5.3	5.0	4.5
Murder and nonnegligent manslaughter	9,015	84	872	8,143	0	13	71	122	247	419	529	632	642	604
Forcible rape	19,884	1,187	3,252	16,632	36	321	830	544	653	868	1,018	1,020	893	891
Robbery	69,369	3,843	16,310	53,059	77	721	3,045	3,074	4,169	5,224	5,749	5,163	4,266	3,785
Aggravated assault	270,905	11,886	33,820	237,085	612	3,502	7,772	5,865	7,421	8,648	9,866	10,439	10,513	11,158
Burglary	178,806	19,533	54,915	123,891	1,032	5,072	13,429	10,135	12,041	13,206	14,050	11,679	9,091	7,799
Larceny-theft	532,274	57,939	150,845	381,429	2,673	16,758	38,508	27,131	31,975	33,800	33,423	28,437	22,323	18,870
Motor vehicle theft	89,463	6,459	26,958	62,505	61	833	5,565	6,216	7,208	7,075	6,773	5,859	4,765	4,079
Arson	10,031	3,301	5,185	4,846	517	1,207	1,577	747	596	541	453	391	288	235
Violent crime[2]	369,173	17,000	54,254	314,919	725	4,557	11,718	9,605	12,490	15,159	17,162	17,254	16,314	16,438
Percent distribution[1]	100.0	4.6	14.7	85.3	0.2	1.2	3.2	2.6	3.4	4.1	4.6	4.7	4.4	4.5
Property crime[3]	810,574	87,232	237,903	572,671	4,283	23,870	59,079	44,229	51,820	54,622	54,699	46,366	36,467	30,983
Percent distribution[1]	100.0	10.8	29.3	70.7	0.5	2.9	7.3	5.5	6.4	6.7	6.7	5.7	4.5	3.8
Crime Index[4]	1,179,747	104,232	292,157	887,590	5,008	28,427	70,797	53,834	64,310	69,781	71,861	63,620	52,781	47,421
Percent distribution[1]	100.0	8.8	24.8	75.2	0.4	2.4	6.0	4.6	5.5	5.9	6.1	5.4	4.5	4.0
Other assaults	701,562	48,824	114,746	586,816	2,359	14,611	31,854	20,250	22,692	22,980	21,617	22,995	23,698	26,433
Forgery and counterfeiting	49,788	301	2,349	47,439	20	36	245	325	647	1,076	2,143	2,623	2,814	2,424
Fraud	127,896	777	4,323	123,573	58	155	564	591	1,081	1,874	3,321	4,732	5,336	5,233
Embezzlement	6,740	62	590	6,150	2	10	50	52	132	344	441	473	368	364
Stolen property; buying, receiving, possessing	74,958	4,091	15,858	59,100	118	813	3,160	2,987	3,902	4,878	5,250	5,034	4,318	3,779
Vandalism	165,574	28,253	65,664	99,910	2,294	8,727	17,232	11,374	13,046	12,991	11,375	9,294	7,291	7,105
Weapons; carrying, possessing, etc.	108,759	7,480	22,502	86,257	415	1,876	5,189	4,007	4,832	6,183	7,103	6,766	6,164	5,898
Prostitution and commercialized vice	20,127	71	366	19,761	2	18	51	43	101	151	306	449	520	591
Sex offenses (except forcible rape and prostitution)	62,234	6,565	12,601	49,633	381	1,978	4,206	2,095	1,926	2,015	2,318	2,281	2,126	2,044
Drug abuse violations	903,656	16,999	112,254	791,402	236	1,970	14,793	18,956	31,320	44,979	60,907	61,957	55,904	50,356
Gambling	6,749	163	1,081	5,668	0	27	136	194	301	423	439	451	415	360
Offenses against the family and children	73,756	1,446	3,996	69,760	207	378	861	708	878	964	1,422	1,608	1,753	2,118
Driving under the influence	842,770	254	12,270	830,500	93	17	144	490	3,024	8,502	20,443	27,740	31,647	41,632
Liquor laws	348,869	5,212	70,249	278,620	112	369	4,731	9,363	20,351	35,323	56,154	61,327	51,697	11,077
Drunkenness	355,973	1,050	10,607	345,366	74	96	880	1,546	2,563	5,448	10,629	11,913	12,132	16,314
Disorderly conduct	364,695	38,239	97,173	267,522	1,240	10,504	26,495	18,612	19,741	20,581	18,516	16,662	15,640	18,629
Vagrancy	16,158	286	1,162	14,996	9	48	229	218	304	354	579	485	439	434
All other offenses (except traffic)	2,036,108	52,758	206,197	1,829,911	2,443	11,517	38,798	37,852	51,788	63,799	82,890	97,475	99,329	99,562
Suspicion	6,103	217	835	5,268	5	40	172	154	220	244	257	265	226	240
Curfew and loitering law violations	70,874	18,999	70,874	—	392	3,489	15,118	15,466	20,376	16,033	—	—	—	—
Runaways	36,339	13,028	36,339	—	689	2,736	9,603	8,667	9,550	5,094	—	—	—	—

[1] Because of rounding, the percentages may not add to 100.0.
[2] Violent crimes are offenses of murder, forcible rape, robbery, and aggravated assault.
[3] Property crimes are offenses of burglary, larceny-theft, motor vehicle theft, and arson.
[4] Includes arson.

SOURCE: Adapted from "Table 39. Arrests, Males, by Age, 2002," in Crime in the United States, 2002, U.S. Department of Justice, Federal Bureau of Investigation, 2003, http://www.fbi.gov/ucr/cius_02/pdf/4sectionfour.pdf (accessed September 16, 2004)

FIGURE 8.3

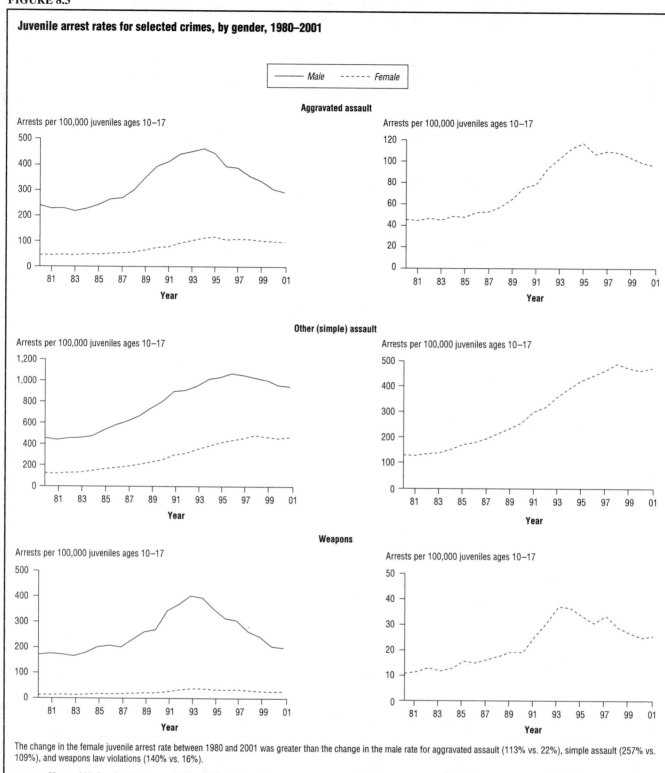

Juvenile arrest rates for selected crimes, by gender, 1980–2001

The change in the female juvenile arrest rate between 1980 and 2001 was greater than the change in the male rate for aggravated assault (113% vs. 22%), simple assault (257% vs. 109%), and weapons law violations (140% vs. 16%).

SOURCE: Howard N. Snyder, "Between 1980 and 2001, Juvenile Arrest Rates Increased Proportionately More for Females Than for Males, Especially for Violent Crimes," in "Juvenile Arrests 2001," *Juvenile Justice Bulletin,* U.S. Department of Justice, Office of Justice Programs, Office of Juvenile Justice and Delinquency Prevention, December 2003, http://www.ncjrs.org/pdffiles1/ojjdp/201370.pdf (accessed September 16, 2004)

PROSECUTING MINORS AS ADULTS

Many people believe that some crimes are so terrible that the courts should focus on the type of offense and not the age of the accused in determining the type of trial court. The increase in violent crime among juveniles from the late 1980s through the mid-1990s saw U.S. juvenile courts handling 84% more criminal homicide cases in 1995 than in 1986. Voters were outraged over the crime wave, and lawmakers responded with tough new policies, including trying more juveniles in adult criminal courts.

TABLE 8.4

Juvenile arrest rates by offense and race, 1980–2001

Offense	White			Black			American Indian			Asian		
	1980	1990	2001	1980	1990	2001	1980	1990	2001	1980	1990	2001
Total including suspicion	6905.8	7232.9	6374.0	11599.9	14077.6	11063.1	7456.2	7242.5	7477.3	3417.0	3407.1	2774.6
Violent crime index*	189.4	253.7	213.4	1190.4	1435.3	765.8	211.8	217.0	239.5	134.0	133.5	110.8
Murder and nonnegligent manslaughter	4.2	5.8	2.4	19.2	45.8	12.3	5.1	3.9	11.7	2.4	3.7	5.9
Forcible rape	8.2	14.3	10.9	60.5	67.7	31.3	16.8	13.3	8.9	7.5	5.6	3.8
Robbery	65.9	68.3	41.6	757.8	642.4	283.3	59.7	42.9	37.8	77.1	49.6	35
Aggravated assault	111.1	165.4	158.5	352.9	679.4	438.9	130.1	156.9	181.1	47.0	74.6	66.2
Property crime index**	2251.6	2341.0	1343.4	4885.9	4412.6	2595.2	2759.1	2566.7	1829.1	1693.8	1248.8	728.6
Burglary	708.9	492.0	257.2	1449.0	765.9	417.4	686.0	485.9	293.8	364.7	208.3	95.9
Larceny-theft	1320.7	1565.9	947.6	3017.7	2731.5	1781.1	1799.1	1783.3	1341.7	1155.6	856.8	560.1
Motor vehicle theft	191.9	252.5	108.9	388.8	882.1	368.9	256.2	272.8	165	164.7	176.0	65.3
Arson	30.2	30.5	29.7	30.4	33.0	27.8	17.9	24.6	28.6	8.8	7.7	7.3
Other assaults	243.6	421.3	594.0	682.9	1288.0	1517.8	257.7	430.1	724.4	171.4	253.7	222.9
Vandalism	445.9	480.8	333.8	376.5	542.4	334.8	308.3	358.3	334	114.8	152.3	93.8
Weapons carrying, possessing, etc.	78.2	112.3	98.5	176.2	354.5	221.9	74.0	54.6	86.9	47.3	61.3	39.1
Drug abuse violations	386.2	188.0	573.2	375.1	966.9	1004.0	208.2	107.7	463.6	107.6	54.4	168.2
Driving under the influence	125.5	84.6	71.8	19.8	16.3	16.2	128.6	97.6	88.9	12.5	11.0	14.6
Liquor laws	589.5	666.9	488.6	80.2	162.2	116.2	608.9	1033.5	975.1	78.2	102.8	87.1
Drunkenness	168.4	98.0	72.5	43.8	55.4	28.9	369.5	124.1	97.8	16.0	8.2	8.1
Disorderly conduct	405.1	376.0	419.4	767.1	931.8	1153.6	414.9	276.3	462.4	51.3	88.3	110.4
Curfew and loitering law violations	236.9	304.0	410	294.3	439.1	734.3	356.2	283.0	350.5	85.2	187.8	177.4
Runaways	512.5	622.7	396.9	499.7	658.6	469.1	684.9	695.9	447.5	316.9	362.5	457

*Violent crime index includes murder and nonnegligent manslaughter, forcible rape, robbery, and aggravated assault.
**Property crime index includes burglary, larceny-theft, motor vehicle theft, and arson.
Note: Persons of Hispanic ethnicity may be of any race. Arrests of Hispanics are not reported separately.

SOURCE: Adapted from "Juvenile Arrest Rates by Offense, Sex, and Race (1980–2001)," National Center for Juvenile Justice, May 31, 2003, http://ojjdp.ncjrs.org/ojstatbb/excel/JAR_053103.xls (accessed July 29, 2004)

FIGURE 8.4

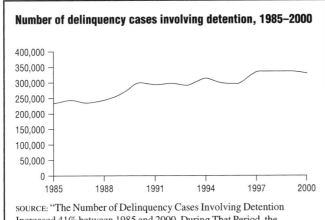

Number of delinquency cases involving detention, 1985–2000

SOURCE: "The Number of Delinquency Cases Involving Detention Increased 41% between 1985 and 2000. During That Period, the Proportion of Detained Delinquency Cases Ranged between 17% and 23%," in *OJJDP Statistical Briefing Book,* U.S. Department of Justice, Office of Justice Programs, Office of Juvenile Justice Delinquency Prevention, August 11, 2003, http://ojjdp.ncjrs.org/ojstatbb/html/qa184.html (accessed August 8, 2004)

FIGURE 8.5

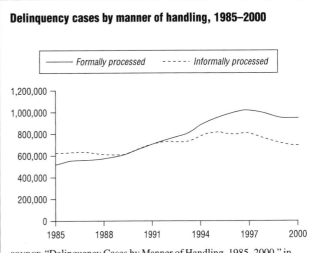

Delinquency cases by manner of handling, 1985–2000

—— Formally processed   - - - - - Informally processed

SOURCE: "Delinquency Cases by Manner of Handling, 1985–2000," in *OJJDP Statistical Briefing Book,* U.S. Department of Justice, Office of Justice Programs, Office of Juvenile Justice Delinquency Prevention, August 11, 2003, http://ojjdp.ncjrs.org/ojstatbb/html/qa188.html (accessed August 8, 2004)

Historically, the states relied mainly on a judge's decision to waive delinquents to adult criminal court, but between 1992 and 1997 all but six states enacted laws that made it easier for more juveniles to be transferred. As a consequence, all states have some provisions to try juveniles as adults in criminal court. In 1999 fourteen states and the District of Columbia had laws that allowed prosecutors to decide in some cases whether to file in juvenile or criminal court.

Twenty-nine states had laws that required certain juvenile offenders to be waived to criminal court. The number of juvenile cases waived to criminal court more than doubled between 1985 and 1994, the peak year, and then declined 58% through 2000. (See Figure 8.7.) In 2000 more offenses against persons were referred to criminal court (2,200) than any other, followed by property offenses (2,000).

FIGURE 8.6

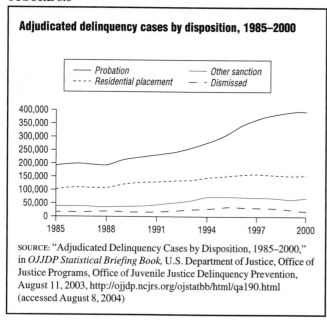

Adjudicated delinquency cases by disposition, 1985–2000

SOURCE: "Adjudicated Delinquency Cases by Disposition, 1985–2000," in *OJJDP Statistical Briefing Book,* U.S. Department of Justice, Office of Justice Programs, Office of Juvenile Justice Delinquency Prevention, August 11, 2003, http://ojjdp.ncjrs.org/ojstatbb/html/qa190.html (accessed August 8, 2004)

FIGURE 8.7

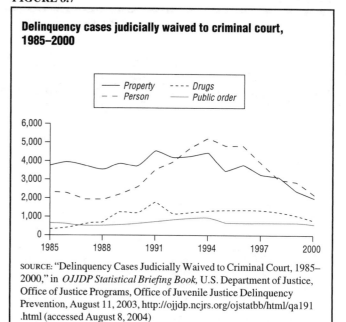

Delinquency cases judicially waived to criminal court, 1985–2000

SOURCE: "Delinquency Cases Judicially Waived to Criminal Court, 1985–2000," in *OJJDP Statistical Briefing Book,* U.S. Department of Justice, Office of Justice Programs, Office of Juvenile Justice Delinquency Prevention, August 11, 2003, http://ojjdp.ncjrs.org/ojstatbb/html/qa191.html (accessed August 8, 2004)

Does the Practice Make a Difference?

An OJJDP study released in 2000 explored the issue of transferring juvenile offenders to adult criminal courts and the impact on recidivism (reoffending) (H. Snyder, M. Sickmund, and E. Poe-Yamagata, *Juvenile Transfers to Criminal Court in the 1990s: Lessons Learned from Four Studies*). The authors of the study discuss research from the 1990s that compared the recidivism rate of juveniles transferred to adult court with the rate of juveniles who were retained in the juvenile system. The research showed that transfers to adult court were more likely than juveniles kept in juvenile court to reoffend within two years. A six-year follow-up study showed that there was no difference between the groups in the proportion of offenders who reoffended, but the transferred juveniles who reoffended did so more quickly and more often than the retained juveniles who reoffended. In explaining these results, the authors found that transfer to adult court is usually reserved for the most serious cases and the most serious juvenile offenders. In making the decision to waive a juvenile offender, judges tended to look upon a history of reoffending after serving time in a correctional facility as a key factor.

Changing Philosophies

Traditionally, the philosophical difference between juvenile delinquency proceedings and adult criminal proceedings was that the juvenile offender was viewed as misguided and correctable rather than as criminal. Juveniles were considered "delinquent," not guilty; they received treatment, not punishment. Juvenile proceedings took place in a closed court to protect the offender and his or her family, and there were wide discretionary powers for probation officers, the court, and correction agencies,

depending upon a youth's history. Long-term incarceration was rare, and cases were disposed of quickly with a broad range of disposition alternatives.

The new trend in juvenile justice is to process juveniles as adults. If they are treated like adults, chronic offenders may receive adult sentences, removing them from society, avoiding the notion of rehabilitation, and replacing it with punishment for a crime committed. On the other hand, in an adult court juveniles are entitled to open courtroom proceedings and jury trials, and they avoid a closed system controlled by one judge.

OPENING JUVENILE RECORDS

Traditionally, juvenile hearings were closed to the public and the records were sealed based on the belief that delinquent behavior by a child should not be held against him or her for the rest of his or her life, but many states are now allowing more openness. According to the National Center for Juvenile Justice, in 2002 twenty-one states required that under certain conditions delinquency hearings be open to the public, and fifteen states had laws that closed all delinquency hearings to the public. Forty-three states required that police departments notify school officials when a student was charged with a crime.

STATUS OFFENSE CASES

Status offenses are behaviors that are law violations only when committed by a juvenile (such as possession of alcohol, truancy, and running away from home). According to the OJJDP, juvenile courts formally handled an estimated 158,500 status offense cases in 1997 (the latest year for which statistics are available). In many communities social service agencies rather than juvenile courts have assumed responsibility for status offenders. National estimates of informally handled status offense cases are not calculated because of differences in screening procedures. The statistics, therefore, focus on formally handled (petitioned) status offense cases.

In 1997 approximately 26% of petitioned status offenses involved a liquor law violation, 26% a truancy charge, 13% ungovernability, and 15% runaway charges. Other types of status offenses, such as curfew violations, accounted for the remaining 20%. Between 1993 and 1997 the rate for runaway cases increased 14%, truancy grew by 14%, liquor law violations rose by 39%, and the case rate for ungovernability offenses increased 35%. The nation's juvenile courts processed 5.5 cases for every one thousand juveniles in the population in 1997.

The FBI reported that more than 55% of formal status offense cases in 1997 involved youths fifteen years old or younger. The most common offense in this age group was truancy (34%), while older youths most often violated the liquor laws (42%).

CHILDREN IN CUSTODY

There are many different types of facilities for delinquent youth, including juvenile detention centers, shelters, reception and diagnostic centers, training schools, and group homes. Not all youths placed in these facilities are accused delinquent and status offenders, however. Some are placed for treatment or as a result of abuse, dependency, or neglect. Others are held temporarily while arrangements are being made.

Prisons and Jails

According to a Bureau of Justice Statistics (BJS) survey, in 1998 1.4% of 592,462 individuals confined in adult jails were seventeen or younger. The number of juveniles confined in the adult jails surveyed increased 366% between 1983 and 1998. The BJS survey revealed that 0.4% (4,775) of one million prisoners confined in state prisons in 1998 were juveniles. Most state prison systems house juveniles. Florida and Connecticut had the highest numbers of juvenile prisoners in adult prisons (572 and 505, respectively), and Hawaii and Rhode Island had the lowest numbers (two and zero, respectively). About 23% of the youths were being held as adjudicated juvenile offenders or pretrial detainees, while 75% had been sentenced as adults.

HOLDING PARENTS RESPONSIBLE

Many Americans became frustrated by the rising juvenile crime rates in the 1980s and early 1990s. In response, communities and states passed laws holding parents responsible for their children's actions. According

to the National Center for Juvenile Justice, a nonprofit research organization, at the end of the 1998 legislative session, thirty-four states had statutes that made parents of delinquent children liable to the victim of the crime. Thirty-nine states had statutes that either allowed or required parents of delinquents to participate in treatment, counseling, or probation with their children.

All states have laws that make it mandatory or optional for the court to require parents to pay at least some of the costs for a child who is delinquent and placed out of the home. Some have laws that hold parents partially responsible for their children's delinquent behavior. A Louisiana law allows parents to be fined up to $1,000 and imprisoned for up to six months if they are found guilty of "improper supervision of a minor" (for example, if the child is associating with drug dealers, members of a street gang, or convicted felons). In 1995 Judge Wayne Creech of Family Court in Columbia, South Carolina, ordered that a fifteen-year-old girl with a history of shoplifting and truancy be chained to her mother for one month. A Florida mother was convicted of truancy and sentenced to a year's probation because three of her five children refused to go to school.

CURFEWS

Because of the rise in rates of juvenile crime from the 1980s through the mid-1990s, many of the nation's jurisdictions imposed youth curfews. A 2000 survey of 490 cities by the National League of Cities found that 69% (337) had nighttime curfews and 14% (68) had daytime curfews. Thirty-five of the cities surveyed reported that they were considering adopting a curfew.

Most curfew laws restrict juveniles to their home or property between the hours of 11 P.M. and 6 A.M. weekdays, allowing them to stay out later on weekends. The laws allow exceptions for young people going to and from school, church events, or work, and for youths who have a family emergency or are accompanied by their parents. Critics of such ordinances argue that they violate the equal protection clause of the U.S. Constitution and abridge parental rights. The critics also argue that no studies have proven the effectiveness of curfew laws.

Court Rulings on Curfews

In 1994 the U.S. Supreme Court let stand a lower court ruling that a Dallas, Texas, curfew law was constitutional. But in 2003 the Washington State Supreme Court struck down the city of Sumner's curfew law (*Walsh v. City of Sumner* [No. 71451–7]). The court ruled that Sumner's curfew ordinance, which makes it unlawful for juveniles to "remain" in a public place during certain hours, is unconstitutionally vague because "it does not provide 'ascertainable standards for locating the line between innocent and unlawful behavior.'" The court noted that "it may be difficult for a city to draft a curfew ordinance that is not unconstitutionally vague" because "curfew ordinances attempt to make activities that are normally considered innocent, unlawful, i.e., walking, driving, going to the store." And in July 2004 the U.S. District Court in the Southern District of Indiana issued an injunction prohibiting enforcement of Indiana's juvenile curfew law.

Do Curfews Reduce Crime?

The U.S. Conference of Mayors conducted a 1997 survey of 276 cities with a nighttime youth curfew and asked city officials how they felt about it. Officials in nine out of ten of the cities thought that curfew enforcement was a good use of police officers' time; 88% felt that enforcing a curfew made their city's streets safer; and 83% said curfews help curb gang violence. Of the 154 cities that had had their curfew in effect for ten years or less, officials in 53% of them noted a decrease in juvenile crime (attributed by them to the curfew), 11% saw no change, and 10% saw an increase in juvenile crime (the remaining 26% of cities had no data on the curfew's effects available because of its recent implementation).

However, the effects of curfews on juvenile crime rates are still controversial. In their study entitled "An Analysis of Curfew Enforcement and Juvenile Crime in California" (*Western Criminology Review*, 1999), Mike Males and Dan Macallair concluded that there was "no support for the proposition that stricter curfew enforcement reduces youth crime or risk of violent fatality. . . . Curfew enforcement generally has no discernible effect on youth crime." A national study done by David McDowall, Colin Loftin, and Brian Wiersma also found that curfew laws had little effect on juvenile arrests ("The Impact of Youth Curfew Laws on Juvenile Crime Rates," *Crime and Delinquency*, 2000).

YOUTH GANGS

The modern street gang takes many forms. Individual members, gang cliques, or entire gang organizations may traffic in drugs; operate car theft rings; commit shootings, assaults, robbery, extortion, and other felonies; and terrorize neighborhoods. The most ambitious gangs spread out from their home jurisdictions to other cities and states. Many are supported by the sale of crack cocaine, heroin, and other illegal drugs, and they often have relatively easy access to high-powered guns and rifles. Furthermore, in many impoverished and transitional neighborhoods, children are born into or must contend with second- and third-generation street gangs.

Defining Gangs

Attempts to collect data about gangs at the national level have been complicated by the fact that definitions differ as to what constitutes a gang. The *1998 National Youth Gang Survey* asked law enforcement officials about the characteristics they consider important in defining a youth gang. The characteristics most often named were that a gang:

- Commits crimes together.
- Has a name.
- Hangs out together.
- Claims a turf or territory of some sort.
- Displays/wears common colors or other insignia.
- Has a leader or several leaders.

In the 2002 *National Youth Gang Survey,* a gang was defined as "a group of youths or young adults in [the respondent's] jurisdiction that [the respondent] or other responsible persons in [the respondent's] agency or community are willing to identify or classify as a 'gang.'" The survey respondents (law enforcement agents) were instructed to exclude motorcycle gangs, hate or ideology groups, prison gangs, and exclusively adult gangs.

Young Juveniles in Gangs

Gangs sometimes serve as families for children whose own families are dysfunctional. Gang members have said there is often little need to intimidate youngsters in order to recruit them because they know what children need and are willing to provide it in return for their commitment. Gangs provide emotional support, shelter, and clothing—in essence, just what the child's family may not be providing. However, some children are intimidated into joining gangs either out of fear or for protection from other gangs.

A Pervasive Problem

According to the OJJDP, only nineteen states reported gang problems in the 1970s, but by the late 1990s youth gangs were reported in all fifty states and the District of Columbia (*The Growth of Youth Gang Problems in the United States: 1970–98,* April 2001). By 1998, 3,700 localities—including about 2,550 cities, towns, and villages, and 1,150 counties—had reported gang problems. Between the mid-1990s and 2002, however, there was a steady decline in reported gang problems, particularly in suburban counties and small cities. (See Figure 8.8.)

Traditionally, gangs were big-city problems. It is still true that the larger the population of a city the greater the likelihood that gangs operate in that city. But gangs have spread to small towns, villages, and rural areas that often do not have their own police departments. In 2002 there were active youth gangs in all of the nation's largest cities, 87% of mid-size cities (with populations between 100,000 and 249,000), 38% percent of suburban counties, 27% of small cities (population below 25,000), and 12% of rural counties. The OJJDP estimated that 21,500 gangs were operating in the United States in 2002, with 731,500 members.

FIGURE 8.8

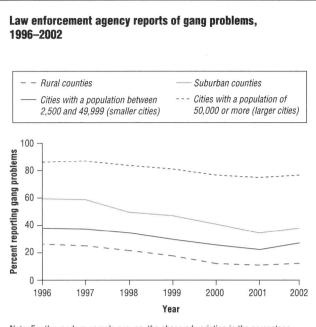

Law enforcement agency reports of gang problems, 1996–2002

- - - Rural counties .... Suburban counties

—— Cities with a population between 2,500 and 49,999 (smaller cities)

- - - Cities with a population of 50,000 or more (larger cities)

Note: For the random-sample groups, the observed variation in the percentage of agencies reporting gang problems from 2000 to 2002 is within the range attributable to sampling error; therefore, it does not represent a definitive change in the estimated number of jurisdictions with gang problems.

SOURCE: "Law Enforcement Agency Reports of Gang Problems," in "Highlights of the 2002 National Youth Gang Survey," *OJJDP Fact Sheet,* Office of Justice Programs, Office of Juvenile Justice and Delinquency Prevention, April 2004, http://www.ncjrs.org/pdffiles1/ojjdp/fs200401.pdf (accessed September 16, 2004)

Portrait of the Modern Youth Gang

The authors of "Hybrid and Other Modern Gangs" examined survey data and the latest research to offer a portrait of the modern youth gang. The stereotypical view holds that youth gangs are tightly organized groups comprised of African-American or Hispanic inner-city males operating under strict codes of conduct with explicit punishments for infractions of the rules. The new "hybrid" gangs may have as members people of both genders, from different racial groups, espousing radically opposing viewpoints; for example, the authors note, a modern gang might be made up of African-Americans, white supremacists, and girls. The gangs are found in schools and the military and in territories as small as shopping malls. Rules or codes of conduct may be unclear. Hybrid gangs sometimes borrow the symbols, graffiti, and even the names of established Los Angeles- or Chicago-based organizations (Bloods and Crips, Black Gangster Disciples, or Vice Lords, for example) but are actually locally based and have no connection to those organizations. Rival gangs may cooperate in criminal activity and mergers of small gangs are common.

The *1998 National Youth Gang Survey* reported that an estimated 36% of youth gangs had members from two or more racial or ethnic groups, and that small cities, par-

ticularly in the Midwest, had the largest proportion of gangs with mixed race/ethnicity. Other studies show that in most cases the modern adolescent may refuse to join a gang without fear of reprisal, even though gangs try to maintain the illusion that leaving is impossible. OJJDP-supported longitudinal studies in Denver, Colorado (1988–99), Rochester, New York (1986–97), and the Seattle Social Development Project in Seattle (1985–2001) showed that well over half (54–69%) of youths who joined gangs in those cities remained for one year or less, while only 9–21% stayed for three or more years.

According to "Hybrid and Other Modern Gangs," in places where gangs are a fairly recent phenomenon, drug sales and distribution are less likely to be major problems. Gang member involvement in drug sales is most prevalent in areas where gangs emerged between 1981 and 1985, at the height of the crack cocaine epidemic. Highly organized, entrepreneurial, gang control of drug distribution across wide areas—and the violent crime that goes with it—are associated with the gangs that emerged in the 1960s and 1970s in Los Angeles and Chicago.

Court Rulings on Gang Loitering

In order to combat the rise in violent and drug-related crime, which was attributed to a rise in criminal street gang activity, the city of Chicago enacted a Gang Congregation Ordinance in 1992. The ordinance prohibited "criminal street gang members from loitering with one another or with other persons in any public place," regardless of whether the others were fellow gang members. Police officers were required to order any group of people standing around "with no apparent purpose" to move along if the officers believed at least one of them belonged to a street gang. The ordinance had considerable support in the high-crime neighborhoods in which it was implemented. During the three years the law was in effect, more than 42,000 people were arrested for refusing to obey police orders to move along. The ordinance was struck down in 2001 when the U.S. Supreme Court agreed with a lower court that it was unconstitutionally vague and encompassed a great deal of harmless behavior (*Chicago v. Morales* [No. 97–1121]).

HOMICIDE

According to the Bureau of Justice Statistics, death rates from homicide doubled from the mid-1960s to the mid-1970s, fell in the mid-1980s, rose again in the late 1980s, then declined sharply through 2001, reaching an overall rate of 7.1 per one hundred thousand people, including those who died in the September 11, 2001, terrorist attacks. But beginning in the mid-1980s the number of teens involved in homicide as either victims and perpetrators rose dramatically. In 2001 homicides were the fourth-leading cause of death in children younger than five years old; the fourth-leading cause for children five to fourteen; and the second-leading cause in fifteen- to twenty-four-year-olds. The youngest victims were more likely to know the perpetrator than adult victims were. More than one-quarter of the victims of gang-related murders were under the age of eighteen. Between 1976 and 1999 children made up 9.8% of the victims of homicide; 10.7% of offenders were under eighteen.

Homicide rates among teens vary dramatically by race. In 2000 young African-Americans of both sexes ages fifteen to twenty-four were six times more likely (20.5 per one hundred thousand) than young whites (3.3 per one hundred thousand) to be murdered. Young African-American men are particularly vulnerable. According to the National Center for Health Statistics, 85.7 out of every one hundred thousand African-American males ages fifteen to twenty-four were victims of homicide, down from a high of 137.1 per one hundred thousand in 1990 (*National Vital Statistics Reports*, vol. 52, no. 9, November 7, 2003).

Trends in Gang Homicides

The number of youth gang homicides declined in the 1990s, but the trends varied by city and also varied between the early and later parts of the decade, according to the OJJDP report "Youth Gang Homicides in the 1990s" (March 2001). From 1990 to 1996 the total number of homicides decreased by 256 (almost 15%) in the 408 cities surveyed, from 1,748 to 1,492 incidents.

Although the total number of gang-related homicides was down even further in 2002 (1,232), 91 out of 142 cities reported at least one gang-related homicide. Los Angeles and Chicago reported more gang-related homicides (655) than the other 89 cities combined (577). In those two cities approximately half the homicides were gang-related.

GUNS AND VIOLENCE

Schools, neighborhoods, and even private homes can be dangerous places for children and adolescents. Knives, handguns, and shotguns turn up in searches of school lockers. News reports describe incidents of children being shot on playgrounds or of youths firing rifles as they cruise the streets in cars. M. H. Swahn et al., in "Prevalence of Youth Access to Alcohol or a Gun in the Home" (*Injury Prevention*, 2002), found that nearly one-quarter (24.3%) of adolescents ages twelve to eighteen have easy access to a gun in their homes.

From 1983 to 1994 gun homicides by juveniles tripled, while homicides involving other types of weapons decreased. (See Figure 8.9.) Between 1994 and 1997, however, gun homicides by young people declined sharply, back to approximately 1989 levels.

FIGURE 8.9

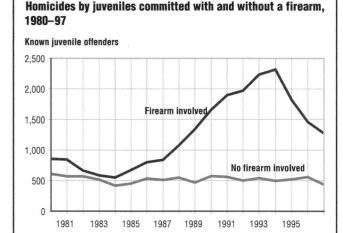

Homicides by juveniles committed with and without a firearm, 1980–97

Between 1980 and 1987, firearms were used in just over half (54%) of all homicides involving a juvenile offender. Then firearm-related homicides began to increase, so that, by 1994, most homicides by juvenile offenders (82%) involved the use of firearms.

SOURCE: "The Sharp Decline in Homicides by Juveniles between 1994 and 1997 Was Attributable Entirely to a Decline in Homicides by Firearm," in "1999 National Report Series, Kids and Guns," *Juvenile Justice Bulletin,* U.S. Department of Justice, Office of Justice Programs, Office of Juvenile Justice and Delinquency Prevention, March 2000, http://www.ncjrs.org/html/ojjdp/jjbul2000_03_2/kid2.html (accessed September 16, 2004)

Young Homicide Victims

In 2002, 1,357 youths under age eighteen were murdered—9.7% of all homicides that year. (See Table 8.5.) A slightly higher percentage of young victims were white (50.8%) than African-American (45%). Almost two-thirds of the young victims (63.9%) were male and one-third (36%) were female. According to the Centers for Disease Control and Prevention (*Injury Fact Book 2001–2002*), in 1998 82% of homicide victims under age eighteen were killed with guns.

Firearm Deaths among Children and Youth

The teen death rate for firearm-related injuries more than doubled between 1970 and 1995 before beginning to decline. During those peak years, the overwhelming majority of deaths among young African-American males were firearm-associated, and American teenage boys were more likely to die from gunshot wounds than from all natural causes combined. In 2001 more than one out of every five deaths among all fifteen- to twenty-four-year-olds and half of all deaths among African-American males fifteen to twenty-four were caused by firearms.

Carrying a Weapon

The 2003 *Youth Risk Behavior Survey* reported that 17.1% of all students in grades nine through twelve claimed to have carried a weapon at least once within the previous thirty days, and 6.1% had carried a gun. (See Table 8.6.) Males were significantly more likely to carry a

TABLE 8.5

Murder victims age 24 and under, by age, sex, and race, 2002

Age	Total	Sex			Race			
		Male	Female	Unknown	White	Black	Other	Unknown
Total	14,054	10,779	3,251	24	6,757	6,730	377	190
Percent distribution[1]	100.0	76.7	23.1	0.2	48.1	47.9	2.7	1.4
Under 18[2]	1,357	867	489	1	689	610	45	13
Under 22[2]	3,398	2,624	772	2	1,581	1,683	104	30
18 and over[2]	12,406	9,703	2,699	4	5,945	6,009	331	121
Infant (under 1)	180	96	84	0	102	71	4	3
1 to 4	328	180	147	1	176	134	14	4
5 to 8	86	35	51	0	50	33	3	0
9 to 12	92	50	42	0	53	35	4	0
13 to 16	390	281	109	0	180	196	11	3
17 to 19	1,184	1,018	166	0	519	615	39	11
20 to 24	2,756	2,356	398	2	1,115	1,560	58	23

[1]Because of rounding, the percentages may not add to 100.0.
[2]Does not include unknown ages.

SOURCE: Adapted from "Table 2.5. Murder Victims by Age, Sex and Race, 2002," in *Crime in the United States 2002,* Federal Bureau of Investigation, 2003, http://www.fbi.gov/ucr/cius_02/pdf/2sectiontwo.pdf (accessed September 16, 2004)

weapon (26.9%) than females (6.7%), and males were even more likely than females to carry a gun (10.2% and 1.6%, respectively). Non-Hispanic white, non-Hispanic African-American, and Hispanic students were equally likely to carry a weapon.

Tracing "Crime Guns"

Rising rates of violent crime involving the use of firearms in the late 1980s and early 1990s led the U.S. Bureau of Alcohol, Tobacco and Firearms (ATF) to initiate the Youth Crime Gun Interdiction Initiative in 1996. In 2000 law enforcement agencies in the forty-four large cities that participated in the program submitted 88,570 trace requests on "crime guns" to the ATF's National Tracing Center. Firearms were traced to the point of original sale as one component of the national effort to reduce youth violence involving firearms.

In 2002 the ATF announced the results of these year-2000 traces (*Crime Gun Trace Reports 2000 National Report,* July 2002). More than 18,000 crime guns (20%) had been confiscated from youths ages eighteen to twenty-four, the peak years of age for being a crime gun possessor. Juveniles made up 8% of crime gun possessors (4,112 guns). Six of every ten handguns confiscated from youths and juveniles were semiautomatic pistols, slightly higher than the five of every ten confiscated from adults. Most of the crime guns had been obtained from firearm traffickers, who illegally sell new, used, or stolen weapons. The serial numbers had been obliterated from most of the traced guns, indicating that someone in the chain of possession assumed that the gun would be used for a crime. The ATF investigation revealed that nearly a third of the crime guns had entered the retail market between December 1996 and December 1997. This short "time to crime" indicated the ease with which a criminal

could "fence" (sell a stolen item to a third party) a gun and the pervasiveness of the illegal firearms market.

Weapons Offenses

Weapons offenses are violations of local, state, and/or federal statutes or regulations that control deadly weapons. Deadly weapons include firearms and their ammunition, silencers, explosives, and certain knives. Between 1985 and 1993 the juvenile arrest rate for weapon offenses more than doubled, from about ninety per one hundred thousand juveniles to about 225 per one hundred thousand. After the peak in 1993, however, the rate of arrests declined sharply to about 1985 levels by 2000. (See Figure 8.10.)

Teenage males arrested for weapons offenses in 1980, 1990, 2000, and 2001 far outnumbered females arrested. (See Table 8.2 and Table 8.3.) However, between 1980 and 2001 the arrest rate for weapons offenses increased two-and-a-half times for females age ten to seventeen, from 10.6 to 25.4 arrests per one hundred thousand; at the same time the rate for males only increased from 169.8 to 197.7 arrests per one hundred thousand. (See Table 8.7.) In 1980 the rate for males was sixteen times that for females; in 2000 the rate for males was not quite eight times that for females.

Survey Results: Teens and Violence

The largest survey of teens ever undertaken in the United States, "Protecting Adolescents from Harm: Findings from the National Longitudinal Study on Adolescent Health" (*Journal of the American Medical Association,* vol. 278, no. 10, September 1997), was conducted by researchers at the University of North Carolina, Chapel Hill, and the University of Minnesota. The researchers questioned 90,000 students in grades seven through

TABLE 8.6

Percentage of high school students who carried a weapon[1] or a gun[2], by sex, race, ethnicity, and grade, 2003

Category	Carried a weapon			Carried a gun		
	Female %	Male %	Total %	Female %	Male %	Total %
Race/ethnicity						
White[3]	5.5	27.1	16.7	1.5	10.0	5.9
Black[3]	9.8	24.9	17.3	1.4	10.6	6.0
Hispanic	8.5	24.3	16.5	2.6	8.2	5.4
Grade						
9	8.8	26.6	18.0	2.1	9.3	5.8
10	5.2	26.5	15.9	1.4	10.4	5.9
11	6.8	29.2	15.2	1.6	10.0	6.3
12	5.2	25.2	15.5	1.0	10.0	5.7
Total	**6.7**	**26.9**	**17.1**	**1.6**	**10.2**	**6.1**

[1]For example, a gun, knife, or club on ≥1 of the 30 days preceding the survey.
[2]On ≥1 of the 30 days preceding the survey.
[3]Non-Hispanic.

SOURCE: "Table 6. Percentage of High School Students Who Carried a Weapon or a Gun, by Sex, Race/Ethnicity, and Grade," in "Youth Risk Behavior Surveillance—United States, 2003," *Centers for Disease Control and Prevention Surveillance Summaries: Morbidity and Mortality Weekly Report,* vol. 53, no. SS–02, May 21, 2004, http://www.cdc.gov/mmwr/PDF/SS/SS5302.pdf (accessed September 16, 2004)

FIGURE 8.10

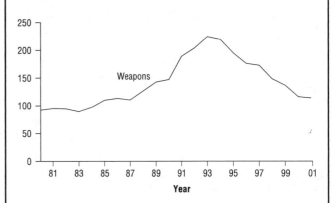

Trends in juvenile arrest rates for weapons law violations, 1980–2001

Arrests per 100,000 juveniles ages 10–17

- The juvenile arrest rates for weapons law violations and for murder more than doubled between 1987 and the peak year of 1993.
- After 1993, both rates fell substantially. The juvenile arrest rate for weapons law violations was cut in half, falling 49% and returning to the 1987 level.

SOURCE: Howard N. Snyder, "Trends in Juvenile Arrest Rates for Weapons Law Violations and for Murder Were Similar between 1980 and 2001," in "Juvenile Arrests 2001," *Juvenile Justice Bulletin,* U.S. Department of Justice, Office of Justice Programs, Office of Juvenile Justice and Delinquency Prevention, December 2003, http://www.ncjrs.org/pdffiles1/ojjdp/201370.pdf (accessed September 16, 2004)

twelve at 145 schools around the country. They found that almost one-fourth of students surveyed had easy access to guns at home. Adolescents living in homes where guns were kept were more likely to behave violently and more likely to contemplate or attempt suicide.

Teens who said they had strong family ties were less likely to be involved in interpersonal violence than those who said they did not have close family ties. Older teens (ninth through twelfth grades) who had a parent present at breakfast, after school, at dinner, and at bedtime were also less likely to behave violently.

More than 10% of males and 5% of females interviewed said they had committed a violent act in the previous year. These acts included participating in fights, injuring someone, threatening someone with a weapon, using a weapon in a fight, or shooting or stabbing someone.

Younger teens (seventh and eighth graders) more often reported having been involved in violent activities than older teens. Urban teens, teens whose families received welfare, and Native American teens seemed more likely than others to have been involved in violence. About one in eight students said that they had brought a weapon to school in the month prior to being surveyed.

VICTIMIZATION OF JUVENILES

Teenagers and young adults—especially African-Americans—are the most likely groups to become victims of violent crime. In 2002 the rate of serious violent crime ranged from a high of more than 58.2 per one thousand persons ages sixteen to nineteen to a low of 3.4 per one thousand persons age sixty-five or older (Callie Marie Rennison and Michael R. Rand, "Table 6. Rates of Violent Crime and Personal Theft, by Gender, Age, Race, and Hispanic Origin, 2002," in "Criminal Victimization, 2002," *National Crime Victimization Survey,* NCJ 199994, U.S. Department of Justice, Bureau of Justic Statistics, Washington, DC, August 2003).

JAMES ALAN FOX EXAMINES TRENDS IN JUVENILE VIOLENCE

Juvenile Violent Crime Rate Jumps in the Late 1980s to Mid-1990s

The late 1980s to 1994 saw a tremendous rise in violent crimes committed by juveniles and in the homicide victimization of teens and young adults. In 1996 James Alan Fox, Ph.D., of Northeastern University wrote in *Trends in Juvenile Violence: A Report to the United States Attorney General on Current and Future Rates of Juvenile Offending* (Bureau of Justice Statistics, Washington, DC) that there were two violent crime trends ongoing in America—one for the young and one for the mature. These trends, Fox theorized, were moving in opposite directions.

For example, between 1990 and 1994, the rate of homicide committed by adults age twenty-five and older declined 18% as the baby boomers matured into their middle-age years. At the same time, however, the homicide rate among teens ages fourteen to seventeen increased

TABLE 8.7

Juvenile arrest rates by offense and gender, selected years, 1980–2001

Offense	1980	1990	2001
Total including suspicion	7414.3	8032.2	6889.8
Violent crime index*	334.1	428.4	296.1
Murder and nonnegligent manslaughter	6.4	11.9	4.3
Forcible rape	15.9	21.8	13.8
Robbery	167.5	155.3	80.8
Aggravated assault	144.3	239.4	197.1
Property crime index**	2562.2	2563.4	1499.1
Burglary	794.2	513.2	270.3
Larceny-theft	1520.9	1677.6	1053.3
Motor vehicle theft	221.9	347.1	150.3
Arson	25.2	25.6	25.3
Other assaults	299.8	537.8	717
Vandalism	398.3	450.1	309.8
Weapons carrying, possessing, etc.	91.9	146.8	113.9
Drug abuse violations	383.7	304.2	623.4
Driving under the influence	109.3	71.8	58.4
Liquor laws	511.4	577.3	413.5
Drunkenness	150.4	88.0	62.1
Disorderly conduct	447.8	443.8	521.3
Curfew and loitering law violations	245.0	319.9	449.3
Runaways	502.5	620.1	403.7

Juvenile male arrest rates (arrests of males ages 10–17/100,000 males ages 10–17)

Offense	1980	1990	2001
Total including suspicion	11543.2	12091.9	9587.8
Violent crime index*	586.7	735.7	470.9
Murder and nonnegligent manslaughter	11.6	22.0	7.5
Forcible rape	30.6	41.7	26.6
Robbery	305.1	276.8	143.9
Aggravated assault	239.4	395.2	292.9
Property crime index**	4081.9	3903.1	1993.8
Burglary	1456.7	920.6	463.2
Larceny-theft	2190.8	2333.3	1244.8
Motor vehicle theft	390.4	604.3	242.9
Arson	44.1	44.9	43
Other assaults	462.7	803.1	949.1
Vandalism	717.2	802.9	523.6
Weapons carrying, possessing, etc.	169.8	268.1	197.7
Drug abuse violations	626.5	526.9	1027.7
Driving under the influence	191.7	120.3	93.5
Liquor laws	773.4	808.3	546.1
Drunkenness	253.9	145.0	95.4
Disorderly conduct	722.0	687.0	710.1
Curfew and loitering law violations	368.7	453.3	603.4
Runaways	401.4	522.4	317.3

TABLE 8.7

Juvenile arrest rates by offense and gender, selected years, 1980–2001 [CONTINUED]

Juvenile female arrest rates (arrests of females ages 10–17/100,000 females ages 10–17)

Offense	1980	1990	2001
Total including suspicion	3104.1	3754.0	4041.7
Violent crime index*	70.4	104.6	111.6
Murder and nonnegligent manslaughter	1.0	1.2	0.9
Forcible rape	0.6	0.8	0.4
Robbery	23.8	27.3	14.3
Aggravated assault	45.0	75.3	96
Property crime index**	975.7	1151.7	976.9
Burglary	102.6	84.0	66.6
Larceny-theft	821.6	986.6	851.1
Motor vehicle theft	45.9	75.9	52.6
Arson	5.6	5.2	6.6
Other assaults	129.7	258.2	471.9
Vandalism	65.4	78.4	84.1
Weapons carrying, possessing, etc.	10.6	19.0	25.4
Drug abuse violations	130.3	69.4	196.7
Driving under the influence	23.2	20.7	21.4
Liquor laws	237.9	333.8	273.5
Drunkenness	42.3	28.0	27
Disorderly conduct	161.6	187.4	321.8
Curfew and loitering law violations	115.8	179.4	286.5
Runaways	608.1	723.2	494.9

*Violent crime index includes murder & nonnegligent manslaughter, forcible rape, robbery, and aggravated assault.
**Property crime index includes burglary, larceny-theft, motor vehicle theft, and arson.
Note: Persons of Hispanic ethnicity may by of any race. Arrests of Hispanics are not reported separately.

SOURCE: Adapted from "Juvenile Arrest Rates by Offense, Sex, and Race (1980–2001)," National Center for Juvenile Justice, May 31, 2003, http://ojjdp.ncjrs.org/ojstatbb/excel/JAR_053103.xls (accessed July 29, 2004)

Dire Predictions in 1996

Fox concluded that too many teenagers, particularly teens in urban areas, were plagued with idleness and even hopelessness. A growing number of teens and preteens saw few feasible or attractive alternatives to violence, drug use, and gang membership. Fox believed that this generation of youth had more dangerous drugs in their bodies, more deadly weapons in their hands, and a seemingly more casual attitude toward violence than previous generations. He predicted in his 1996 report that youth violence would worsen because by the year 2005 the number of teens ages fourteen to seventeen was predicted to be 20% higher than the 1994 level.

Facing the Future—The Rise of Teen Drug Abuse and Teen Violence (Committee on the Judiciary and International Narcotics Control Caucus, Washington, DC, 1995) also warned, "Not only are we facing a rise in violent crime by children, but we are also facing a rising number of children. The combination adds up to expectations that our nation will face an unprecedented number of crimes committed by juveniles."

Predictions Revised in the Face of a Decline in Juvenile Crime

The ominous predictions Fox made in 1996 did not come true. According to the FBI, the juvenile arrest

22% at a time when the population in this age group was declining. Between 1985 and 1994 the rate of homicide committed by teenagers aged fourteen to seventeen years increased 172%. For African-American males the rate of increase was 261 percent. In 1994 African-American males ages fourteen to twenty-four made up slightly more than 1% of the population yet were 17% of the victims of homicide and 30% of the perpetrators of homicide.

Fox also found a rise in the number of killings among family and friends. Guns, he reasoned, made it easy for juveniles to have deadly disputes over small matters such as a pair of athletic shoes or a dirty look. Also, he stated that while the negative impact of drugs, guns, and gang culture became more threatening, the positive socializing forces of family, school, religion, and neighborhood became weaker. The problem of unsupervised youth was reflected in the time-of-day patterns of juvenile violence. The prime time for juvenile crime was during the after-school hours.

rate for murder fell 74% between 1993 and 2000. Fox wrote two follow-ups to his 1996 report. In *Trends in Juvenile Violence: 1997 Update,* Fox warned that teen violence had not disappeared—the rates of homicide had fallen but remained at levels twice as high as in the 1980s. In *Homicide Trends in the United States: 2000 Update,* Fox and his colleagues wrote that teen homicide rates had fallen to levels not seen since the late 1960s, "reversing one of the most dramatic trends in homicide victimization."

CHAPTER 9
RECREATION AND THE USE OF FREE TIME

HISTORICAL CHANGES AND WORKING MOTHERS

Prior to the early twentieth century, when the economy was primarily agricultural, most American families needed their children to work on the farm during their after-school hours and on weekends. When children finished high school—and most left before they graduated (in school year 1899–1900 only 6.4% of seventeen-year-olds graduated high school)—both male and female youth were expected to contribute their full-time labor to the family economy. All activities, including schooling, occupied less time in young people's lives than the very important contribution they made to the economic welfare of the family. At that time, there was no "adolescence" as we know it, no time of relative leisure between childhood and adulthood.

The concept of adolescence as a transitional period between childhood and adulthood, in which young people were still semi-dependent upon parents, began to emerge in the late nineteenth century. By 1904 psychologist G. Stanley Hall began to argue that adolescence was a universal developmental stage—an essential, stormy, stressful period in the sexual maturation process. Since the concept of adolescence came to be culturally accepted, most youths have not been expected to contribute significantly to the economic welfare of the family. Although many teens in the twenty-first century hold part-time or even full-time jobs, greater importance is attached to their education as more young people attend and complete high school and college. The transition into adulthood therefore lasts longer than it did two or three generations ago.

Because of this significant cultural change, most children and adolescents in the late twentieth and early twenty-first century had considerably more discretionary time to themselves than those in pre-1940s America. This trend began to shift somewhat at the close of the twentieth century. A study by the University of Michigan's Institute for Social Research (ISR) (*Changes in American Children's Time, 1981–97,* September 2000) found that free time left

after schooling, eating, and sleeping had decreased 12%, from 56.5 hours per week in 1981 to forty-nine hours in 1997. Researchers found that more time was spent at school, up by an average of more than ninety minutes per week. This increased time at school was not due to longer school days, but because more children were in preschool and before- and after-school programs because more mothers were working outside of the home.

According to the authors of the study, more women entering the paid labor force affected not only the amount of free time children had, but also how they spent that time. Because children spent more time away from their parents in structured environments such as sports practice and educational activities like doing homework, they spent less time in unstructured activities such as playing.

Although more women were in the workforce, children actually spent more time with their mothers in 1997 than in 1981 (John F. Sandberg and Sandra L. Hofferth, *Changes in Children's Time with Parents, U.S. 1981–1997,* May 2001). In 1997 children ages three to twelve spent 4.3 more hours per day with their mothers (a total of nearly 28.6 hours a week) than they did in 1981 (24.3 hours). Children also spent nearly three more hours per day with their fathers in 1997 (18.6 hours a week) than they did in 1981 (15.6 hours). The children were either engaged in activities with their parents (including housework), or the parents were simply accessible to their children during these hours.

Table 9.1 shows the percentage of children who interacted in various ways with a parent in 2000. The amount of interaction decreased as a child aged and went to school, and also tended to be less if the child was living with an unmarried parent. The majority of children under six years old (53%) ate breakfast with a parent every day of the week, three-quarters (76.4%) ate dinner with a parent every day of the week, and almost three-quarters were played with by a parent just for fun three or more times per

TABLE 9.1

Indicators of daily interaction of children under 18 with designated parent, by marital status of designated parent, 2000

(Numbers in thousands)

		Children under 6 years old					Children 6 to 17 years old			
		Living with married parents[2]		Living with unmarried parent(s)[3]			Living with married parents[2]		Living with unmarried parent(s)[3]	
		Interaction with		Interaction with			Interaction with		Interaction with	
Characteristic	Total[1]	Designated parent	Father/ stepfather[4]	Designated parent	Father[4]	Total[1]	Designated parent	Father/ stepfather[4]	Designated parent	Father[4]
Number of children	23,385	17,240	16,649	6,145	835	48,278	34,645	33,114	13,633	636
Percent distribution										
Parent ate breakfast with child in typical week										
No days	14.2	12.6	26.0	18.5	34.8	20.5	18.3	30.2	26.1	38.9
1 to 2 days	16.5	15.6	33.1	19.1	25.4	28.7	27.3	33.1	32.3	32.2
3 to 6 days	16.3	16.7	16.5	15.3	8.8	21.5	22.1	17.3	19.9	12.8
7 days	53.0	55.1	24.3	47.2	31.1	29.3	32.3	19.3	21.7	16.1
Parent ate dinner with child in typical week										
No days	5.3	5.0	7.5	6.2	15.2	3.2	2.8	5.0	4.4	3.6
1 to 2 days	3.3	2.8	8.5	4.6	7.0	5.4	4.9	8.9	6.8	8.2
3 to 6 days	15.1	14.6	24.4	16.4	11.3	26.8	27.0	32.1	26.5	17.7
7 days	76.4	77.7	59.7	72.8	66.5	64.5	65.4	54.0	62.4	70.6
Child praised by parent										
Never—once a week	1.8	1.5	2.5	2.6	5.8	5.2	4.6	6.9	6.8	11.8
A few times per week	7.6	6.1	9.7	12.1	17.0	22.7	21.4	26.5	26.0	24.2
Once or twice per day	20.3	19.3	24.8	23.1	23.0	31.3	31.3	30.6	31.2	36.2
Three or more times per day	70.3	73.2	63.0	62.3	54.2	40.9	42.7	36.0	36.1	27.9
Child talked to or played with for 5 minutes or more just for fun										
Never—once a week	1.0	0.4	1.7	2.6	5.8	5.7	4.9	6.8	7.9	8.5
A few times per week	6.5	5.3	10.6	9.7	17.5	19.6	18.7	24.2	22.1	28.6
Once or twice per day	21.1	19.3	27.7	26.2	22.3	33.4	33.0	33.8	34.7	35.0
Three or more times per day	71.4	75.0	60.0	61.5	54.4	41.2	43.4	35.2	35.4	27.9

[1]Totals given refer to questions of designated parents, regardless of sex of parent.
[2]Married includes married, spouse present and married, spouse absent (excluding separated).
[3]Includes never married, widowed, divorced, and separated.
[4]Question asked of fathers who were not the designated parents. Fathers must be biological, step- or adoptive and must be present in the household. Percent of children eating meals with fathers does not represent presence of both parents at the meals.

SOURCE: Terry A. Lugaila, "Table 2. Selected Indicators of Daily Interaction of Children under 18 with Designated Parent or with Father/Stepfather if Present by Marital Status of Designated Parent: 2000," in *A Child's Day: 2000 (Selected Indicators of Child Well-Being),* Current Population Reports, P70–89, U.S. Census Bureau, August 2003, http://www.census.gov/prod/2003pubs/p70-89.pdf (accessed September 16, 2004)

day (71.4%) and were praised by a parent three or more times per day (70.3%). In contrast, only 29.3% of school-age children ate breakfast with a parent every day, 64.5% ate dinner with a parent every day, and less than half were played with by a parent three or more times per day (41.2%) or praised by a parent three or more times per day (40.9%). If a child lived with an unmarried parent, these kinds of daily parental interaction was less likely to occur.

TELEVISION-WATCHING HABITS OF YOUNG PEOPLE

According to the ISR report *Changes in Children's Time with Parents,* collecting data about the activities children engage in is complicated because observation is the best way but it is expensive, time-consuming, and intrusive. Before 1997 there was only one study, the *Time Use Longitudinal Panel Study, 1975–81,* that contained nationally representative data on U.S. children's use of

time. The 1997 Child Development Supplement to the Panel Study of Income Dynamics had parents maintain twenty-four-hour time diaries; researchers used these diaries to make comparisons between children's time use in 1981 and 1997.

The ISR report *Changes in American Children's Time* revealed that in 1997 children ages three to twelve spent 27% of their weekly time watching television, down from 30% in 1981. Television watching as a primary activity also declined by 23% during the period. The Centers for Disease Control and Prevention, in *National Youth Risk Behavior Survey: 1991–2003, Trends in the Prevalence of Physical Activity,* reported that in 1999 42.8% of high schoolers watched three or more hours of television on an average school day; that percentage had declined to 38.2% in 2003. (See Table 9.2.)

While in general the amount of time children spent watching television declined in the 1980s and 1990s, tele-

TABLE 9.2

Television watching among high school students, by demographic characteristics, 2003

| | Watched ≥3 hours/day of TV | | |
| | Female | Male | Total |
Category	%	%	%
Race/ethnicity			
White**	26.8	31.7	**29.3**
Black**	70.0	64.3	**67.2**
Hispanic	45.1	46.8	**45.9**
Grade			
9	41.2	46.5	**44.0**
10	39.0	42.9	**41.0**
11	34.7	34.1	**34.4**
12	31.3	29.9	**30.6**
Total	**37.0**	**39.3**	**38.2**

*For example, push-ups, sit-ups, or weightlifting on ≥3 of the 7 days preceding the survey to strengthen or tone their muscles.
†Run by their school or community groups during the 12 months preceding the survey.
§On an average school day.
**Non-Hispanic.

SOURCE: Adapted From "Table 56. Percentage of High School Students Who Did Strengthening Exercises, Played on One or More Sports Teams, and Who Watched Three or More Hours/Day of Television, by Sex, Race/Ethnicity, and Grade," in "Youth Risk Behavior Surveillance—United States, 2003," *Surveillance Summaries, Morbidity and Mortality Weekly Report,* vol. 53, no. SS-02, May 21, 2004, http://www.cdc.gov/mmwr/PDF/SS/SS5302.pdf (accessed September 16, 2004)

vision watching varied significantly by age and race. Between 1982 and 1999 the percentage of nine-year-olds who watched at least six hours of television daily decreased from 26% to 19%. The percentage of thirteen-year-olds watching six or more hours of television daily fell from 16% to 12%. However, a greater proportion of seventeen-year-olds (7%) watched six or more hours of television daily in 1999 than in 1982 (6%). In all three age groups African-American children were more likely than white and Hispanic children to watch six or more hours of television each day. (See Figure 9.1.)

In *A Child's Day: 2000* (U.S. Census Bureau, Current Population Reports, P70–89, 2003), Terry A. Lugila outlined the three kinds of television rules a family might use to limit children's television watching: limits on the type of program children watched, rules governing how early or how late the television could be on, and limits on the number of hours children watched television. In 2000 85% of children older than three years lived in households where at least one rule limited their television watching: 89.9% of preschoolers, 92% of children age six to eleven, and 72.6% of children ages twelve to seventeen. (See Table 9.3.) Well over half of children ages three to five (64.4%) and children ages six to eleven (69%) lived in households with all three types of television rules; that percentage dropped to 41.7% of children ages twelve to seventeen.

The percentage of children living in families with television rules also varied by race/ethnicity and by the educational level of parents. Non-Hispanic white children were more likely to have television rules than African-American, Asian, or Hispanic children of any age. (See Table 9.3.) Parents were also more likely to impose television rules as their educational level went up.

The presence or absence of television rules was also correlated with the amount of times per week family members read to young children. In families where there were no television rules, 17.1% of three- to five-year-olds were not read to at all. (See Figure 9.2.) In contrast, in families with one or two television rules only 7.5% of three- to five-year-olds were not read to at all, and in families with all three types of rules, only 5.9% of preschoolers were not read to at all. The percentage of children who were read to seven or more times per week also went up in families with more television rules.

YOUNG PEOPLE AT PLAY

The CDC reported in December 2000 on two different surveys measuring how eleven- to eighteen-year-olds like to spend their free time (*Exploring How to Motivate Behavior Change among Teens in America*, 2000, http://www.cdc.gov/youthcampaign/research/PDF/4.4.04-ReLitSupportDvpRes.pdf). The respondents differed markedly by gender. Girls favored going to the movies: almost two-thirds of girls (62%) and only one-third of boys (31%) listed movies as their favorite leisure activity. Boys, on the other hand, preferred playing video games (33% of boys compared with 7% of girls) and sports (23% of boys compared with 6% of girls). Both boys and girls enjoyed reading and would do more of it if they felt they had the time.

A 1998 Roper youth poll asked youngsters ages six to seventeen what they liked to do in their spare time. Three of five (60%) of the respondents chose hanging out and playing with friends as their favorite way to spend free time. More than half (53%) favored playing sports and participating in outdoor activities. This active play was the first choice of eight- to seventeen-year-old boys and ranked second for boys six to seven years of age and girls ages eight to twelve. The third most popular free-time activities for young people were the ones they did in their rooms, including solitary pursuits such as watching videos or playing video games and social activities such as talking on the phone. More girls (44%) than boys (30%) identified these activities as favorites.

Young children liked games of make-believe. One-third of six- to seven-year-olds (31% of boys and 37% of girls) liked to don costumes and pretend to be superheroes and heroines. Although all children like make-believe games, even at young ages, favorite play activities often varied by gender. Young boys six to seven years of age (44%) were twice as likely as girls the same age (22%) to

FIGURE 9.1

Percentage of students who watched 6 or more hours of television per day, by race and Hispanic origin, selected years 1982–99

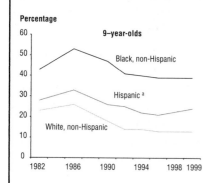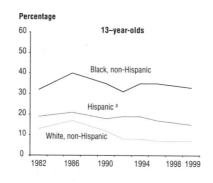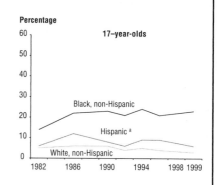

[a] Persons of Hispanic origin may be of any race.

SOURCE: Adapted from "Table SD 1.5.A. Percentage of 9-Year-Old Students in the United States Who Watch 6 or More Hours of Television per Day, by Gender, Race, and Hispanic Origin and Type of School: Selected Years, 1982–1999," "Table SD 1.5.B. Percentage of 13-Year-Old Students in the United States Who Watch 6 or More Hours of Television per Day, by Gender, Race, and Hispanic Origin, Type of School and Parents' Education Level: Selected Years: 1982–1999," and "Table SD 1.5.C. Percentage of 17-Year-Old Students in the United States Who Watch 6 or More Hours of Television per Day, by Gender, Race, and Hispanic Origin, Type of School and Parents' Education Level: Selected Years 1978–1999," in *Trends in the Well-Being of America's Children & Youth 2003*, U.S. Department of Health and Human Services, 2003, http://aspe.hhs.gov/hsp/03trends/ (accessed September 16, 2004)

TABLE 9.3

Family television rules for children 3–17 years old, by selected characteristics, 1994–2000

(Numbers in thousands)

Characteristics	Number of children			Family television rules					
				Percent with at least one television rule			Percent with three types of television rules		
	3 to 5 years	6 to 11 years	12 to 17 years	3 to 5 years	6 to 11 years	12 to 17 years	3 to 5 years	6 to 11 years	12 to 17 years
Total children, 2000	11,780	24,581	23,697	89.9	92.0	72.6	64.4	69.0	41.7
Sex of child									
Female	5,808	11,998	11,526	89.0	91.8	71.5	63.3	69.2	40.9
Male	5,971	12,583	12,171	90.7	92.3	73.6	65.5	68.7	42.5
Race and ethnicity of child									
White	9,420	19,340	18,678	90.3	92.8	73.5	63.9	68.8	41.1
Non-Hispanic	7,631	15,080	15,301	91.8	93.9	74.2	64.0	68.5	40.3
Black	1,813	4,061	3,745	88.3	89.5	69.6	68.3	69.9	45.6
Asian and Pacific Islander	391	846	834	86.2	88.9	70.2	61.3	69.8	44.8
Hispanic (of any race)	1,928	4,520	3,683	83.7	89.1	69.6	64.2	70.3	44.3
Marital status of parent									
Married[1]	8,700	17,858	16,787	91.0	92.8	75.3	66.2	70.5	43.8
Separated, divorced, widowed	1,233	4,047	5,431	89.9	90.9	65.3	63.2	68.1	34.5
Never married	1,846	2,676	1,480	84.4	88.4	68.5	56.9	59.9	44.2
Parent's educational level									
High school or less	5,393	11,990	11,665	86.2	89.6	70.2	60.5	66.8	40.0
Some college	2,083	4,385	4,110	92.4	94.1	73.9	64.2	69.5	44.0
Vocational or associate degree	1,399	3,236	3,420	92.2	92.7	75.6	63.0	68.0	41.5
Bachelor's degree	2,180	3,784	3,063	92.9	95.3	76.4	72.0	73.3	43.9
Advanced degree	725	1,186	1,440	96.6	97.1	72.6	74.0	77.5	45.0
Poverty status[2]									
Below poverty level	2,006	4,379	3,476	84.5	87.4	71.9	59.8	66.0	44.4
On or above poverty level	9,520	19,663	19,861	90.6	93.0	72.7	65.1	69.5	41.3
100 to 199 percent of poverty	2,968	5,956	5,353	88.0	89.4	71.3	64.7	68.0	41.5
200 percent of poverty or higher	6,552	13,707	14,508	91.7	94.6	73.2	65.3	70.1	41.2
Total children, 1998	12,088	24,095	23,345	89.4	93.3	75.3	61.6	65.2	41.0
Total children, 1994[3]	9,576	19,472	17,683	91.3	94.7	79.2	54.0	60.3	40.2

[1]Married includes married, spouse present and married, spouse absent (excluding separated).
[2]For families with income reported.
[3]Based on those children for whom valid answers were reported (no allocation for nonresponse).

SOURCE: Terry A. Lugaila, "Table 5. Family Television Rules for Children 3 to 17 Years Old by Selected Characteristics: 1994 to 2000," in *A Child's Day: 2000 (Selected Indicators of Child Well-Being)*, Current Population Reports, P70–89, U.S. Census Bureau, August 2003, http://www.census.gov/prod/2003pubs/p70-89.pdf (accessed September 16, 2004)

FIGURE 9.2

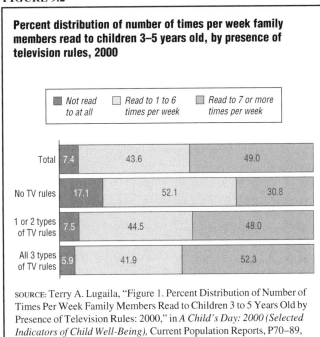

Percent distribution of number of times per week family members read to children 3–5 years old, by presence of television rules, 2000

■ Not read to at all □ Read to 1 to 6 times per week ▨ Read to 7 or more times per week

	Not read to at all	Read to 1 to 6 times per week	Read to 7 or more times per week
Total	7.4	43.6	49.0
No TV rules	17.1	52.1	30.8
1 or 2 types of TV rules	7.5	44.5	48.0
All 3 types of TV rules	5.9	41.9	52.3

SOURCE: Terry A. Lugaila, "Figure 1. Percent Distribution of Number of Times Per Week Family Members Read to Children 3 to 5 Years Old by Presence of Television Rules: 2000," in *A Child's Day: 2000 (Selected Indicators of Child Well-Being)*, Current Population Reports, P70–89, U.S. Census Bureau, August 2003, http://www.census.gov/prod/2003pubs/p70-89.pdf (accessed September 16, 2004)

construct objects with Lego blocks or to make models. Among eight- to twelve-year-olds, girls were more interested than boys in arts (music, crafts, dance, and theater), fashion, and cooking. Boys at this age were more interested in watching and playing sports and in war and military history. Both girls' and boys' levels of interest in music and fashion rose when they became teenagers, but girls' interest was higher at all ages.

Play Trends

The ISR report *Changes in American Children's Time* found that the proportion of discretionary time three- to twelve-year-olds spent on different activities each week has changed significantly since 1981. Changes in children's use of free time varied by age group. For three- to five-year-olds, significant increases were reported in the percentage of discretionary time spent in sports participation (up 173%), reading (up 190%), outdoor activities (up 185%), and art activities (up 157%). Significant decreases were reported for this age group in the amount of discretionary time spent playing (down 33%), attending church (down 58%), and participating in youth groups (down 57%).

For six- to eight-year-olds, there were significant increases in the amount of discretionary time spent shopping (up 168%), studying (up 146%), participating in art activities (up 114%), and pursuing hobbies (up 33%). Significant decreases occurred in discretionary time spent watching television (down 19%), playing (down 25%), playing sports (down 13%), doing chores (down 25%), visiting (down 24%), attending church (down 22%), and talking with family members (down 55%).

For nine- to twelve-year-olds, there were significant increases in the amount of discretionary time spent on arts activities (up 145%), pursuing hobbies (up 133%), playing sports (up 35%), shopping (up 23%), playing (up 20%), and reading (up 17%). Significant decreases occurred in the amount of discretionary time spent watching television (down 32%), doing chores (down 30%), visiting (down 30%), attending church services (down 44%), talking with family members (down 49%), participating in outdoor activities (down 22%), and participating in youth groups (down 13%).

Younger Children's Favorite Sports

According to the National Sporting Goods Association, about 19.9 million children ages seven to eleven participated in sports activities in 2003. Some of the most popular sports among children in this age group were bicycle riding (8.5 million), in-line skating (5.9 million), basketball (6.3 million), soccer (4.7 million), and fishing (3.7 million). Participation of seven- to eleven-year-olds in many of even the most popular sports went down between 1993 and 2003, including bicycle riding (down 24.3%), fishing (down 26.8%), and playing baseball (down 16.7%). Participation of seven- to eleven-year-olds in other sports went way up in that period, including skateboarding (up 60.6%), skiing (up 71.7%), and snowboarding (up 295.2%).

Teens' Favorite Sports

In the 2002–03 school year, approximately four million boys and 2.9 million girls participated in high school athletic programs, according to the National Federation of State High School Associations. The most popular sports among boys in terms of number of participants were football, basketball, track and field, baseball, and soccer. Girls' top sports in terms of number of participants were basketball, track and field, volleyball, softball (fast pitch), and soccer. The 2003 Youth Risk Behavior Survey found that 51% of high school girls and 64% of high school boys played on at least one sports team.

The National Sporting Goods Association reported that 24.7 million children twelve through seventeen participated in sports activities in 2003. Some of the most favored activities among adolescents in this age group were basketball (7.9 million), bicycle riding (6.5 million), in-line skating (3.7 million), fishing (4.1 million), and baseball (4.1 million). Sports that saw substantial gains in participation of twelve- to seventeen-year-olds from 1993 to 2003 included golf (up 35.9%), skateboarding (up 69.1%), and snowboarding (up 184.6%).

TEENAGERS, LEISURE TIME, AND VOLUNTEERISM

While the free time activities of young children can be in large part determined by their parents' schedules, teenagers tend to have more genuinely free time. What do they do with it? Teenagers fill their leisure hours with a variety of activities, some of which are not always agreeable to adults. Some parents claim teens watch too much television; most experts believe teens do not get enough physical exercise; teachers complain their students spend too little time on schoolwork or reading. This unfavorable picture, however, is not entirely accurate.

Volunteerism

Many young people spend a substantial amount of time in a wide variety of volunteer and community service activities, ranging from cooking holiday dinners for homeless people or visiting nursing homes to serving as mentors for children or volunteering at the local animal shelter. According to the U.S. Census Bureau in its *Statistical Abstract of the United States: 2003,* in 1999, the most recent data available, slightly more than fourteen million youngsters (52%) in grades six through twelve performed community service, up from 12.6 million (49%) in 1996. (See Table 9.4.) About 48% of students in grades six through eight, 50% of students in grades nine and ten, and 61% of students in grades eleven and twelve performed community service in 1999. Female students (57%) were more likely than male students (48%) to be engaged in community service. White students (56%) were more likely than African-American (48%) or Hispanic (38%) students to volunteer. The higher the students' parents' level of education, the more likely the student was to participate in community service activities.

During his first term President George W. Bush placed an emphasis on volunteerism. In his 2002 State of the Union address he called on Americans of all ages to pledge at least two years during their lives, or four thousand hours, to volunteer work. Toward this effort, the White House launched the Freedom Corps on January 30, 2002, to foster a culture of service, citizenship, and responsibility. In 2002 more than 130,000 schools received copies of the *Students in Service to America* guidebook. Programs for youth volunteerism described in the *USA Freedom Corps 2003 Annual Report* (January 2004) included Learn and Serve America, designed to provide grants to educational programs linking classroom instruction with community service. In 2003 more than one million students volunteered in community service projects.

Extracurricular Activities

The extracurricular activities engaged in by children and teens vary by age and gender. Adolescents are more likely than younger children to participate in sports (37.2% of twelve- to seventeen-year-olds compared with 30.6% of six- to eleven-year-olds). (See Table 9.5.) Both adolescents and younger children were equally likely to participate in clubs (34.4% and 33.8%, respectively). Younger children (32%) were more likely to take lessons (music, dance, language, computers, and religion, for

TABLE 9.4

Community service participation of students in grades 6–12, 1996 and 1999

(12,627 represents 12,627,000)

Characteristic	Students participating in community service (1,000)		Percent of students participating in community service	
	1996	1999	1996	1999
Total*	12,627	14,010	49	52
Student's grade:				
Grades 6 through 8	5,462	5,573	47	48
Grades 9 and 10	3,370	3,984	45	50
Grades 11 and 12	3,795	4,448	56	61
Sex:				
Male	5,971	6,490	45	48
Female	6,656	7,520	53	57
Race/ethnicity:				
White, non-Hispanic	9,113	9,933	53	56
Black, non-Hispanic	1,761	1,972	43	48
Hispanic	1,246	1,323	38	38
Other race-ethnicity	506	781	50	54
Parent's highest level of education:				
Less than high school	834	935	34	37
High school graduate or equivalent	3,273	3,298	42	46
Voc/tech education after high school or some college	3,617	4,000	48	50
College graduate	2,250	2,648	58	62
Graduate or professional school	2,653	3,129	64	64

*Includes students with no grade reported.

SOURCE: Adapted from "No. 586. Community Service Participation of Students in Grades 6 through 12: 1996 and 1999," in Statistical Abstract of the United States: 2003, U.S. Census Bureau, http://www.census.gov/prod/2004pubs/03statab/socinsur.pdf (accessed September 16, 2004)

example) than were older children (26.2%). Boys of both age groups were more likely to participate in sports than were girls; girls were more likely to join clubs and take lessons. White children, children with parents who were highly educated, and children whose family incomes were above the poverty line were all more likely than other children to take part in extracurricular activities.

Teens' Favorite Leisure Activities

Teens engage in a wide variety of leisure activities. Teenage Research Unlimited (TRU), a marketing research firm based in Northbrook, Illinois, polled more than two thousand teens in 2000 to find out what motivated them. The number-one answer, given by 50% of respondents, was, "We're about fun." The 2000 TRU Teenage Marketing and Lifestyle Study listed leisure activities to determine how many teens participated and how many hours a week the teens spent participating in each activity. The number-one leisure activity was watching TV, with 98% of respondents indicating they participated, spending an average of 11.2 hours a week watching. Other leisure activities chosen by at least three-quarters of respondents were:

TABLE 9.5

Extracurricular activities of school-age children, by selected characteristics, 1994–2000

(Numbers in thousands)

| | Number of children | | Percent participating in specified extracurricular activity | | | | | |
| | | | Sports | | Clubs | | Lessons | |
Characteristic	6 to 11 years	12 to 17 years	6 to 11 years	12 to 17 years	6 to 11 years	12 to 17 years	6 to 11 years	12 to 17 years
Total children, 2000	**24,581**	**23,697**	**30.6**	**37.2**	**33.8**	**34.4**	**32.0**	**26.2**
Sex of child								
Female	11,998	11,526	24.4	32.5	36.0	37.5	36.8	30.2
Male	12,583	12,171	36.5	41.6	31.8	31.4	27.5	22.3
Race and ethnicity of child								
White	19,340	18,678	33.4	39.2	35.7	36.4	33.5	27.5
Non-Hispanic	15,080	15,301	36.7	41.7	39.9	39.4	37.1	29.1
Black	4,061	3,745	20.6	30.5	27.6	25.0	25.4	19.4
Asian and Pacific Islander	846	834	20.4	25.7	27.1	31.5	36.0	33.1
Hispanic (of any race)	4,520	3,683	21.5	28.0	20.2	22.9	20.7	20.3
Marital status of parent								
Married[1]	17,858	16,787	34.7	40.2	37.2	37.9	36.1	29.3
Separated, divorced, widowed	4,047	5,431	25.1	30.3	26.7	27.7	22.5	19.8
Never married	2,676	1,480	18.6	28.3	22.1	19.1	20.0	14.2
Parent's educational level								
High school or less	11,990	11,665	23.5	29.6	24.9	26.2	21.5	19.6
Some college	4,385	4,110	31.1	40.1	36.0	37.6	35.1	28.6
Vocational or associate degree	3,236	3,420	35.1	39.8	40.9	39.6	37.6	29.1
Bachelor's degree	3,784	3,063	42.9	49.3	47.9	46.7	50.0	37.7
Advanced degree	1,186	1,440	48.9	58.4	52.8	52.6	54.6	41.2
Poverty status[2]								
Below poverty level	4,379	3,476	15.9	24.9	22.8	23.2	18.6	17.9
On or above poverty level	19,663	19,861	34.3	39.6	36.6	36.6	35.3	27.9
100 to 199 percent of poverty	5,956	5,353	24.1	30.7	27.2	29.5	23.7	20.8
200 percent of poverty or higher	13,707	14,508	38.7	42.9	40.7	39.2	40.3	30.5
Total children, 1998	**24,095**	**23,345**	**31.7**	**39.4**	**34.4**	**35.3**	**30.8**	**26.9**
Total children, 1994[3]	**19,426**	**17,665**	**34.3**	**42.2**	**38.8**	**42.5**	**23.7**	**19.1**

[1]Married includes married, spouse present and married, spouse absent (excluding separated).
[2]For families with incomes reported.
[3]Number of children varied by activity depending on those reporting valid answers and were approximately 19.4 million 6- to 11-year-olds and 17.6 million.

SOURCE: Terry A. Lugaila, "Table 6. Extracurricular Activities of School Age Children by Selected Characteristics: 1994 to 2000," in *A Child's Day: 2000 (Selected Indicators of Child Well-Being),* Current Population Reports, P70–89, U.S. Census Bureau, August 2003, http://www.census.gov/prod/2003pubs/p70-89.pdf (accessed September 16, 2004)

- Listening to FM radio (10.1 hours/week)
- Listening to CDs or tapes (9.5 hours/week)
- Hanging out with friends (8.6 hours/week)
- Talking on the phone (local calls) (6.2 hours/week)
- Exercising/working out (5.1 hours/week)
- Doing chores/running errands (4.3 hours/week)
- Reading magazines for pleasure (2.8 hours/week)
- Reading newspapers (2.5 hours/week)

READING AND WRITING

According to "Survey Finds Teens Enjoy Reading, Lack Time" (*Teacher Librarian,*, vol. 27, April 2000), teenagers enjoyed reading for pleasure and would read more if they had more time. Among teenagers' favorite books were those by horror writer Stephen King, the Harry Potter series, and some classics like *To Kill a Mockingbird* and *The Catcher in the Rye*. Many teens reported reading magazines (66%), newspapers (59%), and even the backs of cereal boxes (48%) for fun. More girls than boys showed enthusiasm for reading (50% and 31%, respectively).

In *The Condition of Education, 1999,* the U.S. Department of Education reported on the percentage of students who read at home in 1996 and what types of materials they read. Subsequent editions of this publication up to 2005 had not reported on reading. Reading stories and novels was popular with all age groups surveyed in 1996. About 42.6% of nine-year-olds, 38% of thirteen-year-olds, and 27.1% of seventeen-year-olds read stories and novels on their own time. Magazines were also popular reading, enjoyed by 17% of nine-year-olds, 39.5% of thirteen-year-olds, and 41% of seventeen-year-olds. (High school students read more magazines at home than stories and novels.) Newspapers ranked number three, with 5.2% of nine-year-olds reading them at home, 8.4% of thirteen-year-olds, and 21.3% of seventeen-year-olds.

COMPUTER USE

Computer usage is an extremely popular pastime for children. According to *A Nation Online: How Americans*

FIGURE 9.3

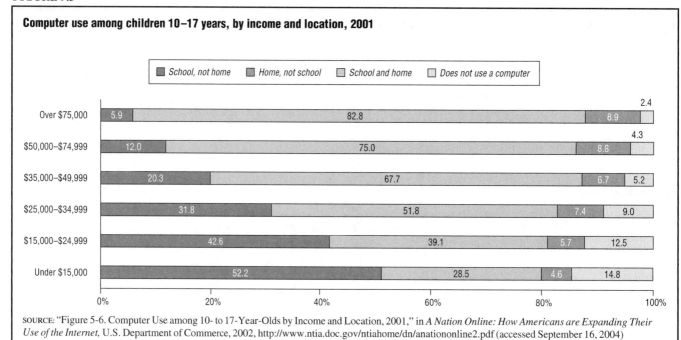

Computer use among children 10–17 years, by income and location, 2001

Legend: ■ *School, not home* ■ *Home, not school* □ *School and home* □ *Does not use a computer*

Income	School, not home	Home, not school	School and home	Does not use a computer
Over $75,000	5.9	82.8	8.9	2.4
$50,000–$74,999	12.0	75.0	8.8	4.3
$35,000–$49,999	20.3	67.7	6.7	5.2
$25,000–$34,999	31.8	51.8	7.4	9.0
$15,000–$24,999	42.6	39.1	5.7	12.5
Under $15,000	52.2	28.5	4.6	14.8

SOURCE: "Figure 5-6. Computer Use among 10- to 17-Year-Olds by Income and Location, 2001," in *A Nation Online: How Americans are Expanding Their Use of the Internet,* U.S. Department of Commerce, 2002, http://www.ntia.doc.gov/ntiahome/dn/anationonline2.pdf (accessed September 16, 2004)

Are Expanding Their Use of the Internet (U.S. Department of Commerce, 2002), in 2001 children and teenagers used computers and the Internet more than any other age group. Almost nine out of ten (89.5%) children between five and seventeen (forty-eight million children) used computers. Three-quarters (75.6%) of fourteen- to seventeen-year-olds and 65.4% of ten- to thirteen-year-olds used the Internet. Even very young children were using computers and accessing the Internet. Nearly three-quarters (71%) of three- to eight-year-olds used computers, and 27.9% of them used the Internet.

The availability of computers at schools has narrowed the gap in computer usage rates between low- and high-income families. (See Figure 9.3.) In the 2002–03 school year 113,637 schools had computers, with an average of one computer for every four students (*Statistical Abstract of the United States, 2003*). In fall 2002 99% of public schools in the United States had access to the Internet, up from 35% in fall 1994 (*Internet Access in U.S. Public Schools and Classrooms: 1994–2002,* National Center for Education Statistics, 2003).

School characteristics affect students' access to computers, according to *Internet Access in U.S. Public Schools and Classrooms: 1994–2002.* Although school characteristics do not affect schools' Internet access, they do affect access to the Internet within instructional rooms. A lower percentage of schools in urban areas where poverty tends to be concentrated had instructional room Internet access (88%) than schools located in towns (96%) and rural areas (93%).

Children and young adults use computers and the Internet for a variety of activities. As children get older, they use the Internet for more and more activities, and the Internet has become integrated into their daily routines. Children of all ages use the Internet for schoolwork, to send e-mail, to play games, to listen to the radio or watch movies, or to talk to others in chat rooms. The percentage of children engaging in each of these activities increases with age, with the exceptions of playing games—which peaks in the ten- to thirteen-year-old age group—and using chatrooms, which peaks in the fourteen- to seventeen-year-old group. (See Figure 9.4.)

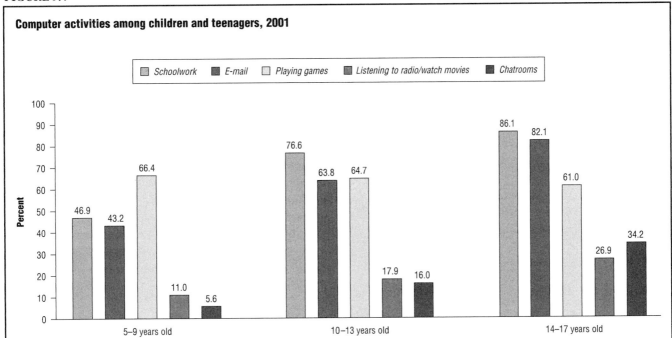

FIGURE 9.4

Computer activities among children and teenagers, 2001

Legend: Schoolwork ▪ E-mail ▪ Playing games ▪ Listening to radio/watch movies ▪ Chatrooms

5–9 years old: 46.9, 43.2, 66.4, 11.0, 5.6
10–13 years old: 76.6, 63.8, 64.7, 17.9, 16.0
14–17 years old: 86.1, 82.1, 61.0, 26.9, 34.2

SOURCE: Adapted from "Figure 5-13: Major Activities among Children and Young Adults, 2001 as a Percentage of U.S. Population under 25 Years Old," in *A Nation Online: How Americans are Expanding their Use of the Internet,* U.S. Department of Commerce, 2002, http://www.ntia.doc.gov/ntiahome/dn/anationonline2.pdf (accessed September 16, 2004)

CHAPTER 10
CHILDREN AROUND THE WORLD

Childhood should be a time of nurturing, growing, learning, playing, and preparing for adulthood. For many children, childhood is essentially a carefree, positive experience. For many others, however, even surviving childhood is a challenge.

A UNITED NATIONS SUMMIT

In 1990 children from all over the world met with more than seventy world leaders at the United Nations (UN) in New York City to ask for a better future for the children of the world. They determined that four of the main problems that face children throughout the world are death, disease, hunger, and illiteracy. Based on this meeting, the United Nations International Children's Emergency Fund (UNICEF) set goals it hoped to achieve by the year 2000. UNICEF goals for the year 2000 included reducing the death rates for children under the age of five by one-third, as well as ensuring access to prenatal care for all women, making family-planning education and services available to all couples, and increasing recognition of the special health and nutritional needs of women at all life stages.

Mortality

According to the U.S. Census Bureau report *World Population Profile: 2002* (2004), the global under-age-five mortality rate in 2002 was seventy-seven per one thousand live births. In more developed countries the mortality rate was ten per one thousand live births for children under five; in less developed countries the under-five rate was eighty-five per one thousand live births. The global AIDS epidemic is responsible for a rise in child mortality rates in many less-developed countries. In some sub-Saharan African countries, the infant mortality rates have doubled due to AIDS. Countries torn by war, disease, or famine also have high child mortality rates. (See Figure 10.1.)

Political upheaval around the world in the late twentieth century (including in Bosnia, Somalia, Rwanda, Koso-vo, Eastern Europe, and the former Soviet Union) subjected untold numbers of children to war, hunger, injury, and death. UNICEF estimated that in the late 1990s alone, 1.5 million children were killed in armed conflicts and four million more were disabled, maimed, blinded, or brain-damaged. At least five million became refugees and twelve million more were uprooted from their communities. Many other children suffered harm to their health, nutrition, and education as conflicts destroyed their countries' crops, schools, clinics, and infrastructure.

In the early twenty-first century UNICEF made the humanitarian situation of the children of Iraq a priority. In 2003 Iraq was at war for the third time in twenty years—this time with the United States—making conditions for Iraqi children even worse than they had been under the previous twelve years of United Nations sanctions. Even before the war, one in eight Iraqi children died before his or her fifth birthday. After the initial wave of combat ended, UNICEF determined that 8% of children in Iraq suffered from acute malnutrition, double the percentage from just one year before. Children in Iraq were injured or killed daily from playing with live ammunition that littered the cities and countryside. And no immunizations had been available since before the start of the war.

THE UNICEF GOALS. The UNICEF goal was to reduce the child mortality rate to seventy deaths per one thousand live births, or to two-thirds of the 1990 level—whichever was less—by 2000. The objective for 2015 was for fewer than forty-five deaths per one thousand births—a goal that most experts consider ambitious.

PROGRESS TOWARD GOALS AND THE FUTURE. In 1999 the United Nations invited countries around the world to review the progress they had made since the 1990 World Summit for Children and to submit a report. The results were summarized in two 2001 UN reports, *Progress since the World Summit for Children: A Statisti-*

FIGURE 10.1

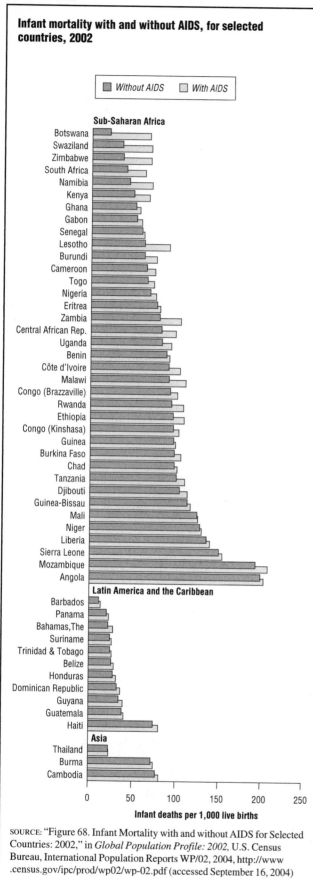

Infant mortality with and without AIDS, for selected countries, 2002

□ Without AIDS   □ With AIDS

Sub-Saharan Africa

Botswana, Swaziland, Zimbabwe, South Africa, Namibia, Kenya, Ghana, Gabon, Senegal, Lesotho, Burundi, Cameroon, Togo, Nigeria, Eritrea, Zambia, Central African Rep., Uganda, Benin, Côte d'Ivoire, Malawi, Congo (Brazzaville), Rwanda, Ethiopia, Congo (Kinshasa), Guinea, Burkina Faso, Chad, Tanzania, Djibouti, Guinea-Bissau, Mali, Niger, Liberia, Sierra Leone, Mozambique, Angola

Latin America and the Caribbean

Barbados, Panama, Bahamas,The, Suriname, Trinidad & Tobago, Belize, Honduras, Dominican Republic, Guyana, Guatemala, Haiti

Asia

Thailand, Burma, Cambodia

0   50   100   150   200   250

Infant deaths per 1,000 live births

SOURCE: "Figure 68. Infant Mortality with and without AIDS for Selected Countries: 2002," in *Global Population Profile: 2002,* U.S. Census Bureau, International Population Reports WP/02, 2004, http://www.census.gov/ipc/prod/wp02/wp-02.pdf (accessed September 16, 2004)

cal Report and *We the Children: Meeting the Promises of the World Summit for Children.*

The UN reported that the average global under-five mortality rate declined by 11%, from ninety-three deaths per one thousand live births in the early 1990s to eighty-three deaths per one thousand births in 2000, and sixty-three countries achieved the targeted one-third reduction. Looking ahead to 2010, the UN predicted that more than half of all under-five deaths will occur in sub-Saharan Africa, where the child mortality rate in 2002 was 153 per one thousand live births. High rates of HIV/AIDS and low immunization coverage due to weak health care systems contributed to the high child mortality rate there.

Disease

Estimates of the proportion of deaths of children under age five caused by various factors are uncertain, because often vital registration systems that provide cause of death are nonexistent in developing countries, and often there are multiple conditions leading to death. It is estimated that more than half of childhood deaths globally are due to disease and other preventable conditions: diarrhea, respiratory infections and pneumonia, measles, and newborn tetanus. Malnutrition is a factor in half of all of these deaths.

UNICEF hoped to eradicate polio by 2000; eliminate tetanus in newborns; eliminate guinea worm disease; reduce deaths due to acute respiratory infection by one-third among children under five; reduce measles cases by 90% and measles deaths by 95%; cut deaths from diarrhea among children under five in half; and make safe water and sanitation available to every family. Also, immunization rates were to be maintained at "a high level."

PROGRESS REPORT. The UN reported in *Progress since the World Summit for Children* that the results of efforts to reduce childhood disease worldwide were mixed. Polio was nearing eradication, tetanus deaths of newborns had decreased by more than half from 470,000 to 215,000, guinea worm infection—a parasite—had dropped by 88% worldwide and had been eradicated in India, and deaths from diarrhea had been cut in half. Although reported annual cases of measles had declined by 40%, measles continued to be a major killer of children in sub-Saharan Africa and South Asia because many children in those regions were not immunized. Over a billion people still lacked access to safe drinking water, and 2.4 billion people lacked access to sanitation facilities (although that coverage had increased, from 51% to 61%). In more than forty countries, fewer than half the children with acute respiratory infection were taken to the doctor to be treated with antibiotics. Immunization levels globally remained above 70% through the 1990s (72% in 1999), but in sub-Saharan Africa less than half of the children received routine immunizations in 2000.

SEXUALLY TRANSMITTED DISEASES AND HIV/AIDS. According to the World Health Organization (WHO) fact sheet "Young People and Sexually Transmitted Diseases" (December 1997), 333 million new cases of sexually transmitted diseases (STDs) occur worldwide each year, and at least one-third of them (111 million) are contracted by young people under twenty-five years old. Adolescents are at high risk for STDs because they tend to engage in short-term relationships and do not use condoms consistently. In some countries cultural expectations encourage young men to express their sexual masculinity at a young age, have multiple partners, or visit prostitutes, increasing the risk of STDs and AIDS.

In countries like Thailand, Guatemala, and Ecuador, young men are as likely to experience their first intercourse with a prostitute as with a girlfriend or wife. In some countries girls are sold into prostitution. Throughout Latin America, sexual activity begins earlier for males than for females, and first partners are frequently older women. These factors potentially jeopardize the reproductive health of young men by increasing the number and type of their sexual contacts.

Cultural factors can also make young women vulnerable to STDs. When young women are paired with older men with more experience and more prior sexual contacts, they are more likely to become infected. They are also less likely to be able to demand condom use. Furthermore, STDs are often asymptomatic in women, and young women often lack the information to identify STD symptoms when they do encounter them.

Sexually transmitted diseases increase the risk of HIV transmission as much as fivefold. The WHO, in *The World Health Report 2004—Changing History* (2004), reported that by 2004 thirty-four to forty-six million people were living with HIV/AIDS, and more than twenty million people had already died of the disease. Of the five million people who became infected in 2003 alone, seven hundred thousand were children, infected by transmission from HIV-infected mothers during pregnancy, birth, or breastfeeding. Because of lack of treatment of HIV-positive pregnant women, almost one-third of babies born to HIV-infected mothers in sub-Saharan Africa contract HIV.

One impact of AIDS and HIV on children is the loss of one or both parents to the disease. A joint U.S. Agency for International Development (USAID), UNICEF, and UNAIDS report, *Children on the Brink 2004* (July 2004), noted that at the end of 2003, fifteen million children had lost one or both parents to AIDS, up from 11.5 million just two years previously.

Other consequences of the epidemic are also dire. In *The World Health Report 2004—Changing History,* WHO emphasized that people in poverty are the most likely to become infected and are also the hardest hit by the suffering caused by HIV/AIDS. The financial burden of the disease forces poor families even deeper into poverty, causing them to turn in desperation to child labor, sale of assets, and migration. Decreasing numbers of working adults in the African countries with the most AIDS cases increases the numbers of children and elderly people who depend on each wage earner. And, WHO argued, as children and adolescents watch their parents and other adults die, the psychological impact is immeasurable; in addition, the high rate of premature deaths of young adults "weakens the process through which human capital—people's experience, skill and knowledge—is accumulated and transmitted across generations." It would be difficult to overestimate the impact the epidemic is having on the countries most affected.

Hunger and Malnutrition

According to 2001 UNICEF data, an estimated 150 million children under age five in developing countries were malnourished. Malnutrition contributes to about half of child deaths globally, because malnourished children have low resistance to common infections. In 1990 UNICEF set as one of its goals the reduction of malnutrition among children under five by 50% by the year 2000. Although this goal was not achieved, prevalence of low weight in developing countries dropped from 32% to 28% between 1990 and 2000. However, South Asia and sub-Saharan Africa still suffer high malnutrition levels. In South Asia nearly half of all children under age five were underweight in 2000. Half of all malnourished children lived in South Asia, and another one-fifth in sub-Saharan Africa.

Other UNICEF goals related to nutrition were the elimination of vitamin A deficiency, which can cause blindness, and the elimination of iodine deficiency, which can cause mental retardation. According to UNICEF data, one million child deaths were prevented between 1998 and 2000 simply by providing vitamin A supplements. In addition, the goal of elimination of iodine deficiency disorders encouraged programs that increased the use of iodized salt from 20% of households in the developing world to 70% in 2000.

Education and Illiteracy

According to UNICEF's report *The State of the World's Children 2004,* 121 million primary-school-age children worldwide were not in school. The children most likely not to attend school were children who were working; those who had been affected by HIV/AIDS, conflict, or disability; those who were poor or minorities; and those who lived in rural areas. Worldwide, girls were less likely to receive education than boys. UNICEF argues that the negative effects of not attending school are greater for girls than for boys—mothers' lack of education puts the next generation in danger of repeating the cycle, and uneducated girls are at a greater risk for sexual exploitation and exposure to sexually transmitted diseases and HIV/AIDS.

Education of girls has a big impact on the next generation. According to the UN, fertility rates decline as education rises. Children of mothers with no education are more than twice as likely to die or to be malnourished than are children of mothers with a secondary or higher-level education. Education for girls also leads to reduced infant and mother mortality, as well as better nourished and healthier children and families.

The 2000 World Education Forum in Dakar, Senegal, underscored the importance of ensuring education for girls and women. Following that conference, initiatives were formed with the goal of accelerating progress in girls' education and achieving the Millennium Development Goal of gender parity in primary and secondary education by 2005: thirteen agencies formed the United Nations Girls' Education Initiative; and UNICEF launched the "25 by 2005 Girls Education Campaign," which focuses on getting girls into schools in twenty-five specified countries.

In spite of formal commitments by governments, funding for elementary education generally receives low priority, and, according to *The State of the World's Children 2004,* when money gets tight, girls' education is sacrificed first. *We the Children* reported that only a small percent of government budgets in the developing world and less than 2% of all international aid for development are directed toward elementary education. Many countries are unable to meet their educational goals because war or political conflicts and the high cost of HIV/AIDS are decimating their budgets.

AN INTERNATIONAL COMPARISON

In 2002 29% of the world's population of six billion people were fourteen or younger, but the proportion of young people to the total global population is projected to decrease until 2050 (*Global Population Profile: 2002,* U.S. Census Bureau, International Population Reports WP/02, 2004). The population pyramids of regions around the world, however, reflected remarkable diversity in the age makeup of populations. (See Figure 10.2.) More than one-third of the population in the Middle East/North Africa (34.6%) and almost half the population in Sub-Saharan Africa (43.8%) were fourteen years old or younger.

Birth Rates for Teens and Adults

According to the United Nations report *World Population Prospects: The 2002 Revision: Highlights* (http://www.un.org/esa/population/publications/wpp2002/WPP2002-HIGHLIGHTSrev1.PDF), in 2000 there were 2.7 births per woman, but there were great regional differences. Fertility rates were far lower in developed nations than in developing countries. The forty-nine least-developed countries had a fertility rate of 5.46 children per woman, well above the global population replacement rate of 2.3. In the most developed regions the total fertility rate was 1.58 children per woman, well below the population replacement rate for developed countries of 2.1. In these countries more people died each year than new children were born; their populations were either declining or would have been declining if not for immigration from other countries.

According to the U.S. Census Bureau's *Global Population Profile,* a few regions contribute most of the world's population increase. Of the 128.6 million babies born in 2002, one of every three was born either in India (24.6 million) or mainland China (17.2 million). Another one-third of the globe's babies were born in the rest of Asia (43.5 million). More than 26.5 million babies were born in sub-Saharan Africa, nearly 11.3 million in Latin America and the Caribbean, and 8.5 million in the Near East and North Africa. Figure 10.3 shows the contributors to world population by region and the proportion of growth attributable to the largest contributors in each region. According to the United Nations report, *World Population Prospects: The 2002 Revision,* by about 2050, fertility levels in the majority of developing countries are expected to fall below the population replacement rate.

Globally, the period of adolescence is lengthening. Girls are reaching puberty at a younger age at the same time that the age of marriage is rising. Thus, young people face a longer period of time during which they are sexually mature and may be sexually active. Many youths are postponing marriage to stay in school or for socioeconomic reasons. As a consequence, many first pregnancies and first births occur outside of marriage.

The UN predicts that between 2000 and 2005 about thirteen million babies will be born worldwide to young women fifteen to nineteen years old. About 9.5 of ten of these babies (12.8 million) will be born in the developing countries of Asia, Africa, and Latin America. The proportion of teens having a child by the age of twenty in these regions is high—around 50% in West Africa and South-Central Asia, and one-third in Latin America. The UN reported that in sub-Saharan Africa, adolescent females (aged fifteen to nineteen) had a fertility rate in 2002 of 116 births per one thousand women, far higher than in any other region of the world. The number of adolescent women capable of bearing children was projected to increase in the less developed countries between 1998 and 2025. Because childbearing among older women has declined more rapidly than among teens, a larger proportion of all births now occur among adolescents.

Among developed countries the United States has the highest rate of teen childbearing. According to the UN, the five countries with the lowest teenage birth rates are Korea, Japan, Switzerland, the Netherlands, and Sweden; all have teen birth rates of fewer than seven per one thousand.

Young women are more likely than mature women to have pregnancy-related complications that can endanger

FIGURE 10.2

Population pyramids by region and selected countries, 2002

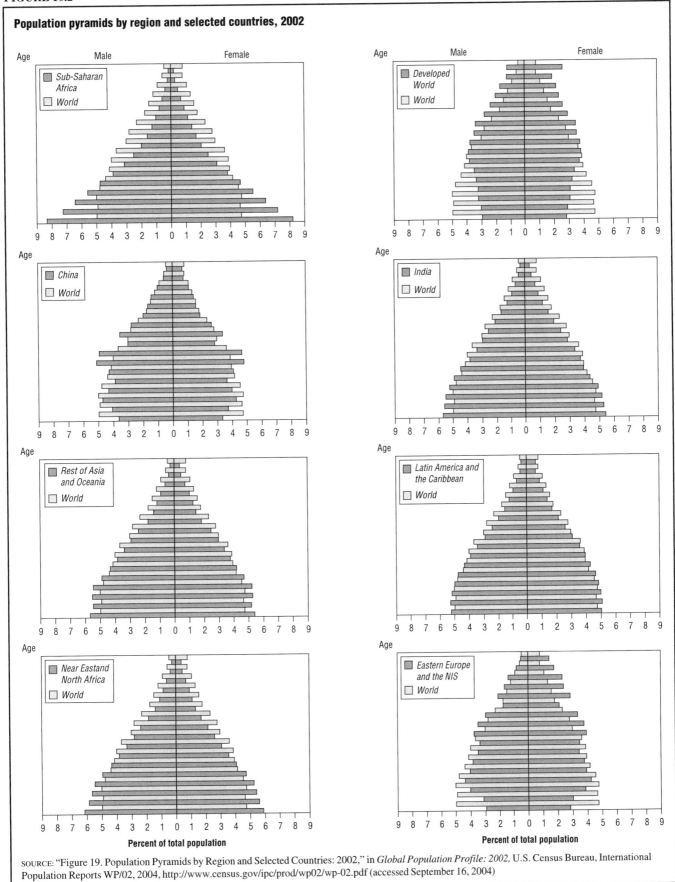

SOURCE: "Figure 19. Population Pyramids by Region and Selected Countries: 2002," in *Global Population Profile: 2002*, U.S. Census Bureau, International Population Reports WP/02, 2004, http://www.census.gov/ipc/prod/wp02/wp-02.pdf (accessed September 16, 2004)

FIGURE 10.3

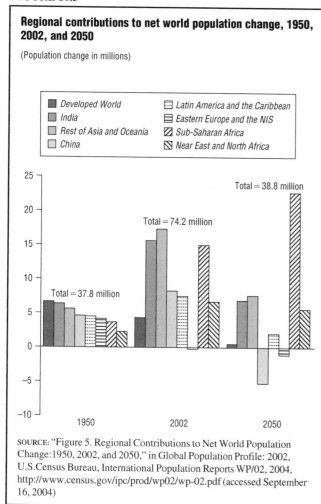

Regional contributions to net world population change, 1950, 2002, and 2050

(Population change in millions)

Legend:
- Developed World
- India
- Rest of Asia and Oceania
- China
- Latin America and the Caribbean
- Eastern Europe and the NIS
- Sub-Saharan Africa
- Near East and North Africa

Total = 37.8 million (1950)
Total = 74.2 million (2002)
Total = 38.8 million (2050)

SOURCE: "Figure 5. Regional Contributions to Net World Population Change:1950, 2002, and 2050," in Global Population Profile: 2002, U.S.Census Bureau, International Population Reports WP/02, 2004, http://www.census.gov/ipc/prod/wp02/wp-02.pdf (accessed September 16, 2004)

their lives or lead to infertility. Maternal mortality rates for women fifteen to nineteen may be double those of older women, and young women are also more likely to consider unsafe late-term abortions as an alternative to carrying a pregnancy to term.

SOME DIFFERENCES AMONG DEVELOPED NATIONS

Children in Families

The structure of family life is undergoing profound change around the world. Trends such as single motherhood, rising divorce rates, smaller households, and increased poverty among women and their children are not unique to the United States but are a worldwide phenomenon. For example, the percentage of children in single-parent families among member countries of the Paris-based Organisation for Economic Co-operation and Development (OECD) was 21.3% for Sweden, 20% for the United Kingdom, and 16.6% for the United States (UNICEF Innocenti Research Centre, Florence, Italy, *A League Table of Child Poverty in Rich Nations,* June 2000). OECD countries with the lowest percentage of children in single-parent families were Turkey (0.7%), Spain (2.3%), and Italy (2.8%).

Economic Status

According to *Social Policies, Family Type, and Child Outcomes in Selected OECD Countries* (2003), a report from the Organisation for Economic Co-operation and Development, child poverty was of particular concern in the United States and the United Kingdom because in those two countries poverty among young children was more pronounced and persistent than among the adult population. UNICEF Innocenti Research Centre's *A League Table of Child Poverty in Rich Nations* (2000) reported that children in the United States were more likely to experience poverty than children in every other industrialized nation except Mexico. More than 22% of American children lived in households with incomes below 50% of the national median. In comparison, only 2.6% of Swedish children lived in poor households. UNICEF concluded that one in six of the "rich world's" children (forty-six million) lived in poverty.

Infant Mortality

Differences in infant mortality rates reflect differences in the health status of women before and during pregnancy, and the quality of health care available to women and their infants. Although the United States greatly reduced its infant mortality rate from twenty-six per one thousand live births in 1960 to 6.8 per one thousand live births in 2001, in 1999 the nation ranked twenty-eighth out of thirty-seven among developed countries with at least one million population. (See Table 10.1.) The U.S. infant mortality rate for children twelve months old or younger in 1999 was 7.1 deaths per one thousand births, one of the highest in the industrialized world. In comparison, the 1999 rate in Japan was 3.4 deaths per one thousand births, and Hong Kong, the top-ranked country, reported less than half the U.S. rate (3.1).

CHILD LABOR

Child labor is a problem for which the world community has sought solutions and has seen some successes, according to the International Labor Organization (ILO). The ILO, created in 1919 and incorporated into the UN in the 1940s, brings together unions, employers, and governments from UN member states to pursue safe and just work environments. In 2002 the ILO report "Every Child Counts: New Global Estimates on Child Labour" estimated that 211 million five- to fourteen-year-old children worked in 2000, a 16% decrease from the 250 million who were working in 1996. Nearly one-fifth (17.6%) of the world's five- to fourteen-year-olds worked and about one-third (seventy-three million) of working children were under the age of ten.

According to another ILO publication, *Investing in Every Child: An Economic Study of the Costs and Benefits of Eliminating Child Labor* (2004), 60.6% of working

TABLE 10.1

Infant mortality rates and international rankings, selected countries, selected years 1960–99

(Data are based on reporting by countries)

Country[2]	1960	1970	1980	1990	1995	1998	1999[3]	International rankings[1] 1960	International rankings[1] 1999
				Infant[4] deaths per 1,000 live births					
Australia	20.2	17.9	10.7	8.2	5.7	5.0	5.7	5	22
Austria	37.5	25.9	14.3	7.8	5.4	4.9	4.4	24	9
Belgium	31.2	21.1	12.1	8.0	6.1	5.6	4.9	20	14
Bulgaria	45.1	27.3	20.2	14.8	14.8	14.4	14.5	30	35
Canada	27.3	18.8	10.4	6.8	6.0	5.3	5.3	14	18
Chile	125.1	78.8	33.0	16.0	11.1	10.9	10.1	36	32
Costa Rica	67.8	65.4	20.3	15.3	13.3	12.6	11.8	33	34
Cuba	37.3	38.7	19.6	10.7	9.4	7.1	6.4	23	26
Czech Republic	20.0	20.2	16.9	10.8	7.7	5.2	4.6	4	12
Denmark	21.5	14.2	8.4	7.5	5.1	4.7	4.2	8	7
England and Wales	22.5	18.5	12.1	7.9	6.2	5.7	5.8	8	24
Finland	21.0	13.2	7.6	5.6	4.0	4.1	3.7	6	5
France	27.5	18.2	10.0	7.3	4.9	4.6	4.3	15	8
Germany[5]	35.0	22.5	12.4	7.0	5.3	4.7	4.5	22	10
Greece	40.1	29.6	17.9	9.7	8.1	6.7	6.2	25	25
Hong Kong	41.5	19.2	11.2	6.2	4.6	3.2	3.1	26	1
Hungary	47.6	35.9	23.2	14.8	10.7	9.7	8.4	31	30
Ireland	29.3	19.5	11.1	8.2	6.3	6.2	5.5	17	19
Israel[6]	31.0	18.9	15.2	9.9	6.8	5.7	5.7	19	22
Italy	43.9	29.6	14.6	8.2	6.2	5.4	5.1	29	16
Japan	30.7	13.1	7.5	4.6	4.3	3.6	3.4	18	2
Netherlands	17.9	12.7	8.6	7.1	5.5	5.2	5.2	2	17
New Zealand	22.6	16.7	13.0	8.4	6.7	5.5	5.5	10	19
Northern Ireland	27.2	22.9	13.4	7.5	7.1	5.6	6.4	13	26
Norway	18.9	12.7	8.1	7.0	4.1	4.0	3.9	3	6
Poland	54.8	36.7	25.5	19.3	13.6	9.5	8.9	32	31
Portugal	77.5	55.5	24.3	11.0	7.5	6.0	5.6	35	21
Puerto Rico	43.3	27.9	18.5	13.4	12.7	10.5	10.6	27	33
Romania	75.7	49.4	29.3	26.9	21.2	20.5	18.6	34	37
Russian Federation[7]	—	—	22.0	17.6	18.2	16.4	17.1	—	36
Scotland	26.4	19.6	12.1	7.7	6.2	5.5	5.0	12	15
Singapore	34.8	21.4	11.7	6.7	4.0	4.2	3.5	21	4
Slovakia	28.6	25.7	20.9	12.0	11.0	8.8	8.3	16	29
Spain	43.7	28.1	12.3	7.6	5.5	4.9	4.5	28	10
Sweden	16.6	11.0	6.9	6.0	4.1	3.5	3.4	1	2
Switzerland	21.1	15.1	9.1	6.8	5.0	4.8	4.6	7	12
United States	26.0	20.0	12.6	9.2	7.6	7.2	7.1	11	28

— Data not available.

[1]Rankings are from lowest to highest infant mortality rates (IMR). Countries with the same IMR receive the same rank. The country with the next highest IMR is assigned the rank it would have received had the lower-ranked countries not been tied, i.e., skip a rank. Some of the variation in infant mortality rate is due to differences among countries in distinguishing between fetal and infant deaths.
[2]Refers to countries, territories, cities, or geographic areas with at least 1 million population and with "complete" counts of live births and infant deaths as indicated in the United Nations Demographic yearbook.
[3]Rates for Israel and New Zealand are from 1998.
[4]Under 1 year of age.
[5]Rates for 1990 and earlier years were calculated by combining information from the Federal Republic of Germany and the German Democratic Republic.
[6]Includes data for East Jerusalem and Israeli residents in certain other territories under occupation by Israel military forces since June 1967.
[7]Excludes infants born alive after less than 28 weeks' gestation, of less than 1,000 grams in weight and 35 centimeters in length, who die within 7 days of birth.
Note: Some rates were revised.

SOURCE: "Table 25. Infant Mortality Rates and International Rankings: Selected Countries, Selected Years 1960–99," in *Health, United States, 2003,* Centers for Disease Control and Prevention, National Center for Health Statistics, 2003, http://WWW.cdc.gov/nchs/products/pubs/pubd/hus/trendtables.htm (accessed September 16, 2004)

children (110.4 million) lived in the Asia-Pacific region, 20.8% (37.9 million) lived in sub-Saharan Africa, and 9% (16.5 million) lived in Latin America and the Caribbean.

Every Child Counts noted that 55% of working children under age twelve worked in hazardous situations. In Sri Lanka, for example, those hazards resulted in more child deaths each year from pesticide poisoning than from malaria, tetanus, diphtheria, whooping cough, and polio combined. Child-trafficking, forced labor, armed conflict, prostitution, pornography, and illegal activities—what the

authors called the "unconditional worst forms of child labor"—employed 8.4 million of the world's children.

Working conditions for children in overseas factories became a growing concern in the United States in the early 1990s as imports of apparel steadily climbed. A 1996 ILO report, "Child Labour: Targeting the Intolerable," noted that more than half the $178 billion worth of garments sold in the United States in 1995 were imported, compared with 30% in 1980. By 1996, thirty-six of the forty-two largest apparel companies had adopted formal standards prohibiting child labor, and the number of children working overseas to make apparel sold in the United States appeared to be decreasing. However, the ILO report stressed that American companies did not adequately enforce their own standards. Child labor remained pervasive in some countries, particularly in Asia, where children in India, Pakistan, and the Philippines worked for small contractors or in their parents' homes.

Finding Solutions

A 2002 report from the U.S. Department of Labor ("Advancing the Campaign against Child Labor, Volume II: Addressing the Worst Forms of Child Labor") described some projects that have been implemented in Nicaragua, Costa Rica, and Nepal to eradicate the worst and most hazardous child labor. The projects were carried out by the ILO with financial contributions from the U.S. Department of Labor. For example, one project undertaken in the poor Municipality of León in Nicaragua in the fall of 1998 was called "The Elimination of Child Labor and Risk of Sexual Exploitation of Girls and Teenagers in the Bus Station of León." A four-phase action plan was developed. First the bus station was identified as a center of informal trade, where child vendors and beggars congregated. Some of the girls who gathered there were victims of abuse, and some depended on income from prostitution to survive. Influential people in the community were educated about the physical and mental consequences of child commercial sexual exploitation and their role in helping the children. Families that participated in the project were given loans to make improvements to an existing business or start a new business. Finally, attention was devoted to rehabilitation of the girls and their families (most often, the families were headed by poverty-stricken single mothers). With a U.S. contribution of $148,940, forty-nine girls were removed completely from commercial sexual exploitation work, and fifty-nine girls working in other activities decreased their workloads and began attending school.

The ILO undertook a study published in 2004 (*Investing in Every Child: An Economic Study of the Costs and Benefits of Eliminating Child Labor*) that estimated the costs associated with eliminating child labor. The study found that the economic benefits associated with a more highly educated and healthier populace would far out-

weigh the costs of supplying quality education for all children, of defraying the loss of income from child labor for families, and of the social and governmental interventions needed to eliminate the worst forms of child labor. The ILO hoped to give countries an idea of the economic benefits of eliminating child labor.

The U.S. Department of Labor produced a 2004 report that detailed the progress made around the world in eliminating the worst forms of child labor—slavery, prostitution or the production of pornography, production or trafficking of drugs, or work that is harmful to the health, safety, or morale of children (*2003 Findings on the Worst Forms of Child Labor*, U.S. Department of Labor, Bureau of International Labor Affairs). The report noted that many governments (including those of Afghanistan, Indonesia, Nepal, Bulgaria, Haiti, and others) were implementing new trafficking laws meant to protect children from abduction, slavery, and forced prostitution; that the government of Costa Rica was at the forefront of global efforts to end the commercial sexual exploitation of children; that several countries (including Costa Rica, El Salvador, Honduras, Guatemala, Nicaragua, Panama, and the Dominican Republic) were working to eliminate hazardous child labor in agriculture; and that many governments (including those of Indonesia, Bulgaria, and Russia) were working to remove children from illegal activities like drug trafficking and provide them with education, counseling, and rehabilitation programs.

Many scholars who study the subject of child labor suggest that general economic development will help to reduce its prevalence. Anne O. Krueger, First Deputy Managing Director of the International Monetary Fund, summed this theory up in a speech before the attendees of the conference "National Security for the Twenty-first Century: Anticipated Challenges, Seizing Opportunities, Building Capabilities" in September, 2002:

> Child labor is something prevalent in developing countries because the alternatives are so much worse: starvation or malnutrition, forced early marriages (for girls) or prostitution, or begging on the streets. Ample evidence suggests that parents in developing countries, like parents everywhere, choose schooling for their young when they can afford to do so, and the quickest path to that outcome is through more rapid economic growth.

CHAPTER 11
ATTITUDES AND BEHAVIORS OF AMERICAN YOUTH

A few national studies periodically survey the attitudes, opinions, and behavior of American teenagers on a range of topics. For example, since 1979 the University of Michigan has conducted the annual study *Monitoring the Future*; the study's primary focus is monitoring drug- and alcohol-related behaviors among American secondary school students, college students, and other young adults. Market research firms can also be depended upon to conduct frequent surveys of teens, since teens have significant buying power.

What do teenagers think about? How do they feel about their parents and families, dating, the media, the government, social issues, their personal safety, and other issues? This chapter discusses some of the surveys.

GENERAL SATISFACTION

In *Teens Today 2003,* an annual survey compiled by the Liberty Mutual Group and Students Against Destructive Decisions/Students Against Drunk Driving (SADD), researchers reported that 61.3% of teens said they feel happy every day or almost every day. About half of the respondents felt stressed at least once a week, however, and older teens were more likely than younger teens to feel this way (58.8% compared to 28.2%).

FAMILY LIFE

Home and Family

According to *Trends in the Well-Being of America's Children and Youth 2002,* a 2003 report from the U.S. Department of Health and Human Services, in 2000 about 69% of children lived with two parents. (See Table 11.1.) About 22% of children lived with their mother only, 4% lived with their father only, and 4% did not live with a parent. Among non-Hispanic whites, 77% of children lived with two parents, 16% lived with their mother only, 4% lived with their father only, and 3% did not live with a

parent. The majority of African-American children lived with only one parent, 38% lived with two parents, 49% lived with their mother only, 4% lived with their father only, and 9% did not live with a parent. Among Hispanic children, 65% lived with two parents, 25% lived with their mother only, 4% lived with their father only, and 5% lived with no parent.

State of Our Nation's Youth, 2004–2005, a 2004 survey of 1,007 students nationwide done by the Horatio Alger Association, found that despite widespread perception of adolescence as being a time of rocky relationships with parents, 77% of teens say they get along very well or extremely well with their parents. More than half (51%) say that if forced to pick only one role model to emulate, they would choose a family member.

A May 2000 report by the Council of Economic Advisers, *Teenagers and Their Parents in the Twenty-first Century: An Examination of Trends in Teen Behavior and the Role of Parental Involvement,* used the criteria "eating dinner with a parent" and "feeling close to at least one parent" to measure parental involvement with teens. The survey found that 74% of children ages twelve to fourteen, 61% of children ages fifteen to sixteen, and 42% of children ages seventeen to nineteen had eaten at least five evening meals with a parent in the last week. The report indicated that parental involvement was a major influence in helping teens avoid risky behaviors such as smoking, drinking, drug use, sexual activity, violence, and suicide attempts. Parental involvement was also helpful in increasing educational achievement and expected attainment.

The report showed that behaviors such as lying to parents, getting into fights, and getting suspended from school were also affected by the amount of closeness teens felt to their parents. More than three-quarters of teens ages fifteen to sixteen who did not have close relationships with their parents said that they lied to their parents. About half of those who did have close relationships

TABLE 11.1

Percentage distribution of living arrangements of children by race and Hispanic origin, selected years, 1970–2000

	1970	1980	1990	1995[b]	1996[b]	1997[b]	1998[b]	1999[b]	2000[b]
All children									
Two parents[c]	85	77	73	69	68	68	68	68	69
Mother only[d]	11	18	22	23	24	24	23	23	22
Father only[d]	1	2	3	4	4	4	4	4	4
No parent	3	4	3	4	4	4	4	4	4
White, non-Hispanic									
Two parents[c]	90	83	81	78	77	77	76	77	77
Mother only[d]	8	14	15	16	16	17	16	161	6
Father only[d]	1	2	3	3	4	4	5	4	4
No parent	2	2	2	3	3	3	3	3	3
Black									
Two parents[c]	58	42	38	33	33	35	36	35	38
Mother only[d]	30	44	51	52	53	52	51	52	49
Father only[d]	2	2	4	4	4	5	4	4	4
No parent	10	12	8	11	9	8	9	10	9
Hispanic									
Two parents[c]	78	75	67	63	62	64	64	63	65
Mother only[d]	—	20	27	28	29	27	27	27	25
Father only[d]	—	2	3	4	4	4	4	5	4
No parent	—	3	3	4	5	5	5	5	5

[a]Persons of Hispanic origin may be of any race. Estimates for Blacks include Hispanics of that race.
[b]Numbers in these years may reflect changes in the Current Population Survey because of newly instituted computer-assisted interviewing techniques and/or because of the change in the population controls to the 1990 Census-based estimates, with adjustments.
[c]Excludes families where parents are not living as a married couple.
[d]Because of data limitations, includes some families where both parents are present in the household, but living as unmarried partners.
— Data not available.

SOURCE: "Table PF 2.2.A. Percentage Distribution of Living Arrangements of Children by Race and Hispanic Origin: Selected Years, 1970–2000," in *Trends in the Well-Being of America's Children & Youth, 2002*, U.S. Department of Health and Human Services, 2003, http://aspe.hhs.gov/hsp/02trends/index.htm (accessed September 16, 2004)

with their parents lied to their parents. The likelihood of ever being involved in a serious fight or ever getting suspended from school were also lower for teens who felt close to their parents.

Spending Time with Parents

Teens Today 2003 found that more than a quarter of youth (28%) would like to spend more time with their parents. In an April 2000 Young Men's Christian Association (YMCA) survey of two hundred children ages twelve to fifteen and their parents, children and parents reported spending about eighty minutes per day together. In that survey 25% of teens surveyed said they would rather spend time with their friends than their families, a sentiment that was more common among boys (31%) than girls (19%). Only 12% of parents surveyed believed their child would rather spend time with friends than family.

Communicating with Parents

Communication between parents and teens is an important influence on teens' emotional maturity and success in life. But according to *Teens Today 2000,* an earlier survey compiled by the Liberty Mutual Group and Students Against Destructive Decisions/Students Against Drunk Driving (SADD), 57% of teens reported that they wanted to discuss topics such as alcohol and drug use and sex with their friends, compared with 15% who wanted to discuss these topics with parents, 15% with an older sibling, 7% with other adults, and 1% with clergy. The *Teens Today 2003* survey found that less than half of teens were completely honest with their parents, particularly about problems they struggled with and their feelings about dating relationships.

Parents' and teens' perceptions of their communication differs. The *Teens Today 2000* survey found that while almost all parents (98%) believed they communicated with their teens about alcohol use, drug use, and sex, only 76% of teens reported that these discussions occurred. And teens did not always let parents know about their most pressing worries. Suicide ranked as the fifth-leading concern of teenagers but ranked seventeenth with parents.

DISCUSSION OF SEXUALITY. A study published in the *Journal for Adolescent Health* (Angela J. Huebner and Laurie W. Howell, "Examining the Relationship between Adolescent Sexual Risk-Taking and Perceptions of Monitoring, Communication, and Parenting Styles," 2003) found that high rates of parental supervision of adolescents (such as knowing where they were after school and at night, knowing the parents of their adolescents' friends, and monitoring television and Internet use) was correlated with lower sexual risk-taking. While the researchers found no relationship between the quantity of general communication between parents and adolescents and adolescent sexual risk-taking, they suggested that talking specifically about sexual topics might have an effect on the sexual behavior of teens as well. Peter S. Karofsky, Lan Zeng, and Michael R. Kosorok reported in "Relationship between Adolescent-Parental Communication and Initiation of First Intercourse by Adolescent" (*Journal of Adolescent Health,* 2001) that teens who believed they had good communication with their parents were less likely than other teens to engage in sexual intercourse.

DISCUSSION OF MENTAL HEALTH ISSUES. A 2001 survey by the National Association of Pediatric Nurse Practitioners and the University of Rochester School of Nursing also found differences in how parents and children perceived their communication about anxiety, stress, and depression. About 80% of parents reported that they talked with their children about anxiety at least sometimes, but only 37% of the children said their parents talked with them about this issue. In addition, while 72% of parents said they talked with their children about depression at least sometimes, only 36% of children said their parents had discussed depression with them.

The survey also found that perceptions of communication between parents and their children differed before and after the terrorist attacks of September 11, 2001. Before the terrorist attacks, about 21% of children and teens reported that they often worried about stressful situations and 39% of parents said they often worried about their children's ability to cope with stress. The perceptions of parents and children became more similar after September 11; at that time 32% of children reported worrying about stressful things and 26% of parents worried about their children's ability to cope. The decreasing gap between perceptions of parents and children may have been due to increased communication between them.

SHARING OF VALUES. A survey conducted in April 1999 for the YMCA illustrated differences between parents' and teens' perceptions of the role parents play in shaping their children's values. The survey found that while 94% of parents believed that their children learned values from them, 20% of teens said that they did not learn their values from their parents. A 2000 survey by the YMCA also showed that parents underestimated the influence of friends on their children's values. About 11% of parents believed that friends played an important role in forming the values of their children, but 26% of teens said their friends were a critical influence on their value systems. In addition, more parents (62%) than teens (46%) believed that parents and teens shared the same basic values.

SPENDING HABITS

Spending by teens in fall 2003 averaged $1,742 annually, up from $1,400 in spring 2003 and $1,536 in fall 2001, according to U.S. Bancorp Piper Jaffray. In fall 2003 girls spent an average of $1,964, compared with

$1,572 in spring 2003 and $1,342 in fall 2002. Boys' spending fell from $1,661 in spring 2002 to $834 in fall 2003. Spending trends for females on apparel increased 25% over spring 2003. Spending trends for males on apparel declined 10% over spring 2003. While *The New York Times* (Ruth Le Ferla, "Boys to Men: Fashion Pack Turns Younger," July 14, 2002) reported in 2002 that boys were catching up to girls in money spent on clothing, according to the Piper Jaffray survey, by fall 2003 that trend seemed to be reversing.

According to a press release from the U.S. Department of the Treasury's Office of Public Affairs (November 13, 2000), never before in history have children had more money of their own to spend and never before have children had more influence over the spending decisions of their families. Children between the ages of four and twelve influence an estimated $190 billion in purchases and teenagers spend another $140 billion of their own and their parents' money. Despite the control teenagers exert over money, however, their financial literacy is quite low. In its 2004 survey of high school seniors, the Jump$tart Coalition for Personal Financial Literacy found that 65.5% of high school seniors failed a test of financial literacy. Although the failing rate was still huge, it was down for the first time since 1997.

JUNK FOOD

A July 2002 report from the market research firm BuzzBack, *Understanding Teen Attitudes and Behaviors around Health and Nutrition,* found that a majority of teens (69%) would like to improve the way they eat, especially girls (78%, compared with 60% of boys), but fewer than half (42%) said they regularly tried to eat foods that were good for them. Sixty-four percent of teens consumed carbonated soft drinks, 64% ate whatever was available, and only 29% of teens thought about nutrition when they selected foods. Researchers found in 2002 that more than half of bag lunches brought to school by young adolescents had more than the recommended amount of fat; bag lunches averaged about twenty-one grams of sugar; only one in twenty bag lunches contained vegetables; and chips, snacks, or cookies were found in 40% of lunches (Terry L. Conway et al., "What Do Middle School Children Bring in Their Bag Lunches?" *Preventive Medicine,* vol. 24, 2002).

DATING, SEX, MARRIAGE, AND CHILDREN

Female Adolescents and Dating

In December 2002 about 250 women ages thirteen to twenty-four were surveyed by 360 Youth, a young adult sales and marketing firm; the survey results were reported in the firm's e-newsletter, *Beats Per Minute.* One-third of girls ages thirteen to fifteen (33%) believed it was "extremely important" to have a boyfriend, compared with only 4% of sixteen- and seventeen-year-olds. Of the young women ages thirteen to twenty-four who were dating, 48% said they looked for someone with whom they could have a serious relationship but they were not thinking of marriage. When asked to rate traits they looked for in a potential partner, respondents ranked personality and intelligence more highly than looks and athletic ability. On a five-point scale, personality (94%), sense of humor (90%), intelligence (77%), and common interests (72%) were ranked either "extremely" or "very" important. Popularity (64%) and athleticism (63%) were ranked "not very important" or "not important at all."

Sex

The Council of Economic Advisors' May 2000 report presented data on the link between regularly dining with parents and the likelihood of teens being sexually active. Among children ages twelve to fourteen, those who regularly ate dinner with a parent were about half as likely to have had sex as other teens their age, and young teens who were close to a parent were less than half as likely to have had sex. These patterns were similar for older teens. About 50% of teens ages fifteen to sixteen who did not regularly eat dinner with a parent had had sex, compared with 32% of teens in this age group who did regularly eat dinner with a parent. Among teens ages seventeen to nineteen, 68% who did not regularly eat dinner with a parent had had sex, compared with 49% who did eat dinner regularly with a parent.

The *Teens Today 2003* survey found that 46.3% of teens had engaged in a sexual activity other than kissing, and 38% had had sexual intercourse. The most common motivations among teens for having sex were to strengthen dating relationships and to have fun, but younger teens also said they sometimes had sex in order to feel more grown up. According to *The State of Our Nation's Youth, 2004–2005* (Horatio Alger Association, 2004), one in three teens said they struggled with pressure to engage in sexual activity before they felt ready.

Relationships

In 2003 a survey of teens was conducted by the Henry J. Kaiser Family Foundation and *Seventeen* magazine, and the results were reported in *Research Alert.* The survey found that traditional gender roles still defined teen relationships. Three-quarters (76%) of boys and 64% of girls said boys should ask for a first date. About two-thirds of both boys (69%) and girls (66%) said boys generally made the first move sexually. More than half (56%) of boys and 69% of girls said girls should be solely responsible for ensuring that some form of birth control was used. About 67% of boys and 72% of girls said girls were more likely to say "no" to sex.

Marriage and Children

The results of a *Teen People* poll of one thousand teens between the ages of thirteen and nineteen were reported in the February 1, 2003, issue of the magazine. The majority of teens believed monogamy was important, with girls more likely than boys to think it was "very important" (94% versus 89%) or "extremely important" (77% versus 65%). In general, survey respondents expected to have had an average of five sexual partners in the next ten years, and 92% planned to marry someday. Nearly two-thirds (63%) of teens believed that ten years in the future they would have to worry about practicing safe sex, but the results varied by age. Younger teens (ages thirteen to fourteen) were more likely to think they would have to worry than older teens (ages seventeen to nineteen)—76% versus 49%. More girls (68%) than boys (61%) planned on having children some day, and 87% of boys said that it would be someone other than themselves who would perform most of the child-rearing chores.

DEATH

At least one study (B. Halpern-Felsher and S. G. Millstein, "The Effects of Terrorism on Teens' Perceptions of Dying: The New World Is Riskier Than Ever," *Journal of Adolescent Health,* vol. 30, 2002) found that teens' fears of death rose after the terrorist attacks of September 11, 2001. Researchers from the University of California at San Francisco found that ninth graders attending public schools in northern California felt their likelihood of dying was 15.25% before the attacks and 20.87% one month after. The teens' perception of vulnerability was higher after the attacks even in non-terrorist scenarios—for example, students believed they were more at risk of dying during an earthquake (24.64% pre-9/11 versus 41.94% post-9/11) or a tornado (34.62% pre-9/11 versus 64.33% post-9/11).

SUICIDE

In 2001 suicide was the fifth-leading cause of death for children ages five to fourteen, and the third-leading cause of death for teens fifteen to nineteen. According to the May 2000 report by the Council of Economic Advisers, for teens of all ages suicidal thoughts were higher among those who do not feel close to a parent. The report showed that younger teens who regularly ate dinner with their parents were about half as likely as other teens to think about suicide. Among teens ages twelve to fourteen, those who didn't feel close to their parents were about three times as likely to think about suicide. Teens ages seventeen to nineteen who didn't feel close to at least one parent were more than twice as likely to think about suicide.

The 2003 *Youth Risk Behavior Survey* questioned high school students regarding their thoughts about suicide. Almost one in six (16.9%) claimed that they had thought about attempting suicide in the previous twelve months. (See Table 5.6 in Chapter 5.) Of all students, 16.5% had made a specific plan to attempt suicide, 8.5% had attempted suicide in the previous year, and 2.9% said they suffered injuries from the attempt that required medical attention.

A *New York Times*/CBS News poll of American teenagers reported in January 2000 that nearly half (46%) of respondents knew of someone their age who had attempted suicide. Using data from the National Longitudinal Survey of Adolescent Health, authors of an article entitled "Suicide and Friendships among American Adolescents" in *American Journal of Public Health* (2004) reported that having had a friend who had committed suicide increased suicidal thoughts and attempts among both male and female adolescents. A feeling of social isolation was an additional risk factor for adolescent girls.

RELIGION

Religion plays an important and positive role in the lives of many American teens, according to the National Study of Youth and Religion, a research project being conducted at the University of North Carolina, Chapel Hill. This four-year project, which used data from the 1996 Monitoring the Future Survey, began in August 2001 and continues until August 2005. The first report based on the project (*Religion and the Life Attitudes and Self-Images of American Adolescents,* December 2002) found that 31% of twelfth graders surveyed attended religious services weekly and 30% said religion was important to them. Teenagers who attended worship services and rated religion as important tended to have positive self-images, to be optimistic, and to enjoy school. According to "Adolescents' Transition to First Intercourse, Religiosity, and Attitudes about Sex," strong religious views appear to help adolescents avoid some risky behaviors (*Social Forces,* March 2003). Researchers found that female adolescents with a strong religious faith were less likely to become sexually active than other girls.

A 2004 publication from the National Study of Youth and Religion reported that 28% of teens thought religion should exert as much influence as it currently does on American society, and a full 41% thought religion should exert more influence (*Are American Youth Alienated from Organized Religion?*). Nearly 85% of respondents in the National Longitudinal Study on Adolescent Health reported that they belonged to a religious group; most of these teenagers had a positive relationship with religious institutions.

APPRAISING SCHOOLS

The Bureau of Justice Statistics (BJS) reported that in 2002 a little more than one-third (37.7%) of high school seniors rated the nation's public schools as "good" or "very good," a higher approval rating than the nation's public schools had had in twelve years. (See Table 11.2.) Students believed that colleges and universities were doing a better job; 69.4% of high school seniors approved of colleges and universities.

According to the National Center for Education Statistics (NCES), twelfth graders reported a declining interest in school between the years 1983 and 2000. In 1983 40.2% of high school seniors said their schoolwork was "often or always meaningful," but only 28.5% gave the same response in 2000. (See Table 11.3.) The proportion of high school seniors who said most of their courses were "quite or very interesting" dropped from 34.6% in 1983 to 21.2% in 2000, and the percentage of students who said what they were learning in school will be "quite or very important later in life" also declined. Moreover, students became more likely to find their school courses "very or slightly dull"—31.9% gave this response in 2000 compared with only 19.8% in 1983. The Horatio Alger Association found in its annual survey *State of Our Nation's Youth, 2004–2005* that high schoolers would give their schools only a 2.9 grade point average (GPA)—the equivalent of a B-minus.

Despite the declining interest in school, the amount of effort expended on schoolwork by high school seniors did not change significantly between 1990 and 2000. The proportion of seniors who said they "often or always try to do their best work" remained between 61% and 66%. Those who reported they "seldom or never fail to complete and hand in school assignments" remained steady at about 60%, and the proportion of those who said they "seldom or never" fool around in class remained at about 35%. The Horatio Alger Association survey found that most students (60%) only do about one to five hours of homework per week; 26% do six to ten hours per week; and 11% do eleven or more hours per week.

SOCIAL ISSUES

Problems That Concern Teens

High school seniors were polled on selected social problems for the 2002 *Monitoring the Future* study. More than three-quarters (75.5%) of the respondents said they worried about crime and violence at least sometimes, down from 81% the previous year. (See Table 11.4.) Race relations troubled 46.9% of students, down from 55.6% in 1999. Drug abuse concerned 56.9% of seniors; economic problems worried 47%; pollution worried 44.2%; and hunger and poverty concerned 49.7%. More than a third (35.9%) of students were concerned about nuclear war, up from the previous year but down from 52.4% in 1989.

Violence in Schools

According to the *Youth Risk Behavior Survey,* high school students were less fearful for their safety in 2001 than they had been in previous years. In 2003 5.4% of all students in this age group skipped school at least once in the past thirty days because they were afraid, down from 6.6% in 2001. (See Table 11.5.) Hispanic students were the most likely to not go to school because of safety concerns (9.4%), African-American students were the next most likely (8.4%), and white students were least likely to not go to school because of safety concerns (3.1%). Male

TABLE 11.2

Public opinion of high school seniors on the performance of selected institutions, 1990–2002

NOW WE'D LIKE YOU TO MAKE SOME RATINGS OF HOW GOOD OR BAD A JOB IS BEING DONE FOR THE COUNTRY AS A WHOLE . . . HOW GOOD OR BAD A JOB IS BEING DONE FOR THE COUNTRY AS A WHOLE BY HOW GOOD OR BAD A JOB YOU FEEL EACH OF THE FOLLOWING ORGANIZATIONS IS DOING FOR THE COUNTRY AS A WHOLE BY. . .?

(Percent responding "good" or "very good")

	Class of 1990 (N=2,600)	Class of 1991 (N=2,582)	Class of 1992 (N=2,684)	Class of 1993 (N=2,773)	Class of 1994 (N=2,642)	Class of 1995 (N=2,658)	Class of 1996 (N=2,455)	Class of 1997 (N=2,648)	Class of 1998 (N=2,608)	Class of 1999 (N=2,357)	Class of 2000 (N=2,216)	Class of 2001 (N=2,201)	Class of 2002 (N=2,250)
Large corporations	38.4%	36.3%	31.8%	31.5%	34.6%	37.9%	36.3%	35.3%	43.0%	42.1%	43.0%	39.3%	38.4%
Major labor unions	31.7	31.3	28.9	27.2	29.2	28.0	30.8	29.2	32.8	34.5	32.0	33.1	32.5
The nation's colleges and universities	73.8	70.2	67.2	61.1	67.7	66.6	70.5	65.7	70.1	72.5	71.0	71.0	69.4
The nation's public schools	36.1	33.6	32.5	29.0	27.2	31.8	30.6	30.0	32.2	34.1	34.7	34.5	37.7
Churches and religious organizations	47.0	49.2	50.3	46.9	50.3	50.2	49.0	48.3	52.6	52.4	50.1	52.1	48.8
The national news media (TV, magazines, news services)	54.7	51.1	47.9	40.5	37.9	33.1	34.5	34.8	36.1	39.8	37.6	38.8	43.0
The President and his administration	41.8	56.8	23.8	24.9	22.1	19.7	24.0	26.8	34.1	33.3	35.7	32.8	54.0
Congress—that is, the U.S. Senate and House of Representatives	32.9	38.3	15.9	16.6	18.8	20.6	18.1	21.7	28.7	29.9	31.4	33.0	42.2
The U.S. Supreme Court	40.9	44.1	35.7	31.0	31.0	29.8	30.4	30.5	36.6	38.9	38.2	37.1	41.5
All the courts and the justice system in general	27.8	31.2	23.4	21.1	19.3	20.6	21.2	22.4	25.7	29.4	28.9	30.7	32.9
The police and other law enforcement agencies	34.3	28.0	26.9	27.1	29.3	28.7	27.6	28.7	33.0	33.7	33.6	33.2	38.9
The U.S. military	58.8	80.6	62.2	57.0	54.3	54.8	55.6	52.9	56.7	59.4	55.5	55.7	70.1

Note: Response categories were "very poor," "poor," "fair," "good," "very good," and "no opinion."

SOURCE: "Table 2.70. High School Seniors Reporting Positive Attitudes toward the Performance of Selected Institutions," in *Public Attitudes toward Crime and Criminal Justice–Related Topics,* Sourcebook of Criminal Justice Statistics, 2002 http://www.albany.edu/sourcebook/pdf/t270.pdf (accessed September 16, 2004)

TABLE 11.3

Percentage distribution of 12th-graders according to their ratings of school work's meaningfulness, courses' degree of interest, and the importance of their school learning in later life, by sex, high school program, and average grades, 1983, 1990, 1995, and 2000

Student characteristics	How often school work is meaningful			How interesting most courses are			How important school learning will be in later life		
	Seldom or never	Sometimes	Often or always	Very or slightly dull	Fairly interesting	Quite or very interesting	Not or slightly important	Fairly important	Quite or very important
				1983					
Total	**18.3**	**41.5**	**40.2**	**19.8**	**45.5**	**34.6**	**19.9**	**29.6**	**50.5**
Sex									
Male	22.2	40.9	36.8	22.7	45.1	32.2	22.4	29.5	48.1
Female	14.8	41.8	43.4	17.3	45.6	37.1	17.8	29.7	52.5
High school program[1]									
Academic/college-prep	13.1	41.0	45.9	18.1	42.9	39.0	16.6	29.0	54.4
General	23.4	42.6	33.9	23.1	49.3	27.5	26.5	31.2	42.3
Vocational/technical	19.0	44.6	36.5	15.9	43.2	40.9	15.6	26.2	58.2
Average grades in high school[2]									
A's	11.2	36.3	52.5	14.5	37.5	48.0	14.9	26.0	59.2
B's	16.6	43.8	39.6	17.1	47.5	35.4	16.7	30.6	52.7
C's or D's	25.5	40.8	33.7	27.9	47.8	24.2	28.9	30.6	40.4
				1990					
Total	**20.0**	**44.5**	**35.5**	**24.6**	**46.7**	**28.7**	**20.7**	**32.3**	**47.0**
Sex									
Male	21.1	44.9	34.1	26.4	46.1	27.4	21.6	30.7	47.7
Female	18.6	44.5	36.9	22.1	47.8	30.2	19.4	34.3	46.3
High school program[1]									
Academic/college-prep	17.9	46.1	35.9	22.4	48.1	29.4	18.8	34.9	46.3
General	23.1	45.7	31.2	28.8	48.0	23.2	24.5	31.9	43.6
Vocational/technical	22.9	37.3	39.8	21.7	41.1	37.3	16.1	25.8	58.1
Average grades in high school[2]									
A's	18.1	41.2	40.8	19.8	45.5	34.7	17.6	30.8	51.6
B's	18.1	45.1	36.8	20.8	48.1	31.1	17.8	34.0	48.2
C's or D's	25.3	46.3	28.5	35.6	45.8	18.6	28.8	31.0	40.1
				1995					
Total	**23.7**	**45.4**	**30.9**	**29.0**	**47.2**	**23.8**	**23.7**	**34.9**	**41.4**
Sex									
Male	26.6	43.7	29.7	31.4	44.0	24.6	24.5	33.1	42.3
Female	20.4	47.7	31.9	26.4	50.6	23.0	22.6	37.0	40.4
High school program[1]									
Academic/college-prep	20.4	46.7	33.0	25.7	47.8	26.5	20.6	36.9	42.6
General	28.4	47.3	24.4	35.1	50.5	14.4	28.9	34.2	36.9
Vocational/technical	29.6	39.1	31.3	27.2	41.6	31.1	24.5	26.8	48.7
Average grades in high school[2]									
A's	18.6	44.2	37.2	22.2	48.0	29.9	20.0	35.1	44.9
B's	22.9	47.3	29.8	27.8	48.3	23.9	22.9	35.2	41.9
C's or D's	33.0	42.7	24.2	42.2	43.6	14.2	31.4	33.9	34.7

and female students were almost equally likely to skip school because of safety concerns (5.5% of male students and 5.3% of female students). Younger students were more likely to stay away from school because of safety concerns than were older students (6.9% of ninth graders compared with 3.8% of twelfth graders).

According to the survey, in 2003 6.1% of high school students carried a weapon (gun, knife, or club) to school on one of the thirty days preceding the survey. (See Table 11.5.) Males were more likely (8.9%) to have carried a

weapon to school than females (3.1%). African-American students (6.9%) were more likely than Hispanic students (6%) and white students (5.5%) to carry a weapon to school.

About one in ten high school seniors (9.2%) reported being threatened or injured with a weapon on school property one or more times during the twelve months prior to the survey. (See Table 11.5.) Non-Hispanic African-American high school students were more likely to have been threatened or injured (10.9%) than were His-

TABLE 11.3

Percentage distribution of 12th-graders according to their ratings of school work's meaningfulness, courses' degree of interest, and the importance of their school learning in later life, by sex, high school program, and average grades, 1983, 1990, 1995, and 2000 [CONTINUED]

Student characteristics	How often school work is meaningful			How interesting most courses are			How important school learning will be in later life		
	Seldom or never	Sometimes	Often or always	Very or slightly dull	Fairly interesting	Quite or very interesting	Not or slightly important	Fairly important	Quite or very important
				2000					
Total	**26.6**	**44.9**	**28.5**	**31.9**	**46.9**	**21.2**	**26.5**	**34.3**	**39.2**
Sex									
Male	31.3	40.8	27.9	35.2	43.9	20.9	28.5	32.2	39.2
Female	22.4	48.9	28.7	29.0	49.3	21.7	24.9	35.9	39.3
High school program [1]									
Academic/college-prep	22.2	47.9	29.9	27.6	49.2	23.3	24.1	35.9	40.0
General	31.7	44.4	23.9	38.5	46.2	15.2	30.8	34.2	35.0
Vocational/technical	31.0	38.6	30.4	31.2	40.1	28.7	23.8	33.2	43.0
Average grades in high school [2]									
A's	20.7	45.0	34.3	24.1	48.3	27.7	24.8	34.4	40.8
B's	27.0	47.3	25.8	31.6	48.3	20.1	25.4	35.4	39.2
C's or D's	35.4	39.7	24.9	45.5	40.7	13.8	31.4	32.7	35.9

[1]Respondents in a category labeled "Other/don't know," not shown separately, are included in the totals.
[2]Categories were made from students' reports of their average grade in high school.
Note: The data do not meet NCES standards for response rates. Percentages may not add to 100.0 due to rounding.

SOURCE: "Table 18-1. Percentage Distributions of 12th-Graders according to Their Ratings of School Work's Meaningfulness, Courses' Degree of Interest, and the Importance of their School Learning in Later Life, by Sex, High School Program, and Average Grades: 1983, 1990, 1995, and 2000," in "12th-Graders' Effort and Interest in School," *The Condition of Education 2002*, U.S. Department of Education, National Center for Education Statistics, May 2002, http://nces.ed.gov/pubsearch/pubsinfo.asp?pubid=2002025 (accessed September 16, 2004)

panic (9.4%) or non-Hispanic white students (7.8%). Younger students were much more likely than older students to report having been threatened or injured with a weapon at school; more students in ninth grade were threatened or injured (12.1%) than students in grades ten (9.2%), eleven (7.3%), or twelve (6.3%).

Terrorism

The 2003 *Teen People* poll found that 80% of teens surveyed believed that in their lifetime there will be another terrorist attack in the United States on the scale of the attacks of September 11, 2001. More than half of teens (57%) believed the United States government is prepared for such an attack, and 26% believed that in ten years terrorist attacks and suicide bombings will be the greatest threat to the world.

Substance Abuse

Data from *Monitoring the Future,* as reported by the BJS, show that starting in 1993 high school seniors' disapproval of marijuana use began to decline. More than two-thirds of students in the class of 1992 (69.9%) expressed disapproval of adults who tried marijuana once or twice. By 2002 only about half of high school seniors (51.6%) expressed disapproval of this behavior. Rates of disapproval of drinking alcohol and taking steroids also declined over the period, while disapproval of smoking one or more packs of cigarettes per day remained relative-

ly steady. In 2002 30.8% of high school seniors thought that marijuana use should be made legal, and 29.1% believed it should be considered a crime. According to the Horatio Alger Association 2004 survey, over a third of students (38%) struggled with peer pressure to drink alcohol or use illicit drugs.

Corporations and Government

The Bureau of Justice Statistics, in *Sourcebook of Criminal Justice Statistics: 2002,* reported that 38.4% of high school seniors in the class of 2002 believed that U.S. corporations were doing a "good" or "very good" job, up from a low of 31.5% in the class of 1994. (See Table 11.2.) During the 1990s high school seniors' approval of most areas of the government declined, but approval ratings in most areas were up in 2002 over the year before, perhaps due to the governmental and military responses to the terrorist attacks of September 11, 2001. In 2001 32.8% of high school seniors believed that the president and his administration were doing a "good" or "very good" job; in 2002 54% believed the president was doing a good job. In 2002 42.2% approved of the Congress, up significantly from the year before, when only 33% of high school seniors approved of the work Congress was doing. In 2001 55.7% of seniors thought the U.S. military was doing a good job; in 2002 the approval rating was up to 70.1%, the highest approval rating of all rated institutions.

TABLE 11.4

Public opinion of high school seniors on selected social problems, 1990–2002

OF ALL THE PROBLEMS FACING THE NATION TODAY, HOW OFTEN DO YOU WORRY ABOUT EACH OF THE FOLLOWING?

(Percent responding "sometimes" or "often")

	Class of 1990 (N=2,595)	Class of 1991 (N=2,595)	Class of 1992 (N=2,736)	Class of 1993 (N=2,807)	Class of 1994 (N=2,664)	Class of 1995 (N=2,646)	Class of 1996 (N=2,502)	Class of 1997 (N=2,651)	Class of 1998 (N=2,621)	Class of 1999 (N=2,348)	Class of 2000 (N=2,204)	Class of 2001 (N=2,222)	Class of 2002 (N=2,267)
Crime and violence	88.8%	88.1%	91.6%	90.8%	92.7%	90.2%	90.1%	86.5%	84.4%	81.8%	83.5%	81.0%	75.5%
Drug abuse	82.6	79.5	77.8	75.5	76.7	72.6	71.0	71.1	65.3	62.7	60.9	61.1	56.9
Hunger and poverty	65.9	66.4	68.1	71.1	65.7	62.3	62.6	61.1	55.5	54.5	54.4	51.3	49.7
Chance of nuclear war	45.1	41.5	33.4	28.8	27.9	20.0	21.6	20.4	29.0	32.1	23.7	23.9	35.9
Economic problems	56.8	63.9	70.6	71.8	62.6	55.7	57.9	51.5	47.6	44.8	45.2	47.0	47.0
Pollution	67.2	72.1	71.9	72.8	66.5	63.6	62.9	61.6	57.1	49.8	53.3	49.6	44.2
Race relations	57.1	59.4	68.7	75.4	71.6	68.9	70.7	64.7	56.0	55.6	51.2	52.6	46.9
Energy shortages	32.6	38.2	35.2	29.8	23.8	17.9	19.2	19.4	18.3	20.8	22.0	31.2	22.6
Using open land for housing or industry	33.9	33.8	34.7	32.9	32.7	28.9	32.6	32.7	30.8	27.5	32.6	30.6	28.5
Population growth	33.0	30.6	35.2	38.9	35.4	34.9	37.4	38.2	34.8	31.7	36.3	36.7	28.3
Urban decay	20.4	21.7	25.8	25.3	25.6	23.0	25.1	22.1	18.8	17.2	20.5	20.3	15.6

Note: These data are from a series of nationwide surveys of high school seniors conducted by the Monitoring the Future Project at the University of Michigan's Institute for Social Research from 1975 through 2002. The survey design is a multistage random sample of high school seniors in public and private schools throughout the continental United States. All percentages reported are based on weighted cases; the Ns that are shown in the tables refer to the number of weighted cases. Response categories were "never," "seldom," "sometimes," and "often."

SOURCE: "Table 2.68. High School Seniors Reporting that They Worry about Selected Social Problems," in *Public Attitudes toward Crime and Criminal Justice–Related Topics*, Sourcebook of Criminal Justice Statistics, 2002, http://www.albany.edu/sourcebook/1995/pdf/t268.pdf (accessed September 16, 2004)

TABLE 11.5

Percentage of high school students who reported violence-related behaviors by sex, race, ethnicity, and grade, 1991–2003

Behavior	1991 %	1993 %	1995 %	1997 %	1999 %	2001 %	2003 %
Carried a weapon (e.g., a gun, knife, or club)§							
Overall	26.1	22.1	20.0	18.3	17.3	17.4	17.1
Sex							
Female	10.9	9.2	8.3	7.0	6.0	6.2	6.7
Male	40.6	34.3	31.1	27.7	28.6	29.3	26.9
Race/Ethnicity							
White, non-Hispanic	25.1	20.6	18.9	17.0	16.4	17.9	16.7
Black, non-Hispanic	32.7	28.5	21.8	21.7	17.2	15.2	17.3
Hispanic	25.8	24.4	24.7	23.3	18.7	16.5	16.5
Grade							
9th	27.5	25.5	22.6	22.6	17.6	19.8	18.0
10th	26.8	21.4	21.1	17.4	18.7	16.7	15.9
11th	29.0	21.5	20.3	18.2	16.1	16.8	18.2
12th	21.3	19.9	16.1	15.4	15.9	15.1	15.5
In a physical fight††							
Overall	42.5	41.8	38.7	36.6	35.7	33.2	33.0
Sex							
Female	34.4	31.7	30.6	26.6	27.3	23.9	25.1
Male	50.2	51.2	46.1	45.5	44.0	43.1	40.5
Race/Ethnicity							
White, non-Hispanic	41.0	40.3	36.0	33.7	33.1	32.2	30.5
Black, non-Hispanic	50.6	49.5	41.6	43.0	41.4	36.5	39.7
Hispanic	41.3	43.2	47.9	40.7	39.9	35.8	36.1
Grade							
9th	50.5	50.4	47.3	44.8	41.1	39.5	38.6
10th	43.1	42.2	40.4	40.2	37.7	34.7	33.5
11th	43.0	40.5	36.9	34.2	31.3	29.1	30.9
12th	33.9	34.8	31.0	28.8	30.4	26.5	26.5
Injured in a physical fight††§§							
Overall	4.4	4.0	4.2	3.5	4.0	4.0	4.2
Sex							
Female	2.7	2.7	2.5	2.2	2.8	2.9	2.6
Male	6.0	5.2	5.7	4.6	5.3	5.2	5.7
Race/Ethnicity							
White, non-Hispanic	3.8	3.2	3.3	2.5	3.2	3.4	2.9
Black, non-Hispanic	6.6	6.4	4.3	5.7	6.3	5.3	5.5
Hispanic	4.3	5.1	6.4	4.3	5.8	4.4	5.2
Grade							
9th	5.2	4.1	4.7	4.6	4.4	4.5	5.0
10th	4.7	4.0	3.4	4.0	4.1	4.6	4.2
11th	3.9	4.0	4.3	2.8	3.7	3.1	3.6
12th	3.6	3.7	4.3	2.8	3.7	3.4	3.1
Carried a weapon (e.g., a gun, knife, or club) on school property§							
Overall	—	11.8	9.8	8.5	6.9	6.4	6.1
Sex							
Female	—	5.1	4.9	3.7	2.8	2.9	3.1
Male	—	17.9	14.3	12.5	11.0	10.2	8.9
Race/Ethnicity							
White, non-Hispanic	—	10.9	9.0	7.8	6.4	6.1	5.5
Black, non-Hispanic	—	15.0	10.3	9.2	5.0	6.3	6.9
Hispanic	—	13.3	14.1	10.4	7.9	6.4	6.0
Grade							
9th	—	12.6	10.7	10.2	7.2	6.7	5.3
10th	—	11.5	10.4	7.7	6.6	6.7	6.0
11th	—	11.9	10.2	9.4	7.0	6.1	6.6
12th	—	10.8	7.6	7.0	6.2	6.0	6.4
In a physical fight on school property††							
Overall	—	16.2	15.5	14.8	14.2	12.5	12.8
Sex							
Female	—	8.6	9.5	8.6	9.8	7.2	8.0
Male	—	23.5	21.0	20.0	18.5	18.0	17.1
Race/Ethnicity							
White, non-Hispanic	—	15.0	12.9	13.3	12.3	11.2	10.0
Black, non-Hispanic	—	22.0	20.3	20.7	18.7	16.8	17.1
Hispanic	—	17.9	21.1	19.0	15.7	14.1	16.7
Grade							
9th	—	23.1	21.6	21.3	18.6	17.3	18.0
10th	—	17.2	16.5	17.0	17.2	13.5	12.8
11th	—	13.8	13.6	12.5	10.8	9.4	10.4
12th	—	11.4	10.6	9.5	8.1	7.5	7.3

TABLE 11.5

Percentage of high school students who reported violence-related behaviors by sex, race, ethnicity, and grade, 1991–2003 (CONTINUED)

Behavior	1991 %	1993 %	1995 %	1997 %	1999 %	2001 %	2003 %
Threatened or injured with a weapon (e.g., a gun, knife or club) on school property[††]							
Overall	—	7.3	8.4	7.4	7.7	8.9	9.2
Sex							
Female	—	5.4	5.8	4.0	5.8	6.5	6.5
Male	—	9.2	10.9	10.2	9.5	11.5	11.6
Race/Ethnicity							
White, non-Hispanic	—	6.3	7.0	6.2	6.6	8.5	7.8
Black, non-Hispanic	—	11.2	11.0	9.9	7.6	9.3	10.9
Hispanic	—	8.6	12.4	9.0	9.8	8.9	9.4
Grade							
9th	—	9.4	9.6	10.1	10.5	12.7	12.1
10th	—	7.3	9.6	7.9	8.2	9.1	9.2
11th	—	7.3	7.7	5.9	6.1	6.9	7.3
12th	—	5.5	6.7	5.8	5.1	5.3	6.3
Did not go to school because of safety concerns[§]							
Overall	—	4.4	4.5	4.0	5.2	6.6	5.4
Sex							
Female	—	4.4	4.3	3.9	5.7	7.4	5.3
Male	—	4.3	4.7	4.1	4.8	5.8	5.5
Race/Ethnicity							
White, non-Hispanic	—	3.0	2.8	2.4	3.9	5.0	3.1
Black, non-Hispanic	—	7.1	7.7	6.8	6.0	9.8	8.4
Hispanic	—	10.1	8.5	7.2	11.2	10.2	9.4
Grade							
9th	—	6.1	5.6	5.5	7.0	8.8	6.9
10th	—	5.2	5.0	4.0	4.8	6.3	5.2
11th	—	3.3	4.1	4.2	4.5	5.9	4.5
12th	—	3.0	3.3	2.6	3.9	4.4	3.8

[§]On ≥1 of the 30 days preceding the survey.
[††]One or more lines during the 12 months preceding the survey.
[§§]Injuries had to be treated by a doctor or nurse.

SOURCE: "Percentage of High School Students Who Reported Violence-Related Behaviors, by Sex, Race/Ethnicity, and Grade—Youth Risk Behavior Survey, United States, 1991–2003," in "Violence-Related Behaviors among High School Students—United States, 1991–2003," *Morbidity and Mortality Weekly Report,* vol. 53, no. 29, July 30, 2004. http://www.cdc.gov/mmwr/preview/mmwrhtml/mm5329a1.htm#tab (accessed September 16, 2004)

The Criminal Justice System

In 2002 38.9% of high school seniors believed that police and other law enforcement agencies were doing a "good" or "very good" job, up from the level of confidence seniors expressed the year before (33.2%). (See Table 11.6.) White students (43.5%) were more likely than African-American students (23.7%) to express approval, as were students who had never used illegal drugs (42.4%).

The War in Iraq

According to *The State of Our Nation's Youth, 2004–2005,* a survey done by the Horatio Alger Association, less than half of students surveyed (44%) believed in 2004 that the United States had been right to go to war in Iraq in March 2003. A third of the students (33%) believed the United States was wrong to go to war, while nearly a quarter (23%) had no opinion. Male students were more likely than female students (53% of males compared with 35% of females) to approve of the war; white students (51%) were much more likely than African-American students (25%) or Hispanic students (29%) to approve of the war. Most students (55%) also

expected the United States to institute a military draft, but almost three-quarters (70%) opposed that possibility.

THE FUTURE

College

According to the Horatio Alger Association survey, 87% of high school students believed that it is critical or very important to graduate from college. Still, in 2002 less than half of tenth graders expected they would attain a bachelor's degree, although expectations of college achievement had risen steadily since 1980. (See Figure 11.1.) The National Education Longitudinal Study found that 40% of tenth graders thought they would attain a bachelor's degree; that percentage varied little by the socioeconomic status (SES) of the student. However, the percentage of students who believed they would attain a graduate or professional degree varied significantly by socioeconomic status: 28% of students with a low SES believed they would attain a graduate or professional degree; 55% of students with a high SES believed they would attain one. The same study found that females were outpacing males in their expectations of educational achievement; in 2002 46.6% of female tenth graders

TABLE 11.6

Public opinion of high school seniors on the performance of the police and other law enforcement agencies, 1990–2002

NOW WE'D LIKE YOU TO MAKE SOME RATINGS OF HOW GOOD OR BAD A JOB YOU FEEL EACH OF THE FOLLOWING ORGANIZATIONS IS DOING FOR THE COUNTRY AS A WHOLE. ... HOW GOOD OR BAD A JOB IS BEING DONE FOR THE COUNTRY AS A WHOLE BY ... THE POLICE AND OTHER LAW ENFORCEMENT AGENCIES?

(Percent responding "good" or "very good")

	Class of 1990 (N = 2,600)	Class of 1991 (N = 2,582)	Class of 1992 (N = 2,684)	Class of 1993 (N = 2,773)	Class of 1994 (N = 2,642)	Class of 1995 (N = 2,658)	Class of 1996 (N = 2,455)	Class of 1997 (N = 2,648)	Class of 1998 (N = 2,608)	Class of 1999 (N = 2,357)	Class of 2000 (N = 2,216)	Class of 2001 (N = 2,201)	Class of 2002 (N = 2,250)
Total	34.3%	28.0%	26.9%	27.1%	29.3%	28.7%	27.6%	28.7%	33.0%	33.7%	33.6%	33.2%	38.9%
Sex													
Male	33.4	29.3	27.4	30.1	30.2	29.1	28.6	30.3	33.9	36.3	35.7	33.8	37.1
Female	35.0	27.2	26.8	24.3	28.4	28.1	26.5	27.7	32.1	31.5	32.7	33.5	41.4
Race													
White	35.4	31.5	30.0	31.1	32.2	31.5	30.7	32.1	35.7	35.2	38.0	37.2	43.5
Black	22.4	11.0	12.4	9.2	16.9	16.8	14.6	16.3	22.5	25.4	16.6	20.0	23.7
Region													
Northeast	28.3	26.3	26.6	28.0	29.5	25.5	30.7	32.7	33.4	29.9	36.1	35.8	42.8
North Central	35.2	35.7	27.7	28.5	29.9	29.9	24.5	25.4	32.8	34.3	33.2	35.7	39.2
South	36.0	22.1	24.5	25.4	29.3	27.3	26.5	28.9	32.4	34.6	31.7	32.9	38.5
West	36.3	30.0	30.7	27.8	28.4	32.9	31.1	28.6	34.2	35.0	35.3	27.7	35.9
College plans													
Yes	34.0	28.5	25.8	26.9	29.5	28.9	27.8	29.3	33.0	34.5	34.1	34.9	40.2
No	33.8	28.7	31.0	27.3	29.7	29.4	28.1	26.6	32.2	32.4	33.5	29.0	36.0
Lifetime illicit drug use													
None	37.7	31.1	29.5	29.7	32.9	31.7	29.4	33.0	39.3	38.1	39.5	37.1	42.4
Marijuana only	33.6	27.0	23.5	24.0	25.8	26.3	25.5	27.7	30.2	33.4	29.6	32.0	41.1
Few pills	31.5	29.4	23.3	25.2	26.7	24.2	36.3	26.1	29.1	34.2	32.3	34.2	38.5
More pills	26.6	17.5	21.3	22.2	22.9	25.8	20.0	21.6	25.9	24.9	28.8	26.8	30.8

Note: Response categories were "very poor," "poor," "fair," "good," "very good," and "no opinion."

SOURCE: "Table 2.71. High School Seniors Reporting Positive Attitudes toward the Performance of the Police and Other Law Enforcement Agencies," in *Public Attitudes toward Crime and Criminal Justice-Related Topics*," Sourcebook of Criminal Justice Statistics, 2002, http://www.albany.edu/sourcebook/1995/pdf/t271.pdf (accessed September 16, 2004)

FIGURE 11.1

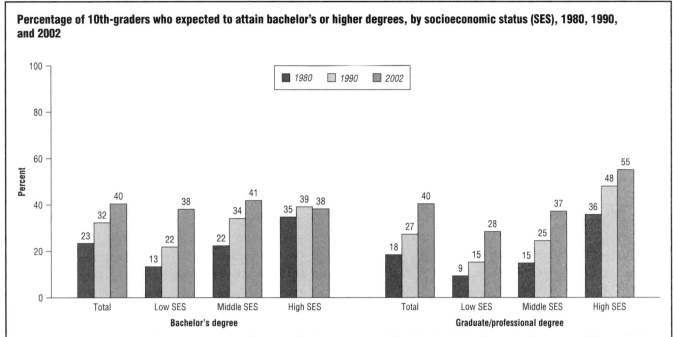

Percentage of 10th-graders who expected to attain bachelor's or higher degrees, by socioeconomic status (SES), 1980, 1990, and 2002

SOURCE: "Postsecondary Expectations: Percentage of 10th-Graders Who Expected to Attain Bachelor's or Higher Degrees, by Socioeconomic Status (SES): 1980, 1990, and 2002," in *The Condition of Education: 2004,* National Center for Education Statistics, 2004, http://nces.ed.gov/programs/coe/2004/pdf/15_2004.pdf (accessed September 16, 2004)

expected to receive a graduate or professional degree, compared with only 32.8% of males.

Beyond College: Money Matters

The 2003 *Teen People* poll found that the majority (97%) of teens expected to make as much or more money than their parents. This expectation was more true of non-white teens (77%) than white teens (61%). Half of teens expected to earn at least $50,000 a year, and 29% believed that they would make upwards of $100,000 a year.

The survey revealed gender differences in attitudes about "bringing home the bacon." More than three-quarters (77%) of girls expected to be one of two equal breadwinners, compared with only 42% of boys. More than half (55%) of boys expected to be the "main breadwinner,"

compared with only 15% of girls. Only 5% of female respondents expected to be supported by their mate.

Students surveyed for the *1999 Phoenix Student Fiscal Fitness Survey,* a Yankelovich Partners study conducted for the Phoenix Home Life Mutual Insurance Company (now the Phoenix Companies, Inc.), expressed an interest in overcoming their lack of confidence in money management skills. Only one in five young people felt they were "very good" at managing money, while 13% said they were not. About 29% of students said their parents provided a lot of financial guidance, and 74% agreed that schools should teach money management. The No Child Left Behind Act, passed in 2002, authorized the use of federal funds for teaching basic economic principles and personal finance skills.

IMPORTANT NAMES AND ADDRESSES

Administration for Children and Families
U.S. Department of Health and Human Services
370 L'Enfant Promenade, SW
Washington, DC 20201
URL: http://www.acf.hhs.gov

American Association for Marriage and Family Therapy
112 South Alfred St.
Alexandria, VA 22314-3061
(703) 838-9808
FAX: (703) 838-9805
E-mail: Central@aamft.org
URL: http://www.aamft.org

America's Second Harvest
35 E. Wacker Dr.
#2000
Chicago, IL 60601
(312) 263-2303
Toll-free: 1-800-771-2303
URL: http://www.secondharvest.org

Bureau of Justice Statistics
810 7th St., NW
Washington, DC 20531
(202) 307-0765
FAX: (301) 519-5212
Toll-free: 1-800-851-3240
E-mail: askbjs@usdoj.gov
URL: http://www.ojp.usdoj.gov/bjs/

Centers for Disease Control and Prevention
1600 Clifton Rd.
Atlanta, GA 30333
(404) 639-3311
Toll-free: 1-800-311-3435
URL: http://www.cdc.gov/

Child Trends Organization
4301 Connecticut Ave., NW
Suite 100
Washington, DC 20008

(202) 572-6000
FAX: (202) 362-8420
URL: http://www.childtrends.org

Child Welfare League of America
440 First St., NW
Third Floor
Washington, DC 20001-2085
(202) 638-2952
FAX: (202) 638-4004
URL: http://www.cwla.org

Children's Defense Fund
25 E St., NW
Washington, DC 20001
(202) 628-8787
E-mail: cdinfo@childrensdefense.org
URL: http://www.childrensdefense.org

Children's Foundation
725 15th St., NW
Suite 505
Washington, DC 20005-2109
(202) 347-3300
FAX: (202)347-3382
E-mail: info@childrensfoundation.net
URL: http://www.childrensfoundation.net

Food Research and Action Center
1875 Connecticut Ave., NW
Suite 540
Washington, DC 20009
(202) 986-2200
FAX: (202) 986-2525
E-mail: webmaster@frac.org
URL: http://www.frac.org/

March of Dimes
1275 Mamaroneck Ave.
White Plains, NY 10605
URL: http://www.modimes.org

NARAL Pro-Choice America (formerly National Abortion Rights Action League)
1156 15th St., NW

Suite 700
Washington, DC 20005
(202) 973-3000
FAX: (202) 973-3096
E-mail:
membership@ProChoiceAmerica.org
URL: http://www.naral.org

National Black Child Development Institute
1011 15th St., NW
Suite 900
Washington, DC 20005
(202) 833-2220
FAX: (202)833-8222
Toll-free: 1-800-556-2234
E-mail: moreinfo@nbcdi.org
URL: http://www.nbcdi.org

National Center for Children in Poverty
215 W. 125th St.
3rd Fl.
New York, NY 10027
(646) 284-9600
FAX: (646) 284-9623
E-mail: info@nccp.org
URL: http://www.nccp.org/

National Center for Missing and Exploited Children
Charles B. Wang International Children's Building
699 Prince St.
Alexandria, VA 22314-3175
(703) 274-3900
FAX: (703) 274-2200
Toll-free: 1-800-THE LOST
URL: http://www.missingkids.com

National Child Support Enforcement Association
444 N. Capitol St.
Suite 414
Washington, DC 20001-1512
(202) 624-8180

FAX: (202) 624-8828
E-mail: ncsea@sso.org
URL: http://www.ncsea.org

National Foster Parent Association
7512 Stanich Ave.
#6
Gig Harbor, WA 98335
(253) 853-4000
FAX: (253) 853-4001
Toll-free: 1-800-557-5238
URL: http://www.nfpainc.org

National Library of Education
U.S. Department of Education
400 Maryland Ave., SW
Washington, DC 20202
FAX: (202) 401-0552
Toll-free: 1-800-424-1616
E-mail: library@ed.gov
URL: http://www.ed.gov/NLE

National Network for Youth
1319 F St., NW
Suite 401
Washington, DC 20004-1106
(202) 783-7949
FAX: (202) 783-7955
E-mail: info@nn4youth.org
URL: http://www.nn4youth.org

Planned Parenthood Federation of America
434 West 33rd St.
New York, NY 10001
(212) 541-7800
FAX: (212) 245-1845
E-mail: communications@ppfa.org
URL: http://www.plannedparenthood.org

Orphan Foundation of America
Tall Oaks Village Center
12020-D North Shore Drive

Reston, VA 20190-4977
(571) 203-0270
FAX: (571) 203-0273
E-mail: help@orphan.org
URL: http://www.orphan.org

United States Bureau of the Census
4700 Silver Hill Rd.
Washington, DC 20233-0001
E-mail: webmaster@census.gov
URL: http://www.census.gov/

Urban Institute
2100 M St., NW
Washington, DC 20037
(202) 833-7200
E-mail: paffairs@ui.urban.org
URL: http://www.urban.org

RESOURCES

Many government agencies in Washington, D.C., publish timely information on their programs and the American population. The U.S. Bureau of the Census publishes statistics on American life in its *Current Population Reports,* including *Children's Living Arrangements and Characteristics: March 2002* (2003), *Income in the United States: 2002* (2003), *Fertility of American Women: June 2002* (2003), *America's Families and Living Arrangements: March 2002* (2003), *Poverty in the United States: 2002* (2003), *Who's Minding the Kids? Child Care Arrangements: Spring 1999* (1999), *Custodial Mothers and Fathers and Their Child Support: 2001* (2003), *Health Insurance Coverage in the United States: 2002* (2003), *Educational Attainment in the United States: 2003* (2004), and *A Child's Day: 2000* (2003).

The Census Bureau also released a series of *Census 2000 Briefs,* including *Grandparents Living with Grandchildren: 2000* (2001), *Age: 2000* (2001), and *Marital Status: 2000* (2001).

The Federal Interagency Forum on Child and Family Statistics, in *America's Children in Brief: Key National Indicators of Well-Being, 2004* (2004), provided invaluable data on many aspects of children's health and well-being. The U.S. Department of Health and Human Services (HHS) releases a wide assortment of statistical data concerning health issues. Its Centers for Disease Control and Prevention (CDC) issues the *Morbidity and Mortality Weekly Report* (MMWR), which focuses on various aspects of death and disease. The CDC's *Youth Risk Behavior Survey—2003* was the source of survey information on "risk" behaviors among American high school students. The CDC is also a leading source of AIDS statistics with its quarterly *HIV/AIDS Surveillance.*

Child Health USA 2002 (2002), published by the Maternal and Child Health Bureau, part of the U.S. Department of Health and Human Services, reported the health status and needs of America's children. *Child Maltreatment 2002: Reports from the States to the National Child Abuse and Neglect Data System* (2004) counted cases of child abuse reported to state child protective agencies, and the Administration for Children and Families provided data on child support collections as well as reports from the *Adoption and Foster Care Analysis and Reporting System (AFCARS) Report* (2003).

The Social Security Administration, Office of Policy, offered helpful statistics on children receiving Supplemental Security Income (SSI) in 2002. The Bureau of Labor Statistics, part of the U.S. Department of Labor, provided data on employment and unemployment.

The *National Vital Statistics Reports,* published by the National Center for Health Statistics (NCHS), Hyattsville, Maryland, provided statistics on births and infant mortality. NCHS also published *Health, United States, 2003* (2003), which gave invaluable data on many health conditions, birth rates, fertility rates, and life expectancy.

The U.S. Department of Agriculture provided estimates of expenditures on children from birth through age seventeen. Its Center for Nutrition Policy and Promotion calculated how much it costs to raise a child in *Expenditures on Children by Families, 2003 Annual Report* (2004). The Center also gave statistics on households that receive food stamps in *Characteristics of Food Stamp Households: Fiscal Year 2002* (2003) and on WIC participants in *WIC Participant and Program Characteristics, 2002* (2003).

The National Center for Education Statistics, part of the U.S. Department of Education, published *The Digest of Education Statistics 2002* (2003), *Projects of Education Statistics* (2003), and *The Condition of Education 2004* (2004), all of which provided important statistics on education in the United States.

The Federal Bureau of Investigation's *Crime in the United States: 2002* (2003) covered crime and victimization. The Bureau of Justice Statistics' *Sourcebook of Criminal Justice Statistics* covered crime as well as attitudes toward institutions in American society. The *Juvenile Justice Bulletin* (2001), the National Youth Gang Survey 2002, and the OJJDP Statistical Briefing Book (2003), prepared by the Office of Juvenile Justice and Delinquency Prevention (OJJDP), focused on juveniles and crime.

The National Center for Children in Poverty graciously provided information on children in low-income households. The Child Trends Organization provided information on adolescent sexual activity. The Alan Guttmacher Institute provided information from *Perspectives on Sexual and Reproductive Health* on abortion rates among teenagers. Thomson Gale thanks the Henry J. Kaiser Family Foundation for information on risky sexual behavior among adolescents. Thomson Gale also thanks Dr. Philip Johnson and Dr. Gerald Bachman for permission to use tables from *Monitoring the Future,* an annual survey of drug use among young people.

INDEX

interviewed, for at least part of the year, or for more than a year, 1997- 59 (f5.2)

health insurance, percentage of children under age 18 covered by, by type of insurance, age, race, Hispanic origin, 58t

HIV/AIDS, 50–52

homeless children, health of, 56–57, 59

hunger, 62

infant mortality, 47–48

infant mortality rate among selected groups by race, Hispanic origin of mother, 49t

infant mortality rates for 10 leading causes of infant death, by race and Hispanic origin, 51t

infant mortality, ten leading causes of, by race, Hispanic origin, 50t

lead poisoning, 62

life expectancy, 47

life expectancy at birth according to race, sex, 48t

life expectancy at birth, age 65, age 75 by sex, race, 50f

Medicaid, children covered by, by race, ethnicity, 59 (f5.3)

mental, child/parent communication about, 139

mental health issues, 62–63

missing children, 68–70

overweight children, percentage of children 6-18 who are overweight, by gender, race, Hispanic origin, 60t

overweight/obese children, 59, 61

physical activity, high school participation in, by demographic characteristics, 61 (t5.13)

suicide, percentage of high school students who felt sad or hopeless, who seriously considered attempting suicide, who made suicide plan, who attempted suicide, by sex, race, ethnicity, grade, 53t

tobacco, percentage of high school students who used, by sex, race, ethnicity, grade, 66t

tobacco use, 64–65, 67

weight control percentage of high school students who engaged in healthy/unhealthy behaviors associated with weight control, by sex, race, ethnicity, grade, 63t

weight, percentage of high school students who had or thought they had a problem with weight, by demographic characteristics, 61 (t5.12)

Health care
for children, 52–53

health care visits to doctor's offices, emergency departments, home visits over 12-month period, according to selected characteristics, 56t–57t

percentage of children vaccinated for selected diseases, by poverty status, race, Hispanic origin, 55t

Health insurance
for children, 53–54, 56

Medicaid, children covered by, by race, ethnicity, 59 (f5.3)

percent of children under 18 years of age who lacked health insurance coverage when interviewed, for at least part of the year, or for more than a year, 59 (f5.2)

percentage of children under age 18 covered by, by type of insurance, age, race, Hispanic origin, 58t

Health Insurance Coverage: Estimates from the National Health Interview Survey, 2003 (Cohen and Coriaty-Nelson), 53

Health, United States, 2003 (Centers for Disease Control and Prevention), 47

HHS. *See* U.S. Department of Health and Human Services

The High Cost of Child Care Puts Quality Care out of Reach for Many Families (Children's Defense Fund), 28–29

High school. *See* Education; Secondary school

High school dropouts
percentage of high school dropouts (status dropouts) among persons 16-24 years old, by sex, race, ethnicity, 83t

percentage of high school (status dropouts) among persons 16 to 24 years old by income level, 82f

statistics on, 78

High school students
high school participation in physical activity, by demographic characteristics, 61 (t5.13)

suicide and, 50

suicide, percentage of high school students who felt sad or hopeless, who seriously considered attempting suicide, who made suicide plan, who attempted suicide, by sex, race, ethnicity, grade, 53t

weight, percentage of high school students who had or thought they had a problem with weight, by demographic characteristics, 61 (t5.12)

See also Adolescents

Higher education
average undergraduate tuition, fees, room and board rates paid by full-time equivalent students in degree-granting institutions, by control of institution and by state, 89t

college entrance examinations, 86–88

college, teenagers' thoughts on, 149

educational attainment and earnings, 76–77

enrollment in institutions of, 88f

estimated number of participants in elementary, secondary, higher education, 72t

percentage of 10th-graders who expected to attain bachelor's or higher degrees, by socioeconomic status, 149f

Hispanic Americans
birth rate/fertility rate of, 3

births to unmarried women, 12

births to unmarried women, number, birth rate, and percentage of, by age, race, Hispanic origin of mother, 14t

child care for preschoolers, 24

children living with grandparents, 15

children living with parents, statistics on, 137

children, poverty of, 33

children under age 18 by race/Hispanic origin, 9f

children with single mothers and fathers and proportion with co-habiting parent, 1516f

contraceptive use by, 93–94

crude birth rates, fertility rates, and birth rates by age of mother, according to race and Hispanic origin, 7t

dropout rate, 78

dropouts, percentage of high school dropouts (status dropouts) among persons 16-24 years old, by sex, race, ethnicity, 83t

eating disorders and, 63

educational attainment and earnings, 76

effects of substance use on sexual activity among, 92

family income of, 33

fertility rate projections, 4

foster care, children in, 16–17

grandparents living with grandchildren, responsible for co-resident grandchildren, duration of responsibility, by race, Hispanic origin, 16t

health insurance coverage of, 53, 54

HIV/AIDS and, 51

infant mortality rate among selected groups by race, Hispanic origin of mother, 49t

infant mortality rate for, 47

median age of, 5

overweight/obese children/adolescents, 59

percentage of children under age 18 by presence of married parents in household, race, and Hispanic origin, 13t

percentage of children vaccinated for selected diseases, by poverty status, race, Hispanic origin, 55t

poverty rate for households, 12

pregnancy statistics, 96–97

private school enrollment, 77

projected population of U.S., by race/Hispanic origin, 8 (t1.3)

SAT/ACT test takers, 87

sexual activity among youth, 91, 100

suicide rate of, 50

violence in schools and, 141, 143–144

HIV. *See* Human immunodeficiency virus

Hofferth, Sandra L., 97, 119

Home School Legal Defense Association, 84–85

Homeless children
education for, 84

health of, 56–57, 59

statistics on, 20

effects of substance use on sexual activity and, 92

"The Effects of Terrorism on Teens' Perceptions of Dying: The New World is Riskier Than Ever," 140

"HIV Risk Behavior among Ethnically Diverse Adolescents Living in Low-Income Housing Developments," 95

"Relationship between Adolescent-Parental Communication and Initiation of First Intercourse by Adolescent," 139

on sex and peer pressure, 91

Journal of Child and Family Studies, 44–45

Journal of Consulting and Clinical Psychology, 91

Journal of Educational Research, 44

Journal of Marriage and the Family, 91

Just the Facts about Sexual Orientation and Youth (American Academy of Pediatrics, American Psychological Association, and National Education Association), 98, 100

Juvenile, 103

"Juvenile Arrests 2001" (Synder), 103

Juvenile crime/victimization
   arrests, 103
   arrests, female arrests for ages 21 and under, by age, 106t
   arrests, juvenile arrest rate for Property Crime Index offenses, 105 (f8.2)
   arrests, juvenile arrest rate for Violent Crime Index offenses, 105 (f8.1)
   arrests, juvenile arrest rates by offense and gender, 117t
   arrests, juvenile arrest rates by offense and race, 109t
   arrests, juvenile arrest rates for selected crimes, by gender, 108f
   arrests, male arrests for ages 21 and under, by age, 107t
   arrests, number of juveniles arrested, by gender, age group, type of offense, 104t
   children in custody, 111
   curfew, 111–112
   delinquency cases by disposition, adjudicated, 110 (f8.6)
   delinquency cases by manner of handling, 109 (f8.5)
   delinquency cases involving detention, number of, 109 (f8.4)
   delinquency cases judicially waived to criminal court, 110 (f8.7)
   delinquency court cases, 104–105
   gangs, 112–113
   gangs, law enforcement agency reports of gang problems, 113f
   guns and violence, 114–116
   homicide, 113–114
   homicides by juveniles committed with/without firearm, 114f
   juvenile records, opening, 110
   juvenile violence trends, 116–118
   murder victims age 24 and under, by age, sex, race, 115t
   parental responsibility, 111
   prosecution of minors as adults, 108–110
   status offense cases, 110–111
   victimization of juveniles, 116

weapons law violations, trends in juvenile arrests for, 116f
weapons, percentage of high school students who carried a weapon or gun, by sex, race, ethnicity, grade, 116t
Juvenile records, opening, 110
Juvenile Transfers to Criminal Court in the 1990s: Lessons Learned from Four Studies (Snyder, Sickmund and Poe-Yamagata), 110

K

Kaiser Family Foundation
   condom use/nonuse among teens, 95
   effect of television on teen sexual activity, 91–92
   effects of substance use on sexual activity, 92–93
   HIV/AIDS among teens, 100
   teen relationships, 140
Kaposi's sarcoma, 51
Karofsky, Peter S., 139
Karr, Catherine, 59
Key Facts: Essential Information about Child Care, Early Education and School-Age Care (Children's Defense Fund), 31
Kids Count Data Book: State Profiles of Child Wellbeing (Annie E. Casey Foundation), 22
Kinney, Hannah, 48
Klitsch, M., 97
Kosorok, Michael R., 139
Krueger, Anne O., 136
Kunkel, Dale, 92

L

Labor, child, 134–136
"Labor Force Participation of Mothers with Infants in 2003" (*Monthly Labor Review*), 21
La Ferla, Ruth, 139
"Latchkey kids," 22
Latin America
   child labor in, 135
   fertility rate in, 132
   STDs in, 131
Law enforcement
   public opinion of high school seniors on the performance of police and other law enforcement agencies, 148t
   teenagers' opinions about, 147
Lead poisoning, 62
A League Table of Child Poverty in Rich Nations (UNICEF Innocenti Research Centre), 134
Legislation and international treaties
   Adoption and Safe Families Act of 1997, 16, 17
   Aid to Families with Dependent Children, 21, 27
   Balanced Budget Act, 54
   Child Care and Development Block Grant, 27, 29–31
   Child Support Recovery Act, 40
   Education of the Handicapped Act, 84
   Family and Medical Leave Act, 21, 32
   Family Support Act, 27

Goals 2000: Educate America Act, 79
   Individuals with Disabilities Education Act, 84
   McKinney-Vento Homeless Assistance Act, 84
   Missing Children's Assistance Act, 68
   No Child Left Behind Act, 71, 73, 80–84, 149
   Personal Responsibility and Work Opportunity Reconciliation Act, 27, 33–34, 40, 97
   Pregnancy Discrimination Act, 21
   Temporary Assistance to Needy Families, 21
   Twenty-First-Century Community Learning Centers and, 22–23
Liberty Mutual Group
   survey on teen sexuality, 91
   on teen communication with parents, 138
   Teens Today 2003, 137
Licensing, state child care licensing regulations, 30t–31t
Life expectancy
   at birth according to race, sex, 48t
   at birth, age 65, age 75 by sex, race, 50f
   increase in, 47
Living arrangements
   adoption, children waiting to be adopted on September 30, 19 (t2.7)
   births to unmarried women, number, birth rate, and percentage of, by age, race, Hispanic origin of mother, 14t
   children with single mothers and fathers and proportion with co-habiting parent, 15f
   family households, 1970 and 12t
   foster care, children who exited, 17t
   foster care system, children adopted from, 18t
   grandparents living with grandchildren, responsible for co-resident grandchildren, and duration of responsibility, by race and Hispanic origin, 16t
   homeless children/youth, 20
   households by type, 12f
   living arrangements of children, 12, 14–18
   living arrangements of children by race and Hispanic origin, percentage distribution of, 138t
   living arrangements of young adults, 18–20
   nonfamily households, rise in, 11–12
   percentage of children under age 18 by presence of married parents in household, race, and Hispanic origin, 13t
   percentage of population aged 15 and over, by sex, age, marital status, 20t
   young adults living at home, 19 (t2.8)
Loftin, Colin, 112
Low-income families
   block grants for child care, 29–31
   child care regulations/quality of care, 27, 28
   cost of child care, 29

increase of, 21

primary child care arrangements for children under age 5 with employed mothers, by age, family income, 29 (*t3.6*)

Working toward Independence (White House report), 100

World Health Organization (WHO), 53, 131

The World Health Report (World Health Organization), 131

World Population Profile: 2002 (U.S. Census Bureau), 129

World Population Prospects: The 2002 Revision: Highlights (United Nations), 132

World Summit for Children, 129

World War II, 1

drug/alcohol use statistics, 64
eating disorders, 63